CONSTITUTIONAL CONFLICTS
2020-2021 ACADEMIC YEAR

I. INSTRUCTOR CONTACT INFORMATION

Han

Email:	han.sam@immaculateheartcoop.net
Home Phone:	(937) 429-0255 (between 7:30pm and 11:00pm)
Mobile Phone:	(937) 401-0070 (before 6:00pm)

Piña

Email:	pina.tom@immaculateheartcoop.net
Mobile Phone:	(801) 390-5344

II. CLASS TIME

Thursdays, Third (3rd) Period, Beginning at 10:15am, Eastern.

III. REQUIREMENTS

This is a <u>very</u> rigorous course with nearly 100-pages of <u>dense</u> reading every four (4) weeks and a <u>heavy demand</u> on students to have deep discussions with their parents. The reason for requiring high parental involvement is because the course addresses <u>very</u> controversial topics and pushes the boundaries of faith, human decency, and our own responses in the face of these controversial topics (e.g., death penalty, equal rights (gay rights, women's rights, etc.), hate speech, etc.).

Students should <u>not</u> enroll in this class if they cannot commit to discussions with their parents on the designated topics. This is because a full quarter (1/4) of the class will be dedicated to discussing the viewpoints of the students' families.

IV. COURSE GOAL AND GENERAL CLASS STRUCTURE

A. *Course Goal*

The primary objective of this course is to expose students to the United States (U.S.) justice system through the lens of federal appellate court decisions.

It is important to note that this course focuses on depth rather than breadth. This is because two (2) semesters cannot cover all topics relating to federal law. In other words, only a handful of topics are covered, but they are covered in great depth.

The main goal is to equip students to rigorously and systematically examine any topic and evaluate the topic in view of their own belief system (including their own individual beliefs and the viewpoints of their families). Thus, when a new topic arises (which is not covered in class), the student can apply the same rigor to the new topic as they did to the in-class topics.

Because the Catholic perspective will be covered in depth for each topic, a major objective is for each of us to own our beliefs. This course will be a step in that direction. By the end, the student will have substantially exercised the life-long skill of reconciling one's beliefs with that of others and the Catholic Church using controversial court decisions. Thus, by the end of the course, each student should be able to:

1. Look at all things through the lens of faith and for the glory of God.
2. Understand what and why we believe what we do.
3. Understand what and why the Church believes what she does.
4. Gracefully wrestle with dissenting views (even our own).
5. Contemplate all views enough to get to the TRUTH.

B. *Cardinal Rule for the Class = Discuss; Not Disrupt*

Because the topics are controversial, disagreement is to be expected. Hearty discussion will be encouraged. However, disruption will not be tolerated. Simply stated, discuss (respectfully focused on the topic) but not disrupt (personal attacks or irrelevant issues).

C. *Daily Structure*

The first few minutes of every class will be dedicated to reviewing the important concepts from the prior class. The last few minutes of every class will be dedicated to reviewing the important concepts from the current class. Because the beginning and ending minutes are for review, those minutes will be lecture style.

The remainder of each class will be dedicated to the lesson for that particular day. Much of the substantive material will be taught during this middle portion of class.

Week-by-week details of the course are appended at the end of this syllabus

D. *Overall Structure*

Each case will have four (4) separate modules. Thus, the study for each case will be divided into four (4) weeks, with one (1) module covered in each of the four (4) weeks. Specifically, Instructor Han will be responsible for Module-1 and Module-2, while Instructor Piña will be responsible for Module-3 and Module-4.

1. *__Module-1 (by Han)__*: Objective Observation Relating to the Case

For the first module, the students will focus on the objective portions of the case, including:

(a) the parties to the case;
(b) the underlying facts that led to the case;
(c) the procedural history of what happened before the case arrived at the appellate courts;
(d) the issues addressed by the court;
(e) the ruling from the highest court to review the case; and
(f) the reasons for why the court ruled as it did.

To be clear, Module-1 will not discuss our own personal opinions about the substance of the case but, instead, will focus mainly on the court's ruling and the court's reasons behind the ruling. This is because it is important to understand and examine (as objectively as possible) the court's decision-making processes and their corresponding results before we can begin forming our own opinions about the case.

Because of the importance of understanding the objective aspects of legal cases, and because the objective facts form the foundation of future modules, the course dedicates a full quarter (1/4) of the material to Module-1.

Insofar as Module-1 is largely a legal analysis, Instructor Han will be primarily responsible for Module-1.

    2.   <u>***Module-2 (by Han)***</u>: Critical Analysis of the Court's Decision

During the second module, the students will analyze and dissect the reasoning behind the case. Unlike Module-1, the students will focus on their respective opinions on the subject-matter of the case. In other words, rather than simply reciting the objective aspects of the case, students will form their own opinions about:

(a) the implications of the case to modern times;
(b) whether or not the rulings are correct;
(c) whether the students agree or disagree with the outcome;
(d) why the students agree or disagree;
(e) whether or not the reasoning of the court is convincing; and
(f) whether or not there are better arguments that could have been presented (and whether or not those additional arguments would have changed the outcome of the case).

For cases that have been decided by the Supreme Court of the United States (SCOTUS), the students will have an opportunity to advocate for the decision (as it stands) or criticize the decision.

For cases that have not yet reached the highest court, the students will have an opportunity to play the role of the SCOTUS and debate whether or not the lower court's decision should be affirmed (or upheld), reversed, or modified in some way.

Instructor Han will be largely responsible for the discussions in Module-2, which serves as a transition for Instructor Piña's Module-3 and Module-4.

At the end of the second module, and in preparation for Module-3 and Module-4, the students will be assigned homework that will require them to:

(a) engage in a similar discussion with their parents; and
(b) determine how and to what degree the family viewpoints coincide with the teachings of the church.

Insofar as the following Module-3 will be substantially dedicated to viewing the cases through the lens of the Catholic Church, it is imperative that the students complete this homework assignment as thoroughly as possible.

3. **_Module-3 (by Piña)_**: Viewing the Case Through the Lens of the Catholic Church

The third module focuses on the position of the Catholic Church (if any) on the particular issues that are raised in the case.

Instructor Piña (being the Catholic instructor) will be largely responsible for the discussions in Module-3. Here, the students will be required to:

(a) explain their families' viewpoints on the issues covered by the case;
(b) determine how and to what degree the family viewpoints coincide with the teachings of the Church;
(c) discuss to what extent the students (as individuals) agree or disagree with their families' viewpoints; and
(d) discuss to what extent the students (as individuals) agree or disagree with the position of the Church.

During this third module, the students will be exposed to the viewpoints of all of the other students and their families, along with how each family views and interprets the teachings of the Church on controversial issues.

To be clear, Module-3 will not address why we (as students, as a family, or as a Church) subscribe to certain beliefs; rather, Module-3 will focus on what are those beliefs. This is because we need to know (with some degree of certainty) what we believe before we can intelligently discuss why we believe.

4. ***Module-4 (by Piña)***: <u>Reconciling the Catholic Perspective with Our Own Opinions and Thoughts</u>

The fourth (and final) module is dedicated to why we (as students, as family members, and as a Church) subscribe to certain beliefs. In other words, Module-4 continues directly from Module-3.

Because Module-4 is substantially dedicated to reconciling the position of the Catholic Church with the rulings from the Court, our own beliefs, and the influence of our families' beliefs, Instructor Piña will continue as the lead instructor for Module-4.

During Module-4, students will be required to:

(a) take a position with reference to the issues that were raised in the case (irrespective of whether or not their own position agrees or disagrees with the ruling of the Court; irrespective of whether or not their own position agrees or disagrees with other members of their own family; and irrespective of whether or not their own position agrees with the position of the Catholic Church);

(b) explain why they subscribe to those particular beliefs; and

(c) defend their respective beliefs, should there be differing opinions from others.

In the final five (5) to ten (10) minutes of the class (at the conclusion of Module-4), both Instructors Han and Piña will provide a quick summary of the important points that were discussed in all four (4) Modules.

[REMAINDER OF PAGE INTENTIONALLY LEFT BLANK]
[CONTINUED ON NEXT PAGE]

CONSTITUTIONAL CONFLICTS
2020-2021 ACADEMIC YEAR

V. GRADING

The student's grade will be determined from:

(a) the student's understanding and exposition of the cases (Module-1);
(b) the in-class discussions (Module-2 and Module-4);
(c) completion of the assignment in preparation for Module-4 (namely, discussions with the family); and
(d) if there are questions or posts on the Google classroom, then both:
   (i) the student's online participation in the Google classrooms; and
   (ii) the depth of the student's online input.

At bottom, the student's grade will depend on both the in-class component and the online component.

VI. CASES THAT WILL BE COVERED IN 2021-2022

Although the students will be required to read the full scope of the Court's rulings (including majority, concurring, and dissenting opinions), some of the cases have an overview on Wikipedia (and, for those cases, a link is provided). The following cases will be covered in this course and in the sequence set forth below:

A. *Employment Division v. Smith*, **494 U.S. 872 (1990)**
[First Amendment; Religion]
https://en.wikipedia.org/wiki/Employment_Division_v._Smith

B. *Cruzan v. Director MDH*, **497 U.S. 261 (1990)**
[Right to Die; Sanctity of Human Life]
https://en.wikipedia.org/wiki/Cruzan_v._Director,_Missouri_Department_of_Health

C. *Kennedy v. Louisiana*, **554 U.S. 407 (2008)**
[Death Penalty; Sanctity of Human Life]
https://en.wikipedia.org/wiki/Kennedy_v._Louisiana

CONSTITUTIONAL CONFLICTS
2020-2021 ACADEMIC YEAR

D. *Snyder v. Phelps*, **562 U.S. 443 (2011)**
[Fundamental Rights; First Amendment]
https://en.wikipedia.org/wiki/Snyder_v._Phelps

E. *New Hampshire v. Zidel*, **Case Number 2006-549 (Supreme Court of New Hampshire, January 18, 2008)**
[Fundamental Rights; First Amendment; Online Content]
[No Wikipedia Entry]

F. *New Hampshire v. Lilley*, **Case Number 2017-0116 (Supreme Court of New Hampshire, February 8, 2019)**
[Equality]
[No Wikipedia Entry]

G. *Hecox v. Little*, **Case Number 1:20-cv-00184-DCN (D. Idaho, August 17, 2020)**
[Equality; Transgender Atheletes]
[No Wikipedia Entry]

[REMAINDER OF PAGE INTENTIONALLY LEFT BLANK]
[CONTINUED ON NEXT PAGE]

CONSTITUTIONAL CONFLICTS
2020-2021 ACADEMIC YEAR

VII. CLASS-BY-CLASS SCHEDULE FOR 2020-2021

SEMESTER 1

WEEK	CASE	MODULE	SUBSTANTIVE MATERIAL
01			Course Introduction, Course Outline, and Expectations of Students
02			Introduction to the Legal System; Assignment of *Employment Division v. Smith* (Religion and First Amendment)
03	01	01 (Han)	Objective Review of *Employment Division v. Smith*
04		02 (Han)	Critical Legal Analysis of *Employment Division v. Smith*
05		03 (Piña)	*Employment Division v. Smith* Viewed Through the Lens of the Catholic Church
06		04 (Piña)	Personal Reflections on *Employment Division v. Smith*; Assignment of *Cruzan v. Director* (Right to Die)
07	02	01 (Han)	Objective Review of *Cruzan v. Director*
08		02 (Han)	Critical Legal Analysis of *Cruzan v. Director*
09		03 (Piña)	*Cruazn v. Director* Viewed Through the Lens of the Catholic Church
10		04 (Piña)	Personal Reflections on *Cruzan v. Director*; Assignment of *Kennedy v. Louisiana* (Death Penalty)
11	03	01 (Han)	Objective Review of *Kennedy v. Louisiana*
12		02 (Han)	Critical Legal Analysis of *Kennedy v. Louisiana*
13		03 (Piña)	*Kennedy v. Louisiana* Viewed Through the Lens of the Catholic Church
14		04 (Piña)	Personal Reflections on *Kennedy v. Louisiana*; Assignment of *Snyder v. Phelps* (Fundamental Rights)

[REMAINDER OF PAGE INTENTIONALLY LEFT BLANK]
[CONTINUED ON NEXT PAGE]

CONSTITUTIONAL CONFLICTS
2020-2021 ACADEMIC YEAR

SEMESTER 2

WEEK	TOPIC	MODULE	
15	04	01 (Han)	Objective Review of *Snyder v. Phelps*
16		02 (Han)	Critical Legal Analysis of *Snyder v. Phelps*
17		03 (Piña)	*Snyder v. Phelps* Viewed Through the Lens of the Catholic Church
18		04 (Piña)	Personal Reflections on *Snyder v. Phelps*; Assignment of *New Hampshire v. Zidel* (Fundamental Rights)
19	05	01 (Han)	Objective Review of *New Hampshire v. Zidel*
20		02 (Han)	Critical Legal Analysis of *New Hampshire v. Zidel*
21		03 (Piña)	*New Hampshire v. Zidel* Viewed Through the Lens of the Catholic Church
22		04 (Piña)	Personal Reflections on *New Hampshire v. Zidel*; Assignment of *New Hampshire v. Lilley* (Equality)
23	06	01 (Han)	Objective Review of *New Hampshire v. Lilley*
24		02 (Han)	Critical Legal Analysis of *New Hampshire v. Lilley*
25		03 (Piña)	*New Hampshire v. Lilley* Viewed Through the Lens of the Catholic Church
26		04 (Piña)	Personal Reflections on *New Hampshire v. Lilley*; Assignment of *Hecox v. Little* (Equality)
27	07	01 (Han)	Objective Review of *Hecox v. Little*
28		02 (Han)	Critical Legal Analysis of *Hecox v. Little*
29		03 (Piña)	*Hecox v. Little* Viewed Through the Lens of the Catholic Church
30		04 (Piña)	Personal Reflections on *Hecox v. Little*
31			Semester Summary

[REMAINDER OF PAGE INTENTIONALLY LEFT BLANK]
[END OF DOCUMENT]

494 U.S. 872
110 S.Ct. 1595
108 L.Ed.2d 876
EMPLOYMENT DIVISION, DEPARTMENT OF HUMAN RESOURCES OF OREGON, et al.,
Petitioners

v.

Alfred L. SMITH et al.
No. 88-1213.

Argued Nov. 6, 1989.

Decided April 17, 1990.

Rehearing Denied June 4, 1990.

See 496 U.S. 913, 110 S.Ct. 2605.

Syllabus

Respondents Smith and Black were fired by a private drug rehabilitation organization because they ingested peyote, a hallucinogenic drug, for sacramental purposes at a ceremony of their Native American Church. Their applications for unemployment compensation were denied by the State of Oregon under a state law disqualifying employees discharged for work-related "misconduct." Holding that the denials violated respondents' First Amendment free exercise rights, the State Court of Appeals reversed. The State Supreme Court affirmed, but this Court vacated the judgment and remanded for a determination whether sacramental peyote use is proscribed by the State's controlled substance law, which makes it a felony to knowingly or intentionally possess the drug. Pending that

Employment Division, Department of Human Resources of Oregon v. Smith, 494 U.S. 872, 110 S.Ct. 1595, 108 L.Ed.2d 876 (1990)

determination, the Court refused to decide whether such use is protected by the Constitution. On remand, the State Supreme Court held that sacramental peyote use violated, and was not excepted from, the state-law prohibition, but concluded that that prohibition was invalid under the Free Exercise Clause.

Held: The Free Exercise Clause permits the State to prohibit sacramental peyote use and thus to deny unemployment benefits to persons discharged for such use. Pp. 876-890.

(a) Although a State would be "prohibiting the free exercise [of religion]" in violation of the Clause if it sought to ban the performance of (or abstention from) physical acts solely because of their religious motivation, the Clause does not relieve an individual of the obligation to comply with a law that incidentally forbids (or requires) the performance of an act that his religious belief requires (or forbids) if the law is not specifically directed to religious practice and is otherwise constitutional as applied to those who engage in the specified act for nonreligious reasons. See, *e.g., Reynolds v. United States,* 98 U.S. 145, 166-167, 25 L.Ed. 244. The only decisions in which this Court has held that the First Amendment bars application of a neutral, generally applicable law to religiously motivated action are distinguished on the ground that they involved not the Free Exercise Clause alone, but that Clause in conjunction with other constitutional protections. See,

Employment Division, Department of Human Resources of Oregon v. Smith, 494 U.S. 872, 110 S.Ct. 1595, 108 L.Ed.2d 876 (1990)

e.g., Cantwell v. Connecticut, 310 U.S. 296, 304-307, 60 S.Ct. 900, 903-905, 84 L.Ed. 1213; *Wisconsin v. Yoder,* 406 U.S. 205, 92 S.Ct. 1526, 32 L.Ed.2d 15. Pp. 876-882.

(b) Respondents' claim for a religious exemption from the Oregon law cannot be evaluated under the balancing test set forth in the line of cases following *Sherbert v. Verner,* 374 U.S. 398, 402-403, 83 S.Ct. 1790, 1792-1794, 10 L.Ed.2d 965, whereby governmental actions that substantially burden a religious practice must be justified by a "compelling governmental interest." That test was developed in a context—unemployment compensation eligibility rules—that lent itself to individualized governmental assessment of the reasons for the relevant conduct. The test is inapplicable to an across-the-board criminal prohibition on a particular form of conduct. A holding to the contrary would create an extraordinary right to ignore generally applicable laws that are not supported by "compelling governmental interest" on the basis of religious belief. Nor could such a right be limited to situations in which the conduct prohibited is "central" to the individual's religion, since that would enmesh judges in an impermissible inquiry into the centrality of particular beliefs or practices to a faith. Cf. *Hernandez v. Commissioner,* 490 U.S. 680, 699, 109 S.Ct. 2136, 2148-2149, 104 L.Ed.2d 766. Thus, although it is constitutionally permissible to exempt sacramental peyote use from the operation of drug laws, it is not constitutionally required. Pp. 882-890.

Employment Division, Department of Human Resources of Oregon v. Smith, 494 U.S. 872, 110 S.Ct. 1595, 108 L.Ed.2d 876 (1990)

307 Or. 68, 763 P.2d 146, reversed.

SCALIA, J., delivered the opinion of the Court, in which REHNQUIST, C.J., and WHITE, STEVENS, and KENNEDY, JJ., joined. O'CONNOR, J., filed an opinion concurring in the judgment, in Parts I and II of which BRENNAN, MARSHALL, and BLACKMUN, JJ., joined without concurring in the judgment, *post,* p. 891. BLACKMUN, J., filed a dissenting opinion, in which BRENNAN and MARSHALL, JJ., joined, *post,* p. 907.

David B. Frohnmayer, for petitioners.

Craig J. Dorsay, Portland, Or., for respondents.

Employment Division, Department of Human Resources of Oregon v. Smith, 494 U.S. 872, 110 S.Ct. 1595, 108 L.Ed.2d 876 (1990)

Justice SCALIA delivered the opinion of the Court.

This case requires us to decide whether the Free Exercise Clause of the First Amendment permits the State of Oregon to include religiously inspired peyote use within the reach of its general criminal prohibition on use of that drug, and thus permits the State to deny unemployment benefits to persons dismissed from their jobs because of such religiously inspired use.

I

Oregon law prohibits the knowing or intentional possession of a "controlled substance" unless the substance has been prescribed by a medical practitioner. Ore.Rev.Stat. § 475.992(4) (1987). The law defines "controlled substance" as a drug classified in Schedules I through V of the Federal Controlled Substances Act, 21 U.S.C. §§ 811-812, as modified by the State Board of Pharmacy. Ore.Rev.Stat. § 475.005(6) (1987). Persons who violate this provision by possessing a controlled substance listed on Schedule I are "guilty of a Class B felony." § 475.992(4)(a). As compiled by the State Board of Pharmacy under its statutory authority, see, § 475.035, Schedule I contains the drug peyote, a hallucinogen derived from the plant *Lophophora williamsii Lemaire.* Ore.Admin.Rule 855-80-021(3)(s) (1988).

Respondents Alfred Smith and Galen Black (hereinafter respondents) were fired from their jobs with

Employment Division, Department of Human Resources of Oregon v. Smith, 494 U.S. 872, 110 S.Ct. 1595, 108 L.Ed.2d 876 (1990)

a private drug rehabilitation organization because they ingested peyote for sacramental purposes at a ceremony of the Native American Church, of which both are members. When respondents applied to petitioner Employment Division (hereinafter petitioner) for unemployment compensation, they were determined to be ineligible for benefits because they had been discharged for work-related "misconduct." The Oregon Court of Appeals reversed that determination, holding that the denial of benefits violated respondents' free exercise rights under the First Amendment.

On appeal to the Oregon Supreme Court, petitioner argued that the denial of benefits was permissible because respondents' consumption of peyote was a crime under Oregon law. The Oregon Supreme Court reasoned, however, that the criminality of respondents' peyote use was irrelevant to resolution of their constitutional claim—since the purpose of the "misconduct" provision under which respondents had been disqualified was not to enforce the State's criminal laws but to preserve the financial integrity of the compensation fund, and since that purpose was inadequate to justify the burden that disqualification imposed on respondents' religious practice. Citing our decisions in *Sherbert v. Verner,* 374 U.S. 398, 83 S.Ct. 1790, 10 L.Ed.2d 965 (1963), and *Thomas v. Review Bd., Indiana Employment Security Div.,* 450 U.S. 707, 101 S.Ct. 1425, 67 L.Ed.2d 624 (1981), the court concluded that respondents were entitled to payment of unemployment benefits. *Smith v.*

Employment Division, Department of Human Resources of Oregon v. Smith, 494 U.S. 872, 110 S.Ct. 1595, 108 L.Ed.2d 876 (1990)

Employment Div., Dept. of Human Resources, 301 Or. 209, 217-219, 721 P.2d 445, 449-450 (1986). We granted certiorari. 480 U.S. 916, 107 S.Ct. 1368, 94 L.Ed.2d 684 (1987).

Before this Court in 1987, petitioner continued to maintain that the illegality of respondents' peyote consumption was relevant to their constitutional claim. We agreed, concluding that "if a State has prohibited through its criminal laws certain kinds of religiously motivated conduct without violating the First Amendment, it certainly follows that it may impose the lesser burden of denying unemployment compensation benefits to persons who engage in that conduct." *Employment Div., Dept. of Human Resources of Oregon v. Smith,* 485 U.S. 660, 670, 108 S.Ct. 1444, 1450, 99 L.Ed.2d 753 (1988) (*Smith I*). We noted, however, that the Oregon Supreme Court had not decided whether respondents' sacramental use of peyote was in fact proscribed by Oregon's controlled substance law, and that this issue was a matter of dispute between the parties. Being "uncertain about the legality of the religious use of peyote in Oregon," we determined that it would not be "appropriate for us to decide whether the practice is protected by the Federal Constitution." *Id.,* at 673, 108 S.Ct., at 1452. Accordingly, we vacated the judgment of the Oregon Supreme Court and remanded for further proceedings. *Id.,* at 674, 108 S.Ct., at 1452.

On remand, the Oregon Supreme Court held that respondents' religiously inspired use of peyote fell within the prohibition of the Oregon statute, which "makes no exception for the sacramental use" of the drug. 307 Or. 68, 72-73, 763 P.2d 146, 148 (1988). It then considered whether that prohibition was valid under the Free Exercise Clause, and concluded that it was not. The court therefore reaffirmed its previous ruling that the State could not deny unemployment benefits to respondents for having engaged in that practice.

We again granted certiorari. 489 U.S. 1077, 109 S.Ct. 1526, 103 L.Ed.2d 832 (1989).

II

Respondents' claim for relief rests on our decisions in *Sherbert v. Verner, supra, Thomas v. Review Bd. of Indiana Employment Security Div., supra,* and *Hobbie v. Unemployment Appeals Comm'n of Florida,* 480 U.S. 136, 107 S.Ct. 1046, 94 L.Ed.2d 190 (1987), in which we held that a State could not condition the availability of unemployment insurance on an individual's willingness to forgo conduct required by his religion. As we observed in *Smith I,* however, the conduct at issue in those cases was not prohibited by law. We held that distinction to be critical, for "if Oregon does prohibit the religious use of peyote, and if that prohibition is consistent with the Federal Constitution, there is no federal right to engage in that conduct in Oregon," and "the State is free to withhold unemployment compensation from respondents for engaging in work-related misconduct, despite its religious motivation." 485 U.S., at 672, 108 S.Ct., at

Employment Division, Department of Human Resources of Oregon v. Smith, 494 U.S. 872, 110 S.Ct. 1595, 108 L.Ed.2d 876 (1990)

1451. Now that the Oregon Supreme Court has confirmed that Oregon does prohibit the religious use of peyote, we proceed to consider whether that prohibition is permissible under the Free Exercise Clause.

A.

The Free Exercise Clause of the First Amendment, which has been made applicable to the States by incorporation into the Fourteenth Amendment, see *Cantwell v. Connecticut,* 310 U.S. 296, 303, 60 S.Ct. 900, 903, 84 L.Ed. 1213 (1940), provides that "Congress shall make no law respecting an establishment of religion, or *prohibiting the free exercise thereof. . . .*" U.S. Const., Amdt. 1 (emphasis added.) The free exercise of religion means, first and foremost, the right to believe and profess whatever religious doctrine one desires. Thus, the First Amendment obviously excludes all "governmental regulation of religious *beliefs* as such." *Sherbert v. Verner, supra,* 374 U.S., at 402, 83 S.Ct., at 1793. The government may not compel affirmation of religious belief, see *Torcaso v. Watkins,* 367 U.S. 488, 81 S.Ct. 1680, 6 L.Ed.2d 982 (1961), punish the expression of religious doctrines it believes to be false, *United States v. Ballard,* 322 U.S. 78, 86-88, 64 S.Ct. 882, 886-87, 88 L.Ed. 1148 (1944), impose special disabilities on the basis of religious views or religious status, see *McDaniel v. Paty,* 435 U.S. 618, 98 S.Ct. 1322, 55 L.Ed.2d 593 (1978); *Fowler v. Rhode Island,* 345 U.S. 67, 69, 73 S.Ct. 526, 527, 97 L.Ed. 828 (1953); cf. *Larson v. Valente,* 456

Employment Division, Department of Human Resources of Oregon v. Smith, 494 U.S. 872, 110 S.Ct. 1595, 108 L.Ed.2d 876 (1990)

U.S. 228, 245, 102 S.Ct. 1673, 1683-84, 72 L.Ed.2d 33 (1982), or lend its power to one or the other side in controversies over religious authority or dogma, see *Presbyterian Church in U.S. v. Mary Elizabeth Blue Hull Memorial Presbyterian Church*, 393 U.S. 440, 445 452, 89 S.Ct. 601, 604-608, 21 L.Ed.2d 658 (1969); *Kedroff v. St. Nicholas Cathedral*, 344 U.S. 94, 95-119, 73 S.Ct. 143, 143-56, 97 L.Ed. 120 (1952); *Serbian Eastern Orthodox Diocese v. Milivojevich*, 426 U.S. 696, 708-725, 96 S.Ct. 2372, 2380-2388, 49 L.Ed.2d 151 (1976).

But the "exercise of religion" often involves not only belief and profession but the performance of (or abstention from) physical acts: assembling with others for a worship service, participating in sacramental use of bread and wine, proselytizing, abstaining from certain foods or certain modes of transportation. It would be true, we think (though no case of ours has involved the point), that a State would be "prohibiting the free exercise [of religion]" if it sought to ban such acts or abstentions only when they are engaged in for religious reasons, or only because of the religious belief that they display. It would doubtless be unconstitutional, for example, to ban the casting of "statues that are to be used for worship purposes," or to prohibit bowing down before a golden calf.

Respondents in the present case, however, seek to carry the meaning of "prohibiting the free exercise [of religion]" one large step further. They contend that their religious motivation for using peyote places them beyond

Employment Division, Department of Human Resources of Oregon v. Smith, 494 U.S. 872, 110 S.Ct. 1595, 108 L.Ed.2d 876 (1990)

the reach of a criminal law that is not specifically directed at their religious practice, and that is concededly constitutional as applied to those who use the drug for other reasons. They assert, in other words, that "prohibiting the free exercise [of religion]" includes requiring any individual to observe a generally applicable law that requires (or forbids) the performance of an act that his religious belief forbids (or requires). As a textual matter, we do not think the words must be given that meaning. It is no more necessary to regard the collection of a general tax, for example, as "prohibiting the free exercise [of religion]" by those citizens who believe support of organized government to be sinful, than it is to regard the same tax as "abridging the freedom . . . of the press" of those publishing companies that must pay the tax as a condition of staying in business. It is a permissible reading of the text, in the one case as in the other, to say that if prohibiting the exercise of religion (or burdening the activity of printing) is not the object of the tax but merely the incidental effect of a generally applicable and otherwise valid provision, the First Amendment has not been offended. Compare *Citizen Publishing Co. v. United States,* 394 U.S. 131, 139, 89 S.Ct. 927, 931-32, 22 L.Ed.2d 148 (1969) (upholding application of antitrust laws to press), with *Grosjean v. American Press Co.,* 297 U.S. 233, 250-251, 56 S.Ct. 444, 449, 80 L.Ed. 660 (1936) (striking down license tax applied only to newspapers with weekly circulation above a specified level); see generally *Minneapolis Star*

Employment Division, Department of Human Resources of Oregon v. Smith, 494 U.S. 872, 110 S.Ct. 1595, 108 L.Ed.2d 876 (1990)

& Tribune Co. v. Minnesota Comm'r of Revenue, 460 U.S. 575, 581, 103 S.Ct. 1365, 1369-70, 75 L.Ed.2d 295 (1983).

Our decisions reveal that the latter reading is the correct one. We have never held that an individual's religious beliefs excuse him from compliance with an otherwise valid law prohibiting conduct that the State is free to regulate. On the contrary, the record of more than a century of our free exercise jurisprudence contradicts that proposition. As described succinctly by Justice Frankfurter in *Minersville School Dist. Bd. of Ed. v. Gobitis,* 310 U.S. 586, 594-595, 60 S.Ct. 1010, 1012-1013, 84 L.Ed. 1375 (1940): "Conscientious scruples have not, in the course of the long struggle for religious toleration, relieved the individual from obedience to a general law not aimed at the promotion or restriction of religious beliefs. The mere possession of religious convictions which contradict the relevant concerns of a political society does not relieve the citizen from the discharge of political responsibilities (footnote omitted)." We first had occasion to assert that principle in *Reynolds v. United States,* 98 U.S. 145, 25 L.Ed. 244 (1879), where we rejected the claim that criminal laws against polygamy could not be constitutionally applied to those whose religion commanded the practice. "Laws," we said, "are made for the government of actions, and while they cannot interfere with mere religious belief and opinions, they may with practices. . . . Can a man excuse his practices to the contrary because of his religious

Employment Division, Department of Human Resources of Oregon v. Smith, 494 U.S. 872, 110 S.Ct. 1595, 108 L.Ed.2d 876 (1990)

belief? To permit this would be to make the professed doctrines of religious belief superior to the law of the land, and in effect to permit every citizen to become a law unto himself." *Id.,* at 166-167.

Subsequent decisions have consistently held that the right of free exercise does not relieve an individual of the obligation to comply with a "valid and neutral law of general applicability on the ground that the law proscribes (or prescribes) conduct that his religion prescribes (or proscribes)." *United States v. Lee,* 455 U.S. 252, 263, n. 3, 102 S.Ct. 1051, 1058, n. 3, 71 L.Ed.2d 127 (1982) (STEVENS, J., concurring in judgment); see *Minersville School Dist. Bd. of Ed. v. Gobitis, supra,* 310 U.S., at 595, 60 S.Ct., at 1013 (collecting cases). In *Prince v. Massachusetts,* 321 U.S. 158, 64 S.Ct. 438, 88 L.Ed. 645 (1944), we held that a mother could be prosecuted under the child labor laws for using her children to dispense literature in the streets, her religious motivation notwithstanding. We found no constitutional infirmity in "excluding [these children] from doing there what no other children may do." *Id.,* at 171, 64 S.Ct., at 444. In *Braunfeld v. Brown,* 366 U.S. 599, 81 S.Ct. 1144, 6 L.Ed.2d 563 (1961) (plurality opinion), we upheld Sunday-closing laws against the claim that they burdened the religious practices of persons whose religions compelled them to refrain from work on other days. In *Gillette v. United States,* 401 U.S. 437, 461, 91 S.Ct. 828, 842, 28 L.Ed.2d 168 (1971), we sustained the military Selective Service System against the claim that it

Employment Division, Department of Human Resources of Oregon v. Smith, 494 U.S. 872, 110 S.Ct. 1595, 108 L.Ed.2d 876 (1990)

violated free exercise by conscripting persons who opposed a particular war on religious grounds.

Our most recent decision involving a neutral, generally applicable regulatory law that compelled activity forbidden by an individual's religion was *United States v. Lee,* 455 U.S., at 258-261, 102 S.Ct., at 1055-1057. There, an Amish employer, on behalf of himself and his employees, sought exemption from collection and payment of Social Security taxes on the ground that the Amish faith prohibited participation in governmental support programs. We rejected the claim that an exemption was constitutionally required. There would be no way, we observed, to distinguish the Amish believer's objection to Social Security taxes from the religious objections that others might have to the collection or use of other taxes. "If, for example, a religious adherent believes war is a sin, and if a certain percentage of the federal budget can be identified as devoted to war-related activities, such individuals would have a similarly valid claim to be exempt from paying that percentage of the income tax. The tax system could not function if denominations were allowed to challenge the tax system because tax payments were spent in a manner that violates their religious belief." *Id.,* at 260, 102 S.Ct., at 1056-57. Cf. *Hernandez v. Commissioner,* 490 U.S. 680, 109 S.Ct. 2136, 104 L.Ed.2d 766 (1989) (rejecting free exercise challenge to payment of income taxes alleged to make religious activities more difficult).

The only decisions in which we have held that the

Employment Division, Department of Human Resources of Oregon v. Smith, 494 U.S. 872, 110 S.Ct. 1595, 108 L.Ed.2d 876 (1990)

First Amendment bars application of a neutral, generally applicable law to religiously motivated action have involved not the Free Exercise Clause alone, but the Free Exercise Clause in conjunction with other constitutional protections, such as freedom of speech and of the press, see *Cantwell v. Connecticut,* 310 U.S., at 304-307, 60 S.Ct., at 903-905 (invalidating a licensing system for religious and charitable solicitations under which the administrator had discretion to deny a license to any cause he deemed nonreligious); *Murdock v. Pennsylvania,* 319 U.S. 105, 63 S.Ct. 870, 87 L.Ed. 1292 (1943) (invalidating a flat tax on solicitation as applied to the dissemination of religious ideas); *Follett v. McCormick,* 321 U.S. 573, 64 S.Ct. 717, 88 L.Ed. 938 (1944) (same), or the right of parents, acknowledged in *Pierce v. Society of Sisters,* 268 U.S. 510, 45 S.Ct. 571, 69 L.Ed. 1070 (1925), to direct the education of their children, see *Wisconsin v. Yoder,* 406 U.S. 205, 92 S.Ct. 1526, 32 L.Ed.2d 15 (1972) (invalidating compulsory school-attendance laws as applied to Amish parents who refused on religious grounds to send their children to school).[1]

Some of our cases prohibiting compelled expression, decided exclusively upon free speech grounds, have also involved freedom of religion, cf. *Wooley v. Maynard,* 430 U.S. 705, 97 S.Ct. 1428, 51 L.Ed.2d 752 (1977) (invalidating compelled display of a license plate slogan that offended individual religious beliefs); *West Virginia Bd. of Education v. Barnette,* 319

U.S. 624, 63 S.Ct. 1178, 87 L.Ed. 1628 (1943) (invalidating compulsory flag salute statute challenged by religious objectors). And it is easy to envision a case in which a challenge on freedom of association grounds would likewise be reinforced by Free Exercise Clause concerns. *Cf. Roberts v. United States Jaycees,* 468 U.S. 609, 622, 104 S.Ct. 3244, 3251-52, 82 L.Ed.2d 462 (1984) ("An individual's freedom to speak, to worship, and to petition the government for the redress of grievances could not be vigorously protected from interference by the State [if] a correlative freedom to engage in group effort toward those ends were not also guaranteed").

The present case does not present such a hybrid situation, but a free exercise claim unconnected with any communicative activity or parental right. Respondents urge us to hold, quite simply, that when otherwise prohibitable conduct is accompanied by religious convictions, not only the convictions but the conduct itself must be free from governmental regulation. We have never held that, and decline to do so now. There being no contention that Oregon's drug law represents an attempt to regulate religious beliefs, the communication of religious beliefs, or the raising of one's children in those beliefs, the rule to which we have adhered ever since *Reynolds* plainly controls. "Our cases do not at their farthest reach support the proposition that a stance of conscientious opposition relieves an objector from any colliding duty fixed by a democratic government."

Employment Division, Department of Human Resources of Oregon v. Smith, 494 U.S. 872, 110 S.Ct. 1595, 108 L.Ed.2d 876 (1990)

Gillette v. United States, supra, 401 U.S., at 461, 91 S.Ct., at 842.

B

Respondents argue that even though exemption from generally applicable criminal laws need not automatically be extended to religiously motivated actors, at least the claim for a religious exemption must be evaluated under the balancing test set forth in *Sherbert v. Verner,* 374 U.S. 398, 83 S.Ct. 1790, 10 L.Ed.2d 965 (1963). Under the *Sherbert* test, governmental actions that substantially burden a religious practice must be justified by a compelling governmental interest. See *id.,* at 402-403, 83 S.Ct., at 1792-1794; see also *Hernandez v. Commissioner,* 490 U.S., at 699, 109 S.Ct., at 2148. Applying that test we have, on three occasions, invalidated state unemployment compensation rules that conditioned the availability of benefits upon an applicant's willingness to work under conditions forbidden by his religion. See *Sherbert v. Verner, supra; Thomas v. Review Bd. of Indiana Employment Security Div.,* 450 U.S. 707, 101 S.Ct. 1425, 67 L.Ed.2d 624 (1981); *Hobbie v. Unemployment Appeals Comm'n of Florida,* 480 U.S. 136, 107 S.Ct. 1046, 94 L.Ed.2d 190 (1987). We have never invalidated any governmental action on the basis of the *Sherbert* test except the denial of unemployment compensation. Although we have sometimes purported to apply the *Sherbert* test in contexts other than that, we have always found the test satisfied, see *United States v. Lee,* 455 U.S. 252, 102 S.Ct. 1051, 71 L.Ed.2d 127 (1982); *Gillette v. United States,* 401 U.S. 437, 91 S.Ct. 828, 28 L.Ed.2d 168 (1971). In recent years we have abstained from applying the *Sherbert* test (outside the unemployment compensation field) at all. In *Bowen v. Roy,* 476 U.S. 693, 106 S.Ct. 2147, 90 L.Ed.2d 735 (1986), we declined to apply *Sherbert* analysis to a federal statutory scheme that required benefit applicants and recipients to provide their Social Security numbers. The plaintiffs in that case asserted that it would violate their religious beliefs to obtain and provide a Social Security number for their daughter. We held the statute's application to the plaintiffs valid regardless of whether it was necessary to effectuate a compelling interest. See 476 U.S., at 699-701, 106 S.Ct., at 2151-53. In *Lyng v. Northwest Indian Cemetery Protective Assn.,* 485 U.S. 439, 108 S.Ct. 1319, 99 L.Ed.2d 534 (1988), we declined to apply *Sherbert* analysis to the Government's logging and road construction activities on lands used for religious purposes by several Native American Tribes, even though it was undisputed that the activities "could have devastating effects on traditional Indian religious practices," 485 U.S., at 451, 108 S.Ct., at 1326.

In *Goldman v. Weinberger,* 475 U.S. 503, 106 S.Ct. 1310, 89 L.Ed.2d 478 (1986), we rejected application of the *Sherbert* test to military dress regulations that forbade the wearing of yarmulkes. In *O'Lone v. Estate of Shabazz,* 482 U.S. 342, 107 S.Ct.

Employment Division, Department of Human Resources of Oregon v. Smith, 494 U.S. 872, 110 S.Ct. 1595, 108 L.Ed.2d 876 (1990)

2400, 96 L.Ed.2d 282 (1987), we sustained, without mentioning the *Sherbert* test, a prison's refusal to excuse inmates from work requirements to attend worship services.

Even if we were inclined to breathe into *Sherbert* some life beyond the unemployment compensation field, we would not apply it to require exemptions from a generally applicable criminal law. The *Sherbert* test, it must be recalled, was developed in a context that lent itself to individualized governmental assessment of the reasons for the relevant conduct. As a plurality of the Court noted in *Roy*, a distinctive feature of unemployment compensation programs is that their eligibility criteria invite consideration of the particular circumstances behind an applicant's unemployment: "The statutory conditions [in *Sherbert* and *Thomas*] provided that a person was not eligible for unemployment compensation benefits if, 'without good cause,' he had quit work or refused available work. The 'good cause' standard created a mechanism for individualized exemptions." *Bowen v. Roy, supra,* 476 U.S., at 708, 106 S.Ct., at 2156 (opinion of Burger, C.J., joined by Powell and REHNQUIST, JJ.). See also *Sherbert, supra,* 374 U.S., at 401, n. 4, 83 S.Ct., at 1792, n. 4 (reading state unemployment compensation law as allowing benefits for unemployment caused by at least some "personal reasons"). As the plurality pointed out in *Roy*, our decisions in the unemployment cases stand for the proposition that where the State has in place a system of individual exemptions, it may not refuse to extend that system to cases of "religious hardship" without compelling reason. *Bowen v. Roy, supra,* 476 U.S., at 708, 106 S.Ct., at 2156-57.

Whether or not the decisions are that limited, they at least have nothing to do with an across-the-board criminal prohibition on a particular form of conduct. Although, as noted earlier, we have sometimes used the *Sherbert* test to analyze free exercise challenges to such laws, see *United States v. Lee*, supra, 455 U.S., at 257-260, 102 S.Ct., at 1055-1057; *Gillette v. United States, supra,* 401 U.S., at 462, 91 S.Ct., at 842-43, we have never applied the test to invalidate one. We conclude today that the sounder approach, and the approach in accord with the vast majority of our precedents, is to hold the test inapplicable to such challenges. The government's ability to enforce generally applicable prohibitions of socially harmful conduct, like its ability to carry out other aspects of public policy, "cannot depend on measuring the effects of a governmental action on a religious objector's spiritual development." *Lyng, supra,* 485 U.S., at 451, 108 S.Ct., at 1326. To make an individual's obligation to obey such a law contingent upon the law's coincidence with his religious beliefs, except where the State's interest is "compelling"—permitting him, by virtue of his beliefs, "to become a law unto himself," *Reynolds v. United States,* 98 U.S., at 167—contradicts both constitutional tradition and common sense.[2]

Employment Division, Department of Human Resources of Oregon v. Smith, 494 U.S. 872, 110 S.Ct. 1595, 108 L.Ed.2d 876 (1990)

The "compelling government interest" requirement seems benign, because it is familiar from other fields. But using it as the standard that must be met before the government may accord different treatment on the basis of race, see, *e.g.,* Palmore v. Sidoti, 466 U.S. 429, 432, 104 S.Ct. 1879, 1881-82, 80 L.Ed.2d 421 (1984), or before the government may regulate the content of speech, see, *e.g., Sable Communications of California v. FCC,* 492 U.S. 115, 126, 109 S.Ct. 2829, 2836, 106 L.Ed.2d 93 (1989), is not remotely comparable to using it for the purpose asserted here. What it produces in those other fields—equality of treatment and an unrestricted flow of contending speech—are constitutional norms; what it would produce here—a private right to ignore generally applicable laws—is a constitutional anomaly.[3]

Nor is it possible to limit the impact of respondents' proposal by requiring a "compelling state interest" only when the conduct prohibited is "central" to the individual's religion. Cf. *Lyng v. Northwest Indian Cemetery Protective Assn.,* 485 U.S., at 474-476, 108 S.Ct., at 1338-1339 (BRENNAN, J., dissenting). It is no more appropriate for judges to determine the "centrality" of religious beliefs before applying a "compelling interest" test in the free exercise field, than it would be for them to determine the "importance" of ideas before applying the "compelling interest" test in the free speech field. What principle of law or logic can be brought to bear to contradict a believer's assertion that a particular act is "central" to his personal faith? Judging the centrality of different religious practices is akin to the unacceptable "business of evaluating the relative merits of differing religious claims." *United States v. Lee,* 455 U.S., at 263 n. 2, 102 S.Ct., at 1058 n. 2 (STEVENS, J., concurring). As we reaffirmed only last Term, "[i]t is not within the judicial ken to question the centrality of particular beliefs or practices to a faith, or the validity of particular litigants' interpretations of those creeds." *Hernandez v. Commissioner,* 490 U.S., at 699, 109 S.Ct., at 2148. Repeatedly and in many different contexts, we have warned that courts must not presume to determine the place of a particular belief in a religion or the plausibility of a religious claim. See, *e.g., Thomas v. Review Bd. of Indiana Employment Security Div.,* 450 U.S., at 716, 101 S.Ct., at 1431; *Presbyterian Church in U.S. v. Mary Eliza beth Blue Hull Memorial Presbyterian Church,* 393 U.S., at 450, 89 S.Ct., at 606-07; *Jones v. Wolf,* 443 U.S. 595, 602-606, 99 S.Ct. 3020, 3024-3027, 61 L.Ed.2d 775 (1979); *United States v. Ballard,* 322 U.S. 78, 85-87, 64 S.Ct. 882, 885-87, 88 L.Ed. 1148 (1944).[4]

If the "compelling interest" test is to be applied at all, then, it must be applied across the board, to all actions thought to be religiously commanded. Moreover, if "compelling interest" really means what it says (and watering it down here would subvert its rigor in the other fields where it is applied), many laws will not meet the test. Any society adopting such a system would be courting anarchy, but that danger increases in direct

Employment Division, Department of Human Resources of Oregon v. Smith, 494 U.S. 872, 110 S.Ct. 1595, 108 L.Ed.2d 876 (1990)

proportion to the society's diversity of religious beliefs, and its determination to coerce or suppress none of them. Precisely because "we are a cosmopolitan nation made up of people of almost every conceivable religious preference," *Braunfeld v. Brown,* 366 U.S., at 606, 81 S.Ct., at 1147, and precisely because we value and protect that religious divergence, we cannot afford the luxury of deeming *presumptively invalid,* as applied to the religious objector, every regulation of conduct that does not protect an interest of the highest order. The rule respondents favor would open the prospect of constitutionally required religious exemptions from civic obligations of almost every conceivable kind ranging from compulsory military service, see, *e.g., Gillette v. United States,* 401 U.S. 437, 91 S.Ct. 828, 28 L.Ed.2d 168 (1971), to the payment of taxes, see, *e.g., United States v. Lee, supra;* to health and safety regulation such as manslaughter and child neglect laws, see, *e.g., Funkhouser v. State,* 763 P.2d 695 (Okla.Crim.App.1988), compulsory vaccination laws, see, *e.g., Cude v. State,* 237 Ark. 927, 377 S.W.2d 816 (1964), drug laws, see, *e.g., Olsen v. Drug Enforcement Administration,* 279 U.S.App.D.C. 1, 878 F.2d 1458 (1989), and traffic laws, see *Cox v. New Hampshire,* 312 U.S. 569, 61 S.Ct. 762, 85 L.Ed. 1049 (1941); to social welfare legislation such as minimum wage laws, see *Tony and Susan Alamo Foundation v. Secretary of Labor,* 471 U.S. 290, 105 S.Ct. 1953, 85 L.Ed.2d 278 (1985), child labor laws, see *Prince v. Massachusetts,*

321 U.S. 158, 64 S.Ct. 438, 88 L.Ed. 645 (1944), animal cruelty laws, see, *e.g., Church of the Lukumi Babalu Aye Inc. v. City of Hialeah,* 723 F.Supp. 1467 (SD Fla.1989), cf. *State v. Massey,* 229 N.C. 734, 51 S.E.2d 179, appeal dism'd, 336 U.S. 942, 69 S.Ct. 813, 93 L.Ed. 1099 (1949), environmental protection laws, see *United States v. Little,* 638 F.Supp. 337 (Mont.1986), and laws providing for equality of opportunity for the races, see, *e.g., Bob Jones University v. United States,* 461 U.S. 574, 603-604, 103 S.Ct. 2017, 2034-2035, 76 L.Ed.2d 157 (1983). The First Amendment's protection of religious liberty does not require this.[5]

Values that are protected against government interference through enshrinement in the Bill of Rights are not thereby banished from the political process. Just as a society that believes in the negative protection accorded to the press by the First Amendment is likely to enact laws that affirmatively foster the dissemination of the printed word, so also a society that believes in the negative protection accorded to religious belief can be expected to be solicitous of that value in its legislation as well. It is therefore not surprising that a number of States have made an exception to their drug laws for sacramental peyote use. See, *e.g.,* Ariz.Rev.Stat.Ann. §§ 13-3402(B)(1)-(3) (1989); Colo.Rev.Stat. § 12-22-317(3) (1985); N.M.Stat.Ann. § 30-31-6(D) (Supp.1989). But to say that a nondiscriminatory religious-practice exemption is permitted, or even that it is desirable, is not to say that it is constitutionally required, and that the appropriate

Employment Division, Department of Human Resources of Oregon v. Smith, 494 U.S. 872, 110 S.Ct. 1595, 108 L.Ed.2d 876 (1990)

occasions for its creation can be discerned by the courts. It may fairly be said that leaving accommodation to the political process will place at a relative disadvantage those religious practices that are not widely engaged in; but that unavoidable consequence of democratic government must be preferred to a system in which each conscience is a law unto itself or in which judges weigh the social importance of all laws against the centrality of all religious beliefs.

* * *

Because respondents' ingestion of peyote was prohibited under Oregon law, and because that prohibition is constitutional, Oregon may, consistent with the Free Exercise Clause, deny respondents unemployment compensation when their dismissal results from use of the drug. The decision of the Oregon Supreme Court is accordingly reversed.

It is so ordered.

[*] Although Justice BRENNAN, Justice MARSHALL, and Justice BLACKMUN join Parts I and II of this opinion, they do not concur in the judgment.

[1.] Both lines of cases have specifically adverted to the non-free-exercise principle involved. *Cantwell,* for example, observed that "[t]he fundamental law declares ns # Employment Division, Department of Human Resources of Oregon v. Smith, 494 U.S. 872, 110 S.Ct. 1595, 108 L.Ed.2d 876 (1990)

the interest of the United States that the free exercise of religion be not prohibited and that freedom to communicate information and opinion be not abridged." 310 U.S., at 307, 60 S.Ct., at 905. *Murdock* said:

"We do not mean to say that religious groups and the press are free from all financial burdens of government. . . . We have here something quite different, for example, from a tax on the income of one who engages in religious activities or a tax on property used or employed in connection with those activities. It is one thing to impose a tax on the income or property of a preacher. It is quite another thing to exact a tax from him for the privilege of delivering a sermon. . . . Those who can deprive religious groups of their colporteurs can take from them a part of the vital power of the press which has survived from the Reformation." 319 U.S., at 112, 63 S.Ct., at 874.

Yoder said that "the Court's holding in *Pierce* stands as a charter of the rights of parents to direct the religious upbringing of their children. And, when the interests of parenthood are combined with a free exercise claim of the nature revealed by this record, more than merely a 'reasonable relation to some purpose within the competency of the State' is required to sustain the validity of the State's requirement under the First Amendment." 406 U.S., at 233, 92 S.Ct., at 1542.

2. Justice O'CONNOR seeks to distinguish *Lyng v. Northwest Indian Cemetery Protective Assn.,* 485 U.S.

Employment Division, Department of Human Resources of Oregon v. Smith, 494 U.S. 872, 110 S.Ct. 1595, 108 L.Ed.2d 876 (1990)

439, 108 S.Ct. 1319, 99 L.Ed.2d 534 (1988), and *Bowen v. Roy,* 476 U.S. 693, 106 S.Ct. 2147, 90 L.Ed.2d 735 (1986), on the ground that those cases involved the government's conduct of "its own internal affairs," which is different because, as Justice Douglas said in *Sherbert,* " 'the Free Exercise Clause is written in terms of what the government cannot do to the individual, not in terms of what the individual can exact from the government.' " *Post,* at 900 (O'CONNOR, J., concurring in judgment), quoting *Sherbert v. Verner,* 374 U.S. 398, 412, 83 S.Ct. 1790, 1798, 10 L.Ed.2d 965 (1963) (Douglas, J., concurring). But since Justice Douglas voted with the majority in *Sherbert,* that quote obviously envisioned that what "the government cannot do to the individual" includes not just the prohibition of an individual's freedom of action through criminal laws but also the running of its programs (in *Sherbert,* state unemployment compensation) in such fashion as to harm the individual's religious interests. Moreover, it is hard to see any reason in principle or practicality why the government should have to tailor its health and safety laws to conform to the diversity of religious belief, but should not have to tailor its management of public lands, *Lyng, supra,* or its administration of welfare programs, *Roy, supra.*

[3.] Justice O'CONNOR suggests that "[t]here is nothing talismanic about neutral laws of general applicability," and that all laws burdening religious practices should be subject to compelling-interest scrutiny because "the First

Employment Division, Department of Human Resources of Oregon v. Smith, 494 U.S. 872, 110 S.Ct. 1595, 108 L.Ed.2d 876 (1990)

Amendment unequivocally makes freedom of religion, like freedom from race discrimination and freedom of speech, a 'constitutional nor[m],' not an 'anomaly.' " *Post,* at 901 (opinion concurring in judgment). But this comparison with other fields supports, rather than undermines, the conclusion we draw today. Just as we subject to the most exacting scrutiny laws that make classifications based on race, see *Palmore v. Sidoti,* 466 U.S. 429, 104 S.Ct. 1879, 80 L.Ed.2d 421 (1984), or on the content of speech, see *Sable Communications of California v. FCC,* 492 U.S. 115, 109 S.Ct. 2829, 106 L.Ed.2d 93 (1989), so too we strictly scrutinize governmental classifications based on religion, see *McDaniel v. Paty,* 435 U.S. 618, 98 S.Ct. 1322, 55 L.Ed.2d 593 (1978); see also *Torcaso v. Watkins,* 367 U.S. 488, 81 S.Ct. 1680, 6 L.Ed.2d 982 (1961). But we have held that race-neutral laws that have the *effect* of disproportionately disadvantaging a particular racial group do not thereby become subject to compelling-interest analysis under the Equal Protection Clause, see *Washington v. Davis,* 426 U.S. 229, 96 S.Ct. 2040, 48 L.Ed.2d 597 (1976) (police employment examination); and we have held that generally applicable laws unconcerned with regulating speech that have the *effect* of interfering with speech do not thereby become subject to compelling-interest analysis under the First Amendment, see *Citizen Publishing Co. v. United States,* 394 U.S. 131, 139, 89 S.Ct. 927, 22 L.Ed.2d 148 (1969) (antitrust laws). Our conclusion that generally applicable,

Employment Division, Department of Human Resources of Oregon v. Smith, 494 U.S. 872, 110 S.Ct. 1595, 108 L.Ed.2d 876 (1990)

religion-neutral laws that have the effect of burdening a particular religious practice need not be justified by a compelling governmental interest is the only approach compatible with these precedents.

4. While arguing that we should apply the compelling interest test in this case, Justice O'CONNOR nonetheless agrees that "our determination of the constitutionality of Oregon's general criminal prohibition cannot, and should not, turn on the centrality of the particular religious practice at issue," *post,* at 906-907 (opinion concurring in judgment). This means, presumably, that compelling interest scrutiny must be applied to generally applicable laws that regulate or prohibit *any* religiously motivated activity, no matter how unimportant to the claimant's religion. Earlier in her opinion, however, Justice O'CONNOR appears to contradict this, saying that the proper approach is "to determine whether the burden on the specific plaintiffs before us is constitutionally significant and whether the particular criminal interest asserted by the State before us is compelling." *Post,* at 899. "Constitutionally significant burden" would seem to be "centrality" under another name. In any case, dispensing with a "centrality" inquiry is utterly unworkable. It would require, for example, the same degree of "compelling state interest" to impede the practice of throwing rice at church weddings as to impede the practice of getting married in church. There is no way out of the difficulty that, if general laws are to be

subjected to a "religious practice" exception, *both* the importance of the law at issue *and* the centrality of the practice at issue must reasonably be considered.

Nor is this difficulty avoided by Justice BLACKMUN's assertion that "although . . . courts should refrain from delving into questions whether, as a matter of religious doctrine, a particular practice is 'central' to the religion, . . . I do not think this means that the courts must turn a blind eye to the severe impact of a State's restrictions on the adherents of a minority religion." *Post,* at 919 (dissenting opinion). As Justice BLACKMUN's opinion proceeds to make clear, inquiry into "severe impact" is no different from inquiry into centrality. He has merely substituted for the question "How important is X to the religious adherent?" the question "How great will be the harm to the religious adherent if X is taken away?" There is no material difference.

5. Justice O'CONNOR contends that the "parade of horribles" in the text only "demonstrates . . . that courts have been quite capable of . . . strik[ing] sensible balances between religious liberty and competing state interests." *Post,* at 902 (opinion concurring in judgment). But the cases we cite have struck "sensible balances" only because they have all applied the general laws, despite the claims for religious exemption. In any event, Justice O'CONNOR mistakes the purpose of our parade: it is not to suggest that courts would necessarily permit harmful exemptions from these laws (though they might),

but to suggest that courts would constantly be in the business of determining whether the "severe impact" of various laws on religious practice (to use Justice BLACKMUN's terminology *post,* at 919) or the "constitutiona[l] significan[ce]" of the "burden on the specific plaintiffs" (to use Justice O'CONNOR's terminology *post,* at 899) suffices to permit us to confer an exemption. It is a parade of horribles because it is horrible to contemplate that federal judges will regularly balance against the importance of general laws the significance of religious practice.

Employment Division, Department of Human Resources of Oregon v. Smith, 494 U.S. 872, 110 S.Ct. 1595, 108 L.Ed.2d 876 (1990)

Justice O'CONNOR, with whom Justice BRENNAN, Justice MARSHALL, and Justice BLACKMUN join as to Parts I and II, concurring in the judgment.*

Although I agree with the result the Court reaches in this case, I cannot join its opinion. In my view, today's holding dramatically departs from well-settled First Amendment jurisprudence, appears unnecessary to resolve the question presented, and is incompatible with our Nation's fundamental commitment to individual religious liberty.

I

At the outset, I note that I agree with the Court's implicit determination that the constitutional question upon which we granted review—whether the Free Exercise Clause protects a person's religiously motivated use of peyote from the reach of a State's general criminal law prohibition—is properly presented in this case. As the Court recounts, respondents Alfred Smith and Galen Black (hereinafter respondents) were denied unemployment compensation benefits because their sacramental use of peyote constituted work-related "misconduct," not because they violated Oregon's general criminal prohibition against possession of peyote. We held, however, in *Employment Div., Dept. of Human Resources of Oregon v. Smith,* 485 U.S. 660, 108 S.Ct. 1444, 99 L.Ed.2d 753 (1988) (*Smith I*), that whether a

Employment Division, Department of Human Resources of Oregon v. Smith, 494 U.S. 872, 110 S.Ct. 1595, 108 L.Ed.2d 876 (1990)

State may, consistent with federal law, deny unemployment compensation benefits to persons for their religious use of peyote depends on whether the State, as a matter of state law, has criminalized the underlying conduct. See *id.,* at 670-672, 108 S.Ct., at 1450-51. The Oregon Supreme Court, on remand from this Court, concluded that "the Oregon statute against possession of controlled substances, which include peyote, makes no exception for the sacramental use of peyote." 307 Or. 68, 72-73, 763 P.2d 146, 148 (1988) (footnote omitted).

Respondents contend that, because the Oregon Supreme Court declined to decide whether the Oregon Constitution prohibits criminal prosecution for the religious use of peyote, see *id.,* at 73, n. 3, 763 P.2d, at 148, n. 3, any ruling on the federal constitutional question would be premature. Respondents are of course correct that the Oregon Supreme Court may eventually decide that the Oregon Constitution requires the State to provide an exemption from its general criminal prohibition for the religious use of peyote. Such a decision would then reopen the question whether a State may nevertheless deny unemployment compensation benefits to claimants who are discharged for engaging in such conduct. As the case comes to us today, however, the Oregon Supreme Court has plainly ruled that Oregon's prohibition against possession of controlled substances does not contain an exemption for the religious use of peyote. In light of our decision in *Smith I,* which makes this finding a "necessary predicate to a correct evaluation of respondents' federal claim," 485 U.S., at 672, 108 S.Ct., at 1451, the question presented and addressed is properly before the Court.

II

The Court today extracts from our long history of free exercise precedents the single categorical rule that "if prohibiting the exercise of religion . . . is . . . merely the incidental effect of a generally applicable and otherwise valid provision, the First Amendment has not been offended." *Ante,* at 878 (citations omitted). Indeed, the Court holds that where the law is a generally applicable criminal prohibition, our usual free exercise jurisprudence does not even apply. *Ante,* at 884. To reach this sweeping result, however, the Court must not only give a strained reading of the First Amendment but must also disregard our consistent application of free exercise doctrine to cases involving generally applicable regulations that burden religious conduct.

A

The Free Exercise Clause of the First Amendment commands that "Congress shall make no law . . . prohibiting the free exercise [of religion]." In *Cantwell v. Connecticut,* 310 U.S. 296, 60 S.Ct. 900, 84 L.Ed. 1213 (1940), we held that this prohibition applies to the States by incorporation into the Fourteenth Amendment and that it categorically forbids government regulation of religious beliefs. *Id.,* at 303, 60 S.Ct., at 903. As the

Employment Division, Department of Human Resources of Oregon v. Smith, 494 U.S. 872, 110 S.Ct. 1595, 108 L.Ed.2d 876 (1990)

Court recognizes, however, the "free *exercise* " of religion often, if not invariably, requires the performance of (or abstention from) certain acts. *Ante,* at 877; cf. 3 A New English Dictionary on Historical Principles 401-402 (J. Murray ed. 1897) (defining "exercise" to include "[t]he practice and performance of rites and ceremonies, worship, etc.; the right or permission to celebrate the observances (of a religion)" and religious observances such as acts of public and private worship, preaching, and prophesying). "[B]elief and action cannot be neatly confined in logic-tight compartments." *Wisconsin v. Yoder,* 406 U.S. 205, 220, 92 S.Ct. 1526, 32 L.Ed.2d 15 (1972). Because the First Amendment does not distinguish between religious belief and religious conduct, conduct motivated by sincere religious belief, like the belief itself, must be at least presumptively protected by the Free Exercise Clause.

The Court today, however, interprets the Clause to permit the government to prohibit, without justification, conduct mandated by an individual's religious beliefs, so long as that prohibition is generally applicable. *Ante,* at 878. But a law that prohibits certain conduct—conduct that happens to be an act of worship for someone—manifestly does prohibit that person's free exercise of his religion. A person who is barred from engaging in religiously motivated conduct is barred from freely exercising his religion. Moreover, that person is barred from freely exercising his religion regardless of whether the law prohibits the conduct only when engaged in for

Employment Division, Department of Human Resources of Oregon v. Smith, 494 U.S. 872, 110 S.Ct. 1595, 108 L.Ed.2d 876 (1990)

religious reasons, only by members of that religion, or by all persons. It is difficult to deny that a law that prohibits religiously motivated conduct, even if the law is generally applicable, does not at least implicate First Amendment concerns.

The Court responds that generally applicable laws are "one large step" removed from laws aimed at specific religious practices. *Ibid.* The First Amendment, however, does not distinguish between laws that are generally applicable and laws that target particular religious practices. Indeed, few States would be so naive as to enact a law directly prohibiting or burdening a religious practice as such. Our free exercise cases have all concerned generally applicable laws that had the effect of significantly burdening a religious practice. If the First Amendment is to have any vitality, it ought not be construed to cover only the extreme and hypothetical situation in which a State directly targets a religious practice. As we have noted in a slightly different context, " '[s]uch a test has no basis in precedent and relegates a serious First Amendment value to the barest level of minimum scrutiny that the Equal Protection Clause already provides.' " *Hobbie v. Unemployment Appeals Comm'n of Florida,* 480 U.S. 136, 141-142, 107 S.Ct. 1046, 1049, 94 L.Ed.2d 190 (1987) (quoting *Bowen v. Roy,* 476 U.S. 693, 727, 106 S.Ct. 2147, 2166-67, 90 L.Ed.2d 735 (1986) (O'CONNOR, J., concurring in part and dissenting in part)).

To say that a person's right to free exercise has

Employment Division, Department of Human Resources of Oregon v. Smith, 494 U.S. 872, 110 S.Ct. 1595, 108 L.Ed.2d 876 (1990)

been burdened, of course, does not mean that he has an absolute right to engage in the conduct. Under our established First Amendment jurisprudence, we have recognized that the freedom to act, unlike the freedom to believe, cannot be absolute. See, *e.g., Cantwell, supra,* 310 U.S., at 304, 60 S.Ct., at 903-04; *Reynolds v. United States,* 98 U.S. 145, 161-167, 25 L.Ed. 244 (1879). Instead, we have respected both the First Amendment's express textual mandate and the governmental interest in regulation of conduct by requiring the government to justify any substantial burden on religiously motivated conduct by a compelling state interest and by means narrowly tailored to achieve that interest. See *Hernandez v. Commissioner,* 490 U.S. 680, 699, 109 S.Ct. 2136, 2148, 104 L.Ed.2d 766 (1989); *Hobbie, supra,* 480 U.S., at 141, 107 S.Ct., at 1049; *United States v. Lee,* 455 U.S. 252, 257-258 (1982); *Thomas v. Review Bd. of Indiana Employment Security Div.,* 450 U.S. 707, 718, 101 S.Ct. 1425, 1432, 67 L.Ed.2d 624 (1981); *McDaniel v. Paty,* 435 U.S. 618, 626-629, 98 S.Ct. 1322, 1327-1329, 55 L.Ed.2d 593 (1978) (plurality opinion); *Yoder, supra,* 406 U.S., at 215, 92 S.Ct., at 1533; *Gillette v. United States,* 401 U.S. 437, 462, 91 S.Ct. 828, 842, 28 L.Ed.2d 168 (1971); *Sherbert v. Verner,* 374 U.S. 398, 403, 83 S.Ct. 1790, 1793-94, 10 L.Ed.2d 965 (1963); see also *Bowen v. Roy, supra,* 476 U.S., at 732, 106 S.Ct., at 2169 (opinion concurring in part and dissenting in part); *West Virginia State Bd. of Ed. v. Barnette,* 319 U.S. 624, 639, 63 S.Ct. 1178, 1186, 87 L.Ed. 1628 (1943). The compelling interest test effectuates the First Amendment's command that religious liberty is an independent liberty, that it occupies a preferred position, and that the Court will not permit encroachments upon this liberty, whether direct or indirect, unless required by clear and compelling governmental interests "of the highest order," *Yoder, supra,* 406 U.S., at 215, 92 S.Ct., at 1533. "Only an especially important governmental interest pursued by narrowly tailored means can justify exacting a sacrifice of First Amendment freedoms as the price for an equal share of the rights, benefits, and privileges enjoyed by other citizens." *Roy, supra,* 476 U.S., at 728, 106 S.Ct., at 2167 (opinion concurring in part and dissenting in part).

The Court attempts to support its narrow reading of the Clause by claiming that "[w]e have never held that an individual's religious beliefs excuse him from compliance with an otherwise valid law prohibiting conduct that the State is free to regulate." *Ante,* at 878-879. But as the Court later notes, as it must, in cases such as *Cantwell* and *Yoder* we have in fact interpreted the Free Exercise Clause to forbid application of a generally applicable prohibition to religiously motivated conduct. See *Cantwell,* 310 U.S., at 304-307, 60 S.Ct., at 903-905; *Yoder,* 406 U.S., at 214-234, 92 S.Ct., at 1532-1542. Indeed, in *Yoder* we expressly rejected the interpretation the Court now adopts:

"[O]ur decisions have rejected the idea that religiously grounded conduct is always outside the

Employment Division, Department of Human Resources of Oregon v. Smith, 494 U.S. 872, 110 S.Ct. 1595, 108 L.Ed.2d 876 (1990)

protection of the Free Exercise Clause. It is true that activities of individuals, even when religiously based, are often subject to regulation by the States in the exercise of their undoubted power to promote the health, safety, and general welfare, or the Federal Government in the exercise of its delegated powers. But to agree that religiously grounded conduct must often be subject to the broad police power of the State is not to deny that there are areas of conduct protected by the Free Exercise Clause of the First Amendment and thus beyond the power of the State to control, *even under regulations of general applicability*. . . . " ". . . A regulation neutral on its face may, in its application, nonetheless offend the constitutional requirement for government neutrality if it unduly burdens the free exercise of religion." *Id.,* at 219-220, 92 S.Ct., at 1535-36 (emphasis added; citations omitted).

The Court endeavors to escape from our decisions in *Cantwell* and *Yoder* by labeling them "hybrid" decisions, *ante,* at 892, but there is no denying that both cases expressly relied on the Free Exercise Clause, see *Cantwell,* 310 U.S., at 303-307, 60 S.Ct., at 903-905; *Yoder, supra,* 406 U.S., at 219-229, 92 S.Ct., at 1535-1540, and that we have consistently regarded those cases as part of the mainstream of our free exercise jurisprudence. Moreover, in each of the other cases cited by the Court to support its categorical rule, *ante,* at 879-880, we rejected the particular constitutional claims before us only after carefully weighing the competing interests. See *Prince v. Massachusetts,* 321 U.S. 158, 168-170, 64 S.Ct. 438, 443-444, 88 L.Ed. 645 (1944) (state interest in regulating children's activities justifies denial of religious exemption from child labor laws); *Braunfeld v. Brown,* 366 U.S. 599, 608-609, 81 S.Ct. 1144, 1148-1149, 6 L.Ed.2d 563 (1961) (plurality opinion) (state interest in uniform day of rest justifies denial of religious exemption from Sunday closing law); *Gillette, supra,* 401 U.S., at 462, 91 S.Ct., at 842-43 (state interest in military affairs justifies denial of religious exemption from conscription laws); *Lee, supra,* 455 U.S., at 258-259, 102 S.Ct., at 1055-1056 (state interest in comprehensive Social Security system justifies denial of religious exemption from mandatory participation requirement). That we rejected the free-exercise claims in those cases hardly calls into question the applicability of First Amendment doctrine in the first place. Indeed, it is surely unusual to judge the vitality of a constitutional doctrine by looking to the win-loss record of the plaintiffs who happen to come before us.

B

Respondents, of course, do not contend that their conduct is automatically immune from all governmental regulation simply because it is motivated by their sincere religious beliefs. The Court's rejection of that argument, *ante,* at 882, might therefore be regarded as merely harmless dictum. Rather, respondents invoke our traditional compelling interest test to argue that the Free

Employment Division, Department of Human Resources of Oregon v. Smith, 494 U.S. 872, 110 S.Ct. 1595, 108 L.Ed.2d 876 (1990)

Exercise Clause requires the State to grant them a limited exemption from its general criminal prohibition against the possession of peyote. The Court today, however, denies them even the opportunity to make that argument, concluding that "the sounder approach, and the approach in accord with the vast majority of our precedents, is to hold the [compelling interest] test inapplicable to" challenges to general criminal prohibitions. *Ante,* at 885.

In my view, however, the essence of a free exercise claim is relief from a burden imposed by government on religious practices or beliefs, whether the burden is imposed directly through laws that prohibit or compel specific religious practices, or indirectly through laws that, in effect, make abandonment of one's own religion or conformity to the religious beliefs of others the price of an equal place in the civil community. As we explained in *Thomas:*

"Where the state conditions receipt of an important benefit upon conduct proscribed by a religious faith, or where it denies such a benefit because of conduct mandated by religious belief, thereby putting substantial pressure on an adherent to modify his behavior and to violate his beliefs, a burden upon religion exists." 450 U.S., at 717-718, 101 S.Ct., at 1432. See also *Frazee v. Illinois Dept. of Employment Security,* 489 U.S. 829, 832, 109 S.Ct. 1514, 1516-1517, 103 L.Ed.2d 914 (1989); *Hobbie,* 480 U.S., at 141, 107 S.Ct., at 1049. A State that makes criminal an individual's religiously motivated conduct burdens that individual's free exercise

Employment Division, Department of Human Resources of Oregon v. Smith, 494 U.S. 872, 110 S.Ct. 1595, 108 L.Ed.2d 876 (1990)

of religion in the severest manner possible, for it "results in the choice to the individual of either abandoning his religious principle or facing criminal prosecution." *Braunfeld, supra,* 366 U.S., at 605, 81 S.Ct., at 1147. I would have thought it beyond argument that such laws implicate free exercise concerns.

Indeed, we have never distinguished between cases in which a State conditions receipt of a benefit on conduct prohibited by religious beliefs and cases in which a State affirmatively prohibits such conduct. The *Sherbert* compelling interest test applies in both kinds of cases. See, *e.g., Lee,* 455 U.S., at 257-260, 102 S.Ct., at 1055-1057 (applying *Sherbert* to uphold Social Security tax liability); *Gillette,* 401 U.S., at 462, 91 S.Ct., at 842-43 (applying *Sherbert* to uphold military conscription requirement); *Yoder,* 406 U.S., at 215-234, 92 S.Ct., at 1533-1538 (applying *Sherbert* to strike down criminal convictions for violation of compulsory school attendance law). As I noted in *Bowen v. Roy* :

"The fact that the underlying dispute involves an award of benefits rather than an exaction of penalties does not grant the Government license to apply a different version of the Constitution. . . .

". . . The fact that appellees seek exemption from a precondition that the Government attaches to an award of benefits does not, therefore, generate a meaningful distinction between this case and one where appellees seek an exemption from the Government's imposition of penalties upon them." 476 U.S., at 731-

Employment Division, Department of Human Resources of Oregon v. Smith, 494 U.S. 872, 110 S.Ct. 1595, 108 L.Ed.2d 876 (1990)

732, 106 S.Ct., at 2168-2169 (opinion concurring in part and dissenting in part). See also *Hobbie, supra,* 480 U.S., at 141-142, 107 S.Ct., at 1049-1050; *Sherbert,* 374 U.S., at 404, 83 S.Ct., at 1794. I would reaffirm that principle today: A neutral criminal law prohibiting conduct that a State may legitimately regulate is, if anything, *more* burdensome than a neutral civil statute placing legitimate conditions on the award of a state benefit.

Legislatures, of course, have always been "left free to reach actions which were in violation of social duties or subversive of good order." *Reynolds,* 98 U.S., at 164; see also *Yoder, supra,* at 219-220, 92 S.Ct., at 1535-1536; *Braunfeld,* 366 U.S., at 603-604, 81 S.Ct., at 1145-1146. Yet because of the close relationship between conduct and religious belief, "[i]n every case the power to regulate must be so exercised as not, in attaining a permissible end, unduly to infringe the protected freedom." *Cantwell,* 310 U.S., at 304, 60 S.Ct., at 903. Once it has been shown that a government regulation or criminal prohibition burdens the free exercise of religion, we have consistently asked the government to demonstrate that unbending application of its regulation to the religious objector "is essential to accomplish an overriding governmental interest," *Lee, supra,* 455 U.S., at 257-258, 102 S.Ct., at 1055, or represents "the least restrictive means of achieving some compelling state interest," *Thomas, supra,* 450 U.S., at 718, 101 S.Ct., at 1432. See, *e.g., Braunfeld, supra,* 366 U.S. at 607, 81

S.Ct., at 1148; *Sherbert, supra,* 374 U.S., at 406, 83 S.Ct., at 1795; *Yoder, supra,* 406 U.S., at 214-215, 92 S.Ct., at 1532-1533; *Roy,* 476 U.S., at 728-732, 106 S.Ct., at 2167-2169 (opinion concurring in part and dissenting in part). To me, the sounder approach—the approach more consistent with our role as judges to decide each case on its individual merits—is to apply this test in each case to determine whether the burden on the specific plaintiffs before us is constitutionally significant and whether the particular criminal interest asserted by the State before us is compelling. Even if, as an empirical matter, a government's criminal laws might usually serve a compelling interest in health, safety, or public order, the First Amendment at least requires a case-by-case determination of the question, sensitive to the facts of each particular claim. Cf. *McDaniel,* 435 U.S., at 628, n. 8, 98 S.Ct., at 1328, n. 8 (plurality opinion) (noting application of *Sherbert* to general criminal prohibitions and the "delicate balancing required by our decisions in" *Sherbert* and *Yoder*). Given the range of conduct that a State might legitimately make criminal, we cannot assume, merely because a law carries criminal sanctions and is generally applicable, that the First Amendment *never* requires the State to grant a limited exemption for religiously motivated conduct.

Moreover, we have not "rejected" or "declined to apply" the compelling interest test in our recent cases. *Ante,* at 883-884. Recent cases have instead affirmed that test as a fundamental part of our First Amendment

Employment Division, Department of Human Resources of Oregon v. Smith, 494 U.S. 872, 110 S.Ct. 1595, 108 L.Ed.2d 876 (1990)

doctrine. See, *e.g., Hernandez,* 490 U.S., at 699, 109 S.Ct., at 2148-2149; *Hobbie, supra,* 480 U.S., at 141-142, 107 S.Ct., at 1049-1050 (rejecting Chief Justice Burger's suggestion in *Roy, supra,* 476 U.S., at 707-708, 106 S.Ct., at 2156-2157, that free exercise claims be assessed under a less rigorous "reasonable means" standard). The cases cited by the Court signal no retreat from our consistent adherence to the compelling interest test. In both *Bowen v. Roy, supra,* and *Lyng v. Northwest Indian Cemetery Protective Assn.,* 485 U.S. 439, 108 S.Ct. 1319, 99 L.Ed.2d 534 (1988), for example, we expressly distinguished *Sherbert* on the ground that the First Amendment does not "require the Government *itself* to behave in ways that the individual believes will further his or her spiritual development. . . . The Free Exercise Clause simply cannot be understood to require the Government to conduct its own internal affairs in ways that comport with the religious beliefs of particular citizens." *Roy, supra,* 476 U.S., at 699, 106 S.Ct., at 2152; see *Lyng, supra,* 485 U.S., at 449, 108 S.Ct., at 1325. This distinction makes sense because "the Free Exercise Clause is written in terms of what the government cannot do to the individual, not in terms of what the individual can exact from the government." *Sherbert, supra,* 374 U.S., at 412, 83 S.Ct., at 1798 (Douglas, J., concurring). Because the case *sub judice,* like the other cases in which we have applied *Sherbert,* plainly falls into the former category, I would apply those established precedents to the facts of this case.

Employment Division, Department of Human Resources of Oregon v. Smith, 494 U.S. 872, 110 S.Ct. 1595, 108 L.Ed.2d 876 (1990)

Similarly, the other cases cited by the Court for the proposition that we have rejected application of the *Sherbert* test outside the unemployment compensation field, *ante,* at 884, are distinguishable because they arose in the narrow, specialized contexts in which we have not traditionally required the government to justify a burden on religious conduct by articulating a compelling interest. See *Goldman v. Weinberger,* 475 U.S. 503, 507, 106 S.Ct. 1310, 1313, 89 L.Ed.2d 478 (1986) ("Our review of military regulations challenged on First Amendment grounds is far more deferential than constitutional review of similar laws or regulations designed for civilian society"); *O'Lone v. Estate of Shabazz,* 482 U.S. 342, 349, 107 S.Ct. 2400, 2404, 96 L.Ed.2d 282 (1987) ("[P]rison regulations alleged to infringe constitutional rights are judged under a 'reasonableness' test less restrictive than that ordinarily applied to alleged infringements of fundamental constitutional rights") (citation omitted). That we did not apply the compelling interest test in these cases says nothing about whether the test should continue to apply in paradigm free exercise cases such as the one presented here.

The Court today gives no convincing reason to depart from settled First Amendment jurisprudence. There is nothing talismanic about neutral laws of general applicability or general criminal prohibitions, for laws neutral toward religion can coerce a person to violate his religious conscience or intrude upon his religious duties just as effectively as laws aimed at religion. Although the

Employment Division, Department of Human Resources of Oregon v. Smith, 494 U.S. 872, 110 S.Ct. 1595, 108 L.Ed.2d 876 (1990)

Court suggests that the compelling interest test, as applied to generally applicable laws, would result in a "constitutional anomaly," *ante,* at 886, the First Amendment unequivocally makes freedom of religion, like freedom from race discrimination and freedom of speech, a "constitutional nor[m]," not an "anomaly." *Ibid.* Nor would application of our established free exercise doctrine to this case necessarily be incompatible with our equal protection cases. Cf. *Rogers v. Lodge,* 458 U.S. 613, 618, 102 S.Ct. 3272, 3276, 73 L.Ed.2d 1012 (1982) (race-neutral law that " 'bears more heavily on one race than another' " may violate equal protection) (citation omitted); *Castaneda v. Partida,* 430 U.S. 482, 492-495, 97 S.Ct. 1272, 1278-1281, 51 L.Ed.2d 498 (1977) (grand jury selection). We have in any event recognized that the Free Exercise Clause protects values distinct from those protected by the Equal Protection Clause. See *Hobbie,* 480 U.S., at 141-142, 107 S.Ct., at 1049. As the language of the Clause itself makes clear, an individual's free exercise of religion is a preferred constitutional activity. See, *e.g.,* McConnell, Accommodation of Religion, 1985 S.Ct.Rev. 1, 9 ("[T]he text of the First Amendment itself 'singles out' religion for special protections"); P. Kauper, Religion and the Constitution 17 (1964). A law that makes criminal such an activity therefore triggers constitutional concern—and heightened judicial scrutiny even if it does not target the particular religious conduct at issue. Our free speech cases similarly recognize that neutral regulations that affect free speech values are subject to a balancing, rather than categorical, approach. See, *e.g., United States v. O'Brien,* 391 U.S. 367, 377, 88 S.Ct. 1673, 1679, 20 L.Ed.2d 672 (1968); *Renton v. Playtime Theatres, Inc.,* 475 U.S. 41, 46-47, 106 S.Ct. 925, 928-929, 89 L.Ed.2d 29 (1986); cf. *Anderson v. Celebrezze,* 460 U.S. 780, 792-794, 103 S.Ct. 1564, 1571-1573, 75 L.Ed.2d 547 (1983) (generally applicable laws may impinge on free association concerns). The Court's parade of horribles, *ante,* at 888-889, not only fails as a reason for discarding the compelling interest test, it instead demonstrates just the opposite: that courts have been quite capable of applying our free exercise jurisprudence to strike sensible balances between religious liberty and competing state interests.

Finally, the Court today suggests that the disfavoring of minority religions is an "unavoidable consequence" under our system of government and that accommodation of such religions must be left to the political process. *Ante,* at 890. In my view, however, the First Amendment was enacted precisely to protect the rights of those whose religious practices are not shared by the majority and may be viewed with hostility. The history of our free exercise doctrine amply demonstrates the harsh impact majoritarian rule has had on unpopular or emerging religious groups such as the Jehovah's Witnesses and the Amish. Indeed, the words of Justice Jackson in *West Virginia State Bd. of Ed. v. Barnette* (overruling *Minersville School Dist. v. Gobitis,* 310 U.S. 586, 60 S.Ct. 1010, 84 L.Ed. 1375 (1940)) are apt:

Employment Division, Department of Human Resources of Oregon v. Smith, 494 U.S. 872, 110 S.Ct. 1595, 108 L.Ed.2d 876 (1990)

"The very purpose of a Bill of Rights was to withdraw certain subjects from the vicissitudes of political controversy, to place them beyond the reach of majorities and officials and to establish them as legal principles to be applied by the courts. One's right to life, liberty, and property, to free speech, a free press, freedom of worship and assembly, and other fundamental rights may not be submitted to vote; they depend on the outcome of no elections." 319 U.S., at 638, 63 S.Ct., at 1185. See also *United States v. Ballard,* 322 U.S. 78, 87, 64 S.Ct. 882, 886-87, 88 L.Ed. 1148 (1944) ("The Fathers of the Constitution were not unaware of the varied and extreme views of religious sects, of the violence of disagreement among them, and of the lack of any one religious creed on which all men would agree. They fashioned a charter of government which envisaged the widest possible toleration of conflicting views"). The compelling interest test reflects the First Amendment's mandate of preserving religious liberty to the fullest extent possible in a pluralistic society. For the Court to deem this command a "luxury," *ante,* at 888, is to denigrate "[t]he very purpose of a Bill of Rights."

III

The Court's holding today not only misreads settled First Amendment precedent; it appears to be unnecessary to this case. I would reach the same result applying our established free exercise jurisprudence.

Employment Division, Department of Human Resources of Oregon v. Smith, 494 U.S. 872, 110 S.Ct. 1595, 108 L.Ed.2d 876 (1990)

A.

There is no dispute that Oregon's criminal prohibition of peyote places a severe burden on the ability of respondents to freely exercise their religion. Peyote is a sacrament of the Native American Church and is regarded as vital to respondents' ability to practice their religion. See O. Stewart, Peyote Religion: A History 327-336 (1987) (describing modern status of peyotism); E. Anderson, Peyote: The Divine Cactus 41-65 (1980) (describing peyote ceremonies); Teachings from the American Earth: Indian Religion and Philosophy 96-104 (D. Tedlock & B. Tedlock eds. 1975) (same); see also *People v. Woody,* 61 Cal.2d 716, 721-722, 40 Cal.Rptr. 69, 73-74, 394 P.2d 813, 817-818 (1964). As we noted in *Smith I,* the Oregon Supreme Court concluded that "the Native American Church is a recognized religion, that peyote is a sacrament of that church, and that respondent's beliefs were sincerely held." 485 U.S., at 667, 108 S.Ct., at 1449. Under Oregon law, as construed by that State's highest court, members of the Native American Church must choose between carrying out the ritual embodying their religious beliefs and avoidance of criminal prosecution. That choice is, in my view, more than sufficient to trigger First Amendment scrutiny.

There is also no dispute that Oregon has a significant interest in enforcing laws that control the possession and use of controlled substances by its citizens. See, *e.g., Sherbert,* 374 U.S., at 403, 83 S.Ct., at 1793-94 (religiously motivated conduct may be regulated

Employment Division, Department of Human Resources of Oregon v. Smith, 494 U.S. 872, 110 S.Ct. 1595, 108 L.Ed.2d 876 (1990)

where such conduct "pose[s] some substantial threat to public safety, peace or order"); *Yoder,* 406 U.S., at 220, 92 S.Ct., at 1535 ("[A]ctivities of individuals, even when religiously based, are often subject to regulation by the States in the exercise of their undoubted power to promote the health, safety, and general welfare"). As we recently noted, drug abuse is "one of the greatest problems affecting the health and welfare of our population" and thus "one of the most serious problems confronting our society today." *Treasury Employees v. Von Raab,* 489 U.S. 656, 668, 674, 109 S.Ct. 1384, 1395, 103 L.Ed.2d 685 (1989). Indeed, under federal law (incorporated by Oregon law in relevant part, see Ore.Rev.Stat. § 475.005(6) (1987)), peyote is specifically regulated as a Schedule I controlled substance, which means that Congress has found that it has a high potential for abuse, that there is no currently accepted medical use, and that there is a lack of accepted safety for use of the drug under medical supervision. See 21 U.S.C. § 812(b)(1). See generally R. Julien, A Primer of Drug Action 149 (3d ed. 1981). In light of our recent decisions holding that the governmental interests in the collection of income tax, *Hernandez,* 490 U.S., at 699-700, 109 S.Ct., at 2148-2149, a comprehensive Social Security system, see *Lee,* 455 U.S., at 258-259, 102 S.Ct., at 1055-1056, and military conscription, see *Gillette,* 401 U.S., at 460, 91 S.Ct., at 841, are compelling, respondents do not seriously dispute that Oregon has a compelling interest in prohibiting the possession of peyote by its citizens.

Employment Division, Department of Human Resources of Oregon v. Smith, 494 U.S. 872, 110 S.Ct. 1595, 108 L.Ed.2d 876 (1990)

B

Thus, the critical question in this case is whether exempting respondents from the State's general criminal prohibition "will unduly interfere with fulfillment of the governmental interest." *Lee, supra,* 455 U.S. at 259, 102 S.Ct., at 1056; see also *Roy,* 476 U.S., at 727, 106 S.Ct., at 2166 ("[T]he Government must accommodate a legitimate free exercise claim unless pursuing an especially important interest by narrowly tailored means"); *Yoder, supra,* 406 U.S., at 221, 92 S.Ct., at 1536; *Braunfeld,* 366 U.S., at 605-607, 81 S.Ct., at 1146-1148. Although the question is close, I would conclude that uniform application of Oregon's criminal prohibition is "essential to accomplish," *Lee, supra,* at 455 U.S., at 257, 102 S.Ct., at 1055, its overriding interest in preventing the physical harm caused by the use of a Schedule I controlled substance. Oregon's criminal prohibition represents that State's judgment that the possession and use of controlled substances, even by only one person, is inherently harmful and dangerous. Because the health effects caused by the use of controlled substances exist regardless of the motivation of the user, the use of such substances, even for religious purposes, violates the very purpose of the laws that prohibit them. Cf. *State v. Massey,* 229 N.C. 734, 51 S.E.2d 179 (denying religious exemption to municipal ordinance prohibiting handling of poisonous reptiles), appeal dism'd *sub nom. Bunn v. North Carolina,* 336 U.S. 942, 69 S.Ct.

813, 93 L.Ed. 1099 (1949). Moreover, in view of the societal interest in preventing trafficking in controlled substances, uniform application of the criminal prohibition at issue is essential to the effectiveness of Oregon's stated interest in preventing any possession of peyote. Cf. *Jacobson v. Massachusetts*, 197 U.S. 11, 25 S.Ct. 358, 49 L.Ed. 643 (1905) (denying exemption from small pox vaccination requirement).

For these reasons, I believe that granting a selective exemption in this case would seriously impair Oregon's compelling interest in prohibiting possession of peyote by its citizens. Under such circumstances, the Free Exercise Clause does not require the State to accommodate respondents' religiously motivated conduct. See, *e.g., Thomas,* 450 U.S., at 719, 101 S.Ct., at 1432-33. Unlike in *Yoder,* where we noted that "[t]he record strongly indicates that accommodating the religious objections of the Amish by forgoing one, or at most two, additional years of compulsory education will not impair the physical or mental health of the child, or result in an inability to be self-supporting or to discharge the duties and responsibilities of citizenship, or in any other way materially detract from the welfare of society," 406 U.S., at 234, 92 S.Ct., at 1542; see also *id.,* at 238-240, 92 S.Ct., at 1544-1545 (WHITE, J., concurring), a religious exemption in this case would be incompatible with the State's interest in controlling use and possession of illegal drugs.

Respondents contend that any incompatibility is

Employment Division, Department of Human Resources of Oregon v. Smith, 494 U.S. 872, 110 S.Ct. 1595, 108 L.Ed.2d 876 (1990)

belied by the fact that the Federal Government and several States provide exemptions for the religious use of peyote, see 21 CFR § 1307.31 (1989); 307 Or., at 73, n. 2, 763 P.2d, at 148, n. 2 (citing 11 state statutes that expressly exempt sacramental peyote use from criminal proscription). But other governments may surely choose to grant an exemption without Oregon, with its specific asserted interest in uniform application of its drug laws, being *required* to do so by the First Amendment. Respondents also note that the sacramental use of peyote is central to the tenets of the Native American Church, but I agree with the Court, *ante,* at 886-887, that because " '[i]t is not within the judicial ken to question the centrality of particular beliefs or practices to a faith,' " quoting *Hernandez, supra,* at 699, 109 S.Ct., at 2148, our determination of the constitutionality of Oregon's general criminal prohibition cannot, and should not, turn on the centrality of the particular religious practice at issue. This does not mean, of course, that courts may not make factual findings as to whether a claimant holds a sincerely held religious belief that conflicts with, and thus is burdened by, the challenged law. The distinction between questions of centrality and questions of sincerity and burden is admittedly fine, but it is one that is an established part of our free exercise doctrine, see *Ballard,* 322 U.S., at 85-88, 64 S.Ct., at 885-87, and one that courts are capable of making. See *Tony and Susan Alamo Foundation v. Secretary of Labor,* 471 U.S. 290, 303-305, 105 S.Ct.1953, 1962-1963, 85 L.Ed.2d 278 (1985).

Employment Division, Department of Human Resources of Oregon v. Smith, 494 U.S. 872, 110 S.Ct. 1595, 108 L.Ed.2d 876 (1990)

I would therefore adhere to our established free exercise jurisprudence and hold that the State in this case has a compelling interest in regulating peyote use by its citizens and that accommodating respondents' religiously motivated conduct "will unduly interfere with fulfillment of the governmental interest." *Lee, supra,* 455 U.S., at 259, 102 S.Ct., at 1056. Accordingly, I concur in the judgment of the Court.

Employment Division, Department of Human Resources of Oregon v. Smith, 494 U.S. 872, 110 S.Ct. 1595, 108 L.Ed.2d 876 (1990)

Justice BLACKMUN, with whom Justice BRENNAN and Justice MARSHALL join, dissenting.

This Court over the years painstakingly has developed a consistent and exacting standard to test the constitutionality of a state statute that burdens the free exercise of religion. Such a statute may stand only if the law in general, and the State's refusal to allow a religious exemption in particular, are justified by a compelling interest that cannot be served by less restrictive means.[1] Until today, I thought this was a settled and inviolate principle of this Court's First Amendment jurisprudence. The majority, however, perfunctorily dismisses it as a "constitutional anomaly." *Ante,* at 886. As carefully detailed in Justice O'CONNOR's concurring opinion, *ante,* p. 891, the majority is able to arrive at this view only by mischaracterizing this Court's precedents. The Court discards leading free exercise cases such as *Cantwell v. Connecticut,* 310 U.S. 296, 60 S.Ct. 900, 84 L.Ed. 1213 (1940), and *Wisconsin v. Yoder,* 406 U.S. 205, 92 S.Ct. 1526, 32 L.Ed.2d 15 (1972), as "hybrid." *Ante,* at 882. The Court views traditional free exercise analysis as somehow inapplicable to criminal prohibitions (as opposed to conditions on the receipt of benefits), and to state laws of general applicability (as opposed, presumably, to laws that expressly single out religious practices). *Ante,* at 884-885. The Court cites cases in which, due to various exceptional circumstances, we found strict scrutiny inapposite, to hint that the Court

Employment Division, Department of Human Resources of Oregon v. Smith, 494 U.S. 872, 110 S.Ct. 1595, 108 L.Ed.2d 876 (1990)

has repudiated that standard altogether. *Ante,* at 882-884. In short, it effectuates a wholesale overturning of settled law concerning the Religion Clauses of our Constitution. One hopes that the Court is aware of the consequences, and that its result is not a product of overreaction to the serious problems the country's drug crisis has generated.

This distorted view of our precedents leads the majority to conclude that strict scrutiny of a state law burdening the free exercise of religion is a "luxury" that a well-ordered society cannot afford, *ante,* at 888, and that the repression of minority religions is an "unavoidable consequence of democratic government." *Ante,* at 890. I do not believe the Founders thought their dearly bought freedom from religious persecution a "luxury," but an essential element of liberty—and they could not have thought religious intolerance "unavoidable," for they drafted the Religion Clauses precisely in order to avoid that intolerance.

For these reasons, I agree with Justice O'CONNOR's analysis of the applicable free exercise doctrine, and I join parts I and II of her opinion.[2] As she points out, "the critical question in this case is whether exempting respondents from the State's general criminal prohibition 'will unduly interfere with fulfillment of the governmental interest.' " *Ante,* at 905, quoting *United States v. Lee,* 455 U.S. 252, 259, 102 S.Ct. 1051, 1056, 71 L.Ed.2d 127 (1982). I do disagree, however, with her specific answer to that question.

Employment Division, Department of Human Resources of Oregon v. Smith, 494 U.S. 872, 110 S.Ct. 1595, 108 L.Ed.2d 876 (1990)

I

In weighing the clear interest of respondents Smith and Black (hereinafter respondents) in the free exercise of their religion against Oregon's asserted interest in enforcing its drug laws, it is important to articulate in precise terms the state interest involved. It is not the State's broad interest in fighting the critical "war on drugs" that must be weighed against respondents' claim, but the State's narrow interest in refusing to make an exception for the religious, ceremonial use of peyote. See *Bowen v. Roy,* 476 U.S. 693, 728, 106 S.Ct. 2147, 2167, 90 L.Ed.2d 735 (1986) (O'CONNOR, J., concurring in part and dissenting in part) ("This Court has consistently asked the Government to demonstrate that unbending application of its regulation to the religious objector 'is essential to accomplish an overriding governmental interest,' " quoting *Lee,* 455 U.S., at 257-258, 102 S.Ct., at 1055); *Thomas v. Review Bd. of Indiana Employment Security Div.,* 450 U.S. 707, 719, 101 S.Ct. 1425, 1432, 67 L.Ed.2d 624 (1981) ("focus of the inquiry" concerning State's asserted interest must be "properly narrowed"); *Yoder,* 406 U.S., at 221, 92 S.Ct., at 1536 ("Where fundamental claims of religious freedom are at stake," the Court will not accept a State's "sweeping claim" that its interest in compulsory education is compelling; despite the validity of this interest "in the generality of cases, we must searchingly examine the interests that the State seeks to promote . . . and the impediment to those objectives that would flow from recognizing the claimed

Employment Division, Department of Human Resources of Oregon v. Smith, 494 U.S. 872, 110 S.Ct. 1595, 108 L.Ed.2d 876 (1990)

Amish exemption"). Failure to reduce the competing interests to the same plane of generality tends to distort the weighing process in the State's favor. See Clark, Guidelines for the Free Exercise Clause, 83 Harv.L.Rev. 327, 330-331 (1969) ("The purpose of almost any law can be traced back to one or another of the fundamental concerns of government: public health and safety, public peace and order, defense, revenue. To measure an individual interest directly against one of these rarified values inevitably makes the individual interest appear the less significant"); Pound, A Survey of Social Interests, 57 Harv.L.Rev. 1, 2 (1943) ("When it comes to weighing or valuing claims or demands with respect to other claims or demands, we must be careful to compare them on the same plane . . . [or else] we may decide the question in advance in our very way of putting it").

The State's interest in enforcing its prohibition, in order to be sufficiently compelling to outweigh a free exercise claim, cannot be merely abstract or symbolic. The State cannot plausibly assert that unbending application of a criminal prohibition is essential to fulfill any compelling interest, if it does not, in fact, attempt to enforce that prohibition. In this case, the State actually has not evinced any concrete interest in enforcing its drug laws against religious users of peyote. Oregon has never sought to prosecute respondents, and does not claim that it has made significant enforcement efforts against other religious users of peyote.[3] The State's asserted interest thus amounts only to the symbolic preservation of an

Employment Division, Department of Human Resources of Oregon v. Smith, 494 U.S. 872, 110 S.Ct. 1595, 108 L.Ed.2d 876 (1990)

unenforced prohibition. But a government interest in "symbolism, even symbolism for so worthy a cause as the abolition of unlawful drugs," *Treasury Employees v. Von Raab,* 489 U.S. 656, 687, 109 S.Ct. 1384, 1402, 103 L.Ed.2d 685 (1989) (SCALIA, J., dissenting), cannot suffice to abrogate the constitutional rights of individuals.

Similarly, this Court's prior decisions have not allowed a government to rely on mere speculation about potential harms, but have demanded evidentiary support for a refusal to allow a religious exception. See *Thomas,* 450 U.S., at 719, 101 S.Ct., at 1432 (rejecting State's reasons for refusing religious exemption, for lack of "evidence in the record"); *Yoder,* 406 U.S., at 224-229, 92 S.Ct., at 1537-38 (rejecting State's argument concerning the dangers of a religious exemption as speculative, and unsupported by the record); *Sherbert v. Verner,* 374 U.S. 398, 407, 83 S.Ct. 1790, 1795, 10 L.Ed.2d 965 (1963) ("[T]here is no proof whatever to warrant such fears . . . as those which the [State] now advance[s]"). In this case, the State's justification for refusing to recognize an exception to its criminal laws for religious peyote use is entirely speculative.

The State proclaims an interest in protecting the health and safety of its citizens from the dangers of unlawful drugs. It offers, however, no evidence that the religious use of peyote has ever harmed anyone.[4] The factual findings of other courts cast doubt on the State's assumption that religious use of peyote is harmful. See

Employment Division, Department of Human Resources of Oregon v. Smith, 494 U.S. 872, 110 S.Ct. 1595, 108 L.Ed.2d 876 (1990)

State v. Whittingham, 19 Ariz.App. 27, 30, 504 P.2d 950, 953 (1973) ("[T]he State failed to prove that the quantities of peyote used in the sacraments of the Native American Church are sufficiently harmful to the health and welfare of the participants so as to permit a legitimate intrusion under the State's police power"); *People v. Woody,* 61 Cal.2d 716, 722-723, 40 Cal.Rptr. 69, 74, 394 P.2d 813, 818 (1964) ("[A]s the Attorney General . . . admits, . . . the opinion of scientists and other experts is 'that peyote . . . works no permanent deleterious injury to the Indian' ").

The fact that peyote is classified as a Schedule I controlled substance does not, by itself, show that any and all uses of peyote, in any circumstance, are inherently harmful and dangerous. The Federal Government, which created the classifications of unlawful drugs from which Oregon's drug laws are derived, apparently does not find peyote so dangerous as to preclude an exemption for religious use.[5] Moreover, other Schedule I drugs have lawful uses. See *Olsen v. Drug Enforcement Admin.,* 279 U.S.App.D.C. 1, 6, n. 4, 878 F.2d 1458, 1463, n. 4 (medical and research uses of marijuana).

The carefully circumscribed ritual context in which respondents used peyote is far removed from the irresponsible and unrestricted recreational use of unlawful drugs.[6] The Native American Church's internal restrictions on, and supervision of, its members' use of peyote substantially obviate the State's health and safety concerns. See *Olsen, id.,* at 10, 878 F.2d, at 1467 (" 'The Administrator [of the Drug Enforcement Administration (DEA)] finds that . . . the Native American Church's use of peyote is isolated to specific ceremonial occasions,' " and so " 'an accommodation can be made for a religious organization which uses peyote in circumscribed ceremonies' " (quoting DEA Final Order)); *id.,* at 7, 878 F.2d, at 1464 ("[F]or members of the Native American Church, use of peyote outside the ritual is sacrilegious"); *Woody,* 61 Cal.2d, at 721, 394 P.2d, at 817 ("[T]o use peyote for nonreligious purposes is sacrilegious"); R. Julien, A Primer of Drug Action 148 (3d ed. 1981) ("[P]eyote is seldom abused by members of the Native American Church"); Slotkin, The Peyote Way, in Teachings from the American Earth 96, 104 (D. Tedlock & B. Tedlock eds. 1975) ("[T]he Native American Church . . . refuses to permit the presence of curiosity seekers at its rites, and vigorously opposes the sale or use of Peyote for non-sacramental purposes"); Bergman, Navajo Peyote Use: Its Apparent Safety, 128 Am.J. Psychiatry 695 (1971) (Bergman).[7]

Moreover, just as in *Yoder,* the values and interests of those seeking a religious exemption in this case are congruent, to a great degree, with those the State seeks to promote through its drug laws. See *Yoder,* 406 U.S., at 224, 228-229, 92 S.Ct., at 1540 (since the Amish accept formal schooling up to 8th grade, and then provide "ideal" vocational education, State's interest in enforcing its law against the Amish is "less substantial than . . . for

Employment Division, Department of Human Resources of Oregon v. Smith, 494 U.S. 872, 110 S.Ct. 1595, 108 L.Ed.2d 876 (1990)

children generally"); *id.,* at 238, 92 S.Ct., at 1544 (WHITE, J., concurring). Not only does the church's doctrine forbid nonreligious use of peyote; it also generally advocates self-reliance, familial responsibility, and abstinence from alcohol. See Brief for Association on American Indian Affairs et al. as *Amici Curiae* 33-34 (the church's "ethical code" has four parts: brotherly love, care of family, self-reliance, and avoidance of alcohol (quoting from the church membership card)); *Olsen,* 279 U.S.App.D.C., at 7, 878 F.2d, at 1464 (the Native American Church, "for all purposes other than the special, stylized ceremony, reinforced the state's prohibition"); Woody, 61 Cal.2d, at 721-722, n. 3, 394 P.2d, at 818, n. 3 ("[M]ost anthropological authorities hold Peyotism to be a positive, rather than negative, force in the lives of its adherents . . . the church forbids the use of alcohol . . ."). There is considerable evidence that the spiritual and social support provided by the church has been effective in combating the tragic effects of alcoholism on the Native American population. Two noted experts on peyotism, Dr. Omer C. Stewart and Dr. Robert Bergman, testified by affidavit to this effect on behalf of respondent Smith before the Employment Appeal Board. Smith Tr., Exh. 7; see also E. Anderson, Peyote: The Divine Cactus 165-166 (1980) (research by Dr. Bergman suggests "that the religious use of peyote seemed to be directed in an ego-strengthening direction with an emphasis on interpersonal relationships where each individual is assured of his own significance as well

Employment Division, Department of Human Resources of Oregon v. Smith, 494 U.S. 872, 110 S.Ct. 1595, 108 L.Ed.2d 876 (1990)

as the support of the group"; many people have " 'come through difficult crises with the help of this religion. . . . It provides real help in seeing themselves not as people whose place and way in the world is gone, but as people whose way can be strong enough to change and meet new challenges' " (quoting Bergman 698)); Pascarosa & Futterman, Ethnopsychedelic Therapy for Alcoholics: Observations in the Peyote Ritual of the Native American Church, 8 J. of Psychedelic Drugs, No. 3, p. 215 (1976) (religious peyote use has been helpful in overcoming alcoholism); Albaugh & Anderson, Peyote in the Treatment of Alcoholism among American Indians, 131 Am.J. Psychiatry 1247, 1249 (1974) ("[T]he philosophy, teachings, and format of the [Native American Church] can be of great benefit to the Indian alcoholic"); see generally O. Stewart, Peyote Religion 75 *et seq.* (1987) (noting frequent observations, across many tribes and periods in history, of correlation between peyotist religion and abstinence from alcohol). Far from promoting the lawless and irresponsible use of drugs, Native American Church members' spiritual code exemplifies values that Oregon's drug laws are presumably intended to foster.

The State also seeks to support its refusal to make an exception for religious use of peyote by invoking its interest in abolishing drug trafficking. There is, however, practically no illegal traffic in peyote. See *Olsen,* 279 U.S.App.D.C., at 6, 7, 878 F.2d, at 1463, 1467 (quoting DEA Final Order to the effect that total amount of peyote

Employment Division, Department of Human Resources of Oregon v. Smith, 494 U.S. 872, 110 S.Ct. 1595, 108 L.Ed.2d 876 (1990)

seized and analyzed by federal authorities between 1980 and 1987 was 19.4 pounds; in contrast, total amount of marijuana seized during that period was over 15 million pounds). Also, the availability of peyote for religious use, even if Oregon were to allow an exemption from its criminal laws, would still be strictly controlled by federal regulations, see 21 U.S.C. §§ 821-823 (registration requirements for distribution of controlled substances); 21 CFR § 1307.31 (1989) (distribution of peyote to Native American Church subject to registration requirements), and by the State of Texas, the only State in which peyote grows in significant quantities. See Texas Health & Safety Code Ann. § 481.111 (1990 pamphlet); Texas Admin.Code, Tit. 37, pt. 1, ch. 13, Controlled Substances Regulations, §§ 13.35-13.41 (1989); *Woody,* 61 Cal.2d, at 720, 394 P.2d, at 816 (peyote is "found in the Rio Grande Valley of Texas and northern Mexico"). Peyote simply is not a popular drug; its distribution for use in religious rituals has nothing to do with the vast and violent traffic in illegal narcotics that plagues this country.

Finally, the State argues that granting an exception for religious peyote use would erode its interest in the uniform, fair, and certain enforcement of its drug laws. The State fears that, if it grants an exemption for religious peyote use, a flood of other claims to religious exemptions will follow. It would then be placed in a dilemma, it says, between allowing a patchwork of exemptions that would hinder its law enforcement efforts, and risking a violation of the Establishment Clause by arbitrarily limiting its religious exemptions. This argument, however, could be made in almost any free exercise case. See Lupu, Where Rights Begin: The Problem of Burdens on the Free Exercise of Religion, 102 Harv.L.Rev. 933, 947 (1989) ("Behind every free exercise claim is a spectral march; grant this one, a voice whispers to each judge, and you will be confronted with an endless chain of exemption demands from religious deviants of every stripe"). This Court, however, consistently has rejected similar arguments in past free exercise cases, and it should do so here as well. See *Frazee v. Illinois Dept. of Employment Security,* 489 U.S. 829, 835, 109 S.Ct. 1514, 1518, 103 L.Ed.2d 914 (1989) (rejecting State's speculation concerning cumulative effect of many similar claims); *Thomas,* 450 U.S., at 719, 101 S.Ct., at 1432 (same); *Sherbert,* 374 U.S., at 407, 83 S.Ct., at 1795.

The State's apprehension of a flood of other religious claims is purely speculative. Almost half the States, and the Federal Government, have maintained an exemption for religious peyote use for many years, and apparently have not found themselves overwhelmed by claims to other religious exemptions.[8] Allowing an exemption for religious peyote use would not necessarily oblige the State to grant a similar exemption to other religious groups. The unusual circumstances that make the religious use of peyote compatible with the State's interests in health and safety and in preventing drug

Employment Division, Department of Human Resources of Oregon v. Smith, 494 U.S. 872, 110 S.Ct. 1595, 108 L.Ed.2d 876 (1990)

trafficking would not apply to other religious claims. Some religions, for example, might not restrict drug use to a limited ceremonial context, as does the Native American Church. See, *e.g., Olsen,* 279 U.S.App.D.C., at 7, 878 F.2d, at 1464 ("[T]he Ethiopian Zion Coptic Church . . . teaches that marijuana is properly smoked 'continually all day' "). Some religious claims, see n. 8, *supra,* involve drugs such as marijuana and heroin, in which there is significant illegal traffic, with its attendant greed and violence, so that it would be difficult to grant a religious exemption without seriously compromising law enforcement efforts.[9] That the State might grant an exemption for religious peyote use, but deny other religious claims arising in different circumstances, would not violate the Establishment Clause. Though the State must treat all religions equally, and not favor one over another, this obligation is fulfilled by the uniform application of the "compelling interest" *test* to all free exercise claims, not by reaching uniform *results* as to all claims. A showing that religious peyote use does not unduly interfere with the State's interests is "one that probably few other religious groups or sects could make," *Yoder,* 406 U.S., at 236, 92 S.Ct., at 1543; this does not mean that an exemption limited to peyote use is tantamount to an establishment of religion. See *Hobbie v. Unemployment Appeals Comm'n of Fla.,* 480 U.S. 136, 144-145, 107 S.Ct. 1046, 1051, 94 L.Ed.2d 190 (1987) ("[T]he government may (and sometimes must) accommodate religious practices and . . . may do so without violating the Establishment Clause"); *Yoder,* 406 U.S., at 220-221, 92 S.Ct., at 1536 ("Court must not ignore the danger that an exception from a general [law] . . . may run afoul of the Establishment Clause, but that danger cannot be allowed to prevent any exception no matter how vital it may be to the protection of values promoted by the right of free exercise"); *id.,* at 234, n. 22, 92 S.Ct., at 1542, n. 22.

II

Finally, although I agree with Justice O'CONNOR that courts should refrain from delving into questions whether, as a matter of religious doctrine, a particular practice is "central" to the religion, *ante,* at 906-907, I do not think this means that the courts must turn a blind eye to the severe impact of a State's restrictions on the adherents of a minority religion. Cf. *Yoder,* 406 U.S., at 219, 92 S.Ct., at 1535 (since "education is inseparable from and a part of the basic tenets of their religion . . . [, just as] baptism, the confessional, or a sabbath may be for others," enforcement of State's compulsory education law would "gravely endanger if not destroy the free exercise of respondents' religious beliefs").

Respondents believe, and their sincerity has *never* been at issue, that the peyote plant embodies their deity, and eating it is an act of worship and communion. Without peyote, they could not enact the essential ritual of their religion. See Brief for Association on American Indian Affairs et al. as *Amici Curiae* 5-6 ("To the

Employment Division, Department of Human Resources of Oregon v. Smith, 494 U.S. 872, 110 S.Ct. 1595, 108 L.Ed.2d 876 (1990)

members, peyote is consecrated with powers to heal body, mind and spirit. It is a teacher; it teaches the way to spiritual life through living in harmony and balance with the forces of the Creation. The rituals are an integral part of the life process. They embody a form of worship in which the sacrament Peyote is the means for communicating with the Great Spirit"). See also O. Stewart, Peyote Religion 327-330 (1987) (description of peyote ritual); T. Hillerman, People of Darkness 153 (1980) (description of Navajo peyote ritual).

If Oregon can constitutionally prosecute them for this act of worship, they, like the Amish, may be "forced to migrate to some other and more tolerant region." *Yoder,* 406 U.S., at 218, 92 S.Ct., at 1534-1535. This potentially devastating impact must be viewed in light of the federal policy—reached in reaction to many years of religious persecution and intolerance—of protecting the religious freedom of Native Americans. See American Indian Religious Freedom Act, 92 Stat. 469, 42 U.S.C. § 1996 (1982 ed.) ("[I]t shall be the policy of the United States to protect and preserve for American Indians their inherent right of freedom to believe, express, and exercise the traditional religions . . ., including but not limited to access to sites, use and possession of sacred objects, and the freedom to worship through ceremonials and traditional rites").[10] Congress recognized that certain substances, such as peyote, "have religious significance because they are sacred, they have power, they heal, they are necessary to the exercise of the rites of the religion,

Employment Division, Department of Human Resources of Oregon v. Smith, 494 U.S. 872, 110 S.Ct. 1595, 108 L.Ed.2d 876 (1990)

they are necessary to the cultural integrity of the tribe, and, therefore, religious survival." H.R.Rep. No. 95-1308, p. 2 (1978), U.S.Code Cong. & Admin.News 1978, pp. 1262, 1263.

The American Indian Religious Freedom Act, in itself, may not create rights enforceable against government action restricting religious freedom, but this Court must scrupulously apply its free exercise analysis to the religious claims of Native Americans, however unorthodox they may be. Otherwise, both the First Amendment and the stated policy of Congress will offer to Native Americans merely an unfulfilled and hollow promise.

III

For these reasons, I conclude that Oregon's interest in enforcing its drug laws against religious use of peyote is not sufficiently compelling to outweigh respondents' right to the free exercise of their religion. Since the State could not constitutionally enforce its criminal prohibition against respondents, the interests underlying the State's drug laws cannot justify its denial of unemployment benefits. Absent such justification, the State's regulatory interest in denying benefits for religiously motivated "misconduct," see *ante,* at 874, is indistinguishable from the state interests this Court has rejected in *Frazee, Hobbie, Thomas,* and *Sherbert.* The State of Oregon cannot, consistently with the Free Exercise Clause, deny respondents unemployment benefits.

Employment Division, Department of Human Resources of Oregon v. Smith, 494 U.S. 872, 110 S.Ct. 1595, 108 L.Ed.2d 876 (1990)

I dissent.

[1.] See *Hernandez v. Commissioner,* 490 U.S. 680, 699, 109 S.Ct. 2136, 2149, 104 L.Ed.2d 766 (1989) ("The free exercise inquiry asks whether government has placed a substantial burden on the observation of a central religious belief or practice and, if so, whether a compelling governmental interest justifies the burden"); *Hobbie v. Unemployment Appeals Comm'n of Fla.,* 480 U.S. 136, 141, 107 S.Ct. 1046, 1049, 94 L.Ed.2d 190 (1987) (state laws burdening religions "must be subjected to strict scrutiny and could be justified only by proof by the State of a compelling interest"); *Bowen v. Roy,* 476 U.S. 693, 732, 106 S.Ct. 2147, 2169, 90 L.Ed.2d 735 (1986) (O'CONNOR, J., concurring in part and dissenting in part) ("Our precedents have long required the Government to show that a compelling state interest is served by its refusal to grant a religious exemption"); *United States v. Lee,* 455 U.S. 252, 257-258, 102 S.Ct. 1051, 1055, 71 L.Ed.2d 127 (1982) ("The state may justify a limitation on religious liberty by showing that it is essential to accomplish an overriding governmental interest"); *Thomas v. Review Bd. of Indiana Employment Security Div.,* 450 U.S. 707, 718, 101 S.Ct. 1425, 1432, 67 L.Ed.2d 624 (1981) ("The state may justify an inroad on religious liberty by showing that it is the least restrictive means of achieving some compelling state interest"); *Wisconsin v. Yoder,* 406 U.S. 205, 215, 92 S.Ct. 1526, 1533, 32 L.Ed.2d 15 (1972) ("[O]nly those interests of the highest order and those not otherwise served can overbalance legitimate claims to the free exercise of religion"); *Sherbert v. Verner,* 374 U.S. 398, 406, 83 S.Ct. 1790, 1795, 10 L.Ed.2d 965 (1963) (question is "whether some compelling state interest . . . justifies the substantial infringement of appellant's First Amendment right").

2. I reluctantly agree that, in light of this Court's decision in *Employment Division, Dept. of Human Resources of Ore. v. Smith,* 485 U.S. 660, 108 S.Ct. 1444, 99 L.Ed.2d 753 (1988), the question on which certiorari was granted is properly presented in this case. I have grave doubts, however, as to the wisdom or propriety of deciding the constitutionality of a criminal prohibition which the State has not sought to enforce, which the State did not rely on in defending its denial of unemployment benefits before the state courts, and which the Oregon courts could, on remand, either invalidate on state constitutional grounds, or conclude that it remains irrelevant to Oregon's interest in administering its unemployment benefits program.

It is surprising, to say the least, that this Court which so often prides itself about principles of judicial restraint and reduction of federal control over matters of state law would stretch its jurisdiction to the limit in order to reach, in this abstract setting, the constitutionality of Oregon's criminal prohibition of peyote use.

Employment Division, Department of Human Resources of Oregon v. Smith, 494 U.S. 872, 110 S.Ct. 1595, 108 L.Ed.2d 876 (1990)

[3.] The only reported case in which the State of Oregon has sought to prosecute a person for religious peyote use is *State v. Soto,* 21 Ore.App. 794, 537 P.2d 142 (1975), cert. denied, 424 U.S. 955, 96 S.Ct. 1431, 47 L.Ed.2d 361 (1976).

[4.] This dearth of evidence is not surprising, since the State never asserted this health and safety interest before the Oregon courts; thus, there was no opportunity for factfinding concerning the alleged dangers of peyote use. What has now become the State's principal argument for its view that the criminal prohibition is enforceable against religious use of peyote rests on no evidentiary foundation at all.

[5.] See 21 CFR § 1307.31 (1989) ("The listing of peyote as a controlled substance in Schedule I does not apply to the nondrug use of peyote in bona fide religious ceremonies of the Native American Church, and members of the Native American Church so using peyote are exempt from registration. Any person who manufactures peyote for or distributes peyote to the Native American Church, however, is required to obtain registration annually and to comply with all other requirements of law"); see *Olsen v. Drug Enforcement Admin.,* 279 U.S.App.D.C. 1, 6-7, 878 F.2d 1458, 1463-1464 (1989) (explaining DEA's rationale for the exception).

Moreover, 23 States, including many that have significant Native American populations, have statutory

Employment Division, Department of Human Resources of Oregon v. Smith, 494 U.S. 872, 110 S.Ct. 1595, 108 L.Ed.2d 876 (1990)

or judicially crafted exemptions in their drug laws for religious use of peyote. See 307 Ore. 68, 73, n. 2, 763 P.2d 146, 148, n. 2 (1988) (case below). Although this does not prove that Oregon must have such an exception too, it is significant that these States, and the Federal Government, all find their (presumably compelling) interests in controlling the use of dangerous drugs compatible with an exemption for religious use of peyote. Cf. *Boos v. Barry,* 485 U.S. 312, 329, 108 S.Ct. 1157, 1168, 99 L.Ed.2d 333 (1988) (finding that an ordinance restricting picketing near a foreign embassy was not the least restrictive means of serving the asserted government interest; existence of an analogous, but more narrowly drawn, federal statute showed that "a less restrictive alternative is readily available").

[6.] In this respect, respondents' use of peyote seems closely analogous to the sacramental use of wine by the Roman Catholic Church. During Prohibition, the Federal Government exempted such use of wine from its general ban on possession and use of alcohol. See National Prohibition Act, Title II, § 3, 41 Stat. 308. However compelling the Government's then general interest in prohibiting the use of alcohol may have been, it could not plausibly have asserted an interest sufficiently compelling to outweigh Catholics' right to take communion.

[7.] The use of peyote is, to some degree, self-limiting. The

Employment Division, Department of Human Resources of Oregon v. Smith, 494 U.S. 872, 110 S.Ct. 1595, 108 L.Ed.2d 876 (1990)

peyote plant is extremely bitter, and eating it is an unpleasant experience, which would tend to discourage casual or recreational use. See *State v. Whittingham,* 19 Ariz.App. 27, 30, 504 P.2d 950, 953 (1973) (" '[P]eyote can cause vomiting by reason of its bitter taste' "); E. Anderson, Peyote: The Divine Cactus 161 (1980) ("[T]he eating of peyote usually is a difficult ordeal in that nausea and other unpleasant physical manifestations occur regularly. Repeated use is likely, therefore, only if one is a serious researcher or is devoutly involved in taking peyote as part of a religious ceremony"); Slotkin, The Peyote Way, in Teachings from the American Earth 96, 98 (D. Tedlock & B. Tedlock eds. 1975) ("[M]any find it bitter, inducing indigestion or nausea").

[8.] Over the years, various sects have raised free exercise claims regarding drug use. In no reported case, except those involving claims of religious peyote use, has the claimant prevailed. See, *e.g., Olsen v. Iowa,* 808 F.2d 652 (CA8 1986) (marijuana use by Ethiopian Zion Coptic Church); *United States v. Rush,* 738 F.2d 497 (CA1 1984) (same), cert. denied, 470 U.S. 1004, 105 S.Ct. 1355, 84 L.Ed.2d 378 (1985); *United States v. Middleton,* 690 F.2d 820 (CA11 1982) (same), cert. denied, 460 U.S. 1051, 103 S.Ct. 1497, 75 L.Ed.2d 929 (1983) (same); *United States v. Hudson,* 431 F.2d 468 (CA5 1970) (marijuana and heroin use by Moslems), cert. denied, 400 U.S. 1011, 91 S.Ct. 575, 577, 27 L.Ed.2d 624 (1971); *Leary v. United States,* 383 F.2d 851 (CA5 1967) (marijuana use by Hindu), rev'd on other grounds, 395 U.S. 6, 89 S.Ct. 1532, 23 L.Ed.2d 57 (1969); *Commonwealth v. Nissenbaum,* 404 Mass. 575, 536 N.E.2d 592 (1989) (marijuana use by Ethiopian Zion Coptic Church); *State v. Blake,* 5 Haw.App. 411, 695 P.2d 336 (1985) (marijuana use in practice of Hindu Tantrism); *Whyte v. United States,* 471 A.2d 1018 (D.C.App.1984) (marijuana use by Rastafarian); *State v. Rocheleau,* 142 Vt. 61, 451 A.2d 1144 (1982) (marijuana use by Tantric Buddhist); *State v. Brashear,* 92 N.M. 622, 593 P.2d 63 (1979) (marijuana use by nondenominational Christian); *State v. Randall,* 540 S.W.2d 156 (Mo.App.1976) (marijuana, LSD, and hashish use by Aquarian Brotherhood Church). See generally Annotation, Free Exercise of Religion as Defense to Prosecution for Narcotic or Psychedelic Drug Offense, 35 A.L.R.3d 939 (1971 and Supp.1989).

[9.] Thus, this case is distinguishable from *United States v. Lee,* 455 U.S. 252, 102 S.Ct. 1051, 71 L.Ed.2d 127 (1982), in which the Court concluded that there was "no principled way" to distinguish other exemption claims, and the "tax system could not function if denominations were allowed to challenge the tax system because tax payments were spent in a manner that violates their religious belief." *Id.,* at 260, 102 S.Ct., at 1056.

[10.] See Federal Agencies Task Force, Report to Congress on American Indian Religious Freedom Act of 1978, pp.

Employment Division, Department of Human Resources of Oregon v. Smith, 494 U.S. 872, 110 S.Ct. 1595, 108 L.Ed.2d 876 (1990)

1-8 (Aug. 1979) (history of religious persecution); Barsh, The Illusion of Religious Freedom for Indigenous Americans, 65 Ore.L.Rev. 363, 369-374 (1986).

Indeed, Oregon's attitude toward respondents' religious peyote use harkens back to the repressive federal policies pursued a century ago:

"In the government's view, traditional practices were not only morally degrading, but unhealthy. 'Indians are fond of gatherings of every description,' a 1913 public health study complained, advocating the restriction of dances and 'sings' to stem contagious diseases. In 1921, Commissioner of Indian Affairs Charles Burke reminded his staff to punish any Indian engaged in 'any dance which involves . . . the reckless giving away of property . . . frequent or prolonged periods of celebration . . . in fact, any disorderly or plainly excessive performance that promotes superstitious cruelty, licentiousness, idleness, danger to health, and shiftless indifference to family welfare.' Two years later, he forbid Indians under the age of 50 from participating in any dances of any kind, and directed federal employees 'to educate public opinion' against them." *Id.*, at 370-371 (footnotes omitted).

497 U.S. 261
110 S.Ct. 2841
111 L.Ed.2d 224
Nancy Beth CRUZAN, by her Parents and Co-Guardians, Lester L. CRUZAN, et ux., Petitioners
v.
DIRECTOR, MISSOURI DEPARTMENT OF HEALTH, et al.
No. 88-1503.

Argued Dec. 6, 1989.
Decided June 25, 1990.

Syllabus

Petitioner Nancy Cruzan is incompetent, having sustained severe injuries in an automobile accident, and now lies in a Missouri state hospital in what is referred to as a persistent vegetative state: generally, a condition in which a person exhibits motor reflexes but evinces no indications of significant cognitive function. The State is bearing the cost of her care. Hospital employees refused, without court approval, to honor the request of Cruzan's parents, co-petitioners here, to terminate her artificial nutrition and hydration, since that would result in death. A state trial court authorized the termination, finding that a person in Cruzan's condition has a fundamental right under the State and Federal Constitutions to direct or refuse the withdrawal of death-prolonging procedures, and that Cruzan's expression to a former housemate that she would not wish to continue her life if sick or injured unless she could live at least halfway normally suggested that she would not wish to continue on with her nutrition and hydration. The State Supreme Court reversed. While recognizing a right to refuse treatment embodied in the common-law doctrine of informed consent, the court questioned its applicability in this case. It also declined to read into the State Constitution a broad right to privacy that would support an unrestricted right to refuse treatment and expressed doubt that the Federal Constitution embodied such a right. The court then decided that the State Living Will statute embodied a state policy strongly favoring the preservation of life, and that Cruzan's statements to her housemate were unreliable for the purpose of determining her intent. It rejected the argument that her parents were entitled to order the termination of her medical treatment, concluding that no person can assume that choice for an incompetent in the absence of the formalities required by the Living Will statute or clear and convincing evidence of the patient's wishes.

Held:

1. The United States Constitution does not forbid Missouri to require that evidence of an incompetent's wishes as to the withdrawal of life-sustaining treatment be proved by clear and convincing evidence. Pp. 269-285.

(a) Most state courts have based a right to refuse treatment on the common-law right to informed consent, see, *e.g., In re Storar,* 52 N.Y.2d 363, 438 N.Y.S.2d 266, 420 N.E.2d 64, or on both that right and a constitutional privacy right, see, *e.g., Superintendent of Belchertown State School v. Saikewicz,* 373 Mass. 728, 370 N.E.2d 417. In addition to relying on state constitutions and the common law, state courts have also turned to state statutes for guidance, see, *e.g., Conservatorship of Drabick,* 200 Cal.App.3d 185, 245 Cal.Rptr. 840. However, these sources are not available to this Court, where the question is simply whether the Federal Constitution prohibits Missouri from choosing the rule of law which it did. Pp. 269-278.

(b) A competent person has a liberty interest under the Due Process Clause in refusing unwanted medical treatment. Cf., *e.g., Jacobson v. Massachusetts,* 197 U.S. 11, 24-30, 25 S.Ct. 358, 360-363, 49 L.Ed. 643. However, the question whether that constitutional right has been violated must be determined by balancing the liberty interest against relevant state interests. For purposes of this case, it is assumed that a competent person would have a constitutionally protected right to refuse lifesaving hydration and nutrition. This does not mean that an incompetent person should possess the same right, since such a person is unable to make an informed and voluntary choice to exercise that hypothetical right or any other right. While Missouri has in effect recognized that under certain circumstances a surrogate may act for the patient in electing to withdraw hydration and nutrition and thus cause death, it has established a procedural safeguard to assure that the surrogate's action conforms as best it may to the wishes expressed by the patient while competent. Pp. 278-280.

(c) It is permissible for Missouri, in its proceedings, to apply a clear and convincing evidence standard, which is an appropriate standard when the individual interests at stake are both particularly important and more substantial than mere loss of money, *Santosky v. Kramer,* 455 U.S. 745, 756, 102 S.Ct. 1388, 1396, 71 L.Ed.2d 599. Here, Missouri has a general interest in the protection and preservation of human life, as well as other, more particular interests, at stake. It may legitimately seek to safeguard the personal element of an individual's choice between life and death. The State is also entitled to guard against potential abuses by surrogates who may not act to protect the patient. Similarly, it is entitled to consider that a judicial proceeding regarding an incompetent's wishes may not be adversarial, with the added guarantee of accurate factfinding that the adversary process brings with it. The State may also properly decline to make judgments about the "quality" of a particular individual's life and simply assert an unqualified interest in the preservation of human life to be weighed against the constitutionally protected interests of the individual. It is self-evident that these interests are more substantial, both on an individual and societal level, than those involved in a common civil dispute. The clear and convincing evidence standard also serves as a societal judgment about how the risk of error should be distributed between the litigants. Missouri may permissibly place the increased risk of an erroneous decision on those seeking to terminate life-sustaining treatment. An erroneous decision not to terminate results in a maintenance of the status quo, with at least the potential that a wrong decision will eventually be corrected or its impact mitigated by an event such as an advancement in medical science or the patient's unexpected death. However, an erroneous decision to withdraw such treatment is not susceptible of correction. Although Missouri's proof requirement may have frustrated the effectuation of Cruzan's not-fully-expressed desires, the Constitution does not require general rules to work flawlessly. Pp. 280-285.

2. The State Supreme Court did not commit constitutional error in concluding that the evidence adduced at trial did not amount to clear and convincing proof of Cruzan's desire to have hydration and nutrition withdrawn. The trial court had not adopted a clear and convincing evidence standard, and Cruzan's observations that she did not want to live life as a "vegetable" did not deal in terms with withdrawal of medical treatment or of hydration and nutrition. P. 285.

3. The Due Process Clause does not require a State to accept the "substituted judgment" of close family members in the absence of substantial proof that their views reflect the patient's. This Court's decision upholding a State's favored treatment of traditional family relationships, *Michael H. v. Gerald D.*, 491 U.S. 110, 109 S.Ct. 2333, 105 L.Ed.2d 91, may not be turned into a constitutional requirement that a State must recognize the primacy of these relationships in a situation like this. Nor may a decision upholding a State's right to permit family decisionmaking, *Parham v. J.R.*, 442 U.S. 584, 99 S.Ct. 2493, 61 L.Ed.2d 101, be turned into a constitutional requirement that the State recognize such decisionmaking. Nancy Cruzan's parents would surely be qualified to exercise such a right of "substituted judgment" were it required by the Constitution. However, for the same reasons that Missouri may require clear and convincing evidence of a patient's wishes, it may also choose to defer only to those wishes rather than confide the decision to close family members. Pp. 285-287.

760 S.W.2d 408, affirmed.

REHNQUIST, C.J., delivered the opinion of the Court, in which WHITE, O'CONNOR, SCALIA, and

KENNEDY, JJ., joined. O'CONNOR, J., *post,* p. 287, and SCALIA, J., *post,* p. 292, filed concurring opinions. BRENNAN, J., filed a dissenting opinion, in which MARSHALL and BLACKMUN,
JJ., joined, *post,* p. 301. STEVENS, J., filed a dissenting opinion, *post,* p. 330.

William H. Colby, Kansas City, Mo., for petitioners.

Robert L. Presson, Jefferson City, Mo., for respondents.

Sol. Gen. Kenneth W. Starr, Washington, D.C., for U.S., as amicus curiae, supporting the respondents, by special leave of Court.

Chief Justice REHNQUIST delivered the opinion of the Court.

Petitioner Nancy Beth Cruzan was rendered incompetent as a result of severe injuries sustained during an automobile accident. Copetitioners Lester and Joyce Cruzan, Nancy's parents and coguardians, sought a court order directing the withdrawal of their daughter's artificial feeding and hydration equipment after it became apparent that she had virtually no chance of recovering her cognitive faculties. The Supreme Court of Missouri held that because there was no clear and convincing evidence of Nancy's desire to have life-sustaining treatment withdrawn under such circumstances, her parents lacked authority to effectuate such a request. We granted certiorari, 492 U.S. 917, 109 S.Ct. 3240, 106 L.Ed.2d 587 (1989), and now affirm.

On the night of January 11, 1983, Nancy Cruzan lost control of her car as she traveled down Elm Road in Jasper County, Missouri. The vehicle overturned, and Cruzan was discovered lying face down in a ditch without detectable respiratory or cardiac function. Paramedics were able to restore her breathing and heartbeat at the accident site, and she was transported to a hospital in an unconscious state. An attending neurosurgeon diagnosed her as having sustained probable cerebral contusions compounded by significant anoxia (lack of oxygen). The Missouri trial court in this case found that permanent brain damage generally results after 6 minutes in an anoxic state; it was estimated that Cruzan was deprived of oxygen from 12 to 14 minutes. She remained in a coma for approximately three weeks and then progressed to an unconscious state in which she was able to orally ingest some nutrition. In order to ease feeding and further the recovery, surgeons implanted a gastrostomy feeding and hydration tube in Cruzan with the consent of her then husband. Subsequent rehabilitative efforts proved unavailing. She now lies in a Missouri state hospital in what is commonly referred to as a persistent vegetative state: generally, a condition in which a person exhibits motor reflexes but evinces no indications of significant cognitive function.[1] The State of Missouri is bearing the cost of her care. After it had become apparent that Nancy Cruzan had virtually no chance of regaining her mental faculties, her parents asked hospital employees to terminate the artificial nutrition and hydration procedures. All agree that such a removal would cause her death. The employees refused to honor the request without court approval. The parents then sought and received authorization from the state trial court for termination. The court found that a person in Nancy's condition had a fundamental right under the State and Federal Constitutions to refuse or direct the withdrawal of "death prolonging procedures." App. to Pet. for Cert. A99. The court also found that Nancy's "expressed thoughts at age twenty-five in somewhat serious conversation with a housemate friend that if sick or injured she would not wish to continue her life unless she could live at least halfway normally suggests that given her present condition she would not wish to continue on with her nutrition and hydration." *Id.,* at A97-A98.

The Supreme Court of Missouri reversed by a divided vote. The court recognized a right to refuse treatment embodied in the common-law doctrine of informed consent, but expressed skepticism about the application of that doctrine in the circumstances of this case. *Cruzan v. Harmon,* 760 S.W.2d 408, 416-417

(1988) (en banc). The court also declined to read a broad right of privacy into the State Constitution which would "support the right of a person to refuse medical treatment in every circumstance," and expressed doubt as to whether such a right existed under the United States Constitution. *Id.*, at 417-418. It then decided that the Missouri Living Will statute, Mo.Rev.Stat. § 459.010 *et seq.* (1986), embodied a state policy strongly favoring the preservation of life. 760 S.W.2d, at 419-420. The court found that Cruzan's statements to her roommate regarding her desire to live or die under certain conditions were "unreliable for the purpose of determining her intent," *id.*, at 424, "and thus insufficient to support the co-guardians['] claim to exercise substituted judgment on Nancy's behalf." *Id.*, at 426. It rejected the argument that Cruzan's parents were entitled to order the termination of her medical treatment, concluding that "no person can assume that choice for an incompetent in the absence of the formalities required under Missouri's Living Will statutes or the clear and convincing, inherently reliable evidence absent here." *Id.*, at 425. The court also expressed its view that "[b]road policy questions bearing on life and death are more properly addressed by representative assemblies" than judicial bodies. *Id.*, at 426.

We granted certiorari to consider the question whether Cruzan has a right under the United States Constitution which would require the hospital to withdraw life-sustaining treatment from her under these circumstances.

At common law, even the touching of one person by another without consent and without legal justification was a battery. See W. Keeton, D. Dobbs, R. Keeton, & D. Owen, Prosser and Keeton on Law of Torts § 9, pp. 39-42 (5th ed. 1984). Before the turn of the century, this Court observed that "[n]o right is held more sacred, or is more carefully guarded, by the common law, than the right of every individual to the possession and control of his own person, free from all restraint or interference of others, unless by clear and unquestionable authority of law." *Union Pacific R. Co. v. Botsford,* 141 U.S. 250, 251, 11 S.Ct. 1000, 1001, 35 L.Ed. 734 (1891). This notion of bodily integrity has been embodied in the requirement that informed consent is generally required for medical treatment. Justice Cardozo, while on the Court of Appeals of New York, aptly described this doctrine: "Every human being of adult years and sound mind has a right to determine what shall be done with his own body; and a surgeon who performs an operation without his patient's consent commits an assault, for which he is liable in damages." *Schloendorff v. Society of New York Hospital,* 211 N.Y. 125, 129-130, 105 N.E. 92, 93 (1914). The informed consent doctrine has become firmly entrenched in American tort law. See Keeton, Dobbs, Keeton, & Owen, *supra,* § 32, pp. 189-192; F. Rozovsky, Consent to Treatment, A Practical Guide 1-98 (2d ed. 1990).

The logical corollary of the doctrine of informed consent is that the patient generally possesses the right not to consent, that is, to refuse treatment. Until about 15 years ago and the seminal decision in *In re Quinlan,* 70 N.J. 10, 355 A.2d 647, cert. denied *sub nom. Garger v. New Jersey,* 429 U.S. 922, 97 S.Ct. 319, 50 L.Ed.2d 289 (1976), the number of right-to-refuse-treatment decisions was relatively few.[2] Most of the earlier cases involved patients who refused medical treatment forbidden by their religious beliefs, thus implicating First Amendment rights as well as common-law rights of self-determination.[3] More recently, however, with the advance of medical technology capable of sustaining life well past the point where natural forces would have brought certain death in earlier times, cases involving the right to refuse life-sustaining treatment have burgeoned. See 760 S.W.2d, at 412, n. 4 (collecting 54 reported decisions from 1976 through 1988).

In the *Quinlan* case, young Karen Quinlan suffered severe brain damage as the result of anoxia and entered a persistent vegetative state. Karen's father sought judicial approval to disconnect his daughter's respirator. The New Jersey Supreme Court granted the relief, holding that

Karen had a right of privacy grounded in the Federal Constitution to terminate treatment. *In re Quinlan,* 70 N.J., at 38-42, 355 A.2d, at 662-664. Recognizing that this right was not absolute, however, the court balanced it against asserted state interests. Noting that the State's interest "weakens and the individual's right to privacy grows as the degree of bodily invasion increases and the prognosis dims," the court concluded that the state interests had to give way in that case. *Id.,* at 41, 355 A.2d, at 664. The court also concluded that the "only practical way" to prevent the loss of Karen's privacy right due to her incompetence was to allow her guardian and family to decide "whether she would exercise it in these circumstances." *Ibid.*

After *Quinlan,* however, most courts have based a right to refuse treatment either solely on the common-law right to informed consent or on both the common-law right and a constitutional privacy right. See L. Tribe, American Constitutional Law § 15-11, p. 1365 (2d ed. 1988). In *Superintendent of Belchertown State School v. Saikewicz,* 373 Mass. 728, 370 N.E.2d 417 (1977), the Supreme Judicial Court of Massachusetts relied on both the right of privacy and the right of informed consent to permit the withholding of chemotherapy from a profoundly retarded 67-year-old man suffering from leukemia. *Id.,* at 737-738, 370 N.E.2d, at 424. Reasoning that an incompetent person retains the same rights as a competent individual "because the value of human dignity extends to both," the court adopted a "substituted judgment" standard whereby courts were to determine what an incompetent individual's decision would have been under the circumstances. *Id.,* at 745, 752-753, 757-758, 370 N.E.2d, at 427, 431, 434. Distilling certain state interests from prior case law—the preservation of life, the protection of the interests of innocent third parties, the prevention of suicide, and the maintenance of the ethical integrity of the medical profession—the court recognized the first interest as paramount and noted it was greatest when an affliction was curable, "as opposed to the State interest where, as here, the issue is not whether, but when, for how long, and at what cost to the individual [a] life may be briefly extended." *Id.,* at 742, 370 N.E.2d, at 426.

In *In re Storar,* 52 N.Y.2d 363, 438 N.Y.S.2d 266, 420 N.E.2d 64, cert. denied, 454 U.S. 858, 102 S.Ct. 309, 70 L.Ed.2d 153 (1981), the New York Court of Appeals declined to base a right to refuse treatment on a constitutional privacy right. Instead, it found such a right-"adequately supported" by the informed consent doctrine. *Id.,* at 376-377, 438 N.Y.S.2d, at 272, 420 N.E.2d, at 70. In *In re Eichner* (decided with *In re Storar, supra*), an 83-year-old man who had suffered brain damage from anoxia entered a vegetative state and was thus incompetent to consent to the removal of his respirator. The court, however, found it unnecessary to reach the question whether his rights could be exercised by others since it found the evidence clear and convincing from statements made by the patient when competent that he "did not want to be maintained in a vegetative coma by use of a respirator." *Id.,* at 380, 438 N.Y.S.2d, at 274, 420 N.E.2d, at 72. In the companion *Storar* case, a 52-year-old man suffering from bladder cancer had been profoundly retarded during most of his life. Implicitly rejecting the approach taken in *Saikewicz, supra,* the court reasoned that due to such life-long incompetency, "it is unrealistic to attempt to determine whether he would want to continue potentially life prolonging treatment if he were competent." 52 N.Y.2d, at 380, 438 N.Y.S.2d, at 275, 420 N.E.2d, at 72. As the evidence showed that the patient's required blood transfusions did not involve excessive pain and without them his mental and physical abilities would deteriorate, the court concluded that it should not "allow an incompetent patient to bleed to death because someone, even someone as close as a parent or sibling, feels that this is best for one with an incurable disease." *Id.,* at 382, 438 N.Y.S.2d, at 275, 420 N.E.2d, at 73.

Many of the later cases build on the principles established in *Quinlan, Saikewicz,* and *Storar/Eichner.* For instance, in *In re Conroy,* 98 N.J. 321, 486 A.2d

1209 (1985), the same court that decided *Quinlan* considered whether a nasogastric feeding tube could be removed from an 84-year-old incompetent nursing-home resident suffering irreversible mental and physical ailments. While recognizing that a federal right of privacy might apply in the case, the court, contrary to its approach in *Quinlan,* decided to base its decision on the common-law right to self-determination and informed consent. 98 N.J., at 348, 486 A.2d, at 1223. "On balance, the right to self-determination ordinarily outweighs any countervailing state interests, and competent persons generally are permitted to refuse medical treatment, even at the risk of death. Most of the cases that have held otherwise, unless they involved the interest in protecting innocent third parties, have concerned the patient's competency to make a rational and considered choice." *Id.,* at 353-354, 486 A.2d, at 1225.

Reasoning that the right of self-determination should not be lost merely because an individual is unable to sense a violation of it, the court held that incompetent individuals retain a right to refuse treatment. It also held that such a right could be exercised by a surrogate decisionmaker using a "subjective" standard when there was clear evidence that the incompetent person would have exercised it. Where such evidence was lacking, the court held that an individual's right could still be invoked in certain circumstances under objective "best interest" standards. *Id.,* at 361-368, 486 A.2d, at 1229-1233. Thus, if some trustworthy evidence existed that the individual would have wanted to terminate treatment, but not enough to clearly establish a person's wishes for purposes of the subjective standard, and the burden of a prolonged life from the experience of pain and suffering markedly outweighed its satisfactions, treatment could be terminated under a "limited-objective" standard. Where no trustworthy evidence existed, and a person's suffering would make the administration of life-sustaining treatment inhumane, a "pure-objective" standard could be used to terminate treatment. If none of these conditions obtained, the court held it was best to err in favor of preserving life. *Id.,* at 364-368, 486 A.2d, at 1231-1233.

The court also rejected certain categorical distinctions that had been drawn in prior refusal-of-treatment cases as lacking substance for decision purposes: the distinction between actively hastening death by terminating treatment and passively allowing a person to die of a disease; between treating individuals as an initial matter versus withdrawing treatment afterwards; between ordinary versus extraordinary treatment; and between treatment by artificial feeding versus other forms of life-sustaining medical procedures. *Id.,* at 369-374, 486 A.2d, at 1233-1237. As to the last item, the court acknowledged the "emotional significance" of food, but noted that feeding by implanted tubes is a "medical procedur[e] with inherent risks and possible side effects, instituted by skilled health-care providers to compensate for impaired physical functioning" which analytically was equivalent to artificial breathing using a respirator. *Id.,* at 373, 486 A.2d, at 1236.[4]

In contrast to *Conroy,* the Court of Appeals of New York recently refused to accept less than the clearly expressed wishes of a patient before permitting the exercise of her right to refuse treatment by a surrogate decisionmaker. *In re Westchester County Medical Center on behalf of O'Connor,* 72 N.Y.2d 517, 534 N.Y.S.2d 886, 531 N.E.2d 607 (1988) (*O'Connor*). There, the court, over the objection of the patient's family members, granted an order to insert a feeding tube into a 77-year-old woman rendered incompetent as a result of several strokes. While continuing to recognize a common-law right to refuse treatment, the court rejected the substituted judgment approach for asserting it "because it is inconsistent with our fundamental commitment to the notion that no person or court should substitute its judgment as to what would be an acceptable quality of life for another. Consequently, we adhere to the view that, despite its pitfalls and inevitable uncertainties, the inquiry must always be narrowed to the patient's expressed intent, with every effort made to minimize the opportunity for error." *Id.,* at 530, 534 N.Y.S.2d, at 892, 531 N.E.2d, at 613 (citation omitted). The court held that the record lacked the requisite clear and convincing evidence of the patient's expressed intent to withhold life-sustaining treatment. *Id.,* at 531-534, 534 N.Y.S.2d, at 892-894, 531 N.E.2d, at 613-615.

Other courts have found state statutory law relevant to the resolution of these issues. In *Conservatorship of Drabick,* 200 Cal.App.3d 185, 245 Cal.Rptr. 840, cert. denied, 488 U.S. 958, 109 S.Ct. 399, 102 L.Ed.2d 387 (1988), the California Court of Appeal authorized the removal of a nasogastric feeding tube from a 44-year-old man who was in a persistent vegetative state as a result of an auto accident. Noting that the right to refuse treatment was grounded in both the common law and a constitutional right of privacy, the court held that a state probate statute authorized the patient's conservator to order the withdrawal of life-sustaining treatment when such a decision was made in good faith based on medical advice and the conservatee's best interests. While acknowledging that "to claim that [a patient's] 'right to choose' survives incompetence is a legal fiction at best," the court reasoned that the respect society accords to persons as individuals is not lost upon incompetence and is best preserved by allowing others "to make a decision that reflects [a patient's] interests more closely than would a purely technological decision to do whatever is possible." [5] *Id.,* 200 Cal.App.3d, at 208, 245 Cal.Rptr., at 854-855. See also *In re Conservatorship of Torres,* 357 N.W.2d 332 (Minn.1984) (Minnesota court had constitutional and statutory authority to authorize a conservator to order the removal of an incompetent individual's respirator since in patient's best interests).

In *In re Estate of Longeway,* 133 Ill.2d 33, 139 Ill.Dec. 780, 549 N.E.2d 292 (1989), the Supreme Court of Illinois considered whether a 76-year-old woman rendered incompetent from a series of strokes had a right to the discontinuance of artificial nutrition and hydration.

Noting that the boundaries of a federal right of privacy were uncertain, the court found a right to refuse treatment in the doctrine of informed consent. *Id.,* at 43-45, 139 Ill.Dec. at 784-785, 549 N.E.2d, at 296-297. The court further held that the State Probate Act impliedly authorized a guardian to exercise a ward's right to refuse artificial sustenance in the event that the ward was terminally ill and irreversibly comatose. *Id.,* at 45-47, 139 Ill.Dec., at 786, 549 N.E.2d, at 298. Declining to adopt a best interests standard for deciding when it would be appropriate to exercise a ward's right because it "lets another make a determination of a patient's quality of life," the court opted instead for a substituted judgment standard. *Id.,* at 49, 139 Ill.Dec., at 787, 549 N.E.2d, at 299. Finding the "expressed intent" standard utilized in *O'Connor, supra,* too rigid, the court noted that other clear and convincing evidence of the patient's intent could be considered. 133 Ill.2d, at 50-51, 139 Ill.Dec., at 787, 549 N.E.2d, at 300. The court also adopted the "consensus opinion [that] treats artificial nutrition and hydration as medical treatment." *Id.,* at 42, 139 Ill.Dec., at 784, 549 N.E.2d, at 296. Cf. *McConnell v. Beverly Enterprises-Connecticut, Inc.,* 209 Conn. 692, 705, 553 A.2d 596, 603 (1989) (right to withdraw artificial nutrition and hydration found in the Connecticut Removal of Life Support Systems Act, which "provid[es] functional guidelines for the exercise of the common law and constitutional rights of self-determination"; attending physician authorized to remove treatment after finding that patient is in a terminal condition, obtaining consent of family, and considering expressed wishes of patient).[6]

As these cases demonstrate, the common-law doctrine of informed consent is viewed as generally encompassing the right of a competent individual to refuse medical treatment. Beyond that, these cases demonstrate both similarity and diversity in their approaches to decision of what all agree is a perplexing question with unusually strong moral and ethical overtones. State courts have available to them for decision a number of sources—state constitutions, statutes, and common law—which are not available to us. In this Court, the question is simply and starkly whether the United States Constitution prohibits Missouri from choosing the rule of decision which it did. This is the first case in which we have been squarely presented with the issue whether the United States Constitution grants what is in common parlance referred to as a "right to die." We follow the judicious counsel of our decision in *Twin City Bank v. Nebeker,* 167 U.S. 196, 202, 17 S.Ct. 766, 769, 42 L.Ed. 134 (1897), where we said that in deciding "a question of such magnitude and importance . . . it is the [better] part of wisdom not to attempt, by any general statement, to cover every possible phase of the subject."

The Fourteenth Amendment provides that no State shall "deprive any person of life, liberty, or property, without due process of law." The principle that a competent person has a constitutionally protected liberty interest in refusing unwanted medical treatment may be inferred from our prior decisions. In *Jacobson v. Massachusetts,* 197 U.S. 11, 24-30, 25 S.Ct. 358, 360-361, 49 L.Ed. 643 (1905), for instance, the Court balanced an individual's liberty interest in declining an unwanted smallpox vaccine against the State's interest in preventing disease. Decisions prior to the incorporation of the Fourth Amendment into the Fourteenth Amendment analyzed searches and seizures involving the body under the Due Process Clause and were thought to implicate substantial liberty interests. See, *e.g., Breithaupt v. Abram,* 352 U.S. 432, 439, 77 S.Ct. 408, 412, 1 L.Ed.2d 448 (1957) ("As against the right of an individual that his person be held inviolable . . . must be set the interests of society . . .").

Just this Term, in the course of holding that a State's procedures for administering antipsychotic medication to prisoners were sufficient to satisfy due process concerns, we recognized that prisoners possess "a significant liberty interest in avoiding the unwanted administration of antipsychotic drugs under the Due Process Clause of the Fourteenth Amendment." *Washington v. Harper,* 494 U.S. 210, 221-222, 110 S.Ct.

1028, 1036, 108 L.Ed.2d 178 (1990); see also *id.,* at 229, 110 S.Ct., at 1041 ("The forcible injection of medication into a nonconsenting person's body represents a substantial interference with that person's liberty"). Still other cases support the recognition of a general liberty interest in refusing medical treatment. *Vitek v. Jones,* 445 U.S. 480, 494, 100 S.Ct. 1254, 1264, 63 L.Ed.2d 552 (1980) (transfer to mental hospital coupled with mandatory behavior modification treatment implicated liberty interests); *Parham v. J.R.,* 442 U.S. 584, 600, 99 S.Ct. 2493, 2503, 61 L.Ed.2d 101 (1979) ("[A] child, in common with adults, has a substantial liberty interest in not being confined unnecessarily for medical treatment").

But determining that a person has a "liberty interest" under the Due Process Clause does not end the inquiry; [7] "whether respondent's constitutional rights have been violated must be determined by balancing his liberty interests against the relevant state interests." *Youngberg v. Romeo,* 457 U.S. 307, 321, 102 S.Ct. 2452, 2461, 73 L.Ed.2d 28 (1982). See also *Mills v. Rogers,* 457 U.S. 291, 299, 102 S.Ct. 2442, 2448, 73 L.Ed.2d 16 (1982).

Petitioners insist that under the general holdings of our cases, the forced administration of life-sustaining medical treatment, and even of artificially delivered food and water essential to life, would implicate a competent person's liberty interest. Although we think the logic of the cases discussed above would embrace such a liberty interest, the dramatic consequences involved in refusal of such treatment would inform the inquiry as to whether the deprivation of that interest is constitutionally permissible. But for purposes of this case, we assume that the United States Constitution would grant a competent person a constitutionally protected right to refuse lifesaving hydration and nutrition.

Petitioners go on to assert that an incompetent person should possess the same right in this respect as is possessed by a competent person. They rely primarily on our decisions in *Parham v. J.R., supra,* and *Youngberg v. Romeo, supra,* 102 S.Ct. 2452, 73 L.Ed.2d 28 (1982). In

Parham, we held that a mentally disturbed minor child had a liberty interest in "not being confined unnecessarily for medical treatment," 442 U.S., at 600, 99 S.Ct., at 2503, but we certainly did not intimate that such a minor child, after commitment, would have a liberty interest in refusing treatment. In *Youngberg,* we held that a seriously retarded adult had a liberty interest in safety and freedom from bodily restraint, 457 U.S., at 320, 102 S.Ct., at 2460. *Youngberg,* however, did not deal with decisions to administer or withhold medical treatment.

The difficulty with petitioners' claim is that in a sense it begs the question: An incompetent person is not able to make an informed and voluntary choice to exercise a hypothetical right to refuse treatment or any other right. Such a "right" must be exercised for her, if at all, by some sort of surrogate. Here, Missouri has in effect recognized that under certain circumstances a surrogate may act for the patient in electing to have hydration and nutrition withdrawn in such a way as to cause death, but it has established a procedural safeguard to assure that the action of the surrogate conforms as best it may to the wishes expressed by the patient while competent. Missouri requires that evidence of the incompetent's wishes as to the withdrawal of treatment be proved by clear and convincing evidence. The question, then, is whether the United States Constitution forbids the establishment of this procedural requirement by the State. We hold that it does not.

Whether or not Missouri's clear and convincing evidence requirement comports with the United States Constitution depends in part on what interests the State may properly seek to protect in this situation. Missouri relies on its interest in the protection and preservation of human life, and there can be no gainsaying this interest. As a general matter, the States—indeed, all civilized nations—demonstrate their commitment to life by treating homicide as a serious crime. Moreover, the majority of States in this country have laws imposing criminal penalties on one who assists another to commit suicide.[8] We do not think a State is required to remain neutral in the face of an informed and voluntary decision by a physically able adult to starve to death.

But in the context presented here, a State has more particular interests at stake. The choice between life and death is a deeply personal decision of obvious and overwhelming finality. We believe Missouri may legitimately seek to safeguard the personal element of this choice through the imposition of heightened evidentiary requirements. It cannot be disputed that the Due Process Clause protects an interest in life as well as an interest in refusing life-sustaining medical treatment. Not all incompetent patients will have loved ones available to serve as surrogate decisionmakers. And even where family members are present, "[t]here will, of course, be some unfortunate situations in which family members will not act to protect a patient." *In re Jobes*, 108 N.J. 394, 419, 529 A.2d 434, 447 (1987). A State is entitled to guard against potential abuses in such situations. Similarly, a State is entitled to consider that a judicial proceeding to make a determination regarding an incompetent's wishes may very well not be an adversarial one, with the added guarantee of accurate factfinding that the adversary process brings with it.[9] See *Ohio v. Akron Center for Reproductive Health*, 497 U.S. 502, 515-516, 110 S.Ct. 2972, 2981-2982, 111 L.Ed.2d 405 (1990). Finally, we think a State may properly decline to make judgments about the "quality" of life that a particular individual may enjoy, and simply assert an unqualified interest in the preservation of human life to be weighed against the constitutionally protected interests of the individual.

In our view, Missouri has permissibly sought to advance these interests through the adoption of a "clear and convincing" standard of proof to govern such proceedings. "The function of a standard of proof, as that concept is embodied in the Due Process Clause and in the realm of factfinding, is to 'instruct the factfinder concerning the degree of confidence our society thinks he should have in the correctness of factual conclusions for a particular type of adjudication.' " *Addington v. Texas*,

441 U.S. 418, 423, 99 S.Ct. 1804, 1808, 60 L.Ed.2d 323 (1979) (quoting *In re Winship,* 397 U.S. 358, 370, 90 S.Ct. 1068, 1076, 25 L.Ed.2d 368 (1970) (Harlan, J., concurring)). "This Court has mandated an intermediate standard of proof—'clear and convincing evidence' when the individual interests at stake in a state proceeding are both 'particularly important' and 'more substantial than mere loss of money.' " *Santosky v. Kramer,* 455 U.S. 745, 756, 102 S.Ct. 1388, 1397, 71 L.Ed.2d 599 (1982) (quoting *Addington, supra,* at 424, 99 S.Ct., at 1808). Thus, such a standard has been required in deportation proceedings, *Woodby v. INS,* 385 U.S. 276, 87 S.Ct. 483, 17 L.Ed.2d 362 (1966), in denaturalization proceedings, *Schneiderman v. United States,* 320 U.S. 118, 63 S.Ct. 1333, 87 L.Ed. 1796 (1943), in civil commitment proceedings, *Addington, supra,* and in proceedings for the termination of parental rights, *Santosky, supra.*[10] Further, this level of proof, "or an even higher one, has traditionally been imposed in cases involving allegations of civil fraud, and in a variety of other kinds of civil cases involving such issues as . . . lost wills, oral contracts to make bequests, and the like." *Woodby, supra,* 385 U.S., at 285, n. 18, 87 S.Ct., at 488, n. 18.

We think it self-evident that the interests at stake in the instant proceedings are more substantial, both on an individual and societal level, than those involved in a run-of-the-mine civil dispute. But not only does the standard of proof reflect the importance of a particular adjudication, it also serves as "a societal judgment about how the risk of error should be distributed between the litigants." *Santosky, supra,* 455 U.S. at 755, 102 S.Ct., at 1395; *Addington, supra,* 441 U.S., at 423, 99 S.Ct., at 1807-1808. The more stringent the burden of proof a party must bear, the more that party bears the risk of an erroneous decision. We believe that Missouri may permissibly place an increased risk of an erroneous decision on those seeking to terminate an incompetent individual's life-sustaining treatment. An erroneous decision not to terminate results in a maintenance of the status quo; the possibility of subsequent developments such as advancements in medical science, the discovery of new evidence regarding the patient's intent, changes in the law, or simply the unexpected death of the patient despite the administration of life-sustaining treatment at least create the potential that a wrong decision will eventually be corrected or its impact mitigated. An erroneous decision to withdraw life-sustaining treatment, however, is not susceptible of correction. In *Santosky,* one of the factors which led the Court to require proof by clear and convincing evidence in a proceeding to terminate parental rights was that a decision in such a case was final and irrevocable. *Santosky, supra,* 445 U.S., at 759, 102 S.Ct., at 1397-1398. The same must surely be said of the decision to discontinue hydration and nutrition of a patient such as Nancy Cruzan, which all agree will result in her death.

It is also worth noting that most, if not all, States simply forbid oral testimony entirely in determining the wishes of parties in transactions which, while important, simply do not have the consequences that a decision to terminate a person's life does. At common law and by statute in most States, the parol evidence rule prevents the variations of the terms of a written contract by oral testimony. The statute of frauds makes unenforceable oral contracts to leave property by will, and statutes regulating the making of wills universally require that those instruments be in writing. See 2 A. Corbin, Contracts § 398, pp. 360-361 (1950); 2 W. Page, Law of Wills §§ 19.3-19.5, pp. 61-71 (1960). There is no doubt that statutes requiring wills to be in writing, and statutes of frauds which require that a contract to make a will be in writing, on occasion frustrate the effectuation of the intent of a particular decedent, just as Missouri's requirement of proof in this case may have frustrated the effectuation of the not-fully-expressed desires of Nancy Cruzan. But the Constitution does not require general rules to work faultlessly; no general rule can.

In sum, we conclude that a State may apply a clear and convincing evidence standard in proceedings where a guardian seeks to discontinue nutrition and hydration of a person diagnosed to be in a persistent vegetative state. We note that many courts which have adopted some sort of substituted judgment procedure in situations like this, whether they limit consideration of evidence to the prior expressed wishes of the incompetent individual, or whether they allow more general proof of what the individual's decision would have been, require a clear and convincing standard of proof for such evidence. See, *e.g., Longeway,* 133 Ill.2d, at 50-51, 139 Ill.Dec., at 787, 549 N.E.2d, at 300; *McConnell,* 209 Conn., at 707-710, 553 A.2d, at 604-605; *O'Connor,* 72 N.Y.2d, at 529-530, 531 N.E.2d, at 613; *In re Gardner,* 534 A.2d 947, 952-953 (Me.1987); *In re Jobes,* 108 N.J., at 412-413, 529 A.2d, at 443; *Leach v. Akron General Medical Center,* 68 Ohio Misc. 1, 11, 426 N.E.2d 809, 815 (1980).

The Supreme Court of Missouri held that in this case the testimony adduced at trial did not amount to clear and convincing proof of the patient's desire to have hydration and nutrition withdrawn. In so doing, it reversed a decision of the Missouri trial court which had found that the evidence "suggest[ed]" Nancy Cruzan would not have desired to continue such measures, App. to Pet. for Cert. A98, but which had not adopted the standard of "clear and convincing evidence" enunciated by the Supreme Court. The testimony adduced at trial consisted primarily of Nancy Cruzan's statements made to a housemate about a year before her accident that she would not want to live should she face life as a "vegetable," and other observations to the same effect. The observations did not deal in terms with withdrawal of medical treatment or of hydration and nutrition. We cannot say that the Supreme Court of Missouri committed constitutional error in reaching the conclusion that it did.[11]

Petitioners alternatively contend that Missouri must accept the "substituted judgment" of close family members even in the absence of substantial proof that their views reflect the views of the patient. They rely primarily upon our decisions in *Michael H. v. Gerald D.,* 491 U.S. 110, 109 S.Ct. 2333, 105 L.Ed.2d 91 (1989), and *Parham v. J.R.,* 442 U.S. 584, 99 S.Ct. 2493, 61 L.Ed.2d 101 (1979). But we do not think these cases support their claim. In *Michael H.,* we *upheld* the constitutionality of California's favored treatment of traditional family relationships; such a holding may not be turned around into a constitutional requirement that a State *must* recognize the primacy of those relationships in a situation like this. And in *Parham,* where the patient was a minor, we also *upheld* the constitutionality of a state scheme in which parents made certain decisions for mentally ill minors. Here again petitioners would seek to turn a decision which allowed a State to rely on family decisionmaking into a constitutional requirement that the State recognize such decisionmaking. But constitutional law does not work that way.

No doubt is engendered by anything in this record but that Nancy Cruzan's mother and father are loving and caring parents. If the State were required by the United States Constitution to repose a right of "substituted judgment" with anyone, the Cruzans would surely qualify. But we do not think the Due Process Clause requires the State to repose judgment on these matters with anyone but the patient herself. Close family members may have a strong feeling—a feeling not at all ignoble or unworthy, but not entirely disinterested, either—that they do not wish to witness the continuation of the life of a loved one which they regard as hopeless, meaningless, and even degrading. But there is no automatic assurance that the view of close family members will necessarily be the same as the patient's would have been had she been confronted with the prospect of her situation while competent. All of the reasons previously discussed for allowing Missouri to require clear and convincing evidence of the patient's wishes lead us to conclude that the State may choose to defer only to those wishes, rather than confide the decision to close family members.[12]

The judgment of the Supreme Court of Missouri is *Affirmed.*

1. The State Supreme Court, adopting much of the trial court's findings, described Nancy Cruzan's medical condition as follows:

". . . (1) [H]er respiration and circulation are not artificially maintained and are within the normal limits of a thirty-year-old female; (2) she is oblivious to her environment except for reflexive responses to sound and perhaps painful stimuli; (3) she suffered anoxia of the brain resulting in a massive enlargement of the ventricles filling with cerebrospinal fluid in the area where the brain has degenerated and [her] cerebral cortical atrophy is irreversible, permanent, progressive and ongoing; (4) her highest cognitive brain function is exhibited by her grimacing perhaps in recognition of ordinarily painful stimuli, indicating the experience of pain and apparent response to sound; (5) she is a spastic quadriplegic; (6) her four extremities are contracted with irreversible muscular and tendon damage to all extremities;

(7) she has no cognitive or reflexive ability to swallow food or water to maintain her daily essential needs and . . . she will never recover her ability to swallow sufficient [sic] to satisfy her needs. In sum, Nancy is diagnosed as in a persistent vegetative state. She is not dead. She is not terminally ill. Medical experts testified that she could live another thirty years." *Cruzan v. Harmon,* 760 S.W.2d 408, 411 (Mo.1988) (en banc) (quotations omitted; footnote omitted).

In observing that Cruzan was not dead, the court referred to the following Missouri statute:

"For all legal purposes, the occurrence of human death shall be determined in accordance with the usual and customary standards of medical practice, provided that death shall not be determined to have occurred unless the following minimal conditions have been met:

"(1) When respiration and circulation are not artificially maintained, there is an irreversible cessation of spontaneous respiration and circulation; or

"(2) When respiration and circulation are artificially maintained, and there is total and irreversible cessation of all brain function, including the brain stem and that such determination is made by a licensed physician." Mo.Rev.Stat. § 194.005 (1986).

Since Cruzan's respiration and circulation were not being artificially maintained, she obviously fit within the first proviso of the statute.

Dr. Fred Plum, the creator of the term "persistent vegetative state" and a renowned expert on the subject, has described the "vegetative state" in the following terms:

" 'Vegetative state describes a body which is functioning entirely in terms of its internal controls. It maintains temperature. It maintains heart beat and pulmonary ventilation. It maintains digestive activity. It maintains reflex activity of muscles and nerves for low level conditioned responses. But there is no behavioral evidence of either self-awareness or awareness of the surroundings in a learned manner.' " *In re Jobes,* 108 N.J. 394, 403, 529 A.2d 434, 438 (1987).

See also Brief for American Medical Association et al. as *Amici Curiae* 6 ("The persistent vegetative state can best be understood as one of the conditions in which patients have suffered a loss of consciousness").

[2.] See generally Karnezis, Patient's Right to Refuse Treatment Allegedly Necessary to Sustain Life, 93 A.L.R.3d 67 (1979) (collecting cases); Cantor, A Patient's Decision to Decline Life-Saving Medical Treatment: Bodily Integrity Versus the Preservation of Life, 26 Rutgers L.Rev. 228, 229, and n. 5 (1973) (noting paucity of cases).

[3.] See Chapman, The Uniform Rights of the Terminally Ill Act: Too Little, Too Late?, 42 Ark.L.Rev. 319, 324, n. 15 (1989); see also F. Rozovsky, Consent to Treatment, A Practical Guide 415-423 (1984).

[4.] In a later trilogy of cases, the New Jersey Supreme Court stressed that the analytic framework adopted in *Conroy* was limited to elderly, incompetent patients with shortened life expectancies, and established alternative approaches to deal with a different set of situations. See *In re Farrell,* 108 N.J. 335, 529 A.2d 404 (1987) (37-year-old competent mother with terminal illness had right to removal of respirator based on common law and constitutional principles which overrode competing state interests); *In re Peter*, 108 N.J. 365, 529 A.2d 419 (1987) (65-year-old woman in persistent vegetative state had right to removal of nasogastric feeding tube—under *Conroy* subjective test, power of attorney and hearsay testimony constituted clear and convincing proof of patient's intent to have treatment withdrawn); *In re Jobes*, 108 N.J. 394, 529 A.2d 434 (1987) (31-year-old woman in persistent vegetative state entitled to removal of jejunostomy feeding tube—even though hearsay testimony regarding patient's intent insufficient to meet clear and convincing standard of proof, under *Quinlan*, family or close friends entitled to make a substituted judgment for patient).

[5.] The *Drabick* court drew support for its analysis from earlier, influential decisions rendered by California Courts of Appeal. See *Bouvia v. Superior Court*, 179 Cal.App.3d 1127, 225 Cal.Rptr. 297 (1986) (competent 28-year-old quadriplegic had right to removal of nasogastric feeding tube inserted against her will); *Bartling v. Superior Court*, 163 Cal.App.3d 186, 209 Cal.Rptr. 220 (1984) (competent 70-year-old, seriously ill man had right to the removal of respirator); *Barber v. Superior Court*, 147 Cal.App.3d 1006, 195 Cal.Rptr. 484 (1983) (physicians could not be prosecuted for homicide on account of removing respirator and intravenous feeding tubes of patient in persistent vegetative state).

[6.] Besides the Missouri Supreme Court in *Cruzan* and the courts in *McConnell, Longeway, Drabick, Bouvia, Barber, O'Connor, Conroy, Jobes,* and *Peter,* appellate courts of at least four other States and one Federal District Court have specifically considered and discussed the issue of withholding or withdrawing artificial nutrition and hydration from incompetent individuals. See *Gray v. Romeo*, 697 F.Supp. 580 (RI 1988); *In re Gardner*, 534 A.2d 947 (Me.1987); *In re Grant*, 109 Wash.2d 545, 747 P.2d 445 (1987); *Brophy v. New England Sinai Hospital, Inc.*, 398 Mass. 417, 497 N.E.2d 626 (1986); *Corbett v. D'Alessandro*, 487 So.2d 368

(Fla.App.1986). All of these courts permitted or would permit the termination of such measures based on rights grounded in the common law, or in the State or Federal Constitution.

7. Although many state courts have held that a right to refuse treatment is encompassed by a generalized constitutional right of privacy, we have never so held. We believe this issue is more properly analyzed in terms of a Fourteenth Amendment liberty interest. See *Bowers v. Hardwick,* 478 U.S. 186, 194-195, 106 S.Ct. 2841, 2846, 92 L.Ed.2d 140 (1986).

8. See Smith, All's Well That Ends Well: Toward a Policy of Assisted Rational Suicide or Merely Enlightened Self-Determination?, 22 U.C.D.L.Rev. 275, 290-291, and n. 106 (1989) (compiling statutes).

9. Since Cruzan was a patient at a state hospital when this litigation commenced, the State has been involved as an adversary from the beginning. However, it can be expected that many disputes of this type will arise in private institutions, where a guardian *ad litem* or similar party will have been appointed as the sole representative of the incompetent individual in the litigation. In such cases, a guardian may act in entire good faith, and yet not maintain a position truly adversarial to that of the family. Indeed, as noted by the court below, "[t]he guardian *ad litem* [in this case] finds himself in the predicament of believing that it is in Nancy's 'best interest to have the tube feeding discontinued,' but 'feeling that an appeal should be made because our responsibility to her as attorneys and guardians *ad litem* was to pursue this matter to the highest court in the state in view of the fact that this is a case of first impression in the State of Missouri.' " 760 S.W.2d, at 410, n. 1. Cruzan's guardian ad litem has also filed a brief in this Court urging reversal of the Missouri Supreme Court's decision. None of this is intended to suggest that the guardian acted the least bit improperly in this proceeding. It is only meant to illustrate the limits which may obtain on the adversarial nature of this type of litigation.

10. We recognize that these cases involved instances where the government sought to take action against an individual. See *Price Waterhouse v. Hopkins,* 490 U.S. 228, 253, 109 S.Ct. 1775, 1792, 104 L.Ed.2d 268 (1989) (plurality opinion). Here, by contrast, the government seeks to protect the interests of an individual, as well as its own institutional interests, in life. We do not see any reason why important individual interests should be afforded less protection simply because the government finds itself in the position of defending them. "[W]e find it significant that . . . the defendant rather than the plaintiff" seeks the clear and convincing standard of proof—"suggesting that this standard ordinarily serves as a shield rather than . . . a sword." *Id.,* at 253, 109 S.Ct., at 1792. That it is the government that has picked up the shield should be of no moment.

11. The clear and convincing standard of proof has been variously defined in this context as "proof sufficient to persuade the trier of fact that the patient held a firm and settled commitment to the termination of life supports under the circumstances like those presented," *In re Westchester County Medical Center on behalf of O'Connor,* 72 N.Y.2d 517, 531, 534 N.Y.S.2d 886, 892, 531 N.E.2d 607, 613 (1988) (*O'Connor*), and as evidence which "produces in the mind of the trier of fact a firm belief or conviction as to the truth of the allegations sought to be established, evidence so clear, direct and weighty and convincing as to enable [the factfinder] to come to a clear conviction, without hesitancy, of the truth of the precise facts in issue." *In re Jobes,* 108 N.J., at 407-408, 529 A.2d, at 441 (quotation omitted). In both of these cases the evidence of the patient's intent to refuse medical treatment was arguably stronger than that presented here. The New York Court of Appeals and the Supreme Court of New Jersey, respectively, held that the proof failed to meet a clear and convincing threshold. See *O'Connor, supra,* 72 N.Y.2d, at 526-534, 534 N.Y.S.2d, at 889-894, 531 N.E.2d, at 610-615; *Jobes, supra,* 108 N.J., at 442-443, 529 A.2d 434.

12. We are not faced in this case with the question whether a State might be required to defer to the decision of a surrogate if competent and probative evidence established that the patient herself had expressed a desire that the decision to terminate life-sustaining treatment be made for her by that individual.

Petitioners also adumbrate in their brief a claim based on the Equal Protection Clause of the Fourteenth Amendment to the effect that Missouri has impermissibly treated incompetent patients differently from competent ones, citing the statement in *Cleburne v. Cleburne Living Center, Inc.,* 473 U.S. 432, 439, 105 S.Ct. 3249, 3254, 87 L.Ed.2d 313 (1985), that the Clause is "essentially a direction that all persons similarly situated should be treated alike." The differences between the choice made *by* a competent person to refuse medical treatment, and the choice made *for* an incompetent person by someone else to refuse medical treatment, are so obviously different that the State is warranted in establishing rigorous procedures for the latter class of cases which do not apply to the former class.

Justice O'CONNOR, concurring.

I agree that a protected liberty interest in refusing unwanted medical treatment may be inferred from our prior decisions, see *ante,* at 278-279, and that the refusal of artificially delivered food and water is encompassed within that liberty interest. See *ante,* at 279. I write separately to clarify why I believe this to be so.

As the Court notes, the liberty interest in refusing medical treatment flows from decisions involving the State's invasions into the body. See *ante,* at 278-279. Because our notions of liberty are inextricably entwined with our idea of physical freedom and self-determination, the Court has often deemed state incursions into the body repugnant to the interests protected by the Due Process Clause. See, *e.g., Rochin v. California,* 342 U.S. 165, 172, 72 S.Ct. 205, 209-210, 96 L.Ed. 183 (1952) ("Illegally breaking into the privacy of the petitioner, the struggle to open his mouth and remove what was there, the forcible extraction of his stomach's contents . . . is bound to offend even hardened sensibilities"); *Union Pacific R. Co. v. Botsford,* 141 U.S. 250, 251, 11 S.Ct. 1000, 1001, 35 L.Ed. 734 (1891). Our Fourth Amendment jurisprudence has echoed this same concern. See *Schmerber v. California,* 384 U.S. 757, 772, 86 S.Ct. 1826, 1836-1837, 16 L.Ed.2d 908 (1966) ("The integrity of an individual's person is a cherished value of our society"); *Winston v. Lee,* 470 U.S. 753, 759, 105 S.Ct. 1611, 1616, 84 L.Ed.2d 662 (1985) ("A compelled surgical intrusion into an individual's body for evidence . . . implicates expectations of privacy and security of such magnitude that the intrusion may be 'unreasonable' even if likely to produce evidence of a crime"). The State's imposition of medical treatment on an unwilling competent adult necessarily involves some form of restraint and intrusion. A seriously ill or dying patient whose wishes are not honored may feel a captive of the machinery required for life-sustaining measures or other medical interventions. Such forced treatment may burden that individual's liberty interests as much as any state coercion. See, *e.g., Washington v. Harper,* 494 U.S. 210,

221, 110 S.Ct. 1028, 1036, 108 L.Ed.2d 178 (1990); *Parham v. J.R.,* 442 U.S. 584, 600, 99 S.Ct. 2493, 2503, 61 L.Ed.2d 101 (1979) ("It is not disputed that a child, in common with adults, has a substantial liberty interest in not being confined unnecessarily for medical treatment").

The State's artificial provision of nutrition and hydration implicates identical concerns. Artificial feeding cannot readily be distinguished from other forms of medical treatment. See, *e.g.,* Council on Ethical and Judicial Affairs, American Medical Association, AMA Ethical Opinion 2.20, Withholding or Withdrawing Life-Prolonging Medical Treatment, Current Opinions 13 (1989); The Hastings Center, Guidelines on the Termination of Life-Sustaining Treatment and the Care of the Dying 59 (1987). Whether or not the techniques used to pass food and water into the patient's alimentary tract are termed "medical treatment," it is clear they all involve some degree of intrusion and restraint. Feeding a patient by means of a nasogastric tube requires a physician to pass a long flexible tube through the patient's nose, throat, and esophagus and into the stomach. Because of the discomfort such a tube causes, "[m]any patients need to be restrained forcibly and their hands put into large mittens to prevent them from removing the tube." Major, The Medical Procedures for Providing Food and Water: Indications and Effects, in By No Extraordinary Means: The Choice to Forgo Life-Sustaining Food and Water 25 (J. Lynn ed. 1986). A gastrostomy tube (as was used to provide food and water to Nancy Cruzan, see *ante,* at 266) or jejunostomy tube must be surgically implanted into the stomach or small intestine. Office of Technology Assessment Task Force, Life-Sustaining Technologies and the Elderly 282 (1988). Requiring a competent adult to endure such procedures against her will burdens the patient's liberty, dignity, and freedom to determine the course of her own treatment. Accordingly, the liberty guaranteed by the Due Process Clause must protect, if it protects anything, an individual's deeply personal decision to reject medical treatment, including the artificial delivery of food and water.

    I also write separately to emphasize that the Court does not today decide the issue whether a State must also give effect to the decisions of a surrogate decisionmaker. See *ante,* at 287, n. 12. In my view, such a duty may well be constitutionally required to protect the patient's liberty interest in refusing medical treatment. Few individuals provide explicit oral or written instructions regarding their intent to refuse medical treatment should they become incompetent.[1] States which decline to consider any evidence other than such instructions may frequently fail to honor a patient's intent. Such failures might be avoided if the State considered an equally probative source of evidence: the patient's appointment of a proxy to make health care decisions on her behalf. Delegating the authority to make medical decisions to a family member or friend is becoming a common method of planning for the future. See, *e.g.,* Areen, The Legal Status of Consent Obtained from Families of Adult Patients to Withhold or Withdraw Treatment, 258 JAMA 229, 230 (1987). Several States have recognized the practical wisdom of such a procedure by enacting durable power of attorney statutes that specifically authorize an individual to appoint a surrogate to make medical treatment decisions.[2] Some state courts have suggested that an agent appointed pursuant to a general durable power of attorney statute would also be empowered to make health care decisions on behalf of the patient.[3] See, *e.g., In re Peter,* 108 N.J. 365, 378-379, 529 A.2d 419, 426 (1987); see also 73 Op.Md.Atty.Gen. No. 88-046 (1988) (interpreting Md.Est. & Trusts Code Ann. §§ 13-601 to 13-602 (1974), as authorizing a delegatee to make health care decisions). Other States allow an individual to designate a proxy to carry out the intent of a living will.[4] These procedures for surrogate decisionmaking, which appear to be rapidly gaining in acceptance, may be a valuable additional safeguard of the patient's interest in directing his medical care. Moreover, as patients are likely to select a family member as a surrogate, see 2

President's Commission for the Study of Ethical Problems in Medicine and Biomedical and Behavioral Research, Making Health Care Decisions 240 (1982), giving effect to a proxy's decisions may also protect the "freedom of personal choice in matters of . . . family life." *Cleveland Board of Education v. LaFleur,* 414 U.S. 632, 639, 94 S.Ct. 791, 796, 39 L.Ed.2d 52 (1974).

Today's decision, holding only that the Constitution permits a State to require clear and convincing evidence of Nancy Cruzan's desire to have artificial hydration and nutrition withdrawn, does not preclude a future determination that the Constitution requires the States to implement the decisions of a patient's duly appointed surrogate. Nor does it prevent States from developing other approaches for protecting an incompetent individual's liberty interest in refusing medical treatment. As is evident from the Court's survey of state court decisions, see *ante* at 271-277 no national consensus has yet emerged on the best solution for this difficult and sensitive problem. Today we decide only that one State's practice does not violate the Constitution; the more challenging task of crafting appropriate procedures for safeguarding incompetents' liberty interests is entrusted to the "laboratory" of the States, *New State Ice Co. v. Liebmann,* 285 U.S. 262, 311, 52 S.Ct. 371, 386-87, 76 L.Ed. 747 (1932) (Brandeis, J., dissenting), in the first instance.

[1.] See 2 President's Commission for the Study of Ethical Problems in Medicine and Biomedical and Behavioral Research, Making Health Care Decisions 241-242 (1982) (36% of those surveyed gave instructions regarding how they would like to be treated if they ever became too sick to make decisions; 23% put those instructions in writing) (Lou Harris Poll, September 1982); American Medical Association Surveys of Physician and Public Opinion on Health Care Issues 29-30 (1988) (56% of those surveyed had told family members their wishes concerning the use of life-sustaining treatment if they entered an irreversible coma; 15% had filled out a living will specifying those wishes).

2. At least 13 States and the District of Columbia have durable power of attorney statutes expressly authorizing the appointment of proxies for making health care decisions. See Alaska Stat.Ann. §§ 13.26.335, 13.26.344(*l*) (Supp.1989); Cal.Civ.Code Ann. § 2500 (West Supp.1990); D.C.Code Ann. § 21-2205 (1989); Idaho Code § 39-4505 (Supp.1989); Ill.Rev.Stat., ch. 1101/2, &Par; 804-1 to 804-12 (Supp.1988); Kan.Stat.Ann. § 58-625 (Supp.1989); Me.Rev.Stat.Ann., Tit. 18-A, § 5-501 (Supp.1989); Nev.Rev.Stat. § 449.800 (Supp.1989); Ohio Rev.Code Ann. § 1337.11 *et seq.* (Supp.1989); Ore.Rev.Stat. § 127.510 (1989); Pa.Con.Stat.Ann., Tit. 20, § 5603(h) (Purdon Supp.1989); R.I.Gen.Laws § 23-4.10-1 *et seq.* (1989); Tex.Rev.Civ.Stat.Ann., Art. 4590h-1 (Vernon Supp.1990); Vt.Stat.Ann., Tit. 14, § 3451 *et seq.* (1989).

3. All 50 States and the District of Columbia have general durable power of attorney statutes. See Ala.Code § 26-1-2 (1986); Alaska Stat.Ann. §§ 13.26.350 to 13.26.356 (Supp.1989); Ariz.Rev.Stat.Ann. § 14-5501 (1975); Ark.Code Ann. §§ 28-68-201 to 28-68-203 (1987); Cal.Civ.Code Ann. § 2400 (West Supp.1990); Colo.Rev.Stat. § 15-14-501 *et seq.* (1987); Conn.Gen.Stat. § 45-69*o* (Supp.1989); Del.Code Ann., Tit. 12, §§ 4901-4905 (1987); D.C.Code Ann. § 21-2081 *et seq.* (1989); Fla.Stat. § 709.08 (1989); Ga.Code Ann. § 10-6-36 (1989); Haw.Rev.Stat. §§ 551D-1 to 551D-7 (Supp.1989); Idaho Code § 15-5-501 *et seq.* (Supp.1989); Ill.Rev.Stat., ch. 1101/2, ¶ 802-6 (1987); Ind.Code §§ 30-2-11-1 to 30-2-11-7 (1988); Iowa Code § 633.705 (Supp.1989); Kan.Stat.Ann. § 58-610 (1983); Ky.Rev.Stat.Ann. § 386.093 (Baldwin 1983); La.Civ.Code Ann., Art. 3027 (West Supp.1990); Me.Rev.Stat.Ann., Tit. 18-A, § 5-501 *et seq.* (Supp.1989); Md.Est. & Trusts Code Ann. §§ 13-601 to 13-602 (1974) (as interpreted by the Attorney General, see 73 Op.Md.Atty.Gen. No. 88-046 (Oct. 17, 1988)); Mass.Gen.Laws ch. 201B, § 1 to 201B, § 7 (1988); Mich.Comp.Laws §§ 700.495, 700.497 (1979); Minn.Stat. § 523.01 *et seq.* (1988); Miss.Code Ann. § 87-

3-13 (Supp.1989); Mo.Rev.Stat. § 404.700 (Supp.1990); Mont.Code Ann. §§ 72-5-501 to 72-5-502 (1989); Neb.Rev.Stat. §§ 30-2664 to 30-2672, 30-2667 (1985); Nev.Rev.Stat. § 111.460 *et seq.* (1986); N.H.Rev.Stat.Ann. § 506:6 *et seq.* (Supp.1989); N.J.Stat.Ann. § 46:2B-8 (West 1989);
N.M.Stat.Ann. § 45-5-501 et seq. (1989); N.Y.Gen.Oblig.Law § 5-1602 (McKinney 1989); N.C.Gen.Stat. § 32A-1 et seq. (1987); N.D.Cent.Code §§ 30.1-30-01 to 30.1-30-05 (Supp.1989); Ohio Rev.Code Ann. § 1337.09 (Supp.1989); Okla.Stat., Tit. 58, §§ 1071-1077 (Supp.1989); Ore.Rev.Stat. § 127.005 (1989); Pa.Con.Stat.Ann., Tit. 20, §§ 5601 *et seq.*, 5602(a)(9) (Purdon Supp.1989); R.I.Gen.Laws § 34-22-6.1 (1984); S.C.Code Ann. §§ 62-5-501 to 62-5-502 (1987); S.D.Codified Laws § 59-7-2.1 (1978); Tenn.Code Ann. § 34-6-101 *et seq.* (1984); Tex.Prob.Code Ann. § 36A (Supp.1990); Utah Code Ann. § 75-5-501 *et seq.* (1978); Vt.Stat.Ann., Tit. 14, § 3051 *et seq.* (1989); Va.Code Ann. § 11-9.1 *et seq.* (1989); Wash.Rev.Code § 11.94.020 (1989); W.Va.Code § 39-4-1 *et seq.* (Supp.1989); Wis.Stat. § 243.07 (1987-1988) (as interpreted by the Attorney General, see Wis.Op.Atty.Gen. 35-88 (1988)); Wyo.Stat. § 3-5-101 *et seq.* (1985).

[4.] Thirteen States have living will statutes authorizing the appointment of health care proxies. See Ark.Code Ann. § 20-17-202 (Supp.1989); Del.Code Ann., Tit. 16, § 2502 (1983); Fla.Stat. § 765.05(2) (1989); Idaho Code § 39-4504 (Supp.1989); Ind.Code § 16-8-11-14(g)(2) (1988); Iowa Code § 144A.7(1)(a) (1989); La.R.S.Ann., §§ 40:1299.58.1, 40:1299.58.3(C) (West Supp.1990); Minn.Stat. § 145B.01 *et seq.* (Supp.1989); Tex.Health & Safety Code Ann. § 672.003(d) (Supp.1990); Utah Code Ann. §§ 75-2-1105, 75-2-1106 (Supp.1989); Va.Code Ann. § 54.1-2986(2) (1988); 1987 Wash.Laws, ch. 162, § 1, Sec. (1)(b); Wyo.Stat. § 35-22-102 (1988).

Justice SCALIA, concurring.

The various opinions in this case portray quite clearly the difficult, indeed agonizing, questions that are presented by the constantly increasing power of science to keep the human body alive for longer than any reasonable person would want to inhabit it. The States have begun to grapple with these problems through legislation. I am concerned, from the tenor of today's opinions, that we are poised to confuse that enterprise as successfully as we have confused the enterprise of legislating concerning abortion—requiring it to be conducted against a background of federal constitutional imperatives that are unknown because they are being newly crafted from Term to Term. That would be a great misfortune.

While I agree with the Court's analysis today, and therefore join in its opinion, I would have preferred that we announce, clearly and promptly, that the federal courts have no business in this field; that American law has always accorded the State the power to prevent, by force if necessary, suicide—including suicide by refusing to take appropriate measures necessary to preserve one's life; that the point at which life becomes "worthless," and the point at which the means necessary to preserve it become "extraordinary" or "inappropriate," are neither set forth in the Constitution nor known to the nine Justices of this Court any better than they are known to nine people picked at random from the Kansas City telephone directory; and hence, that even when it *is* demonstrated by clear and convincing evidence that a patient no longer wishes certain measures to be taken to preserve his or her life, it is up to the citizens of Missouri to decide, through their elected representatives, whether that wish will be honored. It is quite impossible (because the Constitution says nothing about the matter) that those citizens will decide upon a line less lawful than the one we would choose; and it is unlikely (because we know no more about "life and death" than they do) that they will decide upon a line less reasonable.

The text of the Due Process Clause does not protect individuals against deprivations of liberty *simpliciter*. It protects them against deprivations of liberty "without due process of law." To determine that such a deprivation would not occur if Nancy Cruzan were forced to take nourishment against her will, it is unnecessary to reopen the historically recurrent debate over whether "due process" includes substantive restrictions. Compare *Murray's Lessee v. Hoboken Land and Improvement Co.*, 18 How. 272, 15 L.Ed. 372 (1856), with *Scott v. Sandford*, 19 How. 393, 450, 15 L.Ed. 691 (1857); compare *Tyson & Brother v. Banton*, 273 U.S. 418, 47 S.Ct. 426, 71 L.Ed. 718 (1927), with *Olsen v. Nebraska ex rel. Western Reference & Bond Assn., Inc.*, 313 U.S. 236, 246-247, 61 S.Ct. 862, 865-866, 85 L.Ed. 1305 (1941); compare *Ferguson v. Skrupa*, 372 U.S. 726, 730, 83 S.Ct. 1028, 1031, 10 L.Ed.2d 93 (1963), with *Moore v. East Cleveland*, 431 U.S. 494, 97 S.Ct. 1932, 52 L.Ed.2d 531 (1977) (plurality opinion); see Easterbrook, Substance and Due Process, 1982 S.Ct.Rev. 85; Monaghan, Our Perfect Constitution, 56 N.Y.U.L.Rev. 353 (1981). It is at least true that no "substantive due process" claim can be maintained unless the claimant demonstrates that the State has deprived him of a right historically and traditionally protected against state interference. *Michael H. v. Gerald D.*, 491 U.S. 110, 122, 109 S.Ct. 2333, 2341, 105 L.Ed.2d 91 (1989) (plurality opinion); *Bowers v. Hardwick,* 478 U.S. 186, 192, 106 S.Ct. 2841, 2844-2845, 92 L.Ed.2d 140 (1986); *Moore, supra,* 431 U.S., at 502-503, 97 S.Ct., at 1937-1938 (plurality opinion). That cannot possibly be established here.

At common law in England, a suicide—defined as one who "deliberately puts an end to his own existence, or commits any unlawful malicious act, the consequence of which is his own death," 4 W. Blackstone, Commentaries *189—was criminally liable. *Ibid.* Although the States abolished the penalties imposed by the common law (*i.e.,* forfeiture and ignominious burial), they did so to spare the innocent family and not to legitimize the act. Case law at the time of the adoption of the Fourteenth Amendment generally held that assisting suicide was a criminal offense. See Marzen, O'Dowd, Crone, & Balch, Suicide: A Constitutional Right?, 24 Duquesne L.Rev. 1, 76 (1985) ("In short, twenty-one of the thirty-seven states, and eighteen of the thirty ratifying states prohibited assisting suicide. Only eight of the states, and seven of the ratifying states, definitely did not"); see also 1 F. Wharton, Criminal Law § 122 (6th rev. ed. 1868). The System of Penal Law presented to the House of Representatives by Representative Livingston in 1828 would have criminalized assisted suicide. E. Livingston, A System of Penal Law, Penal Code 122 (1828). The Field Penal Code, adopted by the Dakota Territory in 1877, proscribed attempted suicide and assisted suicide. Marzen, O'Dowd, Crone, & Balch, *supra,* at 76-77. And most States that did not explicitly prohibit assisted suicide in 1868 recognized, when the issue arose in the 50 years following the Fourteenth Amendment's ratification, that assisted and (in some cases) attempted suicide were unlawful. *Id.,* at 77-100; *id.,* at 148-242 (surveying development of States' laws). Thus, "there is no significant support for the claim that a right to suicide is so rooted in our tradition that it may be deemed 'fundamental' or 'implicit in the concept of ordered liberty.' " *Id.,* at 100 (quoting *Palko v. Connecticut,* 302 U.S. 319, 325, 58 S.Ct. 149, 152, 82 L.Ed. 288 (1937)).

Petitioners rely on three distinctions to separate Nancy Cruzan's case from ordinary suicide: (1) that she is permanently incapacitated and in pain; (2) that she would bring on her death not by any affirmative act but by merely declining treatment that provides nourishment; and (3) that preventing her from effectuating her presumed wish to die requires violation of her bodily integrity. None of these suffices. Suicide was not excused even when committed "to avoid those ills which [persons] had not the fortitude to endure." 4 Blackstone, *supra,* at *189. "The life of those to whom life has become a burden—of those who are hopelessly diseased or fatally wounded—nay, even the lives of criminals condemned to death, are under the protection of the law, equally as the lives of those who are in the full tide of life's enjoyment, and anxious to continue to live." *Blackburn v. State,* 23 Ohio St. 146, 163 (1873). Thus, a man who prepared a poison, and placed it within reach of his wife, "to put an end to her suffering" from a terminal illness was convicted of murder, *People v. Roberts,* 211 Mich. 187, 198, 178 N.W. 690, 693 (1920); the "incurable suffering of the suicide, as a legal question, could hardly affect the degree of criminality. . . ." Note, 30 Yale L.J. 408, 412 (1921) (discussing *Roberts*). Nor would the imminence of the patient's death have affected liability. "The lives of all are equally under the protection of the law, and under that protection to their last moment. . . . [Assisted suicide] is declared by the law to be murder, irrespective of the wishes or the condition of the party to whom the poison is administered. . . ." *Blackburn, supra,* at 163; see also *Commonwealth v. Bowen,* 13 Mass. 356, 360 (1816).

The second asserted distinction—suggested by the recent cases canvassed by the Court concerning the right to refuse treatment, *ante,* at 270-277—relies on the dichotomy between action and inaction. Suicide, it is said, consists of an affirmative act to end one's life; refusing treatment is not an affirmative act "causing" death, but merely a passive acceptance of the natural process of dying. I readily acknowledge that the distinction between action and inaction has some bearing upon the legislative judgment of what ought to be prevented as suicide—though even there it would seem to me unreasonable to draw the line precisely between action and inaction, rather than between various forms of inaction. It would not make much sense to say that one may not kill oneself by walking into the sea, but may sit on the beach until submerged by the incoming tide; or that one may not intentionally lock oneself into a cold storage locker, but may refrain from coming indoors when the temperature drops below freezing. Even as a legislative matter, in other words, the intelligent line does not fall between action and inaction but between those forms of inaction that consist of abstaining from "ordinary" care and those that consist of abstaining from "excessive" or "heroic" measures. Unlike action versus inaction, that is not a line to be discerned by logic or legal analysis, and we should not pretend that it is.

But to return to the principal point for present purposes: the irrelevance of the action-inaction distinction. Starving oneself to death is no different from putting a gun to one's temple as far as the common-law definition of suicide is concerned; the cause of death in both cases is the suicide's conscious decision to "pu[t] an end to his own existence." 4 Blackstone, *supra,* at *189. See *In re Caulk,* 125 N.H. 226, 232, 480 A.2d 93, 97 (1984); *State ex rel. White v. Narick,* 170 W.Va. 195, 292 S.E.2d 54 (1982); *Von Holden v. Chapman,* 87 App.Div.2d 66, 450 N.Y.S.2d 623 (1982). Of course the common law rejected the action-inaction distinction in other contexts involving the taking of human life as well. In the prosecution of a parent for the starvation death of her infant, it was no defense that the infant's death was "caused" by no action of the parent but by the natural process of starvation, or by the infant's natural inability to provide for itself. See *Lewis v. State,* 72 Ga. 164 (1883); *People v. McDonald,* 49 Hun 67, 1 N.Y.S. 703 (5th Dept., App.Div.1888); *Commonwealth v. Hall,* 322 Mass. 523, 528, 78 N.E.2d 644, 647 (1948) (collecting cases); F. Wharton, Law of Homicide §§ 134-135, 304 (2d ed. 1875); 2 J. Bishop, Commentaries on Criminal Law § 686 (5th ed. 1872); J. Hawley & M. McGregor, Criminal Law 152 (3d ed. 1899). A physician, moreover, could be criminally liable for failure to provide care that could have extended the patient's life, even if death was immediately caused by the underlying disease that the physician failed to treat. *Barrow v. State,* 17 Okl.Cr. 340, 188 P. 351 (1920); *People v. Phillips,* 64 Cal.2d 574, 414 P.2d 353 (1966).

It is not surprising, therefore, that the early cases considering the claimed right to refuse medical treatment dismissed as specious the nice distinction between "passively submitting to death and actively seeking it. The distinction may be merely verbal, as it would be if an adult sought death by starvation instead of a drug. If the State may interrupt one mode of self-destruction, it may with equal authority interfere with the other." *John F. Kennedy Memorial Hosp. v. Heston,* 58 N.J. 576, 581-582, 279 A.2d 670, 672-673 (1971); see also *Application of President & Directors of Georgetown College, Inc.,* 118 U.S.App.D.C. 80, 88-89, 331 F.2d 1000, 1008-1009 (Wright, J., in chambers), cert. denied, 377 U.S. 978, 84 S.Ct. 1883, 12 L.Ed.2d 746 (1964).

The third asserted basis of distinction—that frustrating Nancy Cruzan's wish to die in the present case requires interference with her bodily integrity—is likewise inadequate, because such interference is impermissible only if one begs the question whether her refusal to undergo the treatment on her own is suicide. It has always been lawful not only for the State, but even for private citizens, to interfere with bodily integrity to prevent a felony. See *Phillips v. Trull,* 11 Johns. 486 (N.Y.1814); *City Council v. Payne,* 2 Nott & McCord 475 (S.C.1821); *Vandeveer v. Mattocks,* 3 Ind. 479 (1852); T. Cooley, Law of Torts 174-175 (1879); Wilgus, Arrest Without a Warrant, 22 Mich.L.Rev. 673 (1924); Restatement of Torts § 119 (1934). That general rule has of course been applied to suicide. At common law, even a private person's use of force to prevent suicide was privileged. *Colby v. Jackson,* 12 N.H. 526, 530-531 (1842); *Look v. Choate,* 108 Mass. 116, 120 (1871); *Commonwealth v. Mink,* 123 Mass. 422, 429 (1877); *In re Doyle,* 16 R.I. 537, 539, 18 A. 159, 159-160 (1889); *Porter v. Ritch,* 70 Conn. 235, 255, 39 A. 169, 175 (1898); *Emmerich v. Thorley,* 35 App.Div. 452, 456, 54 N.Y.S. 791, 793-794 (1898); *State v. Hembd,* 305 Minn. 120, 130, 232 N.W.2d 872, 878 (1975); 2 C. Addison, Law of Torts § 819 (1876); Cooley, *supra,* at 179-180. It is not even reasonable, much less required by the Constitution, to maintain that although the State has the right to prevent a person from slashing his wrists, it does not have the power to apply physical force to prevent him from doing so, nor the power, should he succeed, to apply, coercively if necessary, medical measures to stop the flow of blood. The state-run hospital, I am certain, is not liable under 42 U.S.C. § 1983 for violation of constitutional rights, nor the private hospital liable under general tort law, if, in a State where suicide is unlawful, it pumps out the stomach of a person who has intentionally taken an overdose of barbiturates, despite that person's wishes to the contrary.

The dissents of Justices BRENNAN and STEVENS make a plausible case for our intervention here only by embracing—the latter explicitly and the former by implication—a political principle that the States are free to adopt, but that is demonstrably not imposed by the Constitution. "[T]he State," says Justice BRENNAN, "has no legitimate general interest in someone's life, completely abstracted from the interest of the person living that life, that could outweigh the person's choice *to avoid medical treatment.*" *Post,* at 313 (emphasis added). The italicized phrase sounds moderate enough and is all that is needed to cover the present case—but the proposition cannot *logically* be so limited. One who accepts it must also accept, I think, that the State has no such legitimate interest that could outweigh "the person's choice *to put an end to her life.*" Similarly, if one agrees with Justice BRENNAN that "the State's general interest in life must accede to Nancy Cruzan's particularized and intense interest in self-determination *in her choice of medical treatment,*" *ibid.* (emphasis added), he must also believe that the State must accede to her "particularized and intense interest in self-determination *in her choice whether to continue living or to die.*" For insofar as balancing the relative interests of the State and the individual is concerned, there is nothing distinctive about accepting death through the refusal of "medical treatment," as opposed to accepting it through the refusal of food, or through the failure to shut off the engine and get out of the car after parking in one's garage after work. Suppose that Nancy Cruzan were in precisely the condition she is in today, except that she could be fed and digest food and water *without* artificial assistance. How is the State's "interest" in keeping her alive thereby increased, or her interest in deciding whether she wants to continue living reduced? It seems to me, in other words, that Justice BRENNAN's position ultimately rests upon the proposition that it is none of the State's business if a person wants to commit suicide. Justice STEVENS is explicit on the point: "Choices about death touch the core of liberty. . . . [N]ot much may be said with confidence about death unless it is said from faith, and that alone is reason enough to protect the freedom to conform choices about death to individual conscience." *Post,* at 343. This is a view that some societies have held, and that our States are free to adopt if they wish. But it is not a view imposed by our constitutional traditions, in which the power of the State to prohibit suicide is unquestionable.

What I have said above is not meant to suggest that I would think it desirable, if we were sure that Nancy Cruzan wanted to die, to keep her alive by the means at issue here. I assert only that the Constitution has nothing to say about the subject. To raise up a constitutional right here we would have to create out of nothing (for it exists neither in text nor tradition) some constitutional principle whereby, although the State may insist that an individual come in out of the cold and eat food, it may not insist that he take medicine; and although it may pump his stomach empty of poison he has ingested, it may not fill his stomach with food he has failed to ingest. Are there, then, no reasonable and humane limits that ought not to be exceeded in requiring an individual to preserve his own life? There obviously are, but they are not set forth in the Due Process Clause. What assures us that those limits will not be exceeded is the same constitutional guarantee that is the source of most of our protection—what protects us, for example, from being assessed a tax of 100% of our income above the subsistence level, from being forbidden to drive cars, or from being required to send our children to school for 10 hours a day, none of which horribles are categorically prohibited by the Constitution. Our salvation is the Equal Protection

Clause, which requires the democratic majority to accept for themselves and their loved ones what they impose on you and me. This Court need not, and has no authority to, inject itself into every field of human activity where irrationality and oppression may theoretically occur, and if it tries to do so it will destroy itself.

Justice BRENNAN, with whom Justice MARSHALL and Justice BLACKMUN join, dissenting.

"Medical technology has effectively created a twilight zone of suspended animation where death commences while life, in some form, continues. Some patients, however, want no part of a life sustained only by medical technology. Instead, they prefer a plan of medical treatment that allows nature to take its course and permits them to die with dignity." [1]

Nancy Cruzan has dwelt in that twilight zone for six years. She is oblivious to her surroundings and will remain so. *Cruzan v. Harmon,* 760 S.W.2d 408, 411 (Mo.1988). Her body twitches only reflexively, without consciousness. *Ibid.* The areas of her brain that once thought, felt, and experienced sensations have degenerated badly and are continuing to do so. The cavities remaining are filling with cerebro-spinal fluid. The " 'cerebral cortical atrophy is irreversible, permanent, progressive and ongoing.' " *Ibid.* "Nancy will never interact meaningfully with her environment again. She will remain in a persistent vegetative state until her death." *Id.,* at 422.[2] Because she cannot swallow, her nutrition and hydration are delivered through a tube surgically implanted in her stomach.

A grown woman at the time of the accident, Nancy had previously expressed her wish to forgo continuing medical care under circumstances such as these. Her family and her friends are convinced that this is what she would want. See n. 20, *infra.* A guardian ad litem appointed by the trial court is also convinced that this is what Nancy would want. See 760 S.W.2d, at 444 (Higgins, J., dissenting from denial of rehearing). Yet the Missouri Supreme Court, alone among state courts deciding such a question, has determined that an irreversibly vegetative patient will remain a passive prisoner of medical technology—for Nancy, perhaps for the next 30 years. See *id.,* at 424, 427.

Today the Court, while tentatively accepting that there is some degree of constitutionally protected liberty interest in avoiding unwanted medical treatment, including life-sustaining medical treatment such as artificial nutrition and hydration, affirms the decision of the Missouri Supreme Court. The majority opinion, as I read it, would affirm that decision on the ground that a State may require "clear and convincing" evidence of Nancy Cruzan's prior decision to forgo life-sustaining treatment under circumstances such as hers in order to ensure that her actual wishes are honored. See *ante,* at 282-283, 286-287. Because I believe that Nancy Cruzan has a fundamental right to be free of unwanted artificial nutrition and hydration, which right is not outweighed by any interests of the State, and because I find that the improperly biased procedural obstacles imposed by the Missouri Supreme Court impermissibly burden that right, I respectfully dissent. Nancy Cruzan is entitled to choose to die with dignity.

I

A.

"[T]he timing of death—once a matter of fate—is now a matter of human choice." Office of Technology Assessment Task Force, Life Sustaining Technologies and the Elderly 41 (1988). Of the approximately 2 million people who die each year, 80% die in hospitals and long-term care institutions,[3] and perhaps 70% of those after a decision to forgo life-sustaining treatment has been made.[4] Nearly every death involves a decision whether to undertake some medical procedure that could prolong the process of dying. Such decisions are difficult and personal. They must be made on the basis of individual values, informed by medical realities, yet within a framework governed by law. The role of the courts is confined to defining that framework, delineating the ways in which government may and may not participate in such decisions.

The question before this Court is a relatively narrow one: whether the Due Process Clause allows Missouri to require a now-incompetent patient in an irreversible persistent vegetative state to remain on life support absent rigorously clear and convincing evidence that avoiding the treatment represents the patient's prior, express choice. See *ante*, at 277-278. If a fundamental right is at issue, Missouri's rule of decision must be scrutinized under the standards this Court has always applied in such circumstances. As we said in *Zablocki v. Redhail*, 434 U.S. 374, 388, 98 S.Ct. 673, 682, 54 L.Ed.2d 618 (1978), if a requirement imposed by a State "significantly interferes with the exercise of a fundamental right, it cannot be upheld unless it is supported by sufficiently important state interests and is closely tailored to effectuate only those interests." The Constitution imposes on this Court the obligation to "examine carefully . . . the extent to which [the legitimate government interests advanced] are served by the challenged regulation." *Moore v. East Cleveland*, 431 U.S. 494, 499, 97 S.Ct. 1932, 1936, 52 L.Ed.2d 531 (1977). See also *Carey v. Population Services International*, 431 U.S. 678, 690, 97 S.Ct. 2010, 2018-2019, 52 L.Ed.2d 675 (1977) (invalidating a requirement that bore "no relation to the State's interest"). An evidentiary rule, just as a substantive prohibition, must meet these standards if it significantly burdens a fundamental liberty interest. Fundamental rights "are protected not only against heavy-handed frontal attack, but also from being stifled by more subtle governmental interference." *Bates v. Little Rock*, 361 U.S. 516, 523, 80 S.Ct. 412, 416, 4 L.Ed.2d 480 (1960).

B

The starting point for our legal analysis must be whether a competent person has a constitutional right to avoid unwanted medical care. Earlier this Term, this Court held that the Due Process Clause of the Fourteenth Amendment confers a significant liberty interest in avoiding unwanted medical treatment. *Washington v. Harper*, 494 U.S. 210, 221-222, 110 S.Ct. 1028, 1036-1037, 108 L.Ed.2d 178 (1990). Today, the Court concedes that our prior decisions "support the recognition of a general liberty interest in refusing medical treatment." See *ante*, at 278. The Court, however, avoids discussing either the measure of that liberty interest or its application by assuming, for purposes of this case only, that a competent person has a constitutionally protected liberty interest in being free of unwanted artificial nutrition and hydration. See *ante,* at 279. Justice O'CONNOR's opinion is less parsimonious. She openly affirms that "the Court has often deemed state incursions into the body repugnant to the interests protected by the Due Process Clause," that there is a liberty interest in avoiding unwanted medical treatment, and that it encompasses the right to be free of "artificially delivered food and water." See *ante,* at 287.

But if a competent person has a liberty interest to be free of unwanted medical treatment, as both the majority and Justice O'CONNOR concede, it must be fundamental. "We are dealing here with [a decision] which involves one of the basic civil rights of man." *Skinner v. Oklahoma ex rel. Williamson,* 316 U.S. 535, 541, 62 S.Ct. 1110, 1113, 86 L.Ed. 1655 (1942) (invalidating a statute authorizing sterilization of certain felons). Whatever other liberties protected by the Due Process Clause are fundamental, "those liberties that are 'deeply rooted in this Nation's history and tradition' " are among them. *Bowers v. Hardwick,* 478 U.S. 186, 192, 106 S.Ct. 2841, 2844, 92 L.Ed.2d 140 (1986) (quoting *Moore v. East Cleveland, supra,* 431 U.S., at 503, 97 S.Ct., at 1938 (plurality opinion). "Such a tradition commands respect in part because the Constitution carries the gloss of history." *Richmond Newspapers, Inc. v. Virginia,* 448 U.S. 555, 589, 100 S.Ct. 2814, 2834, 65 L.Ed.2d 973 (1980) (BRENNAN, J., concurring in judgment).

The right to be free from medical attention without consent, to determine what shall be done with one's own body, *is* deeply rooted in this Nation's traditions, as the majority acknowledges. See *ante,* at 270. This right has long been "firmly entrenched in American tort law" and is securely grounded in the earliest common law. *Ibid.* See also *Mills v. Rogers,* 457 U.S. 291, 294, n. 4, 102 S.Ct. 2442, 2446, n. 4, 73 L.Ed.2d 16 (1982) ("[T]he right to refuse any medical treatment emerged from the doctrines of trespass and battery, which were applied to unauthorized touchings by a physician"). "Anglo-American law starts with the premise of thorough-going self determination. It follows that each man is considered to be master of his own body, and he may, if he be of sound mind, expressly prohibit the performance of lifesaving surgery, or other medical treatment." *Natanson v. Kline,* 186 Kan. 393, 406-407, 350 P.2d 1093, 1104 (1960). "The inviolability of the person" has been held as "sacred" and "carefully guarded" as any common-law right. *Union Pacific R. Co. v. Botsford,* 141 U.S. 250, 251-252, 11 S.Ct. 1000, 1001, 35 L.Ed. 734 (1891). Thus, freedom from unwanted medical attention is unquestionably among those principles "so rooted in the traditions and conscience of our people as to be ranked as fundamental." *Snyder v. Massachusetts,* 291 U.S. 97, 105, 54 S.Ct. 330, 332, 78 L.Ed. 674 (1934).[5] That there may be serious consequences involved in refusal of the medical treatment at issue here does not vitiate the right under our common-law tradition of medical self-determination. It is "a well-established rule of general law . . . that it is the patient, not the physician, who ultimately decides if treatment—any treatment—is to be given at all. . . . The rule has never been qualified in its application by either the nature or purpose of the treatment, or the gravity of the consequences of acceding to or foregoing it." *Tune v. Walter Reed Army Medical Hospital,* 602 F.Supp. 1452, 1455 (DC 1985). See also *Downer v. Veilleux,* 322 A.2d 82, 91 (Me.1974) ("The rationale of this rule lies in the fact that every competent adult has the right to forego treatment, or even cure, if it entails what for him are intolerable consequences or risks, however unwise his sense of values may be to others").[6]

No material distinction can be drawn between the treatment to which Nancy Cruzan continues to be subject—artificial nutrition and hydration—and any other medical treatment. See *ante,* at 288-289 (O'CONNOR, J., concurring). The artificial delivery of nutrition and hydration is undoubtedly medical treatment. The technique to which Nancy Cruzan is subject—artificial feeding through a gastrostomy tube—involves a tube implanted surgically into her stomach through incisions in her abdominal wall. It may obstruct the intestinal tract, erode and pierce the stomach wall, or cause leakage of the stomach's contents into the abdominal cavity. See Page, Andrassy, & Sandler, Techniques in Delivery of Liquid Diets, in Nutrition in Clinical Surgery 66-67 (M. Deitel 2d ed. 1985). The tube can cause pneumonia from reflux of the stomach's contents into the lung. See Bernard & Forlaw, Complications and Their Prevention, in Enteral and Tube Feeding 553 (J. Rombeau & M. Caldwell eds. 1984). Typically, and in this case (see Tr. 377), commercially prepared formulas are used, rather than fresh food. See Matarese, Enteral Alimentation, in Surgical Nutrition 726 (J. Fischer ed. 1983). The type of formula and method of administration must be experimented with to avoid gastrointestinal problems. *Id.,* at 748. The patient must be monitored daily by medical personnel as to weight, fluid intake, and fluid output; blood tests must be done weekly. *Id.,* at 749, 751.

Artificial delivery of food and water is regarded as medical treatment by the medical profession and the Federal Government.[7] According to the American Academy of Neurology:

"The artificial provision of nutrition and hydration is a form of medical treatment . . . analogous to other forms of life-sustaining treatment, such as the use of the respirator. When a patient is unconscious, both a respirator and an artificial feeding device serve to support or replace normal bodily functions that are compromised as a result of the patient's illness." Position of the American Academy of Neurology on Certain Aspects of the Care and Management of the Persistent Vegetative State Patient, 39 Neurology 125 (Jan.1989). See also Council on Ethical and Judicial Affairs of the American Medical Association, Current Opinions, Opinion 2.20 (1989) ("Life-prolonging medical treatment includes medication and artifically or technologically supplied respiration, nutrition or hydration"); President's Commission 88 (life-sustaining treatment includes respirators, kidney dialysis machines, and special feeding procedures). The Federal Government permits the cost of the medical devices and formulas used in enteral feeding to be reimbursed under Medicare. See Pub.L. 99-509, § 9340, note following 42 U.S.C. § 1395u, p. 592 (1982 ed., Supp. V). The formulas are regulated by the federal Food and Drug Administration as "medical foods," see 21 U.S.C. § 360ee, and the feeding tubes are regulated as medical devices, 21 CFR § 876.5980 (1989).

Nor does the fact that Nancy Cruzan is now incompetent deprive her of her fundamental rights. See *Youngberg v. Romeo,* 457 U.S. 307, 315-316, 319, 102 S.Ct. 2452, 2459-2460, 73 L.Ed.2d 28 (1982) (holding that severely retarded man's liberty interests in safety, freedom from bodily restraint, and reasonable training survive involuntary commitment); *Parham v. J.R.,* 442 U.S. 584, 600, 99 S.Ct. 2493, 2503, 61 L.Ed.2d 101 (1979) (recognizing a child's substantial liberty interest in not being confined unnecessarily for medical treatment); *Jackson v. Indiana,* 406 U.S. 715, 730, 738, 92 S.Ct. 1845, 1858, 32 L.Ed.2d 435 (1972) (holding that Indiana could not violate the due process and equal protection rights of a mentally retarded deaf mute by committing him for an indefinite amount of time simply because he was incompetent to stand trial on the criminal charges filed against him). As the majority recognizes, *ante,* at 280, the question is not whether an incompetent has constitutional rights, but how such rights may be exercised. As we explained in *Thompson v. Oklahoma,* 487 U.S. 815, 108 S.Ct. 2687, 101 L.Ed.2d 702 (1988): "[T]he law must often adjust the manner in which it affords rights to those whose status renders them unable to exercise choice freely and rationally. Children, the insane, and *those who are irreversibly ill with loss of brain function, for instance, all retain 'rights,'* to be sure, but often such rights are only meaningful as they are exercised by agents acting with the best interests of their principals in mind." *Id.,* at 825, n. 23, 108 S.Ct., at 2693, n. 23 (emphasis added). "To deny [its] exercise because the patient is unconscious or incompetent would be to deny the right." *Foody v. Manchester Memorial Hospital,* 40 Conn.Supp. 127, 133, 482 A.2d 713, 718 (1984).

II

A.

The right to be free from unwanted medical attention is a right to evaluate the potential benefit of treatment and its possible consequences according to one's own values and to make a personal decision whether to subject oneself to the intrusion. For a patient like Nancy Cruzan, the sole benefit of medical treatment is being kept metabolically alive. Neither artificial nutrition nor any other form of medical treatment available today can cure or in any way ameliorate her condition.[8] Irreversibly vegetative patients are devoid of thought, emotion, and sensation; they are permanently and completely unconscious. See n. 2, *supra*.[9] As the President's Commission concluded in approving the withdrawal of life support equipment from irreversibly vegetative patients:

"[T]reatment ordinarily aims to benefit a patient through preserving life, relieving pain and suffering, protecting against disability, and returning maximally effective functioning. If a prognosis of permanent unconsciousness is correct, however, continued treatment cannot confer such benefits. Pain and suffering are absent, as are joy, satisfaction, and pleasure. Disability is total and no return to an even minimal level of social or human functioning is possible." President's Commission 181-182.

There are also affirmative reasons why someone like Nancy might choose to forgo artificial nutrition and hydration under these circumstances. Dying is personal. And it is profound. For many, the thought of an ignoble end, steeped in decay, is abhorrent. A quiet, proud death, bodily integrity intact, is a matter of extreme consequence. "In certain, thankfully rare, circumstances the burden of maintaining the corporeal existence degrades the very humanity it was meant to serve." *Brophy v. New England Sinai Hospital, Inc.,* 398 Mass. 417, 434, 497 N.E.2d 626, 635-636 (1986) (finding the subject of the proceeding "in a condition which [he] has indicated he would consider to be degrading and without human dignity" and holding that "[t]he duty of the State to preserve life must encompass a recognition of an individual's right to avoid circumstances in which the individual himself would feel that efforts to sustain life demean or degrade his humanity"). Another court, hearing a similar case, noted:

> "It is apparent from the testimony that what was on [the patient's] mind was not only the invasiveness of life-sustaining systems, such as the [nasogastric] tube, upon the integrity of his body. It was also the utter helplessness of the permanently comatose person, the wasting of a once strong body, and the submission of the most private bodily functions to the attention of others." *In re Gardner,* 534 A.2d 947, 953 (Me.1987).

Such conditions are, for many, humiliating to contemplate,[10] as is visiting a prolonged and anguished vigil on one's parents, spouse, and children. A long, drawn-out death can have a debilitating effect on family members. See Carnwath & Johnson, Psychiatric Morbidity Among Spouses of Patients With Stroke, 294 Brit.Med.J. 409 (1987); Livingston, Families Who Care, 291 Brit.Med.J. 919 (1985). For some, the idea of being remembered in their persistent vegetative states rather than as they were before their illness or accident may be very disturbing.[11]

B

Although the right to be free of unwanted medical intervention, like other constitutionally protected interests, may not be absolute,[12] no state interest could outweigh the rights of an individual in Nancy Cruzan's position. Whatever a State's possible interests in mandating life-support treatment under other circumstances, there is no good to be obtained here by Missouri's insistence that Nancy Cruzan remain on life-support systems if it is indeed her wish not to do so. Missouri does not claim, nor could it, that society as a whole will be benefited by Nancy's receiving medical treatment. No third party's situation will be improved and no harm to others will be averted. Cf. nn. 6 and 8, *supra*.[13]

The only state interest asserted here is a general interest in the preservation of life.[14] But the State has no legitimate general interest in someone's life, completely abstracted from the interest of the person living that life, that could outweigh the person's choice to avoid medical treatment. "[T]he regulation of constitutionally protected decisions . . . must be predicated on legitimate state concerns *other than* disagreement with the choice the individual has made. . . . Otherwise, the interest in liberty protected by the Due Process Clause would be a nullity." *Hodgson v. Minnesota*, 497 U.S. 417, 435, 110 S.Ct. 2926, 2937, 111 L.Ed.2d 344 (1990) (opinion of STEVENS, J.) (emphasis added). Thus, the State's general interest in life must accede to Nancy Cruzan's particularized and intense interest in self-determination in her choice of medical treatment. There is simply nothing legitimately within the State's purview to be gained by superseding her decision.

Moreover, there may be considerable danger that Missouri's rule of decision would impair rather than serve any interest the State does have in sustaining life. Current medical practice recommends use of heroic measures if there is a scintilla of a chance that the patient will recover, on the assumption that the measures will be discontinued should the patient improve. When the President's Commission in 1982 approved the withdrawal of life-support equipment from irreversibly vegetative patients, it explained that "[a]n even more troubling wrong occurs when a treatment that might save life or improve health is not started because the health care personnel are afraid that they will find it very difficult to stop the treatment if, as is fairly likely, it proves to be of little benefit and greatly burdens the patient." President's Commission 75. A New Jersey court recognized that families as well as doctors might be discouraged by an inability to stop life-support measures from "even attempting certain types of care [which] could thereby force them into hasty and premature decisions to allow a patient to die." *In re Conroy,* 98 N.J. 321, 370, 486 A.2d 1209, 1234 (1985). See also Brief for American Academy of Neurology as *Amicus Curiae* 9 (expressing same concern).[15]

III

This is not to say that the State has no legitimate interests to assert here. As the majority recognizes, *ante,* at 282, Missouri has a *parens patriae* interest in providing Nancy Cruzan, now incompetent, with as accurate as possible a determination of how she would exercise her rights under these circumstances. Second, if and when it is determined that Nancy Cruzan would want to continue treatment, the State may legitimately assert an interest in providing that treatment. But *until* Nancy's wishes have been determined, the only state interest that may be asserted is an interest in safe-guarding the accuracy of that determination.

Accuracy, therefore, must be our touchstone. Missouri may constitutionally impose only those procedural requirements that serve to enhance the accuracy of a determination of Nancy Cruzan's wishes or are at least consistent with an accurate determination. The Missouri "safeguard" that the Court upholds today does not meet that standard. The determination needed in this context is whether the incompetent person would choose to live in a persistent vegetative state on life support or to avoid this medical treatment. Missouri's rule of decision imposes a markedly asymmetrical evidentiary burden. Only evidence of specific statements of treatment choice made by the patient when competent is admissible to support a finding that the patient, now in a persistent vegetative state, would wish to avoid further medical treatment. Moreover, this evidence must be clear and convincing. No proof is required to support a finding that the incompetent person would wish to continue treatment.

A.

The majority offers several justifications for Missouri's heightened evidentiary standard. First, the majority explains that the State may constitutionally adopt this rule to govern determinations of an incompetent's wishes in order to advance the State's substantive interests, including its unqualified interest in the preservation of human life. See *ante,* at 282-283, and n. 10. Missouri's evidentiary standard, however, cannot rest on the State's own interest in a particular substantive result. To be sure, courts have long erected clear and convincing evidence standards to place the greater risk of erroneous decisions on those bringing disfavored claims.[16] In such cases, however, the choice to discourage certain claims was a legitimate, constitutional policy choice. In contrast, Missouri has no such power to disfavor a choice by Nancy Cruzan to avoid medical treatment, because Missouri has no legitimate interest in providing Nancy with treatment until it is established that this represents her choice. See *supra,* at 312-314. Just as a State may not override Nancy's choice directly, it may not do so indirectly through the imposition of a procedural rule.

Second, the majority offers two explanations for why Missouri's clear and convincing evidence standard is a means of enhancing accuracy, but neither is persuasive. The majority initially argues that a clear and convincing evidence standard is necessary to compensate for the possibility that such proceedings will lack the "guarantee of accurate factfinding that the adversary process brings with it," citing *Ohio v. Akron Center for Reproductive Health,* 497 U.S. 502, 515-516, 110 S.Ct. 2972, 2981-2982, 111 L.Ed.2d 405 (1990) (upholding a clear and convincing evidence standard for an *ex parte* proceeding). *Ante,* at 281-282. Without supporting the Court's decision in that case, I note that the proceeding to determine an incompetent's wishes is quite different from a proceeding to determine whether a minor may bypass notifying her parents before undergoing an abortion on the ground that she is mature enough to make the decision or that the abortion is in her best interests.

An adversarial proceeding is of particular importance when one side has a strong personal interest which needs to be counterbalanced to assure the court that the questions will be fully explored. A minor who has a strong interest in obtaining permission for an abortion without notifying her parents may come forward whether or not society would be satisfied that she has made the decision with the seasoned judgment of an adult. The proceeding here is of a different nature. Barring venal motives, which a trial court has the means of ferreting out, the decision to come forward to request a judicial order to stop treatment represents a slowly and carefully considered resolution by at least one adult and more frequently several adults that discontinuation of treatment is the patient's wish.

In addition, the bypass procedure at issue in *Akron, supra,* is *ex parte* and secret. The court may not notify the minor's parents, siblings, or friends. No one may be present to submit evidence unless brought forward by the minor herself. In contrast, the proceeding to determine Nancy Cruzan's wishes was neither *ex parte* nor secret. In a hearing to determine the treatment preferences of an incompetent person, a court is not limited to adjusting burdens of proof as its only means of protecting against a possible imbalance. Indeed, any concern that those who come forward will present a one-sided view would be better addressed by appointing a guardian ad litem, who could use the State's powers of discovery to gather and present evidence regarding the patient's wishes. A guardian ad litem's task is to uncover any conflicts of interest and ensure that each party likely to have relevant evidence is consulted and brought forward for example, other members of the family, friends, clergy, and doctors. See, *e.g., In re Colyer,* 99 Wash.2d 114, 133, 660 P.2d 738, 748-749 (1983). Missouri's heightened evidentiary standard attempts to achieve balance by discounting evidence; the guardian ad litem technique achieves balance by probing for additional evidence. Where, as here, the family members, friends, doctors, and guardian ad litem agree, it is not because the process has failed, as the majority suggests. See *ante,* at 281, n. 9. It is because there is no genuine dispute as to Nancy's preference.

The majority next argues that where, as here, important individual rights are at stake, a clear and convincing evidence standard has long been held to be an appropriate means of enhancing accuracy, citing decisions concerning what process an individual is due before he can be deprived of a liberty interest. See *ante,* at 283. In those cases, however, this Court imposed a clear and convincing standard as a constitutional minimum on the basis of its evaluation that one side's interests clearly outweighed the second side's interests and therefore the second side should bear the risk of error. See *Santosky v. Kramer,* 455 U.S. 745, 753, 766-767, 102 S.Ct. 1388, 1401-1402, 71 L.Ed.2d 599 (1982) (requiring a clear and convincing evidence standard for termination of parental rights because the parent's interest is fundamental but the State has no legitimate interest in termination unless the parent is unfit, and finding that the State's interest in finding the best home for the child does not arise until the parent has been found unfit); *Addington v. Texas,* 441 U.S. 418, 426-427, 99 S.Ct. 1804, 1809-1810, 60 L.Ed.2d 323 (1979) (requiring clear and convincing evidence in an involuntary commitment hearing because the interest of the individual far outweighs that of a State, which has no legitimate interest in confining individuals who are not mentally ill and do not pose a danger to themselves or others). Moreover, we have always recognized that shifting the risk of error reduces the likelihood of errors in one direction at the cost of increasing the likelihood of errors in the other. See *Addington, supra,* at 423, 99 S.Ct., at 1807-1808 (contrasting heightened standards of proof to a preponderance standard in which the two sides "share the risk of error in roughly equal fashion" because society does not favor one outcome over the other). In the cases cited by the majority, the imbalance imposed by a heightened evidentiary standard was not only acceptable but required because the standard was deployed to protect an individual's exercise of a fundamental right, as the majority admits, *ante,* at 282-283, n. 10. In contrast, the Missouri court imposed a clear and convincing evidence standard as an obstacle to the exercise of a fundamental right.

The majority claims that the allocation of the risk of error is justified because it is more important not to terminate life support for someone who would wish it continued than to honor the wishes of someone who would not. An erroneous decision to terminate life support is irrevocable, says the majority, while an erroneous decision not to terminate "results in a maintenance of the status quo." See *ante,* at 283.[17] But, from the point of view of the patient, an erroneous decision in either direction is irrevocable. An erroneous decision to terminate artificial nutrition and hydration, to be sure, will lead to failure of that last remnant of physiological life, the brain stem, and result in complete brain death. An erroneous decision not to terminate life support, however, robs a patient of the very qualities protected by the right to avoid unwanted medical treatment. His own degraded existence is perpetuated; his family's suffering is protracted; the memory he leaves behind becomes more and more distorted.

Even a later decision to grant him his wish cannot undo the intervening harm. But a later decision is unlikely in any event. "[T]he discovery of new evidence," to which the majority refers, *ibid.,* is more hypothetical than plausible. The majority also misconceives the relevance of the possibility of "advancements in medical science," *ibid.,* by treating it as a reason to force someone to continue medical treatment against his will. The possibility of a medical miracle is indeed part of the calculus, but it is a part of the *patient's* calculus. If current research suggests that some hope for cure or even moderate improvement is possible within the life span projected, this is a factor that should be and would be accorded significant weight in assessing what the patient himself would choose.[18]

B

Even more than its heightened evidentiary standard, the Missouri court's categorical exclusion of relevant evidence dispenses with any semblance of accurate factfinding. The court adverted to no evidence supporting its decision, but held that no clear and convincing, inherently reliable evidence had been presented to show that Nancy would want to avoid further treatment. In doing so, the court failed to consider statements Nancy had made to family members and a close friend.[19] The court also failed to consider testimony from Nancy's mother and sister that they were certain that Nancy would want to discontinue artificial nutrition and hydration,[20] even after the court found that Nancy's family was loving and without malignant motive. See 760 S.W.2d, at 412. The court also failed to consider the conclusions of the guardian ad litem, appointed by the trial court, that there was clear and convincing evidence that Nancy would want to discontinue medical treatment and that this was in her best interests. *Id.,* at 444 (Higgins, J., dissenting from denial of rehearing); Brief for Respondent Guardian Ad Litem 2-3. The court did not specifically define what kind of evidence it would consider clear and convincing, but its general discussion suggests that only a living will or equivalently formal directive from the patient when competent would meet this standard. See 760 S.W.2d, at 424-425.

Too few people execute living wills or equivalently formal directives for such an evidentiary rule to ensure adequately that the wishes of incompetent persons will be honored.[21] While it might be a wise social policy to encourage people to furnish such instructions, no general conclusion about a patient's choice can be drawn from the absence of formalities. The probability of becoming irreversibly vegetative is so low that many people may not feel an urgency to marshal formal evidence of their preferences. Some may not wish to dwell on their own physical deterioration and mortality. Even someone with a resolute determination to avoid life support under circumstances such as Nancy's would still need to know that such things as living wills exist and how to execute one. Often legal help would be necessary, especially given the majority's apparent willingness to permit States to insist that a person's wishes are not truly known unless the particular medical treatment is specified. See *ante,* at 285.

As a California appellate court observed: "The lack of generalized public awareness of the statutory scheme and the typically human characteristics of procrastination and reluctance to contemplate the need for such arrangements however makes this a tool which will all too often go unused by those who might desire it." *Barber v. Superior Court,* 147 Cal.App.3d 1006, 1015, 195 Cal.Rptr. 484, 489 (1983). When a person tells family or close friends that she does not want her life sustained artificially, she is "express[ing] her wishes in the only terms familiar to her, and . . . as clearly as a lay person should be asked to express them. To require more is unrealistic, and for all practical purposes, it precludes the rights of patients to forego life-sustaining treatment." *In re O'Connor,* 72 N.Y.2d 517, 551, 534 N.Y.S.2d 886, 905, 531 N.E.2d 607, 626 (1988) (Simons, J., dissenting).[22] When Missouri enacted a living will statute, it specifically provided that the absence of a living will does not warrant a presumption that a patient wishes continued medical treatment. See n. 15, *supra.* Thus, apparently not even Missouri's own legislature believes that a person who does not execute a living will fails to do so because he wishes continuous medical treatment under all circumstances.

The testimony of close friends and family members, on the other hand, may often be the best evidence available of what the patient's choice would be. It is they with whom the patient most likely will have discussed such questions and they who know the patient best. "Family members have a unique knowledge of the patient which is vital to any decision on his or her behalf." Newman, Treatment Refusals for the Critically and Terminally Ill: Proposed Rules for the Family, the Physician, and the State, 3 N.Y.L.S. Human Rights Annual 35, 46 (1985). The Missouri court's decision to ignore this whole category of testimony is also at odds with the practices of other States. See, *e.g., In re Peter,* 108 N.J. 365, 529 A.2d 419 (1987); *Brophy v. New*

England Sinai Hospital, Inc., 398 Mass. 417, 497 N.E.2d 626 (1986); *In re Severns,* 425 A.2d 156 (Del.Ch.1980).

The Missouri court's disdain for Nancy's statements in serious conversations not long before her accident, for the opinions of Nancy's family and friends as to her values, beliefs and certain choice, and even for the opinion of an outside objective factfinder appointed by the State evinces a disdain for Nancy Cruzan's own right to choose. The rules by which an incompetent person's wishes are determined must represent every effort to determine those wishes. The rule that the Missouri court adopted and that this Court upholds, however, skews the result away from a determination that as accurately as possible reflects the individual's own preferences and beliefs. It is a rule that transforms human beings into passive subjects of medical technology.

"[M]edical care decisions must be guided by the individual patient's interests and values. Allowing persons to determine their own medical treatment is an important way in which society respects persons as individuals.

Moreover, the respect due to persons as individuals does not diminish simply because they have become incapable of participating in treatment decisions. . . . [I]t is still possible for others to make a decision that reflects [the patient's] interests more closely than would a purely technological decision to do whatever is possible. Lacking the ability to decide, [a patient] has a right to a decision that takes his interests into account." *Conservatorship of Drabick,* 200 Cal.App.3d 185, 208, 245 Cal.Rptr. 840, 854-855, cert. denied, 488 U.S. 958, 109 S.Ct. 399, 102 L.Ed.2d 387 (1988).

C

I do not suggest that States must sit by helplessly if the choices of incompetent patients are in danger of being ignored. See *ante,* at 281. Even if the Court had ruled that Missouri's rule of decision is unconstitutional, as I believe it should have, States would nevertheless remain free to fashion procedural protections to safeguard the interests of incompetents under these circumstances. The

Constitution provides merely a framework here: Protections must be genuinely aimed at ensuring decisions commensurate with the will of the patient, and must be reliable as instruments to that end. Of the many States which have instituted such protections, Missouri is virtually the only one to have fashioned a rule that lessens the likelihood of accurate determinations. In contrast, nothing in the Constitution prevents States from reviewing the advisability of a family decision, by requiring a court proceeding or by appointing an impartial guardian ad litem.

There are various approaches to determining an incompetent patient's treatment choice in use by the several States today, and there may be advantages and disadvantages to each and other approaches not yet envisioned. The choice, in largest part, is and should be left to the States, so long as each State is seeking, in a reliable manner, to discover what the patient would want. But with such momentous interests in the balance, States must avoid procedures that will prejudice the decision. "To err either way—to keep a person alive under circumstances under which he would rather have been allowed to die, or to allow that person to die when he would have chosen to cling to life—would be deeply unfortunate." *In re Conroy,* 98 N.J., at 343, 486 A.2d, at 1220.

D

Finally, I cannot agree with the majority that where it is not possible to determine what choice an incompetent patient would make, a State's role as *parens patriae* permits the State automatically to make that choice itself. See *ante,* at 286 (explaining that the Due Process Clause does not require a State to confide the decision to "anyone but the patient herself"). Under fair rules of evidence, it is improbable that a court could not determine what the patient's choice would be. Under the rule of decision adopted by Missouri and upheld today by this Court, such occasions might be numerous. But in neither case does it follow that it is constitutionally acceptable for the State invariably to assume the role of deciding for the patient. A State's legitimate interest in safeguarding a patient's choice cannot be furthered by simply appropriating it.

The majority justifies its position by arguing that, while close family members may have a strong feeling about the question, "there is no automatic assurance that the view of close family members will necessarily be the same as the patient's would have been had she been confronted with the prospect of her situation while competent." *Ibid.* I cannot quarrel with this observation. But it leads only to another question: Is there any reason to suppose that a State is *more* likely to make the choice that the patient would have made than someone who knew the patient intimately? To ask this is to answer it. As the New Jersey Supreme Court observed: "Family members are best qualified to make substituted judgments for incompetent patients not only because of their peculiar grasp of the patient's approach to life, but also because of their special bonds with him or her. . . . It is . . . they who treat the patient as a person, rather than a symbol of a cause." *In re Jobes,* 108 N.J. 394, 416, 529 A.2d 434, 445 (1987). The State, in contrast, is a stranger to the patient.

A State's inability to discern an incompetent patient's choice still need not mean that a State is rendered powerless to protect that choice. But I would find that the Due Process Clause prohibits a State from doing more than that. A State may ensure that the person who makes the decision on the patient's behalf is the one whom the patient himself would have selected to make that choice for him. And a State may exclude from consideration anyone having improper motives. But a State generally must either repose the choice with the person whom the patient himself would most likely have chosen as proxy or leave the decision to the patient's family.[23]

IV

As many as 10,000 patients are being maintained in persistent vegetative states in the United States, and the number is expected to increase significantly in the near future. See Cranford, *supra* n. 2, at 27, 31. Medical technology, developed over the past 20 or so years, is often capable of resuscitating people after they have stopped breathing or their hearts have stopped beating. Some of those people are brought fully back to life. Two decades ago, those who were not and could not swallow and digest food, died. Intravenous solutions could not provide sufficient calories to maintain people for more than a short time. Today, various forms of artificial feeding have been developed that are able to keep people metabolically alive for years, even decades. See Spencer & Palmisano, Specialized Nutritional Support of Patients—A Hospital's Legal Duty?, 11 Quality Rev.Bull. 160, 160-161 (1985). In addition, in this century, chronic or degenerative ailments have replaced communicable diseases as the primary causes of death. See R. Weir, Abating Treatment with Critically Ill Patients 12-13 (1989); President's Commission 15-16. The 80% of Americans who die in hospitals are "likely to meet their end . . . 'in a sedated or comatose state; betubed nasally, abdominally and intravenously; and far more like manipulated objects than like moral subjects.'"[24] A fifth of all adults surviving to age 80 will suffer a progressive dementing disorder prior to death. See Cohen & Eisdorfer, Dementing Disorders, in The Practice of Geriatrics 194 (E. Calkins, P. Davis, & A, Ford eds. 1986).

"[L]aw, equity and justice must not themselves quail and be helpless in the face of modern technological marvels presenting questions hitherto unthought of." *In re Quinlan,* 70 N.J. 10, 44, 355 A.2d 647, 665, cert. denied, 429 U.S. 922, 97 S.Ct. 319, 50 L.Ed.2d 289 (1976). The new medical technology can reclaim those who would have been irretrievably lost a few decades ago and restore them to active lives. For Nancy Cruzan, it failed, and for others with wasting incurable disease, it may be doomed to failure. In these unfortunate situations, the bodies and preferences and memories of the victims do not escheat to the State; nor does our Constitution permit the State or any other government to commandeer them. No singularity of feeling exists upon which such a government might confidently rely as *parens patriae.* The President's Commission, after years of research, concluded:

"In few areas of health care are people's evaluations of their experiences so varied and uniquely personal as in their assessments of the nature and value of the processes associated with dying. For some, every moment of life is of inestimable value; for others, life without some desired level of mental or physical ability is worthless or burdensome. A moderate degree of suffering may be an important means of personal growth and religious experience to one person, but only frightening or despicable to another." President's Commission 276.

Yet Missouri and this Court have displaced Nancy's own assessment of the processes associated with dying. They have discarded evidence of her will, ignored her values, and deprived her of the right to a decision as closely approximating her own choice as humanly possible. They have done so disingenuously in her name and openly in Missouri's own. That Missouri and this Court may truly be motivated only by concern for incompetent patients makes no matter. As one of our most prominent jurists warned us decades ago: "Experience should teach us to be most on our guard to protect liberty when the government's purposes are beneficent. . . . The greatest dangers to liberty lurk in insidious encroachment by men of zeal, well meaning but without understanding." *Olmstead v. United States,* 277 U.S. 438, 479, 48 S.Ct. 564, 572-573, 72 L.Ed. 944 (1928) (Brandeis, J., dissenting).

I respectfully dissent.

[1] *Rasmussen v. Fleming,* 154 Ariz. 207, 211, 741 P.2d 674, 678 (1987) (en banc).

[2] Vegetative state patients may *react reflexively* to sounds, movements, and normally painful stimuli, but they do not *feel* any pain or *sense* anybody or anything. Vegetative state patients may appear awake but are completely unaware. See Cranford, The Persistent

Vegetative State: The Medical Reality, 18 Hastings Ctr.Rep. 27, 28, 31 (1988).

[3.] See President's Commission for the Study of Ethical Problems in Medicine and Biomedical and Behavioral Research, Deciding to Forego Life Sustaining Treatment 15, n. 1, and 17-18 (1983) (hereafter President's Commission).

[4.] See Lipton, Do-Not-Resuscitate Decisions in a Community Hospital: Incidence, Implications and Outcomes, 256 JAMA 1164, 1168 (1986).

[5.] See, *e.g., Canterbury v. Spence,* 150 U.S.App.D.C. 263, 271, 464 F.2d 772, 780, cert. denied, 409 U.S. 1064 (1972) ("The root premise" of informed consent "is the concept, fundamental in American jurisprudence, that '[e]very human being of adult years and sound mind has a right to determine what shall be done with his own body' ") (quoting *Schloendorff v. Society of New York Hospital,* 211 N.Y. 125, 129-130, 105 N.E. 92, 93 (1914) (Cardozo, J.)). See generally *Washington v. Harper,* 494 U.S. 210, 241, 110 S.Ct. 1028, 1047, 108 L.Ed.2d 178 (1990) (STEVENS, J., dissenting) ("There is no doubt . . . that a competent individual's right to refuse [psychotropic] medication is a fundamental liberty interest deserving the highest order of protection").

[6.] Under traditional tort law, exceptions have been found only to protect dependent children. See *Cruzan v. Harmon,* 760 S.W.2d 408, 422, n. 17 (Mo.1988) (citing cases where Missouri courts have ordered blood transfusions for children over the religious objection of parents); see also *Winthrop University Hospital v. Hess,* 128 Misc.2d 804, 490 N.Y.S.2d 996 (Sup.Ct. Nassau Cty. 1985) (court ordered blood transfusion for religious objector because she was the mother of an infant and had explained that her objection was to the signing of the consent, not the transfusion itself); *Application of President & Directors of Georgetown College, Inc.,* 118 U.S.App.D.C. 80, 88, 331 F.2d 1000, 1008 (blood transfusion ordered for mother of infant); cert. denied, 377 U.S. 978, 84 S.Ct. 1883, 12 L.Ed.2d 746 (1964). Cf. *In re Estate of Brooks,* 32 Ill.2d 361, 373, 205 N.E.2d

435, 441-442 (1965) (finding that lower court erred in ordering a blood transfusion for a woman—whose children were grown—and concluding: "Even though we may consider appellant's beliefs unwise, foolish or ridiculous, in the absence of an overriding danger to society we may not permit interference therewith in the form of a conservatorship established in the waning hours of her life for the sole purpose of compelling her to accept medical treatment forbidden by her religious principles, and previously refused by her with full knowledge of the probable consequences").

7. The Missouri court appears to be alone among state courts to suggest otherwise, 760 S.W.2d, at 419 and 423, although the court did not rely on a distinction between artificial feeding and other forms of medical treatment. *Id.*, at 423. See, *e.g., Delio v. Westchester County Medical Center,* 129 App.Div.2d 1, 19, 516 N.Y.S.2d 677, 689 (1987) ("[R]eview of the decisions in other jurisdictions . . . failed to uncover a single case in which a court confronted with an application to discontinue feeding by artificial means has evaluated medical procedures to provide nutrition and hydration differently from other types of life-sustaining procedures").

8. While brain stem cells can survive 15 to 20 minutes without oxygen, cells in the cerebral hemispheres are destroyed if they are deprived of oxygen for as few as 4 to 6 minutes. See Cranford & Smith, Some Critical Distinctions Between Brain Death and the Persistent Vegetative State, 6 Ethics Sci. & Med. 199, 203 (1979). It is estimated that Nancy's brain was deprived of oxygen from 12 to 14 minutes. See *ante,* at 266. Out of the 100,000 patients who, like Nancy, have fallen into persistive vegetative states in the past 20 years due to loss of oxygen to the brain, there have been only three even partial recoveries documented in the medical literature. Brief for American Medical Association et al. as *Amici Curiae* 11-12. The longest any person has ever been in a persistent vegetative state and recovered was 22 months. See Snyder, Cranford, Rubens, Bundlie, & Rockswold, Delayed Recovery from Postanoxic

Persistent Vegetative State, 14 Annals Neurol. 156 (1983). Nancy has been in this state for seven years.

[9.] The American Academy of Neurology offers three independent bases on which the medical profession rests these neurological conclusions:

"First, direct clinical experience with these patients demonstrates that there is no behavioral indication of any awareness of pain or suffering.

"Second, in all persistent vegetative state patients studied to date, post-mortem examination reveals overwhelming bilateral damage to the cerebral hemispheres to a degree incompatible with consciousness. . . .

"Third, recent data utilizing positron emission tomography indicates that the metabolic rate for glucose in the cerebral cortex is greatly reduced in persistent vegetative state patients, to a degree incompatible with consciousness." Position of the American Academy of Neurology on Certain Aspects of the Care and Management of the Persistent Vegetative State Patient, 39 Neurology 125 (Jan.1989).

[10.] Nancy Cruzan, for instance, is totally and permanently disabled. All four of her limbs are severely contracted; her fingernails cut into her wrists. App. to Pet. for Cert. A93. She is incontinent of bowel and bladder. The most intimate aspects of her existence are exposed to and controlled by strangers. Brief for Respondent Guardian Ad Litem 2. Her family is convinced that Nancy would find this state degrading. See n. 20, *infra*.

[11.] What general information exists about what most people would choose or would prefer to have chosen for them under these circumstances also indicates the importance of ensuring a means for now-incompetent patients to exercise their right to avoid unwanted medical treatment. A 1988 poll conducted by the American Medical Association found that 80% of those surveyed favored withdrawal of life-support systems from hopelessly ill or irreversibly comatose patients if they or their families requested it. New York Times, June 5, 1988, p. 14, col. 4 (citing American Medical News, June 3, 1988, p. 9, col. 1). Another 1988 poll conducted by the

Colorado University Graduate School of Public Affairs showed that 85% of those questioned would not want to have their own lives maintained with artificial nutrition and hydration if they became permanently unconscious. The Coloradoan, Sept. 29, 1988, p. 1.

Such attitudes have been translated into considerable political action. Since 1976, 40 States and the District of Columbia have enacted natural death Acts, expressly providing for self-determination under some or all of these situations. See Brief for Society for the Right to Die, Inc., as *Amicus Curiae* 8; Weiner, Privacy, Family, and Medical Decision Making for Persistent Vegetative Patients, 11 Cardozo L.Rev. 713, 720 (1990). Thirteen States and the District of Columbia have enacted statutes authorizing the appointment of proxies for making health care decisions. See *ante,* at 290, n. 2 (O'CONNOR, J., concurring).

[12.] See *Jacobson v. Massachusetts,* 197 U.S. 11, 26-27, 25 S.Ct. 358, 361-362, 49 L.Ed. 643 (1905) (upholding a Massachusetts law imposing fines or imprisonment on those refusing to be vaccinated as "of paramount necessity" to that State's fight against a smallpox epidemic).

[13.] Were such interests at stake, however, I would find that the Due Process Clause places limits on what invasive medical procedures could be forced on an unwilling comatose patient in pursuit of the interests of a third party. If Missouri were correct that its interests outweigh Nancy's interest in avoiding medical procedures as long as she is free of pain and physical discomfort, see 760 S.W.2d, at 424, it is not apparent why a State could not choose to remove one of her kidneys without consent on the ground that society would be better off if the recipient of that kidney were saved from renal poisoning. Nancy cannot feel surgical pain. See n. 2, *supra.* Nor would removal of one kidney be expected to shorten her life expectancy. See The American Medical Association Family Medical Guide 506 (J. Kunz ed. 1982). Patches of her skin could also be removed to provide grafts for burn victims, and scrapings of bone marrow to provide grafts for someone with leukemia. Perhaps the State could lawfully remove more vital organs for transplanting into others who would then be cured of their ailments, provided the State placed Nancy on some other life-support equipment to replace the lost function. Indeed, why could the State not perform medical experiments on her body, experiments that might save countless lives, and would cause her no greater burden than she already bears by being fed through the gastrostomy tube? This would be too brave a new world for me and, I submit, for our Constitution.

[14.] The Missouri Supreme Court reviewed the state interests that had been identified by other courts as potentially relevant prevention of homicide and suicide, protection of interests of innocent third parties, maintenance of the ethical integrity of the medical profession, and preservation of life—and concluded that: "In this case, only the state's interest in the preservation of life is implicated." 760 S.W.2d, at 419.

[15.] In any event, the state interest identified by the Missouri Supreme Court—a comprehensive and "unqualified" interest in preserving life, *id.,* at 420, 424—is not even well supported by that State's own enactments. In the first place, Missouri has no law requiring every person to procure any needed medical care nor a state health insurance program to underwrite such care. *Id.,* at 429 (Blackmar, J., dissenting). Second, as the state court admitted, Missouri has a living will statute which specifically "allows and encourages the pre-planned termination of life." *Ibid.*; see Mo.Rev.Stat. § 459.015.1 (1986). The fact that Missouri actively provides for its citizens to choose a natural death under certain circumstances suggests that the State's interest in life is not so unqualified as the court below suggests. It is true that this particular statute does not apply to nonterminal patients and does not include artificial nutrition and hydration as one of the measures that may be declined. Nonetheless, Missouri has also not chosen to require court review of every decision to withhold or withdraw life support made on behalf of an incompetent patient. Such decisions are made every day, without state participation. See 760 S.W.2d, at 428 (Blackmar, J., dissenting).

In addition, precisely what implication can be drawn from the statute's limitations is unclear given the inclusion of a series of "interpretive" provisions in the Act. The first such provision explains that the Act is to be interpreted consistently with the following: "Each person has the primary right to request or refuse medical treatment subject to the state's interest in protecting innocent third parties, preventing homicide and suicide and preserving good ethical standards in the medical profession." Mo.Rev.Stat. § 459.055(1) (1986). The second of these subsections explains that the Act's provisions are cumulative and not intended to increase or decrease the right of a patient to make decisions or lawfully effect the withholding or withdrawal of medical care. § 459.055(2). The third subsection provides that "no presumption concerning the intention of an individual who has not executed a declaration to consent to the use or withholding of medical procedures" shall be created. § 459.055(3).

Thus, even if it were conceivable that a State could assert an interest sufficiently compelling to overcome Nancy Cruzan's constitutional right, Missouri law demonstrates a more modest interest at best. See generally *Capital Cities Cable, Inc. v. Crisp,* 467 U.S. 691, 715, 104 S.Ct. 2694, 2708-2709, 81 L.Ed.2d 580 (1984) (finding that state regulations narrow in scope indicated that State had only a moderate interest in its professed goal).

[16.] See *Colorado v. New Mexico,* 467 U.S. 310, 104 S.Ct. 2433, 81 L.Ed.2d 247 (1984) (requiring clear and convincing evidence before one State is permitted to divert water from another to accommodate society's interests in stabile property rights and efficient use of resources); *New York v. New Jersey,* 256 U.S. 296, 41 S.Ct. 492, 65 L.Ed. 937 (1921) (promoting federalism by requiring clear and convincing evidence before using Court's power to control the conduct of one State at the behest of another); *Maxwell Land-Grant Case,* 121 U.S.

325, 7 S.Ct. 1015, 30 L.Ed. 949 (1887) (requiring clear, unequivocal, and convincing evidence to set aside, annul, or correct a patent or other title to property issued by the Government in order to secure settled expectations concerning property rights); *Marcum v. Zaring,* 406 P.2d 970 (Okla.1965) (promoting stability of marriage by requiring clear and convincing evidence to prove its invalidity); *Stevenson v. Stein,* 412 Pa. 478, 195 A.2d 268 (1963) (promoting settled expectations concerning property rights by requiring clear and convincing evidence to prove adverse possession).

[17.] The majority's definition of the "status quo," of course, begs the question. Artificial delivery of nutrition and hydration represents the "status quo" only if the State has chosen to permit doctors and hospitals to keep a patient on life-support systems over the protests of his family or guardian. The "status quo" absent that state interference would be the natural result of his accident or illness (and the family's decision). The majority's definition of status quo, however, is "to a large extent a predictable, yet accidental confluence of technology, psyche, and inertia. The general citizenry . . . never said that it favored the creation of coma wards where permanently unconscious patients would be tended for years and years. Nor did the populace as a whole authorize the preeminence of doctors over families in making treatment decisions for incompetent patients." Rhoden, Litigating Life and Death, 102 Harv.L.Rev. 375, 433-434 (1988).

[18.] For Nancy Cruzan, no such cure or improvement is in view. So much of her brain has deteriorated and been replaced by fluid, see App. to Pet. for Cert. A94, that apparently the only medical advance that could restore consciousness to her body would be a brain transplant. Cf. n. 22, *infra.*

[19.] The trial court had relied on the testimony of Athena Comer, a long-time friend, co-worker, and housemate for several months, as sufficient to show that Nancy Cruzan would wish to be free of medical treatment under her present circumstances. App. to Pet. for Cert. A94. Ms. Comer described a conversation she and Nancy had while living together, concerning Ms. Comer's sister who had become ill suddenly and died during the night. The Comer family had been told that if she had lived through the night, she would have been in a vegetative state. Nancy had lost a grandmother a few months before. Ms. Comer testified: "Nancy said she would never want to live [in a vegetative state] because if she couldn't be normal or even, you know, like half way, and do things for yourself, because Nancy always did, that she didn't want to live . . . and we talked about it a lot." Tr. 388-389. She said "several times" that "she wouldn't want to live that way because if she was going to live, she wanted to be able to live, not to just lay in a bed and not be able to move because you can't do anything for yourself." *Id.*, at 390, 396. "[S]he said that she hoped that [all the] people in her family knew that she wouldn't want to live [in a vegetative state] because she knew it was usually up to the family whether you lived that way or not." *Id.*, at 399.

The conversation took place approximately a year before Nancy's accident and was described by Ms. Comer as a "very serious" conversation that continued for approximately half an hour without interruption. *Id.*, at 390. The Missouri Supreme Court dismissed Nancy's statement as "unreliable" on the ground that it was an informally expressed reaction to other people's medical conditions. 760 S.W.2d, at 424.

The Missouri Supreme Court did not refer to other evidence of Nancy's wishes or explain why it was rejected. Nancy's sister Christy, to whom she was very close, testified that she and Nancy had had two very serious conversations about a year and a half before the accident. A day or two after their niece was stillborn (but would have been badly damaged if she had lived), Nancy had said that maybe it was part of a "greater plan" that the baby had been stillborn and did not have to face "the possible life of mere existence." Tr. 537. A month later, after their grandmother had died after a long battle with heart problems, Nancy said that "it was better for my grandmother not to be kind of brought back and forth

[by] medical [treatment], brought back from a critical near point of death. . . ." *Id.,* at 541.

[20.] Nancy's sister Christy, Nancy's mother, and another of Nancy's friends testified that Nancy would want to discontinue the hydration and nutrition. Christy said that "Nancy would be horrified at the state she is in." *Id.,* at 535. She would also "want to take that burden away from [her family]." *Id.,* at 544. Based on "a lifetime of experience [I know Nancy's wishes] are to discontinue the hydration and the nutrition." *Id.,* at 542. Nancy's mother testified: "Nancy would not want to be like she is now. [I]f it were me up there or Christy or any of us, she would be doing for us what we are trying to do for her. I know she would, . . . as her mother." *Id.,* at 526.

[21.] Surveys show that the overwhelming majority of Americans have not executed such written instructions. See Emmanuel & Emmanuel, The Medical Directive: A New Comprehensive Advance Care Document, 261 JAMA 3288 (1989) (only 9% of Americans execute advance directives about how they would wish treatment decisions to be handled if they became incompetent); American Medical Association Surveys of Physician and Public Opinion on Health Care Issues 29-30 (1988) (only 15% of those surveyed had executed living wills); 2 President's Commission for the Study of Ethical Problems in Medicine and Biomedical and Behavioral Research, Making Health Care Decisions 241-242 (1982) (23% of those surveyed said that they had put treatment instructions in writing).

[22.] New York is the only State besides Missouri to deny a request to terminate life support on the ground that clear and convincing evidence of prior, expressed intent was absent, although New York did so in the context of very different situations. Mrs. O'Connor, the subject of *In re O'Connor,* had several times expressed her desire not to be placed on life support if she were not going to be able to care for herself. However, both of her daughters testified that they did not know whether their mother would want to decline artificial nutrition and hydration under her present circumstances. Cf. n. 13, *supra.*

Moreover, despite damage from several strokes, Mrs. O'Connor was conscious and capable of responding to simple questions and requests and the medical testimony suggested she might improve to some extent. Cf. *supra,* at 301. The New York Court of Appeals also denied permission to terminate blood transfusions for a severely retarded man with terminal cancer because there was no evidence of a treatment choice made by the man when competent, as he had never been competent. See *In re Storar,* 52 N.Y.2d 363, 438 N.Y.S.2d 266, 420 N.E.2d 64, cert. denied, 454 U.S. 858, 102 S.Ct. 309, 70 L.Ed.2d 153 (1981). Again, the court relied on evidence that the man was conscious, functioning in the way he always had, and that the transfusions did not cause him substantial pain (although it was clear he did not like them).

[23.] Only in the exceedingly rare case where the State cannot find any family member or friend who can be trusted to endeavor genuinely to make the treatment choice the patient would have made does the State become the legitimate surrogate decisionmaker.

[24.] Fadiman, The Liberation of Lolly and Gronky, Life Magazine, Dec. 1986, p. 72 (quoting medical ethicist Joseph Fletcher).

Justice STEVENS, dissenting.

Our Constitution is born of the proposition that all legitimate governments must secure the equal right of every person to "Life, Liberty, and the pursuit of Happiness."[1] In the ordinary case we quite naturally assume that these three ends are compatible, mutually enhancing, and perhaps even coincident.

The Court would make an exception here. It permits the State's abstract, undifferentiated interest in the preservation of life to overwhelm the best interests of Nancy Beth Cruzan, interests which would, according to an undisputed finding, be served by allowing her guardians to exercise her constitutional right to discontinue medical treatment. Ironically, the Court reaches this conclusion despite endorsing three significant propositions which should save it from any such dilemma. First, a competent individual's decision to refuse life-sustaining medical procedures is an aspect of liberty protected by the Due Process Clause of the Fourteenth Amendment. See *ante,* at 278-279. Second, upon a proper evidentiary showing, a qualified guardian may make that decision on behalf of an incompetent ward. See, *e.g., ante,* at 284-285. Third, in answering the important question presented by this tragic case, it is wise " 'not to attempt, by any general statement, to cover every possible phase of the subject.' " See *ante,* at 278 (citation omitted). Together, these considerations suggest that Nancy Cruzan's liberty to be free from medical treatment must be understood in light of the facts and circumstances particular to her.

I would so hold: In my view, the Constitution requires the State to care for Nancy Cruzan's life in a way that gives appropriate respect to her own best interests.

I

This case is the first in which we consider whether, and how, the Constitution protects the liberty of seriously ill patients to be free from life-sustaining medical treatment. So put, the question is both general and profound. We need not, however, resolve the question in the abstract. Our responsibility as judges both enables and compels us to treat the problem as it is illuminated by the facts of the controversy before us.

The most important of those facts are these: "Clear and convincing evidence" established that Nancy Cruzan is "oblivious to her environment except for reflexive responses to sound and perhaps to painful stimuli"; that "she has no cognitive or reflexive ability to swallow food or water"; that "she will never recover" these abilities; and that her "cerebral cortical atrophy is irreversible, permanent, progressive and ongoing." App. to Pet. for Cert. A94-A95. Recovery and consciousness are impossible; the highest cognitive brain function that can be hoped for is a grimace in "recognition of ordinarily painful stimuli" or an "apparent response to sound." *Id.,* at A95.[2]

After thus evaluating Nancy Cruzan's medical condition, the trial judge next examined how the interests of third parties would be affected if Nancy's parents were allowed to withdraw the gastrostomy tube that had been implanted in their daughter. His findings make it clear that the parents' request had no economic motivation,[3] and that granting their request would neither adversely affect any innocent third parties nor breach the ethical standards of the medical profession.[4] He then considered, and rejected, a religious objection to his decision,[5] and explained why he concluded that the ward's constitutional "right to liberty" outweighed the general public policy on which the State relied:

"There is a fundamental natural right expressed in our Constitution as the 'right to liberty,' which permits an individual to refuse or direct the withholding or withdrawal of artificial death prolonging procedures when the person has no more cognitive brain function than our Ward and all the physicians agree there is no hope of further recovery while the deterioration of the brain continues with further overall worsening physical contractures. To the extent that the statute or public policy prohibits withholding or withdrawal of nutrition and hydration or euthanasia or mercy killing, if such be the definition, under all circumstances, arbitrarily and with no exceptions, it is in violation of our Ward's constitutional rights by depriving her of liberty without due process of law. To decide otherwise that medical treatment once undertaken must be continued irrespective of its lack of success or benefit to the patient in effect gives one's body to medical science without their [*sic*] consent.

. . . . .

"The Co-guardians are required only to exercise their legal authority to act in the best interests of their Ward as they discharge their duty and are free to act or not with this authority as they may determine." *Id.,* at A98-A99 (footnotes omitted).

II

Because he believed he had a duty to do so, the independent guardian ad litem appealed the trial court's order to the Missouri Supreme Court. In that appeal, however, the guardian advised the court that he did not disagree with the trial court's decision. Specifically, he endorsed the critical finding that "it was in Nancy Cruzan's best interests to have the tube feeding discontinued." [6]

That important conclusion thus was not disputed by the litigants. One might reasonably suppose that it would be dispositive: If Nancy Cruzan has no interest in continued treatment, and if she has a liberty interest in being free from unwanted treatment, and if the cessation of treatment would have no adverse impact on third parties, and if no reason exists to doubt the good faith of Nancy's parents, then what possible basis could the State have for insisting upon continued medical treatment? Yet, instead of questioning or endorsing the trial court's conclusions about Nancy Cruzan's interests, the State Supreme Court largely ignored them.

The opinion of that court referred to four different state interests that have been identified in other somewhat similar cases, but acknowledged that only the State's general interest in "the preservation of life" was implicated by this case.[7] It defined that interest as follows:

"The state's interest in life embraces two separate concerns: an interest in the prolongation of the life of the individual patient and an interest in the sanctity of life itself." *Cruzan v. Harmon,* 760 S.W.2d 408, 419 (1988).

Although the court did not characterize this interest as absolute, it repeatedly indicated that it outweighs any countervailing interest that is based on the "quality of life" of any individual patient.[8] In the view of the state-court majority, that general interest is strong enough to foreclose any decision to refuse treatment for an incompetent person unless that person had previously evidenced, in clear and convincing terms, such a decision for herself. The best interests of the incompetent individual who had never confronted the issue—or perhaps had been incompetent since birth—are entirely irrelevant and unprotected under the reasoning of the State Supreme Court's four-judge majority.

The three dissenting judges found Nancy Cruzan's interests compelling. They agreed with the trial court's evaluation of state policy. In his persuasive dissent, Judge Blackmar explained that decisions about the care of chronically ill patients were traditionally private:

"My disagreement with the principal opinion lies fundamentally in its emphasis on the interest of and the role of the state, represented by the Attorney General. Decisions about prolongation of life are of recent origin. For most of the world's history, and presently in most parts of the world, such decisions would never arise because the technology would not be available. Decisions about medical treatment have customarily been made by the patient, or by those closest to the patient if the patient, because of youth or infirmity, is unable to make the decisions. This is nothing new in substituted decisionmaking. The state is seldom called upon to be the decisionmaker.

"I would not accept the assumption, inherent in the principal opinion, that, with our advanced technology, the state must necessarily become involved in a decision about using extraordinary measures to prolong life. Decisions of this kind are made daily by the patient or relatives, on the basis of medical advice and their conclusion as to what is best. Very few cases reach court, and I doubt whether this case would be before us but for the fact that Nancy lies in a state hospital. I do not place primary emphasis on the patient's expressions, except possibly in the very unusual case, of which I find no example in the books, in which the patient expresses a view that all available life supports should be made use of. Those closest to the patient are best positioned to make judgments about the patient's best interest." *Id.,* at 428.

Judge Blackmar then argued that Missouri's policy imposed upon dying individuals and their families a controversial and objectionable view of life's meaning:

"It is unrealistic to say that the preservation of life is an absolute, without regard to the quality of life. I make this statement only in the context of a case in which the trial judge has found that there is no chance for amelioration of Nancy's condition. The principal opinion accepts this conclusion. It is appropriate to consider the quality of life in making decisions about the extraordinary medical treatment. Those who have made decisions about such matters without resort to the courts certainly consider the quality of life, and balance this against the unpleasant consequences to the patient. There is evidence that Nancy may react to pain stimuli. If she has any awareness of her surroundings, her life must be a living hell. She is unable to express herself or to do anything at all to alter her situation. Her parents, who are her closest relatives, are best able to feel for her and to decide what is best for her. The state should not substitute its decisions for theirs. Nor am I impressed with the crypto-philosophers cited in the principal opinion, who declaim about the sanctity of any life without regard to its quality. They dwell in ivory towers." *Id.,* at 429.

Finally, Judge Blackmar concluded that the Missouri policy was illegitimate because it treats life as a theoretical abstraction, severed from, and indeed opposed to, the person of Nancy Cruzan.

"The Cruzan family appropriately came before the court seeking relief. The circuit judge properly found the facts and applied the law. His factual findings are supported by the record and his legal conclusions by overwhelming weight of authority. The principal opinion attempts to establish absolutes, but does so at the expense of human factors. In so doing it unnecessarily subjects Nancy and those close to her to continuous torture which no family should be forced to endure." *Id.,* at 429-430.

Although Judge Blackmar did not frame his argument as such, it propounds a sound constitutional objection to the Missouri majority's reasoning: Missouri's regulation is an unreasonable intrusion upon traditionally private matters encompassed within the liberty protected by the Due Process Clause.

The portion of this Court's opinion that considers the merits of this case is similarly unsatisfactory. It, too, fails to respect the best interests of the patient.[9] It, too, relies on what is tantamount to a waiver rationale: The dying patient's best interests are put to one side, and the entire inquiry is focused on her prior expressions of intent.[10] An innocent person's constitutional right to be free from unwanted medical treatment is thereby categorically limited to those patients who had the foresight to make an unambiguous statement of their wishes while competent. The Court's decision affords no protection to children, to young people who are victims of unexpected accidents or illnesses, or to the countless thousands of elderly persons who either fail to decide, or fail to explain, how they want to be treated if they should experience a similar fate. Because Nancy Beth Cruzan did not have the foresight to preserve her constitutional right in a living will, or some comparable "clear and convincing" alternative, her right is gone forever and her fate is in the hands of the state legislature instead of in those of her family, her independent neutral guardian ad litem, and an impartial judge—all of whom agree on the course of action that is in her best interests. The Court's willingness to find a waiver of this constitutional right reveals a distressing misunderstanding of the importance of individual liberty.

III

It is perhaps predictable that courts might undervalue the liberty at stake here. Because death is so profoundly personal, public reflection upon it is unusual. As this sad case shows, however, such reflection must become more common if we are to deal responsibly with the modern circumstances of death. Medical advances have altered the physiological conditions of death in ways that may be alarming: Highly invasive treatment may perpetuate human existence through a merger of body and machine that some might reasonably regard as an insult to life rather than as its continuation. But those same advances, and the reorganization of medical care accompanying the new science and technology, have also transformed the political and social conditions of death: People are less likely to die at home, and more likely to die in relatively public places, such as hospitals or nursing homes.[11]

Ultimate questions that might once have been dealt with in intimacy by a family and its physician [12] have now become the concern of institutions. When the institution is a state hospital, as it is in this case, the government itself becomes involved.[13] Dying nonetheless remains a part of "the life which characteristically has its place in the home," *Poe v. Ullman,* 367 U.S. 497, 551, 81 S.Ct. 1752, 1781, 6 L.Ed.2d 989 (1961) (Harlan, J., dissenting). The "integrity of that life is something so fundamental that it has been found to draw to its protection the principles of more than one explicitly granted Constitutional right," *id.,* at 551-552, 81 S.Ct. at 1781, and our decisions have demarcated a "private realm of family life which the state cannot enter." *Prince v. Massachusetts,* 321 U.S. 158, 166-167, 64 S.Ct. 438, 442, 88 L.Ed. 645 (1944). The physical boundaries of the home, of course, remain crucial guarantors of the life within it. See, *e.g., Payton v. New York,* 445 U.S. 573, 589, 100 S.Ct. 1371, 1381, 63 L.Ed.2d 639 (1980);

Stanley v. Georgia, 394 U.S. 557, 565, 89 S.Ct. 1243, 1248, 22 L.Ed.2d 542 (1969). Nevertheless, this Court has long recognized that the liberty to make the decisions and choices constitutive of private life is so fundamental to our "concept of ordered liberty," *Palko v. Connecticut,* 302 U.S. 319, 325, 58 S.Ct. 149, 152, 82 L.Ed. 288 (1937), that those choices must occasionally be afforded more direct protection. See, *e.g., Meyer v. Nebraska,* 262 U.S. 390, 43 S.Ct. 625, 67 L.Ed. 1042 (1923); *Griswold v. Connecticut,* 381 U.S. 479, 85 S.Ct. 1678, 14 L.Ed.2d 510 (1965); *Roe v. Wade,* 410 U.S. 113, 93 S.Ct. 705, 35 L.Ed.2d 147 (1973); *Thornburgh v. American College of Obstetricians and Gynecologists,* 476 U.S. 747, 772-782, 106 S.Ct. 2169, 2184-2190, 90 L.Ed.2d 779 (1986) (STEVENS, J., concurring).

Respect for these choices has guided our recognition of rights pertaining to bodily integrity. The constitutional decisions identifying those rights, like the common-law tradition upon which they built,[14] are mindful that the "makers of our Constitution . . . recognized the significance of man's spiritual nature." *Olmstead v. United States,* 277 U.S. 438, 478, 48 S.Ct. 564, 572, 72 L.Ed. 944 (1928) (Brandeis, J., dissenting). It may truly be said that "our notions of liberty are inextricably entwined with our idea of physical freedom and self-determination." *Ante,* at 287 (O'CONNOR, J., concurring). Thus we have construed the Due Process Clause to preclude physically invasive recoveries of evidence not only because such procedures are "brutal" but also because they are "offensive to human dignity." *Rochin v. California,* 342 U.S. 165, 174, 72 S.Ct. 205, 210, 96 L.Ed. 183 (1952). We have interpreted the Constitution to interpose barriers to a State's efforts to sterilize some criminals not only because the proposed punishment would do "irreparable injury" to bodily integrity, but because "[m]arriage and procreation" concern "the basic civil rights of man." *Skinner v. Oklahoma ex rel. Williamson,* 316 U.S. 535, 541, 62 S.Ct. 1110, 1113, 86 L.Ed. 1655 (1942). The sanctity, and individual privacy, of the human body is obviously fundamental to liberty. "Every violation of a person's bodily integrity is an invasion of his or her liberty." *Washington v. Harper,* 494 U.S. 210, 237, 110 S.Ct. 1028, 1045, 108 L.Ed.2d 178 (1990) (STEVENS, J., concurring in part and dissenting in part). Yet, just as the constitutional protection for the "physical curtilage of the home . . . is surely . . . a result of solicitude to protect the privacies of the life within," *Poe v. Ullman,* 367 U.S., at 551, 81 S.Ct., at 1781 (Harlan, J., dissenting), so too the constitutional protection for the human body is surely inseparable from concern for the mind and spirit that dwell therein.

It is against this background of decisional law, and the constitutional tradition which it illuminates, that the right to be free from unwanted life-sustaining medical treatment must be understood. That right presupposes no abandonment of the desire for life. Nor is it reducible to a protection against batteries undertaken in the name of treatment, or to a guarantee against the infliction of bodily discomfort. Choices about death touch the core of liberty. Our duty, and the concomitant freedom, to come to terms with the conditions of our own mortality are undoubtedly "so rooted in the traditions and conscience of our people as to be ranked as fundamental," *Snyder v. Massachusetts,* 291 U.S. 97, 105, 54 S.Ct. 330, 332, 78 L.Ed. 674 (1934), and indeed are essential incidents of the unalienable rights to life and liberty endowed us by our Creator. See *Meachum v. Fano,* 427 U.S. 215, 230, 96 S.Ct. 2532, 2541, 49 L.Ed.2d 451 (1976) (STEVENS, J., dissenting).

The more precise constitutional significance of death is difficult to describe; not much may be said with confidence about death unless it is said from faith, and that alone is reason enough to protect the freedom to conform choices about death to individual conscience. We may also, however, justly assume that death is not life's simple opposite, or its necessary terminus,[15] but rather its completion. Our ethical tradition has long regarded an appreciation of mortality as essential to understanding life's significance. It may, in fact, be impossible to live for anything without being prepared to die for something. Certainly there was no disdain for life in Nathan Hale's most famous declaration or in Patrick Henry's; their words instead bespeak a passion for life that forever preserves their own lives in the memories of their countrymen.[16] From such "honored dead we take increased devotion to that cause for which they gave the last full measure of devotion." [17]

These considerations cast into stark relief the injustice, and unconstitutionality, of Missouri's treatment of Nancy Beth Cruzan. Nancy Cruzan's death, when it comes, cannot be an historic act of heroism; it will inevitably be the consequence of her tragic accident. But Nancy Cruzan's interest in life, no less than that of any other person, includes an interest in how she will be thought of after her death by those whose opinions mattered to her. There can be no doubt that her life made her dear to her family and to others. How she dies will affect how that life is remembered. The trial court's order authorizing Nancy's parents to cease their daughter's treatment would have permitted the family that cares for Nancy to bring to a close her tragedy and her death. Missouri's objection to that order subordinates Nancy's body, her family, and the lasting significance of her life to the State's own interests. The decision we review thereby interferes with constitutional interests of the highest order.

To be constitutionally permissible, Missouri's intrusion upon these fundamental liberties must, at a minimum, bear a reasonable relationship to a legitimate state end. See, *e.g., Meyer v. Nebraska,* 262 U.S., at 400, 43 S.Ct., at 627; *Doe v. Bolton,* 410 U.S. 179, 194-195, 199, 93 S.Ct. 739, 748-749, 751, 35 L.Ed.2d 201 (1973). Missouri asserts that its policy is related to a state interest in the protection of life. In my view, however, it is an effort to define life, rather than to protect it, that is the heart of Missouri's policy. Missouri insists, without regard to Nancy Cruzan's own interests, upon equating her life with the biological persistence of her bodily functions. Nancy Cruzan, it must be remembered, is not now simply incompetent. She is in a persistent vegetative state and has been so for seven years. The trial court found, and no party contested, that Nancy has no possibility of recovery and no consciousness.

It seems to me that the Court errs insofar as it characterizes this case as involving "judgments about the 'quality' of life that a particular individual may enjoy," *ante,* at 282. Nancy Cruzan is obviously "*alive* " in a physiological sense. But for patients like Nancy Cruzan, who have no consciousness and no chance of recovery, there is a serious question as to whether the mere persistence of their bodies is "*life* " as that word is commonly understood, or as it is used in both the Constitution and the Declaration of Independence.[18] The State's unflagging determination to perpetuate Nancy Cruzan's physical existence is comprehensible only as an effort to define life's meaning, not as an attempt to preserve its sanctity.

This much should be clear from the oddity of Missouri's definition alone. Life, particularly human life, is not commonly thought of as a merely physiological condition or function.[19] Its sanctity is often thought to derive from the impossibility of any such reduction. When people speak of life, they often mean to describe the experiences that comprise a person's history, as when it is said that somebody "led a good life." [20] They may also mean to refer to the practical manifestation of the human spirit, a meaning captured by the familiar observation that somebody "added life" to an assembly. If there is a shared thread among the various opinions on this subject, it may be that life is an activity which is at once the matrix for, and an integration of, a person's interests. In any event, absent some theological abstraction, the idea of life is not conceived separately from the idea of a living person. Yet, it is by precisely such a separation that Missouri asserts an interest in Nancy Cruzan's life in opposition to Nancy Cruzan's own interests. The resulting definition is uncommon indeed.

The laws punishing homicide, upon which the Court relies, *ante,* at 280, do not support a contrary inference. Obviously, such laws protect both the life *and* interests of those who would otherwise be victims. Even laws against suicide pre-suppose that those inclined to take their own lives have *some* interest in living, and, indeed, that the depressed people whose lives are preserved may later be thankful for the State's intervention. Likewise, decisions that address the "quality of life" of incompetent, but conscious, patients rest upon the recognition that these patients have *some* interest in continuing their lives, even if that interest pales in some eyes when measured against interests in dignity or comfort. Not so here. Contrary to the Court's suggestion, Missouri's protection of life in a form abstracted from the living is not commonplace; it is aberrant.

Nor does Missouri's treatment of Nancy Cruzan find precedent in the various state-law cases surveyed by the majority. Despite the Court's assertion that state courts have demonstrated "both similarity and diversity in their approaches" to the issue before us, *none* of the decisions surveyed by the Court interposed an absolute bar to the termination of treatment for a patient in a persistent vegetative state. For example, *In re Westchester County Medical Center on behalf of O'Connor,* 72 N.Y.2d 517, 534 N.Y.S.2d 886, 531 N.E.2d 607 (1988), pertained to an incompetent patient who "was not in a coma or vegetative state. She was conscious, and capable of responding to simple questions or requests sometimes by squeezing the questioner's hand and sometimes verbally." Id., at 524-525, 534 N.Y.S.2d at 888-889, 531 N.E.2d, at 609-610. Likewise, *In re Storar,* 52 N.Y.2d 363, 438 N.Y.S.2d 266, 420 N.E.2d 64 (1981), involved a conscious patient who was incompetent because "profoundly retarded with a mental age of about 18 months." *Id.,* at 373, 438 N.Y.S.2d, at 270, 420 N.E.2d, at 68. When it decided *In re Conroy,* 98 N.J. 321, 486 A.2d 1209 (1985), the New Jersey Supreme Court noted that "Ms. Conroy was not brain dead, comatose, or in a chronic vegetative state," 98 N.J., at 337, 486 A.2d, at 1217, and then distinguished *In re Quinlan,* 70 N.J. 10, 355 A.2d 647 (1976), on the ground that Karen Quinlan had been in a "persistent vegetative or comatose state." 98 N.J., at 358-359, 486 A.2d, at 1228. By contrast, an unbroken stream of cases has authorized procedures for the cessation of treatment of patients in persistent vegetative states.[21] Considered against the background of other cases involving patients in persistent vegetative states, instead of against the broader and inapt—category of cases involving chronically ill incompetent patients, Missouri's decision is anomolous.

In short, there is no reasonable ground for believing that Nancy Beth Cruzan has any *personal* interest in the perpetuation of what the State has decided is her life. As I have already suggested, it would be possible to hypothesize such an interest on the basis of theological or philosophical conjecture. But even to posit such a basis for the State's action is to condemn it. It is not within the province of secular government to circumscribe the liberties of the people by regulations designed wholly for the purpose of establishing a sectarian definition of life. See *Webster v. Reproductive Health Services,* 492 U.S. 490, 566-572, 109 S.Ct. 3040, 3082-3085, 106 L.Ed.2d 410 (1989) (STEVENS, J., dissenting).

My disagreement with the Court is thus unrelated to its endorsement of the clear and convincing standard of proof for cases of this kind. Indeed, I agree that the controlling facts must be established with unmistakable clarity. The critical question, however, is not how to prove the controlling facts but rather what proven facts should be controlling. In my view, the constitutional answer is clear: The best interests of the individual, especially when buttressed by the interests of all related third parties, must prevail over any general state policy that simply ignores those interests.[22] Indeed, the only apparent *secular* basis for the State's interest in life is the policy's persuasive impact upon people other than Nancy and her family. Yet, "[a]lthough the State may properly perform a teaching function," and although that teaching may foster respect for the sanctity of life, the State may not pursue its project by infringing constitutionally protected interests for "*symbolic* effect." *Carey v. Population Services International,* 431 U.S. 678, 715, 97 S.Ct. 2010, 2031, 52 L.Ed.2d 675 (1977) (STEVENS, J., concurring in part and concurring in judgment). The failure of Missouri's policy to heed the interests of a dying individual with respect to matters so private is ample evidence of the policy's illegitimacy.

Only because Missouri has arrogated to itself the power to define life, and only because the Court permits this usurpation, are Nancy Cruzan's life and liberty put into disquieting conflict. If Nancy Cruzan's life were defined by reference to her own interests, so that her life expired when her biological existence ceased serving *any* of her own interests, then her constitutionally protected interest in freedom from unwanted treatment would not come into conflict with her constitutionally protected interest in life. Conversely, if there were *any* evidence that Nancy Cruzan herself defined life to encompass every form of biological persistence by a human being, so that the continuation of treatment would serve Nancy's own liberty, then once again there would be no conflict between life and liberty. The opposition of life and liberty in this case are thus not the result of Nancy Cruzan's tragic accident, but are instead the artificial consequence of Missouri's effort, and this Court's willingness, to abstract Nancy Cruzan's life from Nancy Cruzan's person.

IV

Both this Court's majority and the state court's majority express great deference to the policy choice made by the state legislature.[23] That deference is, in my view, based upon a severe error in the Court's constitutional logic. The Court believes that the liberty interest claimed here on behalf of Nancy Cruzan is peculiarly problematic because "[a]n incompetent person is not able to make an informed and voluntary choice to exercise a hypothetical right to refuse treatment or any other right." *Ante,* at 280. The impossibility of such an exercise affords the State, according to the Court, some discretion to interpose "a procedural requirement" that effectively compels the continuation of Nancy Cruzan's treatment.

There is, however, nothing "hypothetical" about Nancy Cruzan's constitutionally protected interest in freedom from unwanted treatment, and the difficulties involved in ascertaining what her interests are do not in any way justify the State's decision to oppose her interests with its own. As this case comes to us, the crucial question—and the question addressed by the Court—is not what Nancy Cruzan's interests are, but whether the State must give effect to them. There is certainly nothing novel about the practice of permitting a next friend to assert constitutional rights on behalf of an incompetent patient who is unable to do so. See, *e.g., Youngberg v. Romeo,* 457 U.S. 307, 310, 102 S.Ct. 2452, 2455, 73 L.Ed.2d 28 (1982); *Whitmore v. Arkansas,* 495 U.S. 149, 161-164, 110 S.Ct. 1717, 1734-1735, 109 L.Ed.2d 135 (1990). Thus, if Nancy Cruzan's incapacity to "exercise" her rights is to alter the balance between her interests and the State's, there must be some further explanation of how it does so. The Court offers two possibilities, neither of them satisfactory.

The first possibility is that the State's policy favoring life is by its nature less intrusive upon the patient's interest than any alternative. The Court suggests that Missouri's policy "results in a maintenance of the status quo," and is subject to reversal, while a decision to terminate treatment "is not susceptible of correction" because death is irreversible. *Ante,* at 283. Yet, this explanation begs the question, for it assumes either that the State's policy is consistent with Nancy Cruzan's own interests, or that no damage is done by ignoring her interests. The first assumption is without basis in the record of this case, and would obviate any need for the State to rely, as it does, upon its own interests rather than upon the patient's. The second assumption is unconscionable. Insofar as Nancy Cruzan has an interest in being remembered for how she lived rather than how she died, the damage done to those memories by the prolongation of her death is irreversible. Insofar as Nancy Cruzan has an interest in the cessation of any pain, the continuation of her pain is irreversible. Insofar as Nancy Cruzan has an interest in a closure to her life consistent with her own beliefs rather than those of the Missouri Legislature, the State's imposition of its contrary view is irreversible. To deny the importance of these consequences is in effect to deny that Nancy Cruzan has interests at all, and thereby to deny her personhood in the name of preserving the sanctity of her life.

The second possibility is that the State must be allowed to define the interests of incompetent patients with respect to life-sustaining treatment because there is no procedure capable of determining what those interests are in any particular case. The Court points out various possible "abuses" and inaccuracies that may affect procedures authorizing the termination of treatment. See *ante,* at 281-282. The Court correctly notes that in some cases there may be a conflict between the interests of an incompetent patient and the interests of members of his or her family. A State's procedures must guard against the risk that the survivors' interests are not mistaken for the patient's. Yet, the appointment of the neutral guardian ad litem, coupled with the searching inquiry conducted by the trial judge and the imposition of the clear and convincing standard of proof, all effectively avoided that risk in this case. Why such procedural safeguards should not be adequate to avoid a similar risk in other cases is a question the Court simply ignores.

Indeed, to argue that the mere possibility of error in *any* case suffices to allow the State's interests to override the particular interests of incompetent individuals in *every* case, or to argue that the interests of such individuals are unknowable and therefore may be subordinated to the State's concerns, is once again to deny Nancy Cruzan's personhood. The meaning of respect for her personhood, and for that of others who are gravely ill and incapacitated, is, admittedly, not easily defined: Choices about life and death are profound ones, not susceptible of resolution by recourse to medical or legal rules. It may be that the best we can do is to ensure that these choices are made by those who will care enough about the patient to investigate his or her interests with particularity and caution. The Court seems to recognize as much when it cautions against formulating any general or inflexible rule to govern all the cases that might arise in this area of the law. *Ante,* at 277-278. The Court's deference to the legislature is, however, itself an inflexible rule, one that the Court is willing to apply in this case even though the Court's principal grounds for deferring to Missouri's Legislature are hypothetical circumstances not relevant to Nancy Cruzan's interests.

On either explanation, then, the Court's deference seems ultimately to derive from the premise that chronically incompetent persons have no constitutionally cognizable interests at all, and so are not persons within the meaning of the Constitution. Deference of this sort is patently unconstitutional. It is also dangerous in ways that may not be immediately apparent. Today the State of Missouri has announced its intent to spend several hundred thousand dollars in preserving the life of Nancy Beth Cruzan in order to vindicate its general policy favoring the preservation of human life. Tomorrow, another State equally eager to champion an interest in the "quality of life" might favor a policy designed to ensure quick and comfortable deaths by denying treatment to categories of marginally hopeless cases. If the State in fact has an interest in defining life, and if the State's policy with respect to the termination of life-sustaining treatment commands deference from the judiciary, it is unclear how any resulting conflict between the best interests of the individual and the general policy of the State would be resolved.[24] I believe the Constitution requires that the individual's vital interest in liberty should prevail over the general policy in that case, just as in this.

That a contrary result is readily imaginable under the majority's theory makes manifest that this Court cannot defer to any state policy that drives a theoretical wedge between a person's life, on the one hand, and that person's liberty or happiness, on the other.[25] The consequence of such a theory is to deny the personhood of those whose lives are defined by the State's interests rather than their own. This consequence may be acceptable in theology or in speculative philosophy, see *Meyer,* 262 U.S., at 401-402, 43 S.Ct., at 627-628, but it is radically inconsistent with the foundation of all legitimate government. Our Constitution presupposes a respect for the personhood of every individual, and nowhere is strict adherence to that principle more essential than in the judicial branch. See, *e.g., Thornburgh v. American College of Obstetricians and Gynecologists,* 476 U.S., at 781-782, 106 S.Ct., at 2189-2190 (STEVENS, J., concurring).

V

In this case, as is no doubt true in many others, the predicament confronted by the healthy members of the Cruzan family merely adds emphasis to the best interests finding made by the trial judge. Each of us has an interest in the kind of memories that will survive after death. To that end, individual decisions are often motivated by their impact on others. A member of the kind of family identified in the trial court's findings in this case would likely have not only a normal interest in minimizing the burden that her own illness imposes on others, but also an interest in having their memories of her filled predominantly with thoughts about her past vitality rather than her current condition. The meaning and completion of her life should be controlled by persons who have her best interests at heart—not by a state legislature concerned only with the "preservation of human life."

The Cruzan family's continuing concern provides a concrete reminder that Nancy Cruzan's interests did not disappear with her vitality or her consciousness. However commendable may be the State's interest in human life, it cannot pursue that interest by appropriating Nancy Cruzan's life as a symbol for its own purposes. Lives do not exist in abstraction from persons, and to pretend otherwise is not to honor but to desecrate the State's responsibility for protecting life. A State that seeks to demonstrate its commitment to life may do so by aiding those who are actively struggling for life and health. In this endeavor, unfortunately, no State can lack for opportunities: There can be no need to make an example of tragic cases like that of Nancy Cruzan.

    I respectfully dissent.

1. It is stated in the Declaration of Independence that:

"We hold these truths to be self-evident, that all men are created equal, that they are endowed by their Creator with certain unalienable Rights, that among these are Life, Liberty and the pursuit of Happiness. That to secure these rights, Governments are instituted among Men, deriving their just powers from the consent of the governed,—That whenever any Form of Government becomes destructive of these ends, it is the Right of the People to alter or to abolish it, and to institute new Government, laying its foundation on such principles and organizing its powers in such form, as to them shall seem most likely to effect their Safety and Happiness."

2. The trial court found as follows on the basis of "clear and convincing evidence":

"1. That her respiration and circulation are not artificially maintained and within essentially normal limits for a 30 year old female with vital signs recently reported as BP 130/80; pulse 78 and regular; respiration spontaneous at 16 to 18 per minute.

"2. That she is oblivious to her environment except for reflexive responses to sound and perhaps to painful stimuli.

"3. That she has suffered anoxia of the brain resulting in massive enlargement of the ventricles filling with cerebrospinal fluid in the area where the brain has degenerated. This cerebral cortical atrophy is irreversible, permanent, progressive and ongoing.

"4. That her highest cognitive brain function is exhibited by her grimacing perhaps in recognition of ordinarily painful stimuli, indicating the experience of pain and her apparent response to sound.

"5. That she is spastic quadriplegic.

"6. That she has contractures of her four extremities which are slowly progressive with irreversible muscular and tendon damage to all extremities.

"7. That she has no cognitive or reflexive ability to swallow food or water to maintain her daily essential needs. That she will never recover her ability to swallow sufficient to satisfy her needs." App. to Pet. for Cert. A94-A95.

3. "The only economic considerations in this case rest with Respondent's employer, the State of Missouri, which is bearing the entire cost of care. Our ward is an adult without financial resources other than Social Security whose not inconsiderable medical insurance has been exhausted since January 1986." *Id.,* at A96.

4. "In this case there are no innocent third parties requiring state protection, neither homicide nor suicide will be committed and the consensus of the medical witnesses indicated concerns personal to themselves or the legal consequences of such actions rather than any objections that good ethical standards of the profession would be breached if the nutrition and hydration were withdrawn the same as any other artificial death prolonging procedures the statute specifically authorizes." *Id.,* at A98.

5. "Nancy's present unresponsive and hopeless existence is not the will of the Supreme Ruler but of man's will to forcefully feed her when she herself cannot swallow thus fueling respiratory and circulatory pumps to no cognitive purpose for her except sound and perhaps pain." *Id.,* at A97.

6. "Appellant guardian ad litem advises this court:
" 'we informed the [trial] court that we felt it was in Nancy Cruzan's best interests to have the tube feeding discontinued. We now find ourselves in the position of appealing from a judgment we basically agree with.' " *Cruzan v. Harmon,* 760 S.W.2d 408, 435 (Mo.1988) (Higgins, J., dissenting).

7. "Four state interests have been identified: preservation of life, prevention of homicide and suicide, the protection of interests of innocent third parties and the maintenance of the ethical integrity of the medical profession. *See* Section 459.055(1), RSMo 1986; *Brophy,* 497 N.E.2d at 634. In this case, only the state's interest in the preservation of life is implicated." *Id.,* at 419.

8. "The state's concern with the sanctity of life rests on the principle that life is precious and worthy of preservation without regard to its quality." *Ibid.*

"It is tempting to equate the state's interest in the preservation of life with some measure of quality of life. As the discussion which follows shows, some courts find quality of life a convenient focus when justifying the termination of treatment. But the state's interest is not in quality of life. The broad policy statements of the legislature make no such distinction; nor shall we. Were quality of life at issue, persons with all manner of handicaps might find the state seeking to terminate their lives. Instead, the state's interest is in life; that interest is unqualified." *Id.,* at 420.

"As we previously stated, however, the state's interest is not in quality of life. The state's interest is an unqualified interest in life." *Id.,* at 422. "The argument made here, that Nancy will not recover, is but a thinly veiled statement that her life in its present form is not worth living. Yet a diminished quality of life does not support a decision to cause death." *Ibid.*

"Given the fact that Nancy is alive and that the burdens of her treatment are not excessive for her, we do not believe her right to refuse treatment, whether that right proceeds from a constitutional right of privacy or a common law right to refuse treatment, outweighs the immense, clear fact of life in which the state maintains a vital interest." *Id.,* at 424.

9. See especially *ante,* at 282 ("[W]e think a State may properly decline to make judgments about the 'quality' of life that a particular individual may enjoy, and simply assert an unqualified interest in the preservation of human life to be weighed against the constitutionally protected interests of the individual"); *ante,* at 282, n. 10 (stating that the government is seeking to protect "its own institutional interests" in life).

10. See, *e.g., ante,* at 284.

11. "Until the latter part of this century, medicine had relatively little treatment to offer the dying and the vast majority of persons died at home rather than in the

hospital." Brief for American Medical Association et. al. as *Amici Curiae* 6. "In 1985, 83% of deaths [of] Americans age 65 or over occurred in a hospital or nursing home.

Sager, Easterling, *et al., Changes in the Location of Death After Passage of Medicare's Prospective Payment System: A National Study,* 320 New Eng.J.Med. 433, 435 (1989)." *Id.,* at 6, n. 2.

According to the President's Commission for the Study of Ethical Problems in Medicine and Biomedical and Behavioral Research:

"Just as recent years have seen alterations in the underlying causes of death, the places where people die have also changed. For most of recorded history, deaths (of natural causes) usually occurred in the home. " 'Everyone knew about death at first hand; there was nothing unfamiliar or even queer about the phenomenon. People seem to have known a lot more about the process itself than is the case today. The "deathbed" was a real place, and the dying person usually knew where he was and when it was time to assemble the family and call for the priest.'

"Even when people did get admitted to a medical care institution, those whose conditions proved incurable were discharged to the care of their families. This was not only because the health care system could no longer be helpful, but also because alcohol and opiates (the only drugs available to ease pain and suffering) were available without a prescription. Institutional care was reserved for the poor or those without family support; hospitals often aimed more at saving patients' souls than at providing medical care.

"As medicine has been able to do more for dying patients, their care has increasingly been delivered in institutional settings. By 1949, institutions were the sites of 50% of all deaths; by 1958, the figure was 61%; and by 1977, over 70%. Perhaps 80% of all deaths in the United States now occur in hospitals and long-term care institutions, such as nursing homes. The change in where very ill patients are treated permits health care professionals to marshall the instruments of scientific medicine more effectively. But people who are dying may well find such a setting alienating and unsupportive." Deciding to Forego Life-Sustaining Treatment 17-18 (1983) (footnotes omitted), quoting Thomas, Dying as Failure, 447 Annals Am.Acad.Pol. & Soc.Sci. 1, 3 (1980).

[12.] We have recognized that the special relationship between patient and physician will often be encompassed within the domain of private life protected by the Due Process Clause. See, *e.g., Griswold v. Connecticut,* 381 U.S. 479, 481, 85 S.Ct. 1678, 1679, 14 L.Ed.2d 510 (1965); *Roe v. Wade,* 410 U.S. 113, 152-153, 93 S.Ct. 705, 726-727, 35 L.Ed.2d 147 (1973); *Thornburgh v. American College of Obstetricians and Gynecologists,* 476 U.S. 747, 759, 106 S.Ct. 2169, 2178, 90 L.Ed.2d 779 (1986).

[13.] The Court recognizes that "the State has been involved as an adversary from the beginning" in this case only because Nancy Cruzan "was a patient at a state hospital when this litigation commenced," *ante,* at 281, n. 9. It seems to me, however, that the Court draws precisely the wrong conclusion from this insight. The Court apparently believes that the absence of the State from the litigation would have created a problem, because agreement among the family and the independent guardian ad litem as to Nancy Cruzan's best interests might have prevented her treatment from becoming the focus of a "truly adversarial" proceeding. *Ibid.* It may reasonably be debated whether some judicial process should be required before life-sustaining treatment is discontinued; this issue has divided the state courts. Compare *In re Estate of Longeway,* 133 Ill.2d 33, 51, 139 Ill.Dec. 780, 788, 549 N.E.2d 292, 300 (1989) (requiring judicial approval of guardian's decision), with *In re Hamlin,* 102 Wash.2d 810, 818-819, 689 P.2d 1372, 1377-1378 (1984) (discussing circumstances in which judicial approval is unnecessary). Cf. *In re Conservatorship of Torres,* 357 N.W.2d 332, 341, n. 4 (Minn.1984) ("At oral argument it was disclosed that on an average about 10 life support systems are disconnected weekly in Minnesota"). I tend, however, to agree with Judge Blackmar that the intervention of the State in these proceedings as an *adversary* is not so much a cure as it is part of the disease.

[14.] See *ante,* at 269, 278. "No right is held more sacred, or is more carefully guarded, by the common law, than the right of every individual to the possession and control of his own person, free from all restraint or interference of others, unless by clear and unquestionable authority of law." *Union Pacific R. Co. v. Botsford,* 141 U.S. 250, 251, 11 S.Ct. 1000, 1001, 35 L.Ed. 734 (1891).

[15.] Many philosophies and religions have, for example, long venerated the idea that there is a "life after death," and that the human soul endures even after the human body has perished. Surely Missouri would not wish to define its interest in life in a way antithetical to this tradition.

[16.] See, *e.g.,* H. Johnston, Nathan Hale 1776: Biography and Memorials 128-129 (1914); J. Axelrad, Patrick Henry: The Voice of Freedom 110-111 (1947).

[17.] A. Lincoln, Gettysburg Address, 1 Documents of American History 429 (H. Commager ed.) (9th ed. 1973).

[18.] The Supreme Judicial Court of Massachusetts observed in this connection: "When we balance the State's interest in prolonging a patient's life against the rights of the patient to reject such prolongation, we must recognize that the State's interest in life encompasses a broader interest than mere corporeal existence. In certain, thankfully rare, circumstances the burden of maintaining the corporeal existence degrades the very humanity it was meant to serve." *Brophy v. New England Sinai Hospital, Inc.,* 398 Mass. 417, 433-434, 497 N.E.2d 626, 635 (1986). The *Brophy* court then stressed that this reflection upon the nature of the State's interest in life was distinguishable from any considerations related to the quality of a particular patient's life, considerations which the court regarded as irrelevant to its inquiry. See also *In re Eichner,* 73 App.Div.2d 431, 465, 426 N.Y.S.2d 517, 543 (1980) (A patient in a persistent vegetative state "has *no* health, and, in the true sense, no life, for the State to protect"), modified in *In re Storar,* 52 N.Y.2d 363, 438 N.Y.S.2d 266, 420 N.E.2d 64 (1981).

[19.] One learned observer suggests, in the course of discussing persistent vegetative states, that "few of us would accept the preservation of such a reduced level of function as a proper *goal* for medicine, even though we sadly accept it as an unfortunate and unforeseen *result* of treatment that had higher aspirations, and even if we refuse actively to cause such vegetative life to cease." L. Kass, Toward a More Natural Science 203 (1985). This assessment may be controversial. Nevertheless, I again tend to agree with Judge Blackmar, who in his dissent from the Missouri Supreme Court's decision contended that it would be unreasonable for the State to assume that most people *did* in fact hold a view contrary to the one described by Dr. Kass.

My view is further buttressed by the comments of the President's Commission for the Study of Ethical Problems in Medicine and Biomedical and Behavioral Research:

"The primary basis for medical treatment of patients is the prospect that each individual's interests (specifically, the interest in well-being) will be promoted. Thus, treatment ordinarily aims to benefit a patient through preserving life, relieving pain and suffering, protecting against disability, and returning maximally effective functioning. If a prognosis of permanent unconsciousness is correct, however, continued treatment cannot confer such benefits. Pain and suffering are absent, as are joy, satisfaction, and pleasure. Disability is total and no return to an even minimal level of social or human functioning is possible." Deciding to Forego Life-Sustaining Treatment 181-182 (1983).

[20.] It is this sense of the word that explains its use to describe a biography: for example, Boswell's Life of Johnson or Beveridge's The Life of John Marshall. The reader of a book so titled would be surprised to find that it contained a compilation of biological data.

[21.] See, *e.g., In re Estate of Longeway,* 133 Ill.2d 33, 139 Ill.Dec. 780, 549 N.E.2d 292 (1989) (authorizing removal of a gastrostomy tube from a permanently unconscious patient after judicial approval is obtained); *McConnell v. Beverly Enterprises-Connecticut, Inc.,* 209 Conn. 692, 705, 553 A.2d 596, 603 (1989) (authorizing, pursuant to statute, removal of a gastrostomy tube from patient in a persistent vegetative state, where patient had previously expressed a wish not to have treatment sustained); *Gray v. Romeo,* 697 F.Supp. 580 (RI 1988) (authorizing removal of a feeding tube from a patient in a persistent vegetative state); *Rasmussen v. Fleming,* 154 Ariz. 207, 741 P.2d 674 (1987) (en banc) (authorizing procedures for the removal of a feeding tube from a patient in a persistent vegetative state); *In re Gardner,* 534 A.2d 947 (Me.1987) (allowing discontinuation of life-sustaining procedures for a patient in a persistent vegetative state); *In re Peter,* 108 N.J. 365, 529 A.2d 419 (1987) (authorizing procedures for cessation of treatment to elderly nursing home patient in a persistent vegetative state); *In re Jobes,* 108 N.J. 394, 529 A.2d 434 (1987) (authorizing procedures for cessation of treatment to nonelderly patient determined by "clear and convincing" evidence to be in a persistent vegetative state); *Brophy v. New England Sinai Hospital, Inc.,* 398 Mass. 417, 497 N.E.2d 626 (1986) (permitting removal of a feeding tube from a patient in a persistent vegetative state); *John F. Kennedy Memorial Hospital, Inc. v. Bludworth,* 452 So.2d 921 (Fla.1984) (holding that court approval was not needed to authorize cessation of life-support for patient in a persistent vegetative state who had executed a living will); *In re Conservatorship of Torres,* 357 N.W.2d 332 (Minn.1984) (authorizing removal of a permanently unconscious patient from life-support systems); *In re L.H.R.,* 253 Ga. 439, 321 S.E.2d 716 (1984)
(allowing parents to terminate life support for infant in a chronic vegetative state); *In re Hamlin,* 102 Wash.2d 810, 689 P.2d 1372 (1984) (allowing termination, without judicial intervention, of life support for patient in

a vegetative state if doctors and guardian concur; conflicts among doctors and the guardian with respect to cessation of treatment are to be resolved by a trial court); *In re Colyer,* 99 Wash.2d 114, 660 P.2d 738 (1983), modified on other grounds, *In re Hamlin,* 102 Wash.2d 810, 689 P.2d 1372 (1984) (allowing court-appointed guardian to authorize cessation of treatment of patient in persistent vegetative state); *In re Eichner* (decided with *In re Storar*), 52 N.Y.2d 363, 438 N.Y.S.2d 266, 420 N.E.2d 64 (authorizing the removal of a patient in a persistent vegetative state from a respirator), cert. denied, 454 U.S. 858, 102 S.Ct. 309, 70 L.Ed.2d 153 (1981); *In re Quinlan,* 70 N.J. 10, 355 A.2d 647 (authorizing, on constitutional grounds, the removal of a patient in a persistent vegetative state from a respirator), cert. denied, 429 U.S. 922, 97 S.Ct. 319, 50 L.Ed.2d 289 (1976); *Corbett v. D'Alessandro,* 487 So.2d 368 (Fla.App.1986) (authorizing removal of nasogastric feeding tube from patient in persistent vegetative state); *In re Conservatorship of Drabick,* 200 Cal.App.3d 185, 218, 245 Cal.Rptr. 840, 861 (1988) ("Life sustaining treatment is not 'necessary' under Probate Code section 2355 if it offers no reasonable possibility of returning the conservatee to cognitive life and if it is not otherwise in the conservatee's best interests, as determined by the conservator in good faith") (footnote omitted); *Delio v. Westchester County Medical Center,* 129 App.Div.2d 1, 516 N.Y.S.2d 677 (1987) (authorizing discontinuation of artificial feeding for a 33-year-old patient in a persistent vegetative state); *Leach v. Akron General Medical Center,* 68 Ohio Misc. 1, 426 N.E.2d 809 (1980) (authorizing removal of a patient in a persistent vegetative state from a respirator); *In re Severns,* 425 A.2d 156 (Del.Ch.1980) (authorizing discontinuation of all medical support measures for a patient in a "virtual vegetative state").

These cases are not the only ones which have allowed the cessation of life-sustaining treatment to incompetent patients. See, *e.g., Superintendent of Belchertown State School v. Saikewicz,* 373 Mass. 728, 370 N.E.2d 417

(1977) (holding that treatment could have been withheld from a profoundly mentally retarded patient); *Bouvia v. Superior Court of Los Angeles County,* 179 Cal.App.3d 1127, 225 Cal.Rptr. 297 (1986) (allowing removal of life saving nasogastric tube from competent, highly intelligent patient who was in extreme pain).

[22] Although my reasoning entails the conclusion that the best interests of the incompetent patient must be respected even when the patient is conscious, rather than in a vegetative state, considerations pertaining to the "quality of life," in addition to considerations about the definition of life, might then be relevant. The State's interest in protecting the life, and thereby the interests, of the incompetent patient would accordingly be more forceful, and the constitutional questions would be correspondingly complicated.

[23] Thus, the state court wrote:

"This State has expressed a strong policy favoring life. We believe that policy dictates that we err on the side of preserving life. If there is to be a change in that policy, it must come from the people through their elected representatives. Broad policy questions bearing on life and death issues are more properly addressed by representative assemblies. These have vast fact and opinion gathering and synthesizing powers unavailable to courts; the exercise of these powers is particularly appropriate where issues invoke the concerns of medicine, ethics, morality, philosophy, theology and law. Assuming change is appropriate, this issue demands a comprehensive resolution which courts cannot provide." 760 S.W.2d, at 426.

[24] The Supreme Judicial Court of Massachusetts anticipated this possibility in its *Brophy* decision, where it observed that the "duty of the State to preserve life must encompass a recognition of an individual's right to avoid circumstances in which the individual himself would feel that efforts to sustain life demean or degrade his humanity," because otherwise the State's defense of life would be tantamount to an effort by "the State to make decisions regarding the individual's quality of life."

398 Mass., at 434, 497 N.E.2d, at 635. Accord, *Gray v. Romeo,* 697 F.Supp., at 588.

[25.] Judge Campbell said on behalf of the Florida District Court of Appeal for the Second District:

"[W]e want to acknowledge that we began our deliberations in this matter, as did those who drafted our Declaration of Independence, with the solemnity and the gratefulness of the knowledge 'that all men are . . . endowed by their Creator with . . . Life.' It was not without considerable searching of our hearts, souls, and minds, as well as the jurisprudence of this great Land that we have reached our conclusions. We forcefully affirm that Life having been endowed by our Creator should not be lightly taken nor relinquished. We recognize, however, that we are also endowed with a certain amount of dignity and the right to the 'Pursuit of Happiness.' When, therefore, it may be determined by reason of the advanced scientific and medical technologies of this day that Life has, through causes beyond our control, reached the unconscious and vegetative state where all that remains is the forced function of the body's vital functions, including the artificial sustenance of the body itself, then we recognize the right to allow the natural consequence of the removal of those artificial life sustaining measures." *Corbett v. D'Alessandro,* 487 So.2d, at 371.

(Slip Opinion) OCTOBER TERM, 2007

Syllabus

NOTE: Where it is feasible, a syllabus (headnote) will be released, as is being done in connection with this case, at the time the opinion is issued. The syllabus constitutes no part of the opinion of the Court but has been prepared by the Reporter of Decisions for the convenience of the reader. See *United States* v. *Detroit Timber & Lumber Co.,* 200 U. S. 321, 337.

SUPREME COURT OF THE UNITED STATES

Syllabus

KENNEDY *v.* LOUISIANA

CERTIORARI TO THE SUPREME COURT OF LOUISIANA

No. 07–343. Argued April 16, 2008—Decided June 25, 2008

Louisiana charged petitioner with the aggravated rape of his then-8-year-old stepdaughter. He was convicted and sentenced to death under a state statute authorizing capital punishment for the rape of a child under 12. The State Supreme Court affirmed, rejecting petitioner's reliance on *Coker* v. *Georgia,* 433 U. S. 584, which barred the use of the death penalty as punishment for the rape of an adult woman but left open the question which, if any, other nonhomicide crimes can be punished by death consistent with the Eighth Amendment. Reasoning that children are a class in need of special protection, the state court held child rape to be unique in terms of the harm it inflicts upon the victim and society and concluded that, short of first-degree murder, there is no crime more deserving of death. The court acknowledged that petitioner would be the first person executed since the state law was amended to authorize the death penalty for child rape in 1995, and that Louisiana is in the minority of jurisdictions authorizing death for that crime. However, emphasizing that four more States had capitalized child rape since 1995 and at least eight others had authorized death for other nonhomicide crimes, as well as that, under *Roper* v. *Simmons,* 543 U. S. 551, and *Atkins* v. *Virginia,* 536 U. S. 304, it is the direction of change rather than the numerical count that is significant, the court held petitioner's death sentence to be constitutional.

Held: The Eighth Amendment bars Louisiana from imposing the death penalty for the rape of a child where the crime did not result, and was not intended to result, in the victim's death. Pp. 8–36.

  1. The Amendment's Cruel and Unusual Punishment Clause "draw[s] its meaning from the evolving standards of decency that mark the progress of a maturing society." *Trop* v. *Dulles,* 356 U. S. 86, 101. The standard for extreme cruelty "itself remains the same,

Syllabus

but its applicability must change as the basic mores of society change." *Furman* v. *Georgia*, 408 U. S. 238, 382. Under the precept of justice that punishment is to be graduated and proportioned to the crime, informed by evolving standards, capital punishment must "be limited to those offenders who commit 'a narrow category of the most serious crimes' and whose extreme culpability makes them 'the most deserving of execution.'" *Roper, supra,* at 568. Applying this principle, the Court held in *Roper* and *Atkins* that the execution of juveniles and mentally retarded persons violates the Eighth Amendment because the offender has a diminished personal responsibility for the crime. The Court also has found the death penalty disproportionate to the crime itself where the crime did not result, or was not intended to result, in the victim's death. See, *e.g., Coker, supra; Enmund* v. *Florida*, 458 U. S. 782. In making its determination, the Court is guided by "objective indicia of society's standards, as expressed in legislative enactments and state practice with respect to executions." *Roper, supra,* at 563. Consensus is not dispositive, however. Whether the death penalty is disproportionate to the crime also depends on the standards elaborated by controlling precedents and on the Court's own understanding and interpretation of the Eighth Amendment's text, history, meaning, and purpose. Pp. 8–10.

2. A review of the authorities informed by contemporary norms, including the history of the death penalty for this and other nonhomicide crimes, current state statutes and new enactments, and the number of executions since 1964, demonstrates a national consensus against capital punishment for the crime of child rape. Pp. 11–23.

(a) The Court follows the approach of cases in which objective indicia of consensus demonstrated an opinion against the death penalty for juveniles, see *Roper, supra,* mentally retarded offenders, see *Atkins, supra,* and vicarious felony murderers, see *Enmund, supra.* Thirty-seven jurisdictions—36 States plus the Federal Government—currently impose capital punishment, but only six States authorize it for child rape. In 45 jurisdictions, by contrast, petitioner could not be executed for child rape of any kind. That number surpasses the 30 States in *Atkins* and *Roper* and the 42 in *Enmund* that prohibited the death penalty under the circumstances those cases considered. Pp. 11–15.

(b) Respondent's argument that *Coker*'s general discussion contrasting murder and rape, 433 U. S., at 598, has been interpreted too expansively, leading some States to conclude that *Coker* applies to child rape when in fact it does not, is unsound. *Coker*'s holding was narrower than some of its language read in isolation indicates. The *Coker* plurality framed the question as whether, "with respect to rape of an adult woman," the death penalty is disproportionate punish-

Syllabus

ment, *id.,* at 592, and it repeated the phrase "adult woman" or "adult female" eight times in discussing the crime or the victim. The distinction between adult and child rape was not merely rhetorical; it was central to *Coker*'s reasoning, including its analysis of legislative consensus. See, *e.g., id.,* at 595–596. There is little evidence to support respondent's contention that state legislatures have understood *Coker* to state a broad rule that covers minor victims, and state courts have uniformly concluded that *Coker* did not address that crime. Accordingly, the small number of States that have enacted the death penalty for child rape is relevant to determining whether there is a consensus against capital punishment for the rape of a child. Pp. 15–20.

(c) A consistent direction of change in support of the death penalty for child rape might counterbalance an otherwise weak demonstration of consensus, see, *e.g., Atkins,* 536 U. S., at 315, but no showing of consistent change has been made here. That five States may have had pending legislation authorizing death for child rape is not dispositive because it is not this Court's practice, nor is it sound, to find contemporary norms based on legislation proposed but not yet enacted. Indeed, since the parties submitted their briefs, the legislation in at least two of the five States has failed. Further, evidence that, in the last 13 years, six new death penalty statutes have been enacted, three in the last two years, is not as significant as the data in *Atkins,* where 18 States between 1986 and 2001 had enacted legislation prohibiting the execution of mentally retarded persons. See *id.,* at 314–315. Respondent argues that this case is like *Roper* because, there, only five States had shifted their positions between 1989 and 2005, one less State than here. See 543 U. S., at 565. But the *Roper* Court emphasized that the slow pace of abolition was counterbalanced by the total number of States that had recognized the impropriety of executing juvenile offenders. See *id.,* at 566–567. Here, the fact that only six States have made child rape a capital offense is not an indication of a trend or change in direction comparable to the one in *Roper.* The evidence bears a closer resemblance to that in *Enmund,* where the Court found a national consensus against death for vicarious felony murder despite eight jurisdictions having authorized it. See 458 U. S., at 789, 792. Pp. 20–22.

(d) Execution statistics also confirm that there is a social consensus against the death penalty for child rape. Nine States have permitted capital punishment for adult or child rape for some length of time between the Court's 1972 *Furman* decision and today; yet no individual has been executed for the rape of an adult or child since 1964, and no execution for any other nonhomicide offense has been conducted since 1963. Louisiana is the only State since 1964 that has

Syllabus

sentenced an individual to death for child rape, and petitioner and another man so sentenced are the only individuals now on death row in the United States for nonhomicide offenses. Pp. 22–23.

3. Informed by its own precedents and its understanding of the Constitution and the rights it secures, the Court concludes, in its independent judgment, that the death penalty is not a proportional punishment for the crime of child rape. Pp. 23–35.

(a) The Court's own judgment should be brought to bear on the death penalty's acceptability under the Eighth Amendment. See, *e.g., Coker, supra*, at 597. Rape's permanent and devastating impact on a child suggests moral grounds for questioning a rule barring capital punishment simply because the crime did not result in the victim's death, but it does not follow that death is a proportionate penalty for child rape. The constitutional prohibition against excessive or cruel and unusual punishments mandates that punishment "be exercised within the limits of civilized standards." *Trop,* 356 U. S., at 99–100. Evolving standards of decency counsel the Court to be most hesitant before allowing extension of the death penalty, especially where no life was taken in the commission of the crime. See, *e.g., Coker,* 433 U. S., at 597–598; *Enmund,* 458 U. S., at 797. Consistent with those evolving standards and the teachings of its precedents, the Court concludes that there is a distinction between intentional first-degree murder on the one hand and nonhomicide crimes against individuals, even including child rape, on the other. The latter crimes may be devastating in their harm, as here, but "in terms of moral depravity and of the injury to the person and to the public," they cannot compare to murder in their "severity and irrevocability," *id,* at 598. The Court finds significant the substantial number of executions that would be allowed for child rape under respondent's approach. Although narrowing aggravators might be used to ensure the death penalty's restrained application in this context, as they are in the context of capital murder, all such standards have the potential to result in some inconsistency of application. The Court, for example, has acknowledged that the requirement of general rules to ensure consistency of treatment, see, *e.g., Godfrey* v. *Georgia,* 446 U. S. 420, and the insistence that capital sentencing be individualized, see, *e.g., Woodson* v. *North Carolina,* 428 U. S. 280, have resulted in tension and imprecision. This approach might be sound with respect to capital murder but it should not be introduced into the justice system where death has not occurred. The Court has spent more than 32 years developing a foundational jurisprudence for capital murder to guide the States and juries in imposing the death penalty. Beginning the same process for crimes for which no one has been executed in more than 40 years would require experimentation in an area where

Syllabus

a failed experiment would result in the execution of individuals undeserving of death. Pp. 24–30.

   (b) The Court's decision is consistent with the justifications offered for the death penalty, retribution and deterrence, see, *e.g., Gregg* v. *Georgia,* 428 U. S. 153, 183. Among the factors for determining whether retribution is served, the Court must look to whether the death penalty balances the wrong to the victim in nonhomicide cases. Cf. *Roper, supra,* at 571. It is not at all evident that the child rape victim's hurt is lessened when the law permits the perpetrator's death, given that capital cases require a long-term commitment by those testifying for the prosecution. Society's desire to inflict death for child rape by enlisting the child victim to assist it over the course of years in asking for capital punishment forces a moral choice on the child, who is not of mature age to make that choice. There are also relevant systemic concerns in prosecuting child rape, including the documented problem of unreliable, induced, and even imagined child testimony, which creates a "special risk of wrongful execution" in some cases. Cf. *Atkins, supra,* at 321. As to deterrence, the evidence suggests that the death penalty may not result in more effective enforcement, but may add to the risk of nonreporting of child rape out of fear of negative consequences for the perpetrator, especially if he is a family member. And, by in effect making the punishment for child rape and murder equivalent, a State may remove a strong incentive for the rapist not to kill his victim. Pp. 30–35.

   4. The concern that the Court's holding will effectively block further development of a consensus favoring the death penalty for child rape overlooks the principle that the Eighth Amendment is defined by "the evolving standards of decency that mark the progress of a maturing society," *Trop,* 356 U. S., at 101. Confirmed by the Court's repeated, consistent rulings, this principle requires that resort to capital punishment be restrained, limited in its instances of application, and reserved for the worst of crimes, those that, in the case of crimes against individuals, take the victim's life. P. 36.

957 So. 2d 757, reversed and remanded.

KENNEDY, J., delivered the opinion of the Court, in which STEVENS, SOUTER, GINSBURG, and BREYER, JJ., joined. ALITO, J., filed a dissenting opinion, in which ROBERTS, C. J., and SCALIA and THOMAS, JJ., joined.

Opinion of the Court

NOTICE: This opinion is subject to formal revision before publication in the preliminary print of the United States Reports. Readers are requested to notify the Reporter of Decisions, Supreme Court of the United States, Washington, D. C. 20543, of any typographical or other formal errors, in order that corrections may be made before the preliminary print goes to press.

SUPREME COURT OF THE UNITED STATES

No. 07–343

PATRICK KENNEDY, PETITIONER v. LOUISIANA

ON WRIT OF CERTIORARI TO THE SUPREME COURT OF LOUISIANA

[June 25, 2008]

JUSTICE KENNEDY delivered the opinion of the Court.

The National Government and, beyond it, the separate States are bound by the proscriptive mandates of the Eighth Amendment to the Constitution of the United States, and all persons within those respective jurisdictions may invoke its protection. See Amdts. 8 and 14, §1; *Robinson* v. *California*, 370 U. S. 660 (1962). Patrick Kennedy, the petitioner here, seeks to set aside his death sentence under the Eighth Amendment. He was charged by the respondent, the State of Louisiana, with the aggravated rape of his then-8-year-old stepdaughter. After a jury trial petitioner was convicted and sentenced to death under a state statute authorizing capital punishment for the rape of a child under 12 years of age. See La. Stat. Ann. §14:42 (West 1997 and Supp. 1998). This case presents the question whether the Constitution bars respondent from imposing the death penalty for the rape of a child where the crime did not result, and was not intended to result, in death of the victim. We hold the Eighth Amendment prohibits the death penalty for this offense. The Louisiana statute is unconstitutional.

I

Petitioner's crime was one that cannot be recounted in these pages in a way sufficient to capture in full the hurt and horror inflicted on his victim or to convey the revulsion society, and the jury that represents it, sought to express by sentencing petitioner to death. At 9:18 a.m. on March 2, 1998, petitioner called 911 to report that his stepdaughter, referred to here as L. H., had been raped. He told the 911 operator that L. H. had been in the garage while he readied his son for school. Upon hearing loud screaming, petitioner said, he ran outside and found L. H. in the side yard. Two neighborhood boys, petitioner told the operator, had dragged L. H. from the garage to the yard, pushed her down, and raped her. Petitioner claimed he saw one of the boys riding away on a blue 10-speed bicycle.

When police arrived at petitioner's home between 9:20 and 9:30 a.m., they found L. H. on her bed, wearing a T-shirt and wrapped in a bloody blanket. She was bleeding profusely from the vaginal area. Petitioner told police he had carried her from the yard to the bathtub and then to the bed. Consistent with this explanation, police found a thin line of blood drops in the garage on the way to the house and then up the stairs. Once in the bedroom, petitioner had used a basin of water and a cloth to wipe blood from the victim. This later prevented medical personnel from collecting a reliable DNA sample.

L. H. was transported to the Children's Hospital. An expert in pediatric forensic medicine testified that L. H.'s injuries were the most severe he had seen from a sexual assault in his four years of practice. A laceration to the left wall of the vagina had separated her cervix from the back of her vagina, causing her rectum to protrude into the vaginal structure. Her entire perineum was torn from the posterior fourchette to the anus. The injuries required emergency surgery.

Opinion of the Court

At the scene of the crime, at the hospital, and in the first weeks that followed, both L. H. and petitioner maintained in their accounts to investigators that L. H. had been raped by two neighborhood boys. One of L. H.'s doctors testified at trial that L. H. told all hospital personnel the same version of the rape, although she reportedly told one family member that petitioner raped her. L. H. was interviewed several days after the rape by a psychologist. The interview was videotaped, lasted three hours over two days, and was introduced into evidence at trial. On the tape one can see that L. H. had difficulty discussing the subject of the rape. She spoke haltingly and with long pauses and frequent movement. Early in the interview, L. H. expressed reservations about the questions being asked:

> "I'm going to tell the same story. They just want me to change it.... They want me to say my Dad did it.... I don't want to say it.... I tell them the same, same story." Def. Exh. D–7, 01:29:07–:36.

She told the psychologist that she had been playing in the garage when a boy came over and asked her about Girl Scout cookies she was selling; and that the boy "pulled [her by the legs to] the backyard," *id.,* at 01:47:41–:52, where he placed his hand over her mouth, "pulled down [her] shorts," Def. Exh. D–8, 00:03:11–:12, and raped her, *id.,* at 00:14:39–:40.

Eight days after the crime, and despite L. H.'s insistence that petitioner was not the offender, petitioner was arrested for the rape. The State's investigation had drawn the accuracy of petitioner and L. H.'s story into question. Though the defense at trial proffered alternative explanations, the case for the prosecution, credited by the jury, was based upon the following evidence: An inspection of the side yard immediately after the assault was inconsistent with a rape having occurred there, the grass having been found mostly undisturbed but for a small patch of coagulated blood. Petitioner said that one of the perpetrators fled the crime scene on a blue 10-speed bicycle but gave inconsistent descriptions of the bicycle's features, such as its handlebars. Investigators found a bicycle matching petitioner and L. H.'s description in tall grass behind a nearby apartment, and petitioner identified it as the bicycle one of the perpetrators was riding. Yet its tires were flat, it did not have gears, and it was covered in spider webs. In addition police found blood on the underside of L. H.'s mattress. This convinced them the rape took place in her bedroom, not outside the house.

Police also found that petitioner made two telephone calls on the morning of the rape. Sometime before 6:15 a.m., petitioner called his employer and left a message that he was unavailable to work that day. Petitioner called back between 6:30 and 7:30 a.m. to ask a colleague how to get blood out of a white carpet because his daughter had "'just become a young lady.'" Brief for Respondent 12. At 7:37 a.m., petitioner called B & B Carpet Cleaning and requested urgent assistance in removing bloodstains from a carpet. Petitioner did not call 911 until about an hour and a half later.

About a month after petitioner's arrest L. H. was removed from the custody of her mother, who had maintained until that point that petitioner was not involved in the rape. On June 22, 1998, L. H. was returned home and told her mother for the first time that petitioner had raped her. And on December 16, 1999, about 21 months after the rape, L. H. recorded her accusation in a videotaped interview with the Child Advocacy Center.

The State charged petitioner with aggravated rape of a child under La. Stat. Ann. §14:42 (West 1997 and Supp. 1998) and sought the death penalty. At all times relevant to petitioner's case, the statute provided:

"A. Aggravated rape is a rape committed . . . where the anal or vaginal sexual intercourse is deemed to be without lawful consent of the victim because it is committed under any one or more of the following circumstances:

. . . . .

"(4) When the victim is under the age of twelve years. Lack of knowledge of the victim's age shall not be a defense.

. . . . .

"D. Whoever commits the crime of aggravated rape shall be punished by life imprisonment at hard labor without benefit of parole, probation, or suspension of sentence.

"(1) However, if the victim was under the age of twelve years, as provided by Paragraph A(4) of this Section:

"(a) And if the district attorney seeks a capital verdict, the offender shall be punished by death or life imprisonment at hard labor without benefit of parole, probation, or suspension of sentence, in accordance with the determination of the jury."

(Since petitioner was convicted and sentenced, the statute has been amended to include oral intercourse within the definition of aggravated rape and to increase the age of the victim from 12 to 13. See La. Stat. Ann. §14:42 (West Supp. 2007).)

Aggravating circumstances are set forth in La. Code Crim. Proc. Ann., Art. 905.4 (West 1997 Supp.). In pertinent part and at all times relevant to petitioner's case, the provision stated:

"A. The following shall be considered aggravating circumstances:

"(1) The offender was engaged in the perpetration or attempted perpetration of aggravated rape, forcible rape, aggravated kidnapping, second degree kidnapping, aggravated burglary, aggravated arson, aggravated escape, assault by drive-by shooting, armed robbery, first degree robbery, or simple robbery.

. . . . .

"(10) The victim was under the age of twelve years or sixty-five years of age or older."

The trial began in August 2003. L. H. was then 13 years old. She testified that she "'woke up one morning and Patrick was on top of [her].'" She remembered petitioner bringing her "[a] cup of orange juice and pills chopped up in it" after the rape and overhearing him on the telephone saying she had become a "young lady." 2005–1981, pp. 12, 15, 16 (La. 5/22/07), 957 So. 2d 757, 767, 769, 770. L. H. acknowledged that she had accused two neighborhood boys but testified petitioner told her to say this and that it was untrue. *Id.*, at 769.

The jury having found petitioner guilty of aggravated rape, the penalty phase ensued. The State presented the testimony of S. L., who is the cousin and goddaughter of petitioner's ex-wife. S. L. testified that petitioner sexually abused her three times when she was eight years old and that the last time involved sexual intercourse. *Id.*, at 772. She did not tell anyone until two years later and did not pursue legal action.

The jury unanimously determined that petitioner should be sentenced to death. The Supreme Court of Louisiana affirmed. See *id.*, at 779–789, 793; see also *State* v. *Wilson*, 96–1392, 96–2076 (La. 12/13/96), 685 So. 2d 1063 (upholding the constitutionality of the death penalty for child rape). The court rejected petitioner's reliance on *Coker* v. *Georgia*, 433 U. S. 584 (1977), noting that, while *Coker* bars the use of the death penalty as punishment for the rape of an adult woman, it left open the question which, if any, other nonhomicide crimes can be punished by death consistent with the Eighth Amendment. Because "'children are a class that need special protection,'" the state court reasoned, the rape of a child is unique in terms of the harm it inflicts upon the victim and our society. 957 So. 2d, at 781.

The court acknowledged that petitioner would be the first person executed for committing child rape since La. Stat. Ann. §14:42 was amended in 1995 and that Louisiana is in the minority of jurisdictions that authorize the death penalty for the crime of child rape. But following the approach of *Roper* v. *Simmons*, 543 U. S. 551 (2005), and *Atkins* v. *Virginia*, 536 U. S. 304 (2002), it found significant not the "numerical counting of which [S]tates . . . stand for or against a particular capital prosecution," but "the direction of change." 957 So. 2d, at 783 (emphasis deleted). Since 1993, the court explained, four more States—Oklahoma, South Carolina, Montana, and Georgia—had capitalized the crime of child rape and at least eight States had authorized capital punishment for other nonhomicide crimes. By its count, 14 of the then-38 States permitting capital punishment, plus the Federal Government, allowed the death penalty for nonhomicide crimes and 5 allowed the death penalty for the crime of child rape. See *id.,* at 785–786.

The state court next asked whether "child rapists rank among the worst offenders." *Id.,* at 788. It noted the severity of the crime; that the execution of child rapists would serve the goals of deterrence and retribution; and that, unlike in *Atkins* and *Roper*, there were no characteristics of petitioner that tended to mitigate his moral culpability. *Id.,* at 788–789. It concluded: "[S]hort of first-degree murder, we can think of no other non-homicide crime more deserving [of capital punishment]." *Id.,* at 789.

On this reasoning the Supreme Court of Louisiana rejected petitioner's argument that the death penalty for the rape of a child under 12 years is disproportionate and upheld the constitutionality of the statute. Chief Justice Calogero dissented. *Coker, supra,* and *Eberheart* v. *Georgia,* 433 U. S. 917 (1977), in his view, "set out a bright-line and easily administered rule" that the Eighth Amendment precludes capital punishment for any offense that does not involve the death of the victim. 957 So. 2d, at 794.

We granted certiorari. See 552 U. S. ___ (2008).

II

The Eighth Amendment, applicable to the States through the Fourteenth Amendment, provides that "[e]xcessive bail shall not be required, nor excessive fines imposed, nor cruel and unusual punishments inflicted." The Amendment proscribes "all excessive punishments, as well as cruel and unusual punishments that may or may not be excessive." *Atkins,* 536 U. S., at 311, n. 7. The Court explained in *Atkins, id.,* at 311, and *Roper, supra,* at 560, that the Eighth Amendment's protection against excessive or cruel and unusual punishments flows from the basic "precept of justice that punishment for [a] crime should be graduated and proportioned to [the] offense." *Weems* v. *United States,* 217 U. S. 349, 367 (1910). Whether this requirement has been fulfilled is determined not by the standards that prevailed when the Eighth Amendment was adopted in 1791 but by the norms that "currently prevail." *Atkins, supra,* at 311. The Amendment "draw[s] its meaning from the evolving standards of decency that mark the progress of a maturing society." *Trop* v. *Dulles,* 356 U. S. 86, 101 (1958) (plurality opinion). This is because "[t]he standard of extreme cruelty is not merely descriptive, but necessarily embodies a moral judgment. The standard itself remains the same, but its applicability must change as the basic mores of society change." *Furman* v. *Georgia,* 408 U. S. 238, 382 (1972) (Burger, C. J., dissenting).

Evolving standards of decency must embrace and express respect for the dignity of the person, and the punishment of criminals must conform to that rule. See *Trop, supra,* at 100 (plurality opinion). As we shall discuss, punishment is justified under one or more of three principal rationales: rehabilitation, deterrence, and retribution. See *Harmelin* v. *Michigan,* 501 U. S. 957, 999 (1991) (KENNEDY, J., concurring in part and concurring in judgment); see also Part IV–B, *infra.* It is the last of these, retribution, that most often can contradict the law's own ends. This is of particular concern when the Court interprets the meaning of the Eighth Amendment in capital cases. When the law punishes by death, it risks its own sudden descent into brutality, transgressing the constitutional commitment to decency and restraint.

For these reasons we have explained that capital punishment must "be limited to those offenders who commit 'a narrow category of the most serious crimes' and whose extreme culpability makes them 'the most deserving of execution.'" *Roper, supra,* at 568 (quoting *Atkins, supra,* at 319). Though the death penalty is not invariably unconstitutional, see *Gregg* v. *Georgia,* 428 U. S. 153 (1976), the Court insists upon confining the instances in which the punishment can be imposed.

Applying this principle, we held in *Roper* and *Atkins* that the execution of juveniles and mentally retarded persons are punishments violative of the Eighth Amendment because the offender had a diminished personal responsibility for the crime. See *Roper, supra,* at 571–573; *Atkins, supra,* at 318, 320. The Court further has held that the death penalty can be disproportionate to the crime itself where the crime did not result, or was not intended to result, in death of the victim. In *Coker,* 433 U. S. 584, for instance, the Court held it would be unconstitutional to execute an offender who had raped an adult woman. See also *Eberheart, supra* (holding unconstitutional in light of *Coker* a sentence of death for the kidnaping and rape of an adult woman). And in *Enmund* v. *Florida*, 458 U. S. 782 (1982), the Court overturned the capital sentence of a defendant who aided and abetted a robbery during which a murder was committed but did not himself kill, attempt to kill, or intend that a killing would take place. On the other hand, in *Tison* v. *Arizona*, 481 U. S. 137 (1987), the Court allowed the defendants' death sentences to stand where they did not themselves kill the victims but their involvement in the events leading up to the murders was active, recklessly indifferent, and substantial.

In these cases the Court has been guided by "objective indicia of society's standards, as expressed in legislative enactments and state practice with respect to executions." *Roper*, 543 U. S., at 563; see also *Coker, supra*, at 593–597 (plurality opinion) (finding that both legislatures and juries had firmly rejected the penalty of death for the rape of an adult woman); *Enmund, supra,* at 788 (looking to "historical development of the punishment at issue, legislative judgments, international opinion, and the sentencing decisions juries have made"). The inquiry does not end there, however. Consensus is not dispositive. Whether the death penalty is disproportionate to the crime committed depends as well upon the standards elaborated by controlling precedents and by the Court's own understanding and interpretation of the Eighth Amendment's text, history, meaning, and purpose. See *id.,* at 797–801; *Gregg, supra,* at 182–183 (joint opinion of Stewart, Powell, and STEVENS, JJ.); *Coker, supra*, at 597–600 (plurality opinion).

Based both on consensus and our own independent judgment, our holding is that a death sentence for one who raped but did not kill a child, and who did not intend to assist another in killing the child, is unconstitutional under the Eighth and Fourteenth Amendments.

III

A

The existence of objective indicia of consensus against making a crime punishable by death was a relevant concern in *Roper*, *Atkins*, *Coker*, and *Enmund*, and we follow the approach of those cases here. The history of the death penalty for the crime of rape is an instructive beginning point.

In 1925, 18 States, the District of Columbia, and the Federal Government had statutes that authorized the death penalty for the rape of a child or an adult. See *Coker, supra,* at 593 (plurality opinion). Between 1930 and 1964, 455 people were executed for those crimes. See 5 Historical Statistics of the United States: Earliest Times to the Present, pp. 5–262 to 5–263 (S. Carter et al. eds. 2006) (Table Ec343–357). To our knowledge the last individual executed for the rape of a child was Ronald Wolfe in 1964. See H. Frazier, Death Sentences in Missouri, 1803–2005: A History and Comprehensive Registry of Legal Executions, Pardons, and Commutations 143 (2006).

In 1972, *Furman* invalidated most of the state statutes authorizing the death penalty for the crime of rape; and in *Furman*'s aftermath only six States reenacted their capital rape provisions. Three States—Georgia, North Carolina, and Louisiana—did so with respect to all rape offenses. Three States—Florida, Mississippi, and Tennessee—did so with respect only to child rape. See *Coker, supra,* at 594–595 (plurality opinion). All six statutes were later invalidated under state or federal law. See *Coker, supra* (striking down Georgia's capital rape statute); *Woodson* v. *North Carolina*, 428 U. S. 280, 287, n. 6, 301–305 (1976) (plurality opinion) (striking down North Carolina's mandatory death penalty statute); *Roberts* v. *Louisiana*, 428 U. S. 325 (1976) (striking down Louisiana's mandatory death penalty statute); *Collins* v. *State*, 550 S. W. 2d 643, 646 (Tenn.

1977) (striking down Tennessee's mandatory death penalty statute); *Buford* v. *State*, 403 So. 2d 943, 951 (Fla. 1981) (holding unconstitutional the imposition of death for child rape); *Leatherwood* v. *State*, 548 So. 2d 389, 402–403 (Miss. 1989) (striking down the death penalty for child rape on state-law grounds).

Louisiana reintroduced the death penalty for rape of a child in 1995. See La. Stat. Ann. §14:42 (West Supp. 1996). Under the current statute, any anal, vaginal, or oral intercourse with a child under the age of 13 constitutes aggravated rape and is punishable by death. See La. Stat. Ann. §14:42 (West Supp. 2007). Mistake of age is not a defense, so the statute imposes strict liability in this regard. Five States have since followed Louisiana's lead: Georgia, see Ga. Code Ann. §16–6–1 (2007) (enacted 1999); Montana, see Mont. Code Ann. §45–5–503 (2007) (enacted 1997); Oklahoma, see Okla. Stat., Tit. 10, §7115(K) (West 2007 Supp.) (enacted 2006); South Carolina, see S. C. Code Ann. §16–3–655(C)(1) (Supp. 2007) (enacted 2006); and Texas, see Tex. Penal Code Ann. §12.42(c)(3) (West Supp. 2007) (enacted 2007); see also Tex. Penal Code Ann. §22.021(a) (West Supp. 2007). Four of these States' statutes are more narrow than Louisiana's in that only offenders with a previous rape conviction are death eligible. See Mont. Code Ann. §45–5–503(3)(c); Okla. Stat., Tit. 10, §7115(K); S. C. Code Ann. §16–3–655(C)(1); Tex. Penal Code Ann. §12.42(c)(3). Georgia's statute makes child rape a capital offense only when aggravating circumstances are present, including but not limited to a prior conviction. See Ga. Code Ann. §17–10–30 (Supp. 2007).

By contrast, 44 States have not made child rape a capital offense. As for federal law, Congress in the Federal Death Penalty Act of 1994 expanded the number of federal crimes for which the death penalty is a permissible sentence, including certain nonhomicide offenses; but it did not do the same for child rape or abuse. See 108 Stat.

Opinion of the Court

1972 (codified as amended in scattered sections of 18 U. S. C.). Under 18 U. S. C. §2245, an offender is death eligible only when the sexual abuse or exploitation results in the victim's death.

Petitioner claims the death penalty for child rape is not authorized in Georgia, pointing to a 1979 decision in which the Supreme Court of Georgia stated that "[s]tatutory rape is not a capital crime in Georgia." *Presnell* v. *State*, 243 Ga. 131, 132–133, 252 S. E. 2d 625, 626. But it appears *Presnell* was referring to the separate crime of statutory rape, which is not a capital offense in Georgia, see Ga. Code Ann. §26–2018 (1969); cf. Ga. Code. Ann. §16–6–3 (2007). The State's current capital rape statute, by contrast, is explicit that the rape of "[a] female who is less than ten years of age" is punishable "by death." Ga. Code Ann. §§16–6–1(a)(2), (b) (2007). Based on a recent statement by the Supreme Court of Georgia it must be assumed that this law is still in force: "Neither the United States Supreme Court, nor this Court, has yet addressed whether the death penalty is unconstitutionally disproportionate for the crime of raping a child." *State* v. *Velazquez*, 283 Ga. 206, 208, 657 S. E. 2d 838, 840 (2008).

Respondent would include Florida among those States that permit the death penalty for child rape. The state statute does authorize, by its terms, the death penalty for "sexual battery upon . . . a person less than 12 years of age." Fla. Stat. §794.011(2) (2007); see also §921.141(5) (2007). In 1981, however, the Supreme Court of Florida held the death penalty for child sexual assault to be unconstitutional. See *Buford, supra*. It acknowledged that *Coker* addressed only the constitutionality of the death penalty for rape of an adult woman, 403 So. 2d, at 950, but held that "[t]he reasoning of the justices in *Coker* . . . compels [the conclusion] that a sentence of death is grossly disproportionate and excessive punishment for the crime of sexual assault and is therefore forbidden by the Eighth

Amendment as cruel and unusual punishment," *id.,* at 951. Respondent points out that the state statute has not since been amended. Pursuant to Fla. Stat. §775.082(2) (2007), however, Florida state courts have understood *Buford* to bind their sentencing discretion in child rape cases. See, *e.g., Gibson* v. *State,* 721 So. 2d 363, 367, and n. 2 (Fla. App. 1998) (deeming it irrelevant that "the Florida Legislature never changed the wording of the sexual battery statute"); *Cooper* v. *State,* 453 So. 2d 67 (Fla. App. 1984) ("After *Buford*, death was no longer a possible penalty in Florida for sexual battery"); see also Fla. Stat. §775.082(2) ("In the event the death penalty in a capital felony is held to be unconstitutional by the Florida Supreme Court . . . the court having jurisdiction over a person previously sentenced to death for a capital felony . . . shall sentence such person to life imprisonment").

Definitive resolution of state-law issues is for the States' own courts, and there may be disagreement over the statistics. It is further true that some States, including States that have addressed the issue in just the last few years, have made child rape a capital offense. The summary recited here, however, does allow us to make certain comparisons with the data cited in the *Atkins, Roper,* and *Enmund* cases.

When *Atkins* was decided in 2002, 30 States, including 12 noncapital jurisdictions, prohibited the death penalty for mentally retarded offenders; 20 permitted it. See 536 U. S., at 313–315. When *Roper* was decided in 2005, the numbers disclosed a similar division among the States: 30 States prohibited the death penalty for juveniles, 18 of which permitted the death penalty for other offenders; and 20 States authorized it. See 543 U. S., at 564. Both in *Atkins* and in *Roper*, we noted that the practice of executing mentally retarded and juvenile offenders was infrequent. Only five States had executed an offender known to have an IQ below 70 between 1989 and 2002, see *At-*

kins, supra, at 316; and only three States had executed a juvenile offender between 1995 and 2005, see *Roper, supra,* at 564–565.

The statistics in *Enmund* bear an even greater similarity to the instant case. There eight jurisdictions had authorized imposition of the death penalty solely for participation in a robbery during which an accomplice committed murder, see 458 U. S., at 789, and six defendants between 1954 and 1982 had been sentenced to death for felony murder where the defendant did not personally commit the homicidal assault, *id.,* at 794. These facts, the Court concluded, "weigh[ed] on the side of rejecting capital punishment for the crime." *Id.,* at 793.

The evidence of a national consensus with respect to the death penalty for child rapists, as with respect to juveniles, mentally retarded offenders, and vicarious felony murderers, shows divided opinion but, on balance, an opinion against it. Thirty-seven jurisdictions—36 States plus the Federal Government—have the death penalty. As mentioned above, only six of those jurisdictions authorize the death penalty for rape of a child. Though our review of national consensus is not confined to tallying the number of States with applicable death penalty legislation, it is of significance that, in 45 jurisdictions, petitioner could not be executed for child rape of any kind. That number surpasses the 30 States in *Atkins* and *Roper* and the 42 States in *Enmund* that prohibited the death penalty under the circumstances those cases considered.

B

At least one difference between this case and our Eighth Amendment proportionality precedents must be addressed. Respondent and its *amici* suggest that some States have an "erroneous understanding of this Court's Eighth Amendment jurisprudence." Brief for Missouri Governor Matt Blunt et al. as *Amici Curiae* 10. They submit that the general propositions set out in *Coker,* contrasting murder and rape, have been interpreted in too expansive a way, leading some state legislatures to conclude that *Coker* applies to child rape when in fact its reasoning does not, or ought not, apply to that specific crime.

This argument seems logical at first, but in the end it is unsound. In *Coker,* a four-Member plurality of the Court, plus Justice Brennan and Justice Marshall in concurrence, held that a sentence of death for the rape of a 16-year-old woman, who was a minor under Georgia law, see Ga. Code Ann. §74–104 (1973), yet was characterized by the Court as an adult, was disproportionate and excessive under the Eighth Amendment. See 433 U. S., at 593–600; see also *id.,* at 600 (Brennan, J., concurring in judgment); *ibid.* (Marshall, J., concurring in judgment). (The Court did not explain why the 16-year-old victim qualified as an adult, but it may be of some significance that she was married, had a home of her own, and had given birth to a son three weeks prior to the rape. See Brief for Petitioner in *Coker* v. *Georgia,* O. T. 1976, No. 75–5444, pp. 14–15.)

The plurality noted that only one State had a valid statute authorizing the death penalty for adult rape and that "in the vast majority of cases, at least 9 out of 10, juries ha[d] not imposed the death sentence." *Coker,* 433 U. S., at 597; see also *id.,* at 594 ("Of the 16 States in which rape had been a capital offense, only three provided the death penalty for rape of an adult woman in their revised statutes—Georgia, North Carolina, and Louisiana. In the latter two States, the death penalty was mandatory for those found guilty, and those laws were invalidated by *Woodson* and *Roberts*"). This "history and . . . objective evidence of the country's present judgment concerning the acceptability of death as a penalty for rape of an adult woman," *id.,* at 593, confirmed the Court's independent judgment that punishing adult rape by death was not proportional:

> "Rape is without doubt deserving of serious punishment; but in terms of moral depravity and of the injury to the person and to the public, it does not compare with murder, which does involve the unjustified taking of human life. Although it may be accompanied by another crime, rape by definition does not include the death of . . . another person. The murderer kills; the rapist, if no more than that, does not. . . . We have the abiding conviction that the death penalty, which 'is unique in its severity and irrevocability,' *Gregg* v. *Georgia*, 428 U. S., at 187, is an excessive penalty for the rapist who, as such, does not take human life." *Id.*, at 598 (footnote omitted).

Confined to this passage, *Coker*'s analysis of the Eighth Amendment is susceptible of a reading that would prohibit making child rape a capital offense. In context, however, *Coker*'s holding was narrower than some of its language read in isolation. The *Coker* plurality framed the question as whether, "with respect to rape of an adult woman," the death penalty is disproportionate punishment. *Id.*, at 592. And it repeated the phrase "an adult woman" or "an adult female" in discussing the act of rape or the victim of rape eight times in its opinion. See *Coker, supra*. The distinction between adult and child rape was not merely rhetorical; it was central to the Court's reasoning. The opinion does not speak to the constitutionality of the death penalty for child rape, an issue not then before the Court. In discussing the legislative background, for example, the Court noted:

> "Florida, Mississippi, and Tennessee also authorized the death penalty in some rape cases, but only where the victim was a child and the rapist an adult. The Tennessee statute has since been invalidated because the death sentence was mandatory. The upshot is

that Georgia is the sole jurisdiction in the United States at the present time that authorizes a sentence of death when the rape victim is an adult woman, and only two other jurisdictions provide capital punishment when the victim is a child. . . . [This] obviously weighs very heavily on the side of rejecting capital punishment as a suitable penalty for raping an adult woman." *Id.*, at 595–596 (citation and footnote omitted).

Still, respondent contends, it is possible that state legislatures have understood *Coker* to state a broad rule that covers the situation of the minor victim as well. We see little evidence of this. Respondent cites no reliable data to indicate that state legislatures have read *Coker* to bar capital punishment for child rape and, for this reason, have been deterred from passing applicable death penalty legislation. In the absence of evidence from those States where legislation has been proposed but not enacted we refuse to speculate about the motivations and concerns of particular state legislators.

The position of the state courts, furthermore, to which state legislators look for guidance on these matters, indicates that *Coker* has not blocked the emergence of legislative consensus. The state courts that have confronted the precise question before us have been uniform in concluding that *Coker* did not address the constitutionality of the death penalty for the crime of child rape. See, *e.g., Wilson*, 685 So. 2d, at 1066 (upholding the constitutionality of the death penalty for rape of a child and noting that "[t]he plurality [in *Coker*] took great pains in referring only to the rape of adult women throughout their opinion" (emphasis deleted)); *Upshaw* v. *State*, 350 So. 2d 1358, 1360 (Miss. 1977) ("In *Coker* the Court took great pains to limit its decision to the applicability of the death penalty for the rape of an adult woman. . . . As we view *Coker* the Court carefully refrained from deciding whether the death penalty for the rape of a female child under the age of twelve years is grossly disproportionate to the crime"). See also *Simpson* v. *Owens*, 207 Ariz. 261, 268, n. 8, 85 P. 3d 478, 485, n. 8 (App. 2004) (addressing the denial of bail for sexual offenses against children and noting that "[a]lthough the death penalty was declared in a plurality opinion of the United States Supreme Court to be a disproportionate punishment for the rape of an adult woman . . . the rape of a child remains a capital offense in some states"); *People* v. *Hernandez*, 30 Cal. 4th 835, 869, 69 P. 3d 446, 466 (2003) (addressing the death penalty for conspiracy to commit murder and noting that "the constitutionality of laws imposing the death penalty for crimes not necessarily resulting in death is unresolved").

There is, to be sure, some contrary authority contained in various state-court opinions. But it is either dicta, see *State* v. *Barnum*, 921 So. 2d 513, 526 (Fla. 2005) (addressing the retroactivity of *Thompson* v. *State*, 695 So. 2d 691 (Fla. 1997)); *State* v. *Coleman*, 185 Mont. 299, 327, 605 P. 2d 1000, 1017 (1979) (upholding the defendant's death sentence for aggravated kidnaping); *State* v. *Gardner*, 947 P. 2d 630, 653 (Utah 1997) (addressing the constitutionality of the death penalty for prison assaults); equivocal in its conclusion, see *People* v. *Huddleston*, 212 Ill. 2d 107, 141, 816 N. E. 2d 322, 341–342 (2004) (citing law review articles for the proposition that the constitutionality of the death penalty for nonhomicide crimes "is the subject of debate"); or from a decision of a state intermediate court that has been superseded by a more specific statement of the law by the State's supreme court, compare, *e.g., Parker* v. *State*, 216 Ga. App. 649, 650, n. 1, 455 S. E. 2d 360, 361, n. 1 (1995) (characterizing *Coker* as holding that the death penalty "is no longer permitted for rape where the victim is not killed"), with *Velazquez*, 283 Ga., at 208, 657 S. E. 2d, at 840 ("[T]he United States Supreme Court . . . has yet [to] addres[s] whether the death penalty is unconstitutionally disproportionate for the crime of raping a child").

The Supreme Court of Florida's opinion in *Buford* could be read to support respondent's argument. But even there the state court recognized that "[t]he [Supreme] Court has yet to decide whether [*Coker*'s rationale] holds true for the rape of a child" and made explicit that it was extending the reasoning but not the holding of *Coker* in striking down the death penalty for child rape. 403 So. 2d, at 950, 951. The same is true of the Supreme Court of California's opinion in *Hernandez, supra,* at 867, 69 P. 3d, at 464.

We conclude on the basis of this review that there is no clear indication that state legislatures have misinterpreted *Coker* to hold that the death penalty for child rape is unconstitutional. The small number of States that have enacted this penalty, then, is relevant to determining whether there is a consensus against capital punishment for this crime.

C

Respondent insists that the six States where child rape is a capital offense, along with the States that have proposed but not yet enacted applicable death penalty legislation, reflect a consistent direction of change in support of the death penalty for child rape. Consistent change might counterbalance an otherwise weak demonstration of consensus. See *Atkins*, 536 U. S., at 315 ("It is not so much the number of these States that is significant, but the consistency of the direction of change"); *Roper,* 543 U. S., at 565 ("Impressive in *Atkins* was the rate of abolition of the death penalty for the mentally retarded"). But whatever the significance of consistent change where it is cited to show emerging support for expanding the scope of the death penalty, no showing of consistent change has been made in this case.

Respondent and its *amici* identify five States where, in

their view, legislation authorizing capital punishment for child rape is pending. See Brief for Missouri Governor Matt Blunt et al. as *Amici Curiae* 2, 14. It is not our practice, nor is it sound, to find contemporary norms based upon state legislation that has been proposed but not yet enacted. There are compelling reasons not to do so here. Since the briefs were submitted by the parties, legislation in two of the five States has failed. See, *e.g.*, S. 195, 66th Gen. Assembly, 2d Reg. Sess. (Colo. 2008) (rejected by Senate Appropriations Committee on Apr. 11, 2008); S. 2596, 2008 Leg., Reg. Sess. (Miss. 2008) (rejected by House Committee on Mar. 18, 2008). In Tennessee, the house bills were rejected almost a year ago, and the senate bills appear to have died in committee. See H. R. 601, 105th Gen. Assembly, 1st Reg. Sess. (2007) (taken off Subcommittee Calendar on Apr. 4, 2007); H. R. 662, *ibid.* (failed for lack of second on Mar. 21, 2007); H. R. 1099, *ibid.* (taken off notice for Judiciary Committee calendar on May 16, 2007); S. 22, *ibid.* (referred to General Subcommittee of Senate Finance, Ways, and Means Committee on June 11, 2007); S. 157, *ibid.* (referred to Senate Judiciary Committee on Feb. 7, 2007; action deferred until Jan. 2008); S. 841, *ibid.* (referred to General Subcommittee of Senate Judiciary Committee on Mar. 27, 2007). In Alabama, the recent legislation is similar to a bill that failed in 2007. Compare H. R. 456, 2008 Leg., Reg. Sess. (2008), with H. R. 335, 2007 Leg., Reg. Sess. (2007). And in Missouri, the 2008 legislative session has ended, tabling the pending legislation. See Mo. Const., Art. III, §20(a).

Aside from pending legislation, it is true that in the last 13 years there has been change towards making child rape a capital offense. This is evidenced by six new death penalty statutes, three enacted in the last two years. But this showing is not as significant as the data in *Atkins*, where 18 States between 1986 and 2001 had enacted legislation prohibiting the execution of mentally retarded persons. See *Atkins, supra,* at 313–315. Respondent argues the instant case is like *Roper* because, there, only five States had shifted their positions between 1989 and 2005, one less State than here. See *Roper, supra,* at 565. But in *Roper*, we emphasized that, though the pace of abolition was not as great as in *Atkins*, it was counterbalanced by the total number of States that had recognized the impropriety of executing juvenile offenders. See 543 U. S., at 566–567. When we decided *Stanford* v. *Kentucky*, 492 U. S. 361 (1989), 12 death penalty States already prohibited the execution of any juvenile under 18, and 15 prohibited the execution of any juvenile under 17. See *Roper, supra,* at 566–567 ("If anything, this shows that the impropriety of executing juveniles between 16 and 18 years of age gained wide recognition earlier"). Here, the total number of States to have made child rape a capital offense after *Furman* is six. This is not an indication of a trend or change in direction comparable to the one supported by data in *Roper*. The evidence here bears a closer resemblance to the evidence of state activity in *Enmund*, where we found a national consensus against the death penalty for vicarious felony murder despite eight jurisdictions having authorized the practice. See 458 U. S., at 789, 792.

D

There are measures of consensus other than legislation. Statistics about the number of executions may inform the consideration whether capital punishment for the crime of child rape is regarded as unacceptable in our society. See, *e.g., id.,* at 794–795; *Roper, supra,* at 564–565; *Atkins, supra,* at 316; Cf. *Coker,* 433 U. S., at 596–597 (plurality opinion). These statistics confirm our determination from our review of state statutes that there is a social consensus against the death penalty for the crime of child rape.

Nine States—Florida, Georgia, Louisiana, Mississippi,

Montana, Oklahoma, South Carolina, Tennessee, and Texas—have permitted capital punishment for adult or child rape for some length of time between the Court's 1972 decision in *Furman* and today. See *supra*, at 12; *Coker, supra*, at 595 (plurality opinion). Yet no individual has been executed for the rape of an adult or child since 1964, and no execution for any other nonhomicide offense has been conducted since 1963. See Historical Statistics of the United States, at 5–262 to 5–263 (Table Ec343–357). Cf. *Thompson* v. *Oklahoma*, 487 U. S. 815, 852–853 (1988) (O'Connor, J., concurring in judgment) (that "four decades have gone by since the last execution of a defendant who was younger than 16 at the time of the offense . . . support[s] the inference of a national consensus opposing the death penalty for 15-year-olds").

Louisiana is the only State since 1964 that has sentenced an individual to death for the crime of child rape; and petitioner and Richard Davis, who was convicted and sentenced to death for the aggravated rape of a 5-year-old child by a Louisiana jury in December 2007, see *State* v. *Davis,* Case No. 262,971 (1st Jud. Dist., Caddo Parish, La.) (cited in Brief for Respondent 42, and n. 38), are the only two individuals now on death row in the United States for a nonhomicide offense.

After reviewing the authorities informed by contemporary norms, including the history of the death penalty for this and other nonhomicide crimes, current state statutes and new enactments, and the number of executions since 1964, we conclude there is a national consensus against capital punishment for the crime of child rape.

IV
A

As we have said in other Eighth Amendment cases, objective evidence of contemporary values as it relates to punishment for child rape is entitled to great weight, but it does not end our inquiry. "[T]he Constitution contemplates that in the end our own judgment will be brought to bear on the question of the acceptability of the death penalty under the Eighth Amendment." *Coker, supra,* at 597 (plurality opinion); see also *Roper, supra,* at 563; *Enmund, supra,* at 797 ("[I]t is for us ultimately to judge whether the Eighth Amendment permits imposition of the death penalty"). We turn, then, to the resolution of the question before us, which is informed by our precedents and our own understanding of the Constitution and the rights it secures.

It must be acknowledged that there are moral grounds to question a rule barring capital punishment for a crime against an individual that did not result in death. These facts illustrate the point. Here the victim's fright, the sense of betrayal, and the nature of her injuries caused more prolonged physical and mental suffering than, say, a sudden killing by an unseen assassin. The attack was not just on her but on her childhood. For this reason, we should be most reluctant to rely upon the language of the plurality in *Coker*, which posited that, for the victim of rape, "life may not be nearly so happy as it was" but it is not beyond repair. 433 U. S., at 598. Rape has a permanent psychological, emotional, and sometimes physical impact on the child. See C. Bagley & K. King, Child Sexual Abuse: The Search for Healing 2–24, 111–112 (1990); Finkelhor & Browne, Assessing the Long-Term Impact of Child Sexual Abuse: A Review and Conceptualization in Handbook on Sexual Abuse of Children 55–60 (L. Walker ed. 1988). We cannot dismiss the years of long anguish that must be endured by the victim of child rape.

It does not follow, though, that capital punishment is a proportionate penalty for the crime. The constitutional prohibition against excessive or cruel and unusual punishments mandates that the State's power to punish "be exercised within the limits of civilized standards." *Trop,*

356 U. S., at 99, 100 (plurality opinion). Evolving standards of decency that mark the progress of a maturing society counsel us to be most hesitant before interpreting the Eighth Amendment to allow the extension of the death penalty, a hesitation that has special force where no life was taken in the commission of the crime. It is an established principle that decency, in its essence, presumes respect for the individual and thus moderation or restraint in the application of capital punishment. See *id.,* at 100.

To date the Court has sought to define and implement this principle, for the most part, in cases involving capital murder. One approach has been to insist upon general rules that ensure consistency in determining who receives a death sentence. See *California* v. *Brown,* 479 U. S. 538, 541 (1987) ("[D]eath penalty statutes [must] be structured so as to prevent the penalty from being administered in an arbitrary and unpredictable fashion" (citing *Gregg,* 428 U. S. 153; *Furman,* 408 U. S. 238)); *Godfrey* v. *Georgia,* 446 U. S. 420, 428 (1980) (plurality opinion) (requiring a State to give narrow and precise definition to the aggravating factors that warrant its imposition). At the same time the Court has insisted, to ensure restraint and moderation in use of capital punishment, on judging the "character and record of the individual offender and the circumstances of the particular offense as a constitutionally indispensable part of the process of inflicting the penalty of death." *Woodson,* 428 U. S., at 304 (plurality opinion); *Lockett* v. *Ohio,* 438 U. S. 586, 604–605 (1978) (plurality opinion).

The tension between general rules and case-specific circumstances has produced results not all together satisfactory. See *Tuilaepa* v. *California,* 512 U. S. 967, 973 (1994) ("The objectives of these two inquiries can be in some tension, at least when the inquiries occur at the same time"); *Walton* v. *Arizona,* 497 U. S. 639, 664–665 (1990) (SCALIA, J., concurring in part and concurring in judgment) ("The latter requirement quite obviously destroys whatever rationality and predictability the former requirement was designed to achieve"). This has led some Members of the Court to say we should cease efforts to resolve the tension and simply allow legislatures, prosecutors, courts, and juries greater latitude. See *id.,* at 667–673 (advocating that the Court adhere to the *Furman* line of cases and abandon the *Woodson-Lockett* line of cases). For others the failure to limit these same imprecisions by stricter enforcement of narrowing rules has raised doubts concerning the constitutionality of capital punishment itself. See *Baze* v. *Rees,* 553 U. S. ___, ___–___ (2008) (slip op., at 13–17) (STEVENS, J., concurring in judgment); *Furman, supra,* at 310–314 (White, J., concurring); *Callins* v. *Collins,* 510 U. S. 1141, 1144–1145 (1994) (Blackmun, J., dissenting from denial of certiorari).

Our response to this case law, which is still in search of a unifying principle, has been to insist upon confining the instances in which capital punishment may be imposed. See *Gregg, supra,* at 187, 184 (joint opinion of Stewart, Powell, and STEVENS, JJ.) (because "death as a punishment is unique in its severity and irrevocability," capital punishment must be reserved for those crimes that are "so grievous an affront to humanity that the only adequate response may be the penalty of death" (citing in part *Furman,* 408 U. S., at 286–291 (Brennan, J., concurring); *id.,* at 306 (Stewart, J., concurring))); see also *Roper,* 543 U. S., at 569 (the Eighth Amendment requires that "the death penalty is reserved for a narrow category of crimes and offenders").

Our concern here is limited to crimes against individual persons. We do not address, for example, crimes defining and punishing treason, espionage, terrorism, and drug kingpin activity, which are offenses against the State. As it relates to crimes against individuals, though, the death penalty should not be expanded to instances where the victim's life was not taken. We said in *Coker* of adult rape:

> "We do not discount the seriousness of rape as a crime. It is highly reprehensible, both in a moral sense and in its almost total contempt for the personal integrity and autonomy of the female victim.... Short of homicide, it is the 'ultimate violation of self.'... [But] [t]he murderer kills; the rapist, if no more than that, does not.... We have the abiding conviction that the death penalty, which 'is unique in its severity and irrevocability,' is an excessive penalty for the rapist who, as such, does not take human life." 433 U. S., at 597–598 (plurality opinion) (citation omitted).

The same distinction between homicide and other serious violent offenses against the individual informed the Court's analysis in *Enmund*, 458 U. S. 782, where the Court held that the death penalty for the crime of vicarious felony murder is disproportionate to the offense. The Court repeated there the fundamental, moral distinction between a "murderer" and a "robber," noting that while "robbery is a serious crime deserving serious punishment," it is not like death in its "severity and irrevocability." *Id.,* at 797 (internal quotation marks omitted).

Consistent with evolving standards of decency and the teachings of our precedents we conclude that, in determining whether the death penalty is excessive, there is a distinction between intentional first-degree murder on the one hand and nonhomicide crimes against individual persons, even including child rape, on the other. The latter crimes may be devastating in their harm, as here, but "in terms of moral depravity and of the injury to the person and to the public," *Coker,* 433 U. S., at 598 (plurality opinion), they cannot be compared to murder in their "severity and irrevocability." *Ibid.*

In reaching our conclusion we find significant the number of executions that would be allowed under respondent's approach. The crime of child rape, considering its reported incidents, occurs more often than first-degree murder. Approximately 5,702 incidents of vaginal, anal, or oral rape of a child under the age of 12 were reported nationwide in 2005; this is almost twice the total incidents of intentional murder for victims of all ages (3,405) reported during the same period. See Inter-University Consortium for Political and Social Research, National Incident-Based Reporting System, 2005, Study No. 4720, http://www.icpsr.umich.edu (as visited June 12, 2008, and available in Clerk of Court's case file). Although we have no reliable statistics on convictions for child rape, we can surmise that, each year, there are hundreds, or more, of these convictions just in jurisdictions that permit capital punishment. Cf. Brief for Louisiana Association of Criminal Defense Lawyers et al. as *Amici Curiae* 1–2, and n. 2 (noting that there are now at least 70 capital rape indictments pending in Louisiana and estimating the actual number to be over 100). As a result of existing rules, see generally *Godfrey*, 446 U. S., at 428–433 (plurality opinion), only 2.2% of convicted first-degree murderers are sentenced to death, see Blume, Eisenberg, & Wells, Explaining Death Row's Population and Racial Composition, 1 J. of Empirical Legal Studies 165, 171 (2004). But under respondent's approach, the 36 States that permit the death penalty could sentence to death all persons convicted of raping a child less than 12 years of age. This could not be reconciled with our evolving standards of decency and the necessity to constrain the use of the death penalty.

It might be said that narrowing aggravators could be used in this context, as with murder offenses, to ensure the death penalty's restrained application. We find it difficult to identify standards that would guide the decisionmaker so the penalty is reserved for the most severe

Opinion of the Court

cases of child rape and yet not imposed in an arbitrary way. Even were we to forbid, say, the execution of first-time child rapists, see *supra* at 12, or require as an aggravating factor a finding that the perpetrator's instant rape offense involved multiple victims, the jury still must balance, in its discretion, those aggravating factors against mitigating circumstances. In this context, which involves a crime that in many cases will overwhelm a decent person's judgment, we have no confidence that the imposition of the death penalty would not be so arbitrary as to be "freakis[h]," *Furman,* 408 U. S., at 310 (Stewart, J., concurring). We cannot sanction this result when the harm to the victim, though grave, cannot be quantified in the same way as death of the victim.

It is not a solution simply to apply to this context the aggravating factors developed for capital murder. The Court has said that a State may carry out its obligation to ensure individualized sentencing in capital murder cases by adopting sentencing processes that rely upon the jury to exercise wide discretion so long as there are narrowing factors that have some "'common-sense core of meaning . . . that criminal juries should be capable of understanding.'" *Tuilaepa,* 512 U. S., at 975 (quoting *Jurek* v. *Texas,* 428 U. S. 262, 279 (1976) (White, J., concurring in judgment)). The Court, accordingly, has upheld the constitutionality of aggravating factors ranging from whether the defendant was a "'cold-blooded, pitiless slayer,'" *Arave* v. *Creech,* 507 U. S. 463, 471–474 (1993), to whether the "perpetrator inflict[ed] mental anguish or physical abuse before the victim's death," *Walton,* 497 U. S., at 654, to whether the defendant "'would commit criminal acts of violence that would constitute a continuing threat to society,'" *Jurek, supra,* at 269-270, 274–276 (joint opinion of Stewart, Powell, and STEVENS, JJ.). All of these standards have the potential to result in some inconsistency of application.

Opinion of the Court

As noted above, the resulting imprecision and the tension between evaluating the individual circumstances and consistency of treatment have been tolerated where the victim dies. It should not be introduced into our justice system, though, where death has not occurred.

Our concerns are all the more pronounced where, as here, the death penalty for this crime has been most infrequent. See Part III–D, *supra*. We have developed a foundational jurisprudence in the case of capital murder to guide the States and juries in imposing the death penalty. Starting with *Gregg*, 428 U. S. 153, we have spent more than 32 years articulating limiting factors that channel the jury's discretion to avoid the death penalty's arbitrary imposition in the case of capital murder. Though that practice remains sound, beginning the same process for crimes for which no one has been executed in more than 40 years would require experimentation in an area where a failed experiment would result in the execution of individuals undeserving of the death penalty. Evolving standards of decency are difficult to reconcile with a regime that seeks to expand the death penalty to an area where standards to confine its use are indefinite and obscure.

B

Our decision is consistent with the justifications offered for the death penalty. *Gregg* instructs that capital punishment is excessive when it is grossly out of proportion to the crime or it does not fulfill the two distinct social purposes served by the death penalty: retribution and deterrence of capital crimes. See *id.*, at 173, 183, 187 (joint opinion of Stewart, Powell, and STEVENS, JJ.); see also *Coker,* 433 U. S., at 592 (plurality opinion) ("A punishment might fail the test on either ground").

As in *Coker*, here it cannot be said with any certainty that the death penalty for child rape serves no deterrent or retributive function. See *id.*, at 593, n. 4 (concluding

Opinion of the Court

that the death penalty for rape might serve "legitimate ends of punishment" but nevertheless is disproportionate to the crime). Cf. *Gregg, supra,* at 185–186 (joint opinion of Stewart, Powell, and STEVENS, JJ.) ("[T]here is no convincing empirical evidence either supporting or refuting th[e] view [that the death penalty serves as a significantly greater deterrent than lesser penalties]. We may nevertheless assume safely that there are murderers . . . for whom . . . the death penalty undoubtedly is a significant deterrent"); *id.,* at 186 (the value of capital punishment, and its contribution to acceptable penological goals, typically is a "complex factual issue the resolution of which properly rests with the legislatures"). This argument does not overcome other objections, however. The incongruity between the crime of child rape and the harshness of the death penalty poses risks of overpunishment and counsels against a constitutional ruling that the death penalty can be expanded to include this offense.

The goal of retribution, which reflects society's and the victim's interests in seeing that the offender is repaid for the hurt he caused, see *Atkins,* 536 U. S., at 319; *Furman, supra,* at 308 (Stewart, J., concurring), does not justify the harshness of the death penalty here. In measuring retribution, as well as other objectives of criminal law, it is appropriate to distinguish between a particularly depraved murder that merits death as a form of retribution and the crime of child rape. See Part IV–A, *supra*; *Coker, supra,* at 597–598 (plurality opinion).

There is an additional reason for our conclusion that imposing the death penalty for child rape would not further retributive purposes. In considering whether retribution is served, among other factors we have looked to whether capital punishment "has the potential . . . to allow the community as a whole, including the surviving family and friends of the victim, to affirm its own judgment that the culpability of the prisoner is so serious that the ultimate penalty must be sought and imposed." *Panetti* v. *Quarterman*, 551 U. S. ___, ___ (2007) (slip op., at 26). In considering the death penalty for nonhomicide offenses this inquiry necessarily also must include the question whether the death penalty balances the wrong to the victim. Cf. *Roper,* 543 U. S., at 571.

It is not at all evident that the child rape victim's hurt is lessened when the law permits the death of the perpetrator. Capital cases require a long-term commitment by those who testify for the prosecution, especially when guilt and sentencing determinations are in multiple proceedings. In cases like this the key testimony is not just from the family but from the victim herself. During formative years of her adolescence, made all the more daunting for having to come to terms with the brutality of her experience, L. H. was required to discuss the case at length with law enforcement personnel. In a public trial she was required to recount once more all the details of the crime to a jury as the State pursued the death of her stepfather. Cf. G. Goodman et al., Testifying in Criminal Court: Emotional Effects on Child Sexual Assault Victims 50, 62, 72 (1992); Brief for National Association of Social Workers et al. as *Amici Curiae* 17–21. And in the end the State made L. H. a central figure in its decision to seek the death penalty, telling the jury in closing statements: "[L. H.] is asking you, asking you to set up a time and place when he dies." Tr. 121 (Aug. 26, 2003).

Society's desire to inflict the death penalty for child rape by enlisting the child victim to assist it over the course of years in asking for capital punishment forces a moral choice on the child, who is not of mature age to make that choice. The way the death penalty here involves the child victim in its enforcement can compromise a decent legal system; and this is but a subset of fundamental difficulties capital punishment can cause in the administration and enforcement of laws proscribing child rape.

Opinion of the Court

There are, moreover, serious systemic concerns in prosecuting the crime of child rape that are relevant to the constitutionality of making it a capital offense. The problem of unreliable, induced, and even imagined child testimony means there is a "special risk of wrongful execution" in some child rape cases. *Atkins, supra,* at 321. See also Brief for National Association of Criminal Defense Lawyers et al. as *Amici Curiae* 5–17. This undermines, at least to some degree, the meaningful contribution of the death penalty to legitimate goals of punishment. Studies conclude that children are highly susceptible to suggestive questioning techniques like repetition, guided imagery, and selective reinforcement. See Ceci & Friedman, The Suggestibility of Children: Scientific Research and Legal Implications, 86 Cornell L. Rev. 33, 47 (2000) (there is "strong evidence that children, especially young children, are suggestible to a significant degree—even on abuse-related questions"); Gross, Jacoby, Matheson, Montgomery, & Patil, Exonerations in the United States 1989 Through 2003, 95 J. Crim. L. & C. 523, 539 (2005) (discussing allegations of abuse at the Little Rascals Day Care Center); see also Quas, Davis, Goodman, & Myers, Repeated Questions, Deception, and Children's True and False Reports of Body Touch, 12 Child Maltreatment 60, 61–66 (2007) (finding that 4- to 7-year-olds "were able to maintain [a] lie about body touch fairly effectively when asked repeated, direct questions during a mock forensic interview").

Similar criticisms pertain to other cases involving child witnesses; but child rape cases present heightened concerns because the central narrative and account of the crime often comes from the child herself. She and the accused are, in most instances, the only ones present when the crime was committed. See *Pennsylvania* v. *Ritchie,* 480 U. S. 39, 60 (1987). Cf. Goodman, Testifying in Criminal Court, at 118. And the question in a capital case is not just the fact of the crime, including, say, proof of rape as distinct from abuse short of rape, but details bearing upon brutality in its commission. These matters are subject to fabrication or exaggeration, or both. See Ceci and Friedman, *supra;* Quas, *supra.* Although capital punishment does bring retribution, and the legislature here has chosen to use it for this end, its judgment must be weighed, in deciding the constitutional question, against the special risks of unreliable testimony with respect to this crime.

With respect to deterrence, if the death penalty adds to the risk of non-reporting, that, too, diminishes the penalty's objectives. Underreporting is a common problem with respect to child sexual abuse. See Hanson, Resnick, Saunders, Kilpatrick, & Best, Factors Related to the Reporting of Childhood Rape, 23 Child Abuse & Neglect 559, 564 (1999) (finding that about 88% of female rape victims under the age of 18 did not disclose their abuse to authorities); Smith et al., Delay in Disclosure of Childhood Rape: Results From A National Survey, 24 Child Abuse & Neglect 273, 278–279 (2000) (finding that 72% of women raped as children disclosed their abuse to someone, but that only 12% of the victims reported the rape to authorities). Although we know little about what differentiates those who report from those who do not report, see Hanson, *supra,* at 561, one of the most commonly cited reasons for nondisclosure is fear of negative consequences for the perpetrator, a concern that has special force where the abuser is a family member, see Goodman-Brown, Edelstein, Goodman, Jones, & Gordon, Why Children Tell: A Model of Children's Disclosure of Sexual Abuse, 27 Child Abuse & Neglect 525, 527–528 (2003); Smith, *supra,* at 283–284 (finding that, where there was a relationship between perpetrator and victim, the victim was likely to keep the abuse a secret for a longer period of time, perhaps because of a "greater sense of loyalty or emotional bond"); Hanson, *supra*, at 565–566, and Table 3 (finding that a "significantly greater proportion of reported than nonreported cases involved a stranger"); see also *Ritchie, supra,* at 60. The experience of the *amici* who work with child victims indicates that, when the punishment is death, both the victim and the victim's family members may be more likely to shield the perpetrator from discovery, thus increasing underreporting. See Brief for National Association of Social Workers et al. as *Amici Curiae* 11–13. As a result, punishment by death may not result in more deterrence or more effective enforcement.

In addition, by in effect making the punishment for child rape and murder equivalent, a State that punishes child rape by death may remove a strong incentive for the rapist not to kill the victim. Assuming the offender behaves in a rational way, as one must to justify the penalty on grounds of deterrence, the penalty in some respects gives less protection, not more, to the victim, who is often the sole witness to the crime. See Rayburn, Better Dead Than R(ap)ed?: The Patriarchal Rhetoric Driving Capital Rape Statutes, 78 St. John's L. Rev. 1119, 1159–1160 (2004). It might be argued that, even if the death penalty results in a marginal increase in the incentive to kill, this is counterbalanced by a marginally increased deterrent to commit the crime at all. Whatever balance the legislature strikes, however, uncertainty on the point makes the argument for the penalty less compelling than for homicide crimes.

Each of these propositions, standing alone, might not establish the unconstitutionality of the death penalty for the crime of child rape. Taken in sum, however, they demonstrate the serious negative consequences of making child rape a capital offense. These considerations lead us to conclude, in our independent judgment, that the death penalty is not a proportional punishment for the rape of a child.

V

Our determination that there is a consensus against the death penalty for child rape raises the question whether the Court's own institutional position and its holding will have the effect of blocking further or later consensus in favor of the penalty from developing. The Court, it will be argued, by the act of addressing the constitutionality of the death penalty, intrudes upon the consensus-making process. By imposing a negative restraint, the argument runs, the Court makes it more difficult for consensus to change or emerge. The Court, according to the criticism, itself becomes enmeshed in the process, part judge and part the maker of that which it judges.

These concerns overlook the meaning and full substance of the established proposition that the Eighth Amendment is defined by "the evolving standards of decency that mark the progress of a maturing society." *Trop*, 356 U. S., at 101 (plurality opinion). Confirmed by repeated, consistent rulings of this Court, this principle requires that use of the death penalty be restrained. The rule of evolving standards of decency with specific marks on the way to full progress and mature judgment means that resort to the penalty must be reserved for the worst of crimes and limited in its instances of application. In most cases justice is not better served by terminating the life of the perpetrator rather than confining him and preserving the possibility that he and the system will find ways to allow him to understand the enormity of his offense. Difficulties in administering the penalty to ensure against its arbitrary and capricious application require adherence to a rule reserving its use, at this stage of evolving standards and in cases of crimes against individuals, for crimes that take the life of the victim.

The judgment of the Supreme Court of Louisiana upholding the capital sentence is reversed. This case is remanded for further proceedings not inconsistent with this opinion.

It is so ordered.

Cite as: 554 U. S. ____ (2008)   1

ALITO, J., dissenting

SUPREME COURT OF THE UNITED STATES

No. 07–343

PATRICK KENNEDY, PETITIONER *v.* LOUISIANA

ON WRIT OF CERTIORARI TO THE SUPREME COURT OF LOUISIANA

[June 25, 2008]

JUSTICE ALITO, with whom THE CHIEF JUSTICE, JUSTICE SCALIA, and JUSTICE THOMAS join, dissenting.

The Court today holds that the Eighth Amendment categorically prohibits the imposition of the death penalty for the crime of raping a child. This is so, according to the Court, no matter how young the child, no matter how many times the child is raped, no matter how many children the perpetrator rapes, no matter how sadistic the crime, no matter how much physical or psychological trauma is inflicted, and no matter how heinous the perpetrator's prior criminal record may be. The Court provides two reasons for this sweeping conclusion: First, the Court claims to have identified "a national consensus" that the death penalty is never acceptable for the rape of a child; second, the Court concludes, based on its "independent judgment," that imposing the death penalty for child rape is inconsistent with "'the evolving standards of decency that mark the progress of a maturing society.'" *Ante*, at 8, 15, 16 (citation omitted). Because neither of these justifications is sound, I respectfully dissent.

I
A

I turn first to the Court's claim that there is "a national consensus" that it is never acceptable to impose the death penalty for the rape of a child. The Eighth Amendment's requirements, the Court writes, are "determined not by the standards that prevailed" when the Amendment was adopted but "by the norms that 'currently prevail.'" *Ante,* at 8 (quoting *Atkins* v. *Virginia,* 536 U. S. 304, 311 (2002)). In assessing current norms, the Court relies primarily on the fact that only 6 of the 50 States now have statutes that permit the death penalty for this offense. But this statistic is a highly unreliable indicator of the views of state lawmakers and their constituents. As I will explain, dicta in this Court's decision in *Coker* v. *Georgia,* 433 U. S. 584 (1977), has stunted legislative consideration of the question whether the death penalty for the targeted offense of raping a young child is consistent with prevailing standards of decency. The *Coker* dicta gave state legislators and others good reason to fear that any law permitting the imposition of the death penalty for this crime would meet precisely the fate that has now befallen the Louisiana statute that is currently before us, and this threat strongly discouraged state legislators—regardless of their own values and those of their constituents—from supporting the enactment of such legislation.

As the Court correctly concludes, the *holding* in *Coker* was that the Eighth Amendment prohibits the death penalty for the rape of an "'adult woman,'" and thus *Coker* does not control our decision here. See *ante,* at 17. But the reasoning of the Justices in the majority had broader implications.

Two Members of the *Coker* majority, Justices Brennan and Marshall, took the position that the death penalty is always unconstitutional. 433 U. S., at 600 (Brennan, J., concurring in judgment) and (Marshall, J., concurring in judgment). Four other Justices, who joined the controlling plurality opinion, suggested that the Georgia capital rape statute was unconstitutional for the simple reason that the impact of a rape, no matter how heinous, is not grievous enough to justify capital punishment. In the words of

ALITO, J., dissenting

the plurality: "Life is over for the victim of the murderer; for the rape victim, life may not be nearly so happy as it was, but it is not over and normally is not beyond repair." *Id.,* at 598. The plurality summarized its position as follows: "We have the abiding conviction that the death penalty . . . is an excessive penalty for the rapist who, as such, does not take human life." *Ibid.*

The implications of the *Coker* plurality opinion were plain. Justice Powell, who concurred in the judgment overturning the death sentence in the case at hand, did not join the plurality opinion because he understood it to draw "a bright line between murder and all rapes—regardless of the degree of brutality of the rape or the effect upon the victim." *Id.,* at 603. If Justice Powell read *Coker* that way, it was reasonable for state legislatures to do the same.

Understandably, state courts have frequently read *Coker* in precisely this way. The Court is correct that state courts have generally understood the limited scope of the *holding* in *Coker, ante,* at 18, but lower courts and legislators also take into account—and I presume that this Court wishes them to continue to take into account—the Court's dicta. And that is just what happened in the wake of *Coker*. Four years after *Coker,* when Florida's capital child rape statute was challenged, the Florida Supreme Court, while correctly noting that this Court had not *held* that the Eighth Amendment bars the death penalty for child rape, concluded that "[t]he reasoning of the justices in *Coker v. Georgia* compels us to hold that a sentence of death is grossly disproportionate and excessive punishment for the crime of sexual assault and is therefore forbidden by the Eighth Amendment as cruel and unusual punishment." *Buford* v. *State,* 403 So. 2d 943, 951 (1981).

Numerous other state courts have interpreted the *Coker* dicta similarly. See *State* v. *Barnum,* 921 So. 2d 513, 526 (Fla. 2005) (citing *Coker* as holding that "'a sentence of

ALITO, J., dissenting

death is grossly disproportionate and excessive punishment for the crime of rape,'" not merely the rape of an adult woman); *People* v. *Huddleston*, 212 Ill. 2d. 107, 141, 816 N. E. 2d 322, 341 (2004) (recognizing that "the constitutionality of state statutes that impose the death penalty for nonhomicide crimes is the subject of debate" after *Coker*); *People* v. *Hernandez*, 30 Cal. 4th 835, 867, 69 P. 3d 446, 464–467 (2003) (*Coker* "rais[ed] serious doubts that the federal Constitution permitted the death penalty for any offense not requiring the actual taking of human life" because "[a]lthough the high court did not expressly hold [in *Coker*] that the Eighth Amendment prohibits capital punishment for *all* crimes not resulting in death, the plurality stressed that the crucial difference between rape and murder is that a rapist 'does not take human life'"); *State* v. *Gardner*, 947 P. 2d 630, 653 (Utah 1997) ("The *Coker* holding leaves no room for the conclusion that any rape, even an 'inhuman' one involving torture and aggravated battery but not resulting in death, would constitutionally sustain imposition of the death penalty"); *Parker* v. *State*, 216 Ga. App. 649, n. 1, 455 S. E. 2d 360, 361, n. 1 (1995) (citing *Coker* for the proposition that the death penalty "is no longer permitted for rape where the victim is not killed"); *Leatherwood* v. *State*, 548 So. 2d 389, 406 (Miss. 1989) (Robertson, J., concurring) ("There is as much chance of the Supreme Court sanctioning death as a penalty for *any* non-fatal rape as the proverbial snowball enjoys in the nether regions"); *State* v. *Coleman*, 185 Mont. 299, 327–328, 605 P. 2d 1000, 1017 (1979) (stating that "[t]he decision of the Court in *Coker* v. *Georgia* is relevant only to crimes for which the penalty has been imposed which did *not* result in the loss of a life" (citations omitted)); *Boyer* v. *State*, 240 Ga. 170, 240 S. E. 2d 68 (1977) *(per curiam)* (stating that "[s]ince death to the victim did not result ... the death penalty for rape must be set aside"); see also 2005–1981 (La. Sup. Ct. 5/22/07), 957 So.

ALITO, J., dissenting

2d 757, 794 (case below) (Calogero, C. J., dissenting) (citing the comments of the *Coker* plurality and concluding that the Louisiana child rape law cannot pass constitutional muster).[1]

For the past three decades, these interpretations have posed a very high hurdle for state legislatures considering the passage of new laws permitting the death penalty for the rape of a child. The enactment and implementation of any new state death penalty statute—and particularly a new type of statute such as one that specifically targets the rape of young children—imposes many costs. There is

---

[1] Commentators have expressed similar views. See Fleming, Louisiana's Newest Capital Crime: The Death Penalty for Child Rape, 89 J. Crim. L. & C. 717, 727 (1999) (the *Coker* Court drew a line between "crimes which result in loss of life, and crimes which do not"); Baily, Death is Different, Even on the Bayou: The Disproportionality of Crime, 55 Wash. & Lee L. Rev. 1335, 1357 (1998) (noting that "[m]any post-Coker cases interpreting the breadth of *Coker*'s holding suggest that the Mississippi Supreme Court's narrow reading of *Coker* in Upshaw is a minority position"); Matura, When Will It Stop? The Use of the Death Penalty for Non-homicide Crimes, 24 J. Legis. 249, 255 (1998) (stating that the *Coker* Court did not "draw a distinction between the rape of an adult woman and the rape of a minor"); Garvey, "As the Gentle Rain from Heaven": Mercy in Capital Sentencing, 81 Cornell L. Rev. 989, 1009, n. 74 (1996) (stating that courts generally understand *Coker* to prohibit death sentences for crimes other than murder); Nanda, Recent Developments in the United States and Internationally Regarding Capital Punishment—An Appraisal, 67 St. John's L. Rev. 523, 532 (1993) (finding that *Coker* stands for the proposition that a death sentence is excessive when the victim is not killed); Ellis, Guilty but Mentally Ill and the Death Penalty: Punishment Full of Sound and Fury, Signifying Nothing, 43 Duke L. J. 87, 94 (1994) (referencing *Coker* to require capital offenses to be defined by unjustified human death); Dingerson, Reclaiming the Gavel: Making Sense out of the Death Penalty Debate in State Legislatures, 18 N. Y. U. Rev. L. & Soc. Change 873, 878 (1991) (stating that *Coker* "ruled that the imposition of the death penalty for crimes from which no death results violates the cruel and unusual punishment provision of the eighth amendment" and that "[n]o subsequent Supreme Court decision has challenged this precedent").

the burden of drafting an innovative law that must take into account this Court's exceedingly complex Eighth Amendment jurisprudence. Securing passage of controversial legislation may interfere in a variety of ways with the enactment of other bills on the legislative agenda. Once the statute is enacted, there is the burden of training and coordinating the efforts of those who must implement the new law. Capital prosecutions are qualitatively more difficult than noncapital prosecutions and impose special emotional burdens on all involved. When a capital sentence is imposed under the new law, there is the burden of keeping the prisoner on death row and the lengthy and costly project of defending the constitutionality of the statute on appeal and in collateral proceedings. And if the law is eventually overturned, there is the burden of new proceedings on remand. Moreover, conscientious state lawmakers, whatever their personal views about the morality of imposing the death penalty for child rape, may defer to this Court's dicta, either because they respect our authority and expertise in interpreting the Constitution or merely because they do not relish the prospect of being held to have violated the Constitution and contravened prevailing "standards of decency." Accordingly, the *Coker* dicta gave state legislators a strong incentive not to push for the enactment of new capital child-rape laws even though these legislators and their constituents may have believed that the laws would be appropriate and desirable.

B

The Court expresses doubt that the *Coker* dicta had this effect, but the skepticism is unwarranted. It would be quite remarkable if state legislators were not influenced by the considerations noted above. And although state legislatures typically do not create legislative materials like those produced by Congress, there is evidence that proposals to permit the imposition of the death penalty for

ALITO, J., dissenting

child rape were opposed on the ground that enactment would be futile and costly.

In Oklahoma, the opposition to the State's capital child-rape statute argued that *Coker* had already ruled the death penalty unconstitutional as applied to cases of rape. See Oklahoma Senate News Release, Senator Nichols Targets Child Predators with Death Penalty, Child Abuse Response Team, May 26, 2006, on line at http://www.oksenate.gov/news/press_releases/press_releases_ 2006/pr20060526d.htm (all Internet materials as visited June 23, 2008, and available in Clerk of Court's case file). Likewise, opponents of South Carolina's capital child-rape law contended that the statute would waste state resources because it would undoubtedly be held unconstitutional. See The State, Death Penalty Plan in Spotlight: Attorney General to Advise Senate Panel on Proposal for Repeat Child Rapists, Mar. 28, 2006 (quoting Laura Hudson, spokeswoman for the S. C. Victim Assistance Network, as stating that "'[w]e don't need to be wasting state money to have an appeal to the [United States] Supreme Court, knowing we are going to lose it'"). Representative Fletcher Smith of the South Carolina House of Representatives forecast that the bill would not meet constitutional standards because "death isn't involved." See Davenport, Emotion Drives Child Rape Death Penalty Debate in South Carolina, Associated Press, Apr. 4, 2006.

In Texas, opponents of that State's capital child-rape law argued that *Coker*'s reasoning doomed the proposal. House Research Organization Bill Analysis, Mar. 5, 2007 (stating that "the law would impose an excessive punishment and fail to pass the proportionality test established by the U. S. Supreme Court" and arguing that "Texas should not enact a law of questionable constitutionality simply because it is politically popular, especially given clues by the U. S. Supreme Court that death penalty laws that would be rarely imposed or that are not supported by a broad national consensus would be ruled unconstitutional").

C

Because of the effect of the *Coker* dicta, the Court is plainly wrong in comparing the situation here to that in *Atkins* or *Roper* v. *Simmons*, 543 U. S. 551 (2005). See *ante*, at 14–15. *Atkins* concerned the constitutionality of imposing the death penalty on a mentally retarded defendant. Thirteen years earlier, in *Penry* v. *Lynaugh*, 492 U. S. 302 (1989), the Court had held that this was permitted by the Eighth Amendment, and therefore, during the time between *Penry* and *Atkins,* state legislators had reason to believe that this Court would follow its prior precedent and uphold statutes allowing such punishment.

The situation in *Roper* was similar. *Roper* concerned a challenge to the constitutionality of imposing the death penalty on a defendant who had not reached the age of 18 at the time of the crime. Sixteen years earlier in *Stanford* v. *Kentucky*, 492 U. S. 361 (1989), the Court had rejected a similar challenge, and therefore state lawmakers had cause to believe that laws allowing such punishment would be sustained.

When state lawmakers believe that their decision will prevail on the question whether to permit the death penalty for a particular crime or class of offender, the legislators' resolution of the issue can be interpreted as an expression of their own judgment, informed by whatever weight they attach to the values of their constituents. But when state legislators think that the enactment of a new death penalty law is likely to be futile, inaction cannot reasonably be interpreted as an expression of their understanding of prevailing societal values. In that atmosphere, legislative inaction is more likely to evidence acquiescence.

ALITO, J., dissenting

D

If anything can be inferred from state legislative developments, the message is very different from the one that the Court perceives. In just the past few years, despite the shadow cast by the *Coker* dicta, five States have enacted targeted capital child-rape laws. See Ga. Code Ann. §16–6–1 (1999); Mont. Code Ann. §45–5–503 (1997); Okla. Stat., Tit. 10, §7115(K) (West Supp. 2008); S. C. Code Ann. §16–3–655(C)(1) (Supp. 2007); Tex. Penal Code Ann. §§22.021(a), 12.42(c)(3) (West Supp. 2007). If, as the Court seems to think, our society is "[e]volving" toward ever higher "standards of decency," *ante*, at 36, these enactments might represent the beginning of a new evolutionary line.

Such a development would not be out of step with changes in our society's thinking since *Coker* was decided. During that time, reported instances of child abuse have increased dramatically;[2] and there are many indications of growing alarm about the sexual abuse of children. In 1994, Congress enacted the Jacob Wetterling Crimes Against Children and Sexually Violent Offender Registration Program, 42 U. S. C. §14071 (2000 ed. and Supp. V),

---

[2] From 1976 to 1986, the number of reported cases of child sexual abuse grew from 6,000 to 132,000, an increase of 2,100%. A. Lurigio, M. Jones, & B. Smith, Child Sexual Abuse: Its Causes, Consequences, and Implications for Probation Practice, 59 Sep Fed. Probation 69 (1995). By 1991, the number of cases totaled 432,000, an increase of another 227%. *Ibid.* In 1995, local child protection services agencies identified 126,000 children who were victims of either substantiated or indicated sexual abuse. Nearly 30% of those child victims were between the age of four and seven. Rape, Abuse & Incest National Network Statistics, online at http://www.rainn.org/get-information/ statistics/sexual-assault-victims. There were an estimated 90,000 substantiated cases of child sexual abuse in 2003. Crimes Against Children Research Center, Reports from the States to the National Child Abuse and Neglect Data System, available at www.unh.edu/ccrc/ sexual-abuse/Child%20Sexual%20Abuse.pdf.

ALITO, J., dissenting

which requires States receiving certain federal funds to establish registration systems for convicted sex offenders and to notify the public about persons convicted of the sexual abuse of minors. All 50 States have now enacted such statutes.[3] In addition, at least 21 States and the

---

[3] Ala. Code §§13A–11–200 to 13A–11–203, 1181 (1994); Alaska Stat §§1.56.840, 12.63.010–100, 18.65.087, 28.05.048, 33.30.035 (1994, 1995, and 1995 Cum. Supp.); Ariz. Rev. Stat. Ann. §§13–3821 to –3825 (1989 and Supp. 1995); Ark. Code Ann. §§12–12–901 to –909 (1995); Cal. Penal Code Ann. §§290 to 290.4 (West Supp. 1996); Colo. Rev. Stat. Ann. §18–3–412.5 (Supp. 1996); Conn. Gen. Stat. Ann. §§54–102a to 54–102r (Supp. 1995); Del. Code Ann. Tit. 11, §4120 (1995); Fla. Stat. Ann. §§775.13, 775.22 (1992 and Supp. 1994); Ga. Code Ann. §42–9–44.1 (1994); 1995 Haw. Sess. Laws No. 160 (enacted June 14, 1995); Idaho Code §§9–340(11)(f), 18–8301 to 18–8311 (Supp. 1995); Ill. Comp. Stat. Ann., ch. 730, §§150/1 to 150/10 (2002); Ind. Code §§5–2–12–1 to 5–2–12–13 (West Supp. 1995); 1995 Iowa Legis. Serv. 146 (enacted May 3, 1995); Kan. Stat. Ann. §§22–4901 to 22–4910 (1995); Ky. Rev. Stat. Ann. §§17.500 to 17.540 (West Supp. 1994); La. Stat. Ann. §§15:540 to 15:549 (West Supp. 1995); Me. Rev. Stat. Ann., Tit. 34–A, §§11001 to 11004 (West Supp. 1995); 1995 Md. Laws p. 142 (enacted May 9, 1995); Mass. Gen. Laws Ann., ch. 6, §178D; 1994 Mich. Pub. Acts p. 295 (enacted July 13, 1994); Minn. Stat. §243.166 (1992 and Supp. 1995); Miss. Code Ann. §§45–33–1 to 45–33–19 (Supp. 1995); Mo. Rev. Stat. §§566.600 to 566.625 (Supp. 1996); Mont. Code Ann. §§46–23–501 to 46–23–507 (1994); Neb. Rev. Stat. §§4001 to 4014; Nev. Rev. Stat. §§207.080, 207.151 to 207.157 (1992 and Supp. 1995); N. H. Rev. Stat. Ann. §§632–A:11 to 632–A:19 (Supp. 1995); N. J. Stat. Ann. §§2c:7–1 to 2c:7–11 (1995); N. M. Stat. Ann. §§29–11A–1 to 29–11A–8 (Supp. 1995); N. Y. Correct. Law Ann. §§168 to 168–V (West Supp. 1996); N. C. Gen. Stat. Ann. §§14–208.5–10 (Lexis Supp. 1995); N. D. Cent. Code §12.1–32–15 (Lexis Supp. 1995); Ohio Rev. Code Ann. §§2950.01–.08 (Baldwin 1997); Okla. Stat., Tit. 57, §§582–584 (2003 Supp.); Ore. Rev. Stat. §§181.507 to 181.519 (1993); 1995 Pa. Laws p. 24 (enacted Oct. 24, 1995); R. I. Gen. Laws §11–37–16 (1994); S. C. Code Ann. §23–3–430; S. D. Codified Laws §§22–22–30 to 22–22–41 (Supp. 1995) Tenn. Code Ann. §§40–39–101 to 40–39–108 (2003); Tex. Rev. Civ. Stat. Ann., Art. 6252–13c.1 (Vernon Supp. 1996); Utah Code Ann. §§53–5–212.5, 77–27–21.5 (Lexis Supp. 1995); Vt. Stat. Ann., Tit. 13, §5402; Va. Code Ann. §§19.2–298.1 to 19.2–390.1 (Lexis 1995); Wash. Rev. Code §§4.24.550, 9A.44.130, 9A.44.140, 10.01.200, 70.48.470, 72.09.330 (1992

ALITO, J., dissenting

District of Columbia now have statutes permitting the involuntary commitment of sexual predators,[4] and at least 12 States have enacted residency restrictions for sex offenders.[5]

---

and Supp. 1996); W. Va. Code §§61–8F–1 to 61–8F–8 (Lexis Supp. 1995); Wis. Stat. §175.45 (Supp. 1995); Wyo. Stat. Ann. §§7–19–301 to 7–19–306 (1995).

[4]Those States are Arizona, California, Connecticut, the District of Columbia, Florida, Illinois, Iowa, Kansas, Kentucky, Massachusetts, Minnesota, Missouri, Nebraska, New Jersey, North Dakota, Oregon, Pennsylvania, South Carolina, Texas, Virginia, Washington, and Wisconsin. See Ariz. Rev. Stat. §§36–3701 to 36–3713 (West 2003 and Supp. 2007); Cal. Welf. & Inst. Code Ann. §§6600 to 6609.3 (West 1998 and Supp. 2008); Conn. Gen. Stat. §17a–566 (1998); D. C. Code §§22–3803 to 22–3811 (2001); Fla. Stat. §§394.910 to 394.931 (West 2002 and Supp. 2005); Ill. Comp. Stat., ch. 725, §§207/1 to 207/99 (2002); Iowa Code §§229A.1–.16 (Supp. 2005); Kan. Stat. Ann. §59–29a02 (2004 and Supp. 2005); Ky. Rev. Stat. Ann. §202A.051 (West ___); Mass. Gen. Laws, ch. 123A (1989); Minn. Stat. §253B.02 (1992); Mo. Ann. Stat. §§632.480 to 632.513 (West 2000 and Supp. 2006); Neb. Rev. Stat. §§83–174 to 83–174.05 (2007); N. J. Stat. Ann. §§30:4–27.24 to 30:4–27.38 (West Supp. 2004); N. D. Cent. Code Ann. §25–03.3 (Lexis 2002); Ore. Rev. Stat. §426.005 (1998); Pa. Stat. Ann., Tit. 42, §§9791 to 9799.9 (2007); S. C. Code Ann. §§44–48–10 to 44–48–170 (2002 and Supp. 2007); Tex. Health & Safety Code Ann. §§841.001 to 841.147 (West 2003); Va. Code Ann. §§37.2–900 to 37.2–920 (2006 and Supp. 2007); Wash. Rev. Code §71.09.010 (West 1992 and Supp. 2002); Wis. Stat. §980.01–13 (2005).

[5]See Ala. Code §15–20–26 (Supp. 2000) (restricts sex offenders from residing or accepting employment within 2,000 feet of school or childcare facility); Ark. Code Ann. §5–14–128 (Supp. 2007) (unlawful for level three or four sex offenders to reside within 2,000 feet of school or daycare center); Cal. Penal Code Ann. §3003 (West Supp. 2008) (parolees may not live within 35 miles of victim or witnesses, and certain sex offenders on parole may not live within a quarter mile from a primary school); Fla. Stat. §947.1405(7)(a)(2) (2001) (released sex offender with victim under 18 prohibited from living within 1,000 feet of a school, daycare center, park, playground, or other place where children regularly congregate); Ga. Code Ann. §42–1–13 (Supp. 2007) (sex offenders required to register shall not reside within 1,000 feet of any childcare facility, school, or area where minors congregate); Ill. Comp. Stat., ch. 720, §5/11–9.3(b–5) (Supp. 2008) (child sex offenders prohibited from

Seeking to counter the significance of the new capital child-rape laws enacted during the past two years, the Court points out that in recent months efforts to enact similar laws in five other States have stalled. *Ante*, at 21. These developments, however, all took place after our decision to grant certiorari in this case, see 552 U. S. ___ (2008), which gave state legislators reason to delay the enactment of new legislation until the constitutionality of such laws was clarified. And there is no evidence of which I am aware that these legislative initiatives failed because the proposed laws were viewed as inconsistent with our society's standards of decency.

On the contrary, the available evidence suggests otherwise. For example, in Colorado, the Senate Appropriations Committee in April voted 6 to 4 against Senate Bill 195, reportedly because it "would have cost about $616,000 next year for trials, appeals, public defenders, and prison costs." Associated Press, Lawmakers Reject Death Penalty for Child Sex Abusers, Denver Post, Apr. 11, 2008. Likewise, in Tennessee, the capital child-rape bill was withdrawn in committee "because of the high associated costs." The bill's sponsor stated that "'[b]ecause of the state's budget situation, we thought to with-

---

knowingly residing within 500 feet of schools); Ky. Rev. Stat. Ann. §17.495 (West 2000) (registered sex offenders on supervised release shall not reside within 1,000 feet of school or childcare facility); La. Rev. Stat. Ann. §14:91.1 (West Supp. 2004) (sexually violent predators shall not reside within 1,000 feet of schools unless permission is given by school superintendent); Ohio Rev. Code Ann. §2950.031 (Lexis 2003) (sex offenders prohibited from residing within 1,000 feet of school); Okla. Stat., Tit. 57, §590 (West 2003) (prohibits sex offenders from residing within 2,000 feet of schools or educational institutions); Ore. Rev. Stat. §§144.642, 144.643 (1999) (incorporates general prohibition on supervised sex offenders living near places where children reside); Tenn. Code Ann. §40–39–111 (2006) (repealed by Acts 2004, ch. 921, §4, effective Aug. 1, 2004) (sex offenders prohibited from establishing residence within 1,000 feet of school, childcare facility, or victim).

ALITO, J., dissenting

draw that bill. . . . We'll revisit it next year to see if we can reduce the cost of the fiscal note.'" Green, Small Victory in Big Fight for Tougher Sex Abuse Laws, The Leaf-Chronicle, May 8, 2008, p. 1A. Thus, the failure to enact capital child-rape laws cannot be viewed as evidence of a moral consensus against such punishment.

E

Aside from its misleading tally of current state laws, the Court points to two additional "objective indicia" of a "national consensus," *ante,* at 11, but these arguments are patent makeweights. The Court notes that Congress has not enacted a law permitting the death penalty for the rape of a child, *ante,* at 12–13, but due to the territorial limits of the relevant federal statutes, very few rape cases, not to mention child-rape cases, are prosecuted in federal court. See 18 U. S. C. §§2241, 2242 (2000 ed. and Supp. V); United States Sentencing Commission, Report to Congress: Analysis of Penalties for Federal Rape Cases, p. 10, Table 1. Congress' failure to enact a death penalty statute for this tiny set of cases is hardly evidence of Congress' assessment of our society's values.

Finally, the Court argues that statistics about the number of executions in rape cases support its perception of a "national consensus," but here too the statistics do not support the Court's position. The Court notes that the last execution for the rape of a child occurred in 1964, *ante,* at 23, but the Court fails to mention that litigation regarding the constitutionality of the death penalty brought executions to a halt across the board in the late 1960's. In 1965 and 1966, there were a total of eight executions for all offenses, and from 1968 until 1977, the year when *Coker* was decided, there were no executions for any crimes.[6]

---

[6] Department of Justice, Bureau of Justice Statistics, online at http://www.ojp.usdoj.gov/bjs/glance/tables/exetab.htm; see also Death Penalty Information Center, Executions in the U. S. 1608–2002:

ALITO, J., dissenting

The Court also fails to mention that in Louisiana, since the state law was amended in 1995 to make child rape a capital offense, prosecutors have asked juries to return death verdicts in four cases. See *State* v. *Dickerson*, 01–1287 (La. App. 6/26/02), 822 So. 2d 849 (2002); *State* v. *LeBlanc*, 01–1322 (La. App. 5/13/01), 788 So. 2d 1255; 2005–1981 (La. Sup. Ct. 5/22/07), 957 So. 2d 757; *State* v. *Davis,* Case No. 262,971 (1st Jud. Dist., Caddo Parish, La.) (cited in Brief for Respondent 42, and n. 38). In two of those cases, Louisiana juries imposed the death penalty. See 2005–1981 (La. Sup. Ct. 5/22/07), 957 So. 2d 757; *Davis, supra.* This 50% record is hardly evidence that juries share the Court's view that the death penalty for the rape of a young child is unacceptable under even the most aggravated circumstances.[7]

F

In light of the points discussed above, I believe that the "objective indicia" of our society's "evolving standards of decency" can be fairly summarized as follows. Neither Congress nor juries have done anything that can plausibly be interpreted as evidencing the "national consensus" that the Court perceives. State legislatures, for more than 30 years, have operated under the ominous shadow of the *Coker* dicta and thus have not been free to express their own understanding of our society's standards of decency. And in the months following our grant of certiorari in this case, state legislatures have had an additional reason to pause. Yet despite the inhibiting legal atmosphere that has prevailed since 1977, six States have recently enacted new, targeted child-rape laws.

I do not suggest that six new state laws necessarily

The ESPY File Executions by Date (2007), online at http://www.death penaltyinfo.org/ESPYyear.pdf.

[7] Of course, the other five capital child rape statutes are too recent for any individual to have been sentenced to death under them.

establish a "national consensus" or even that they are sure evidence of an ineluctable trend. In terms of the Court's metaphor of moral evolution, these enactments might have turned out to be an evolutionary dead end. But they might also have been the beginning of a strong new evolutionary line. We will never know, because the Court today snuffs out the line in its incipient stage.

II
A

The Court is willing to block the potential emergence of a national consensus in favor of permitting the death penalty for child rape because, in the end, what matters is the Court's "own judgment" regarding "the acceptability of the death penalty." *Ante,* at 24. Although the Court has much to say on this issue, most of the Court's discussion is not pertinent to the Eighth Amendment question at hand. And once all of the Court's irrelevant arguments are put aside, it is apparent that the Court has provided no coherent explanation for today's decision.

In the next section of this opinion, I will attempt to weed out the arguments that are not germane to the Eighth Amendment inquiry, and in the final section, I will address what remains.

B

A major theme of the Court's opinion is that permitting the death penalty in child-rape cases is not in the best interests of the victims of these crimes and society at large. In this vein, the Court suggests that it is more painful for child-rape victims to testify when the prosecution is seeking the death penalty. *Ante,* at 32. The Court also argues that "a State that punishes child rape by death may remove a strong incentive for the rapist not to kill the victim," *ante,* at 35, and may discourage the reporting of child rape, *ante,* at 34–35.

ALITO, J., dissenting

These policy arguments, whatever their merits, are simply not pertinent to the question whether the death penalty is "cruel and unusual" punishment. The Eighth Amendment protects the right of an accused. It does not authorize this Court to strike down federal or state criminal laws on the ground that they are not in the best interests of crime victims or the broader society. The Court's policy arguments concern matters that legislators should—and presumably do—take into account in deciding whether to enact a capital child-rape statute, but these arguments are irrelevant to the question that is before us in this case. Our cases have cautioned against using "'the aegis of the Cruel and Unusual Punishment Clause' to cut off the normal democratic processes," *Atkins* v. *Virginia*, 536 U. S. 304, 323 (2002) (Rehnquist, C. J., dissenting), in turn quoting *Gregg* v. *Georgia*, 428 U. S. 153, 176 (1976), (joint opinion of Stewart, Powell, and STEVENS, JJ.), but the Court forgets that warning here.

The Court also contends that laws permitting the death penalty for the rape of a child create serious procedural problems. Specifically, the Court maintains that it is not feasible to channel the exercise of sentencing discretion in child-rape cases, *ante*, at 28–29, and that the unreliability of the testimony of child victims creates a danger that innocent defendants will be convicted and executed, *ante*, at 33–34. Neither of these contentions provides a basis for striking down all capital child-rape laws no matter how carefully and narrowly they are crafted.

The Court's argument regarding the structuring of sentencing discretion is hard to comprehend. The Court finds it "difficult to identify standards that would guide the decisionmaker so the penalty is reserved for the most severe cases of child rape and yet not imposed in an arbitrary way." *Ante*, at 28–29. Even assuming that the age of a child is not alone a sufficient factor for limiting sentencing discretion, the Court need only examine the child-

ALITO, J., dissenting

rape laws recently enacted in Texas, Oklahoma, Montana, and South Carolina, all of which use a concrete factor to limit quite drastically the number of cases in which the death penalty may be imposed. In those States, a defendant convicted of the rape of a child may be sentenced to death only if the defendant has a prior conviction for a specified felony sex offense. See Mont. Code Ann. §45–5–503(3)(c) (2007) ("If the offender was previously convicted of [a felony sexual offense] . . . the offender shall be . . . punished by death . . ."); Okla. Stat., Tit. 10, §7115(K) (West Supp. 2008) ("Notwithstanding any other provision of law, any parent or other person convicted of forcible anal or oral sodomy, rape, rape by instrumentation, or lewd molestation of a child under fourteen (14) years of age subsequent to a previous conviction for any offense of forcible anal or oral sodomy, rape, rape by instrumentation, or lewd molestation of a child under fourteen (14) years of age shall be punished by death"); S. C. Code Ann. §16–3–655(C)(1) (Supp. 2007) ("If the [defendant] has previously been convicted of, pled guilty or nolo contendere to, or adjudicated delinquent for first degree criminal sexual conduct with a minor who is less than eleven years of age . . . he must be punished by death or by imprisonment for life"); Tex. Penal Code Ann. §12.42(c)(3) (2007 Supp.); ("[A] defendant shall be punished for a capital felony if it is shown on the trial of an offense under Section 22.021 . . . that the defendant has previously been finally convicted of [a felony sexual offense against a victim younger than fourteen years of age]").

Moreover, it takes little imagination to envision other limiting factors that a State could use to structure sentencing discretion in child rape cases. Some of these might be: whether the victim was kidnapped, whether the defendant inflicted severe physical injury on the victim, whether the victim was raped multiple times, whether the rapes occurred over a specified extended period, and whether there were multiple victims.

The Court refers to limiting standards that are "indefinite and obscure," *ante*, at 30, but there is nothing indefinite or obscure about any of the above-listed aggravating factors. Indeed, they are far more definite and clear-cut than aggravating factors that we have found to be adequate in murder cases. See, *e.g.*, *Arave* v. *Creech*, 507 U. S. 463, 471 (1993) (whether the defendant was a "'cold-blooded, pitiless slayer'"); *Walton* v. *Arizona*, 497 U. S. 639, 646 (1990) (whether the "'perpetrator inflict[ed] mental anguish or physical abuse before the victim's death'"); *Jurek* v. *Texas*, 428 U. S. 262, 269 (1976) (joint opinion of Stewart, Powell, and STEVENS, JJ.) (whether the defendant "'would commit criminal acts of violence that would constitute a continuing threat to society'"). For these reasons, concerns about limiting sentencing discretion provide no support for the Court's blanket condemnation of all capital child-rape statutes.

That sweeping holding is also not justified by the Court's concerns about the reliability of the testimony of child victims. First, the Eighth Amendment provides a poor vehicle for addressing problems regarding the admissibility or reliability of evidence, and problems presented by the testimony of child victims are not unique to capital cases. Second, concerns about the reliability of the testimony of child witnesses are not present in every child-rape case. In the case before us, for example, there was undisputed medical evidence that the victim was brutally raped, as well as strong independent evidence that petitioner was the perpetrator. Third, if the Court's evidentiary concerns have Eighth Amendment relevance, they could be addressed by allowing the death penalty in only those child-rape cases in which the independent evidence is sufficient to prove all the elements needed for conviction and imposition of a death sentence. There is precedent for requiring special corroboration in certain criminal cases. For exam-

ALITO, J., dissenting

ple, some jurisdictions do not allow a conviction based on the uncorroborated testimony of an accomplice. See, *e.g.*, Ala. Code 12–21–222 (1986); Alaska Stat. §12.45.020 (1984); Ark. Code Ann. §16–89–111(e)(1) (1977); Cal. Penal Code Ann. §1111 (West 1985); Ga. Code Ann. §24–4–8 (1995); Idaho Code §19–2117 (Lexis 1979); Minn. Stat. §634.04 (1983); Mont. Code Ann. §46–16–213 (1985); Nev. Rev. Stat. §175.291 (1985); N. D. Cent. Code Ann. §29–21–14 (1974); Okla. St., Tit. 22, §742 (West 1969); Ore. Rev. Stat. §136.440 (1984); S. D. Codified Laws §23A–22–8 (1979). A State wishing to permit the death penalty in child-rape cases could impose an analogous corroboration requirement.

C

After all the arguments noted above are put aside, what is left? What remaining grounds does the Court provide to justify its independent judgment that the death penalty for child rape is categorically unacceptable? I see two.

1

The first is the proposition that we should be "most hesitant before interpreting the Eighth Amendment to allow the *extension* of the death penalty." *Ante,* at 25 (emphasis added); see also *ante,* at 27, 30 (referring to expansion of the death penalty). But holding that the Eighth Amendment does not categorically prohibit the death penalty for the rape of a young child would not "extend" or "expand" the death penalty. Laws enacted by the state legislatures are presumptively constitutional, *Gregg,* 428 U. S., at 175 (joint opinion of Stewart, Powell, and STEVENS, JJ.) ("[I]n assessing a punishment selected by a democratically elected legislature against the constitutional measure, we presume its validity"), and until today, this Court has not held that capital child rape laws are unconstitutional, see *ante,* at 17 (*Coker* "does not speak to the constitutionality of the death penalty for child rape, an issue not then before the Court"). Consequently, upholding the constitutionality of such a law would not "extend" or "expand" the death penalty; rather, it would confirm the status of presumptive constitutionality that such laws have enjoyed up to this point. And in any event, this Court has previously made it clear that "[t]he Eighth Amendment is not a ratchet, whereby a temporary consensus on leniency for a particular crime fixes a permanent constitutional maximum, disabling States from giving effect to altered beliefs and responding to changed social conditions." *Harmelin* v. *Michigan*, 501 U. S. 957, 990 (1991) (principal opinion); see also *Gregg, supra,* at 176 (joint opinion of Stewart, Powell, and STEVENS, JJ.).

2

The Court's final—and, it appears, principal— justification for its holding is that murder, the only crime for which defendants have been executed since this Court's 1976 death penalty decisions,[8] is unique in its moral depravity and in the severity of the injury that it inflicts on the victim and the public. See *ante,* at 27–28. But the Court makes little attempt to defend these conclusions.

With respect to the question of moral depravity, is it really true that every person who is convicted of capital murder and sentenced to death is more morally depraved than every child rapist? Consider the following two cases. In the first, a defendant robs a convenience store and watches as his accomplice shoots the store owner. The defendant acts recklessly, but was not the triggerman and did not intend the killing. See, *e.g., Tison* v. *Arizona,* 481

---

[8] *Gregg* v. *Georgia,* 428 U. S. 153 (1976); *Proffitt* v. *Florida,* 428 U. S. 242 (1976); *Jurek* v. *Texas,* 428 U. S. 262 (1976); *Woodson* v. *North Carolina,* 428 U. S. 280 (1976); *Roberts* v. *Louisiana,* 428 U. S. 325 (1976).

U. S. 137 (1987). In the second case, a previously convicted child rapist kidnaps, repeatedly rapes, and tortures multiple child victims. Is it clear that the first defendant is more morally depraved than the second?

The Court's decision here stands in stark contrast to *Atkins* and *Roper*, in which the Court concluded that characteristics of the affected defendants—mental retardation in *Atkins* and youth in *Roper*—diminished their culpability. See *Atkins*, 536 U. S., at 305; *Roper*, 543 U. S., at 571. Nor is this case comparable to *Enmund* v. *Florida*, 458 U. S. 782 (1982), in which the Court held that the Eighth Amendment prohibits the death penalty where the defendant participated in a robbery during which a murder was committed but did not personally intend for lethal force to be used. I have no doubt that, under the prevailing standards of our society, robbery, the crime that the petitioner in *Enmund* intended to commit, does not evidence the same degree of moral depravity as the brutal rape of a young child. Indeed, I have little doubt that, in the eyes of ordinary Americans, the very worst child rapists—predators who seek out and inflict serious physical and emotional injury on defenseless young children—are the epitome of moral depravity.

With respect to the question of the harm caused by the rape of child in relation to the harm caused by murder, it is certainly true that the loss of human life represents a unique harm, but that does not explain why other grievous harms are insufficient to permit a death sentence. And the Court does not take the position that no harm other than the loss of life is sufficient. The Court takes pains to limit its holding to "crimes against individual persons" and to exclude "offenses against the State," a category that the Court stretches—without explanation—to include "drug kingpin activity." *Ante*, at 26. But the Court makes no effort to explain why the harm caused by such crimes is necessarily greater than the harm caused by the rape of young children. This is puzzling in light of the Court's acknowledgment that "[r]ape has a permanent psychological, emotional, and sometimes physical impact on the child." *Ante,* at 24. As the Court aptly recognizes, "[w]e cannot dismiss the years of long anguish that must be endured by the victim of child rape." *Ibid.*

The rape of any victim inflicts great injury, and "[s]ome victims are so grievously injured physically or psychologically that life *is* beyond repair." *Coker,* 433 U. S., at 603 (opinion of Powell, J.). "The immaturity and vulnerability of a child, both physically and psychologically, adds a devastating dimension to rape that is not present when an adult is raped." Meister, Murdering Innocence: The Constitutionality of Capital Child Rape Statutes, 45 Ariz. L. Rev. 197, 208–209 (2003). See also *State* v. *Wilson,* 96–1392, p. 6 (La. Sup. Ct. 12/13/96),685 So. 2d 1063, 1067; Broughton, "On Horror's Head Horrors Accumulate": A Reflective Comment on Capital Child Rape Legislation, 39 Duquesne L. Rev. 1, 38 (2000). Long-term studies show that sexual abuse is "grossly intrusive in the lives of children and is harmful to their normal psychological, emotional and sexual development in ways which no just or humane society can tolerate." C. Bagley & K. King, Child Sexual Abuse: The Search for Healing 2 (1990).

It has been estimated that as many as 40% of 7- to 13-year-old sexual assault victims are considered "seriously disturbed." A. Lurigio, M. Jones, & B. Smith, Child Sexual Abuse: Its Causes, Consequences, and Implications for Probation Practice, 59 Sep Fed. Probation 69, 70 (1995). Psychological problems include sudden school failure, unprovoked crying, dissociation, depression, insomnia, sleep disturbances, nightmares, feelings of guilt and inferiority, and self-destructive behavior, including an increased incidence of suicide. Meister, *supra,* at 209; Broughton, *supra,* at 38; Glazer, Child Rapists Beware! The Death Penalty and Louisiana's Amended Aggravated

Rape Statute, 25 Am. J. Crim. L. 79, 88 (1997).

The deep problems that afflict child-rape victims often become society's problems as well. Commentators have noted correlations between childhood sexual abuse and later problems such as substance abuse, dangerous sexual behaviors or dysfunction, inability to relate to others on an interpersonal level, and psychiatric illness. Broughton, *supra*, at 38; Glazer, *supra,* at 89; Handbook on Sexual Abuse of Children 7 (L. Walker ed. 1988). Victims of child rape are nearly 5 times more likely than nonvictims to be arrested for sex crimes and nearly 30 times more likely to be arrested for prostitution. *Ibid.*

The harm that is caused to the victims and to society at large by the worst child rapists is grave. It is the judgment of the Louisiana lawmakers and those in an increasing number of other States that these harms justify the death penalty. The Court provides no cogent explanation why this legislative judgment should be overridden. Conclusory references to "decency," "moderation," "restraint," "full progress," and "moral judgment" are not enough.

III

In summary, the Court holds that the Eighth Amendment categorically rules out the death penalty in even the most extreme cases of child rape even though: (1) This holding is not supported by the original meaning of the Eighth Amendment; (2) neither *Coker* nor any other prior precedent commands this result; (3) there are no reliable "objective indicia" of a "national consensus" in support of the Court's position; (4) sustaining the constitutionality of the state law before us would not "extend" or "expand" the death penalty; (5) this Court has previously rejected the proposition that the Eighth Amendment is a one-way ratchet that prohibits legislatures from adopting new capital punishment statutes to meet new problems; (6) the worst child rapists exhibit the epitome of moral depravity;

and (7) child rape inflicts grievous injury on victims and on society in general.

The party attacking the constitutionality of a state statute bears the "heavy burden" of establishing that the law is unconstitutional. *Gregg*, 428 U. S., at 175 (joint opinion of Stewart, Powell, and STEVENS, JJ.). That burden has not been discharged here, and I would therefore affirm the decision of the Louisiana Supreme Court.

Syllabus

NOTE: Where it is feasible, a syllabus (headnote) will be released, as is being done in connection with this case, at the time the opinion is issued. The syllabus constitutes no part of the opinion of the Court but has been prepared by the Reporter of Decisions for the convenience of the reader. See *United States* v. *Detroit Timber & Lumber Co.,* 200 U. S. 321, 337.

SUPREME COURT OF THE UNITED STATES

Syllabus

SNYDER *v.* PHELPS ET AL.

CERTIORARI TO THE UNITED STATES COURT OF APPEALS FOR THE FOURTH CIRCUIT

No. 09–751. Argued October 6, 2010—Decided March 2, 2011

For the past 20 years, the congregation of the Westboro Baptist Church has picketed military funerals to communicate its belief that God hates the United States for its tolerance of homosexuality, particularly in America's military. The church's picketing has also condemned the Catholic Church for scandals involving its clergy. Fred Phelps, who founded the church, and six Westboro Baptist parishioners (all relatives of Phelps) traveled to Maryland to picket the funeral of Marine Lance Corporal Matthew Snyder, who was killed in Iraq in the line of duty. The picketing took place on public land approximately 1,000 feet from the church where the funeral was held, in accordance with guidance from local law enforcement officers. The picketers peacefully displayed their signs—stating, *e.g.,* "Thank God for Dead Soldiers," "Fags Doom Nations," "America is Doomed," "Priests Rape Boys," and "You're Going to Hell"—for about 30 minutes before the funeral began. Matthew Snyder's father (Snyder), petitioner here, saw the tops of the picketers' signs when driving to the funeral, but did not learn what was written on the signs until watching a news broadcast later that night.

Snyder filed a diversity action against Phelps, his daughters—who participated in the picketing—and the church (collectively Westboro) alleging, as relevant here, state tort claims of intentional infliction of emotional distress, intrusion upon seclusion, and civil conspiracy. A jury held Westboro liable for millions of dollars in compensatory and punitive damages. Westboro challenged the verdict as grossly excessive and sought judgment as a matter of law on the ground that the First Amendment fully protected its speech. The District Court reduced the punitive damages award, but left the verdict otherwise intact. The Fourth Circuit reversed, concluding that Westboro's statements were entitled to First Amendment protection because those statements were on matters of public concern, were not provably false, and were expressed solely through hyperbolic rhetoric.

Held: The First Amendment shields Westboro from tort liability for its picketing in this case. Pp. 5–15.

(a) The Free Speech Clause of the First Amendment can serve as a defense in state tort suits, including suits for intentional infliction of emotional distress. *Hustler Magazine, Inc.* v. *Falwell,* 485 U. S. 46, 50-51. Whether the First Amendment prohibits holding Westboro liable for its speech in this case turns largely on whether that speech is of public or private concern, as determined by all the circumstances of the case. "[S]peech on public issues occupies the '"highest rung of the hierarchy of First Amendment values"' and is entitled to special protection." *Connick* v. *Myers,* 461 U. S. 138, 145. Although the boundaries of what constitutes speech on matters of public concern are not well defined, this Court has said that speech is of public concern when it can "be fairly considered as relating to any matter of political, social, or other concern to the community," *id.,* at 146, or when it "is a subject of general interest and of value and concern to the public," *San Diego* v. *Roe,* 543 U. S. 77, 83–84. A statement's arguably "inappropriate or controversial character . . . is irrelevant to the question whether it deals with a matter of public concern." *Rankin* v. *McPherson,* 483 U. S. 378, 387. Pp. 5–7.

To determine whether speech is of public or private concern, this Court must independently examine the "'content, form, and context,'" of the speech "'as revealed by the whole record.'" *Dun & Bradstreet, Inc.* v. *Greenmoss Builders, Inc.,* 472 U. S. 749, 761. In considering content, form, and context, no factor is dispositive, and it is necessary to evaluate all aspects of the speech. Pp. 7–8.

The "content" of Westboro's signs plainly relates to public, rather than private, matters. The placards highlighted issues of public import—the political and moral conduct of the United States and its citizens, the fate of the Nation, homosexuality in the military, and scandals involving the Catholic clergy—and Westboro conveyed its views on those issues in a manner designed to reach as broad a public audience as possible. Even if a few of the signs were viewed as containing messages related to a particular individual, that would not change the fact that the dominant theme of Westboro's demonstration spoke to broader public issues. P. 8.

The "context" of the speech—its connection with Matthew Snyder's funeral—cannot by itself transform the nature of Westboro's speech. The signs reflected Westboro's condemnation of much in modern society, and it cannot be argued that Westboro's use of speech on public issues was in any way contrived to insulate a personal attack on

Cite as: 562 U. S. ____ (2011)　　3

Syllabus

Snyder from liability. Westboro had been actively engaged in speaking on the subjects addressed in its picketing long before it became aware of Matthew Snyder, and there can be no serious claim that the picketing did not represent Westboro's honestly held beliefs on public issues. Westboro may have chosen the picket location to increase publicity for its views, and its speech may have been particularly hurtful to Snyder. That does not mean that its speech should be afforded less than full First Amendment protection under the circumstances of this case. Pp. 8–10.

That said, "'[e]ven protected speech is not equally permissible in all places and at all times.'" *Frisby* v. *Schultz,* 487 U. S. 474, 479. Westboro's choice of where and when to conduct its picketing is not beyond the Government's regulatory reach—it is "subject to reasonable time, place, or manner restrictions." *Clark* v. *Community for Creative Non-Violence,* 468 U. S. 288, 293. The facts here are quite different, however, both with respect to the activity being regulated and the means of restricting those activities, from the few limited situations where the Court has concluded that the location of targeted picketing can be properly regulated under provisions deemed content neutral. *Frisby, supra,* at 477; *Madsen* v. *Women's Health Center, Inc.,* 512 U. S. 753, 768, distinguished. Maryland now has a law restricting funeral picketing but that law was not in effect at the time of these events, so this Court has no occasion to consider whether that law is a "reasonable time, place, or manner restrictio[n]" under the standards announced by this Court. *Clark, supra,* at 293. Pp. 10–12.

The "special protection" afforded to what Westboro said, in the whole context of how and where it chose to say it, cannot be overcome by a jury finding that the picketing was "outrageous" for purposes of applying the state law tort of intentional infliction of emotional distress. That would pose too great a danger that the jury would punish Westboro for its views on matters of public concern. For all these reasons, the jury verdict imposing tort liability on Westboro for intentional infliction of emotional distress must be set aside. Pp. 12–13.

(b) Snyder also may not recover for the tort of intrusion upon seclusion. He argues that he was a member of a captive audience at his son's funeral, but the captive audience doctrine—which has been applied sparingly, see *Rowan* v. *Post Office Dept.,* 397 U. S. 728, 736–738; *Frisby, supra,* at 484–485—should not be expanded to the circumstances here. Westboro stayed well away from the memorial service, Snyder could see no more than the tops of the picketers' signs, and there is no indication that the picketing interfered with the funeral service itself. Pp. 13–14.

(c) Because the First Amendment bars Snyder from recovery for in-

Syllabus

tentional infliction of emotional distress or intrusion upon seclusion—the allegedly unlawful activity Westboro conspired to accomplish—Snyder also cannot recover for civil conspiracy based on those torts. P. 14.

(d) Westboro addressed matters of public import on public property, in a peaceful manner, in full compliance with the guidance of local officials. It did not disrupt Mathew Snyder's funeral, and its choice to picket at that time and place did not alter the nature of its speech. Because this Nation has chosen to protect even hurtful speech on public issues to ensure that public debate is not stifled, Westboro must be shielded from tort liability for its picketing in this case. Pp. 14–15.

580 F. 3d 206, affirmed.

ROBERTS, C. J., delivered the opinion of the Court, in which SCALIA, KENNEDY, THOMAS, GINSBURG, BREYER, SOTOMAYOR, and KAGAN, JJ., joined. BREYER, J., filed a concurring opinion. ALITO, J., filed a dissenting opinion.

Opinion of the Court

NOTICE: This opinion is subject to formal revision before publication in the preliminary print of the United States Reports. Readers are requested to notify the Reporter of Decisions, Supreme Court of the United States, Washington, D. C. 20543, of any typographical or other formal errors, in order that corrections may be made before the preliminary print goes to press.

SUPREME COURT OF THE UNITED STATES

No. 09–751

ALBERT SNYDER, PETITIONER v. FRED W. PHELPS, SR., ET AL.

ON WRIT OF CERTIORARI TO THE UNITED STATES COURT OF APPEALS FOR THE FOURTH CIRCUIT

[March 2, 2011]

CHIEF JUSTICE ROBERTS delivered the opinion of the Court.

A jury held members of the Westboro Baptist Church liable for millions of dollars in damages for picketing near a soldier's funeral service. The picket signs reflected the church's view that the United States is overly tolerant of sin and that God kills American soldiers as punishment. The question presented is whether the First Amendment shields the church members from tort liability for their speech in this case.

I

A

Fred Phelps founded the Westboro Baptist Church in Topeka, Kansas, in 1955. The church's congregation believes that God hates and punishes the United States for its tolerance of homosexuality, particularly in America's military. The church frequently communicates its views by picketing, often at military funerals. In the more than 20 years that the members of Westboro Baptist have publicized their message, they have picketed nearly 600 funerals. Brief for Rutherford Institute as *Amicus Curiae* 7, n. 14.

Opinion of the Court

Marine Lance Corporal Matthew Snyder was killed in Iraq in the line of duty. Lance Corporal Snyder's father selected the Catholic church in the Snyders' hometown of Westminster, Maryland, as the site for his son's funeral. Local newspapers provided notice of the time and location of the service.

Phelps became aware of Matthew Snyder's funeral and decided to travel to Maryland with six other Westboro Baptist parishioners (two of his daughters and four of his grandchildren) to picket. On the day of the memorial service, the Westboro congregation members picketed on public land adjacent to public streets near the Maryland State House, the United States Naval Academy, and Matthew Snyder's funeral. The Westboro picketers carried signs that were largely the same at all three locations. They stated, for instance: "God Hates the USA/Thank God for 9/11," "America is Doomed," "Don't Pray for the USA," "Thank God for IEDs," "Thank God for Dead Soldiers," "Pope in Hell," "Priests Rape Boys," "God Hates Fags," "You're Going to Hell," and "God Hates You."

The church had notified the authorities in advance of its intent to picket at the time of the funeral, and the picketers complied with police instructions in staging their demonstration. The picketing took place within a 10- by 25-foot plot of public land adjacent to a public street, behind a temporary fence. App. to Brief for Appellants in No. 08–1026 (CA4), pp. 2282–2285 (hereinafter App.). That plot was approximately 1,000 feet from the church where the funeral was held. Several buildings separated the picket site from the church. *Id.*, at 3758. The Westboro picketers displayed their signs for about 30 minutes before the funeral began and sang hymns and recited Bible verses. None of the picketers entered church property or went to the cemetery. They did not yell or use profanity, and there was no violence associated with the picketing. *Id.*, at 2168, 2371, 2286, 2293.

Opinion of the Court

The funeral procession passed within 200 to 300 feet of the picket site. Although Snyder testified that he could see the tops of the picket signs as he drove to the funeral, he did not see what was written on the signs until later that night, while watching a news broadcast covering the event. *Id.*, at 2084–2086.[1]

B

Snyder filed suit against Phelps, Phelps's daughters, and the Westboro Baptist Church (collectively Westboro or the church) in the United States District Court for the District of Maryland under that court's diversity jurisdiction. Snyder alleged five state tort law claims: defamation, publicity given to private life, intentional infliction of emotional distress, intrusion upon seclusion, and civil conspiracy. Westboro moved for summary judgment contending, in part, that the church's speech was insulated from liability by the First Amendment. See 533 F. Supp. 2d 567, 570 (Md. 2008).

---

[1] A few weeks after the funeral, one of the picketers posted a message on Westboro's Web site discussing the picketing and containing religiously oriented denunciations of the Snyders, interspersed among lengthy Bible quotations. Snyder discovered the posting, referred to by the parties as the "epic," during an Internet search for his son's name. The epic is not properly before us and does not factor in our analysis. Although the epic was submitted to the jury and discussed in the courts below, Snyder never mentioned it in his petition for certiorari. See Pet. for Cert. *i* ("Snyder's claim arose out of Phelps' intentional acts *at Snyder's son's funeral*" (emphasis added)); this Court's Rule 14.1(g) (petition must contain statement "setting out the facts material to consideration of the question presented"). Nor did Snyder respond to the statement in the opposition to certiorari that "[t]hough the epic was asserted as a basis for the claims at trial, the petition . . . appears to be addressing only claims based on the picketing." Brief in Opposition 9. Snyder devoted only one paragraph in the argument section of his opening merits brief to the epic. Given the foregoing and the fact that an Internet posting may raise distinct issues in this context, we decline to consider the epic in deciding this case. See *Ontario* v. *Quon*, 560 U. S. ___, ___–___ (2010) (slip op., at 10–12).

Opinion of the Court

The District Court awarded Westboro summary judgment on Snyder's claims for defamation and publicity given to private life, concluding that Snyder could not prove the necessary elements of those torts. *Id.,* at 572–573. A trial was held on the remaining claims. At trial, Snyder described the severity of his emotional injuries. He testified that he is unable to separate the thought of his dead son from his thoughts of Westboro's picketing, and that he often becomes tearful, angry, and physically ill when he thinks about it. *Id.,* at 588–589. Expert witnesses testified that Snyder's emotional anguish had resulted in severe depression and had exacerbated pre-existing health conditions.

A jury found for Snyder on the intentional infliction of emotional distress, intrusion upon seclusion, and civil conspiracy claims, and held Westboro liable for $2.9 million in compensatory damages and $8 million in punitive damages. Westboro filed several post-trial motions, including a motion contending that the jury verdict was grossly excessive and a motion seeking judgment as a matter of law on all claims on First Amendment grounds. The District Court remitted the punitive damages award to $2.1 million, but left the jury verdict otherwise intact. *Id.,* at 597.

In the Court of Appeals, Westboro's primary argument was that the church was entitled to judgment as a matter of law because the First Amendment fully protected Westboro's speech. The Court of Appeals agreed. 580 F. 3d 206, 221 (CA4 2009). The court reviewed the picket signs and concluded that Westboro's statements were entitled to First Amendment protection because those statements were on matters of public concern, were not provably false, and were expressed solely through hyperbolic rhetoric. *Id.,* at 222–224.[2]

---

[2] One judge concurred in the judgment on the ground that Snyder had failed to introduce sufficient evidence at trial to support a jury verdict

Opinion of the Court

We granted certiorari. 559 U. S. ___ (2010).

II

To succeed on a claim for intentional infliction of emotional distress in Maryland, a plaintiff must demonstrate that the defendant intentionally or recklessly engaged in extreme and outrageous conduct that caused the plaintiff to suffer severe emotional distress. See *Harris* v. *Jones*, 281 Md. 560, 565–566, 380 A. 2d 611, 614 (1977). The Free Speech Clause of the First Amendment—"Congress shall make no law . . . abridging the freedom of speech"—can serve as a defense in state tort suits, including suits for intentional infliction of emotional distress. See, *e.g.*, *Hustler Magazine, Inc.* v. *Falwell*, 485 U. S. 46, 50–51 (1988).[3]

Whether the First Amendment prohibits holding Westboro liable for its speech in this case turns largely on whether that speech is of public or private concern, as determined by all the circumstances of the case. "[S]peech on 'matters of public concern' . . . is 'at the heart of the First Amendment's protection.'" *Dun & Bradstreet, Inc.* v. *Greenmoss Builders, Inc.*, 472 U. S. 749, 758–759 (1985) (opinion of Powell, J.) (quoting *First Nat. Bank of Boston* v. *Bellotti*, 435 U. S. 765, 776 (1978)). The First Amendment reflects "a profound national commitment to the

---

on any of his tort claims. 580 F. 3d, at 227 (opinion of Shedd, J.). The Court of Appeals majority determined that the picketers had "voluntarily waived" any such contention on appeal. *Id.,* at 216. Like the court below, we proceed on the unexamined premise that respondents' speech was tortious.

[3] The dissent attempts to draw parallels between this case and hypothetical cases involving defamation or fighting words. *Post,* at 10–11 (opinion of ALITO, J.). But, as the court below noted, there is "no suggestion that the speech at issue falls within one of the categorical exclusions from First Amendment protection, such as those for obscenity or 'fighting words.'" 580 F. 3d, at 218, n. 12; see *United States* v. *Stevens,* 559 U. S. ___, ___ (2010) (slip op., at 5).

principle that debate on public issues should be uninhibited, robust, and wide-open." *New York Times Co.* v. *Sullivan,* 376 U. S. 254, 270 (1964). That is because "speech concerning public affairs is more than self-expression; it is the essence of self-government." *Garrison* v. *Louisiana,* 379 U. S. 64, 74–75 (1964). Accordingly, "speech on public issues occupies the highest rung of the hierarchy of First Amendment values, and is entitled to special protection." *Connick* v. *Myers,* 461 U. S. 138, 145 (1983) (internal quotation marks omitted).

"'[N]ot all speech is of equal First Amendment importance,'" however, and where matters of purely private significance are at issue, First Amendment protections are often less rigorous. *Hustler, supra,* at 56 (quoting *Dun & Bradstreet, supra,* at 758); see *Connick, supra,* at 145–147. That is because restricting speech on purely private matters does not implicate the same constitutional concerns as limiting speech on matters of public interest: "[T]here is no threat to the free and robust debate of public issues; there is no potential interference with a meaningful dialogue of ideas"; and the "threat of liability" does not pose the risk of "a reaction of self-censorship" on matters of public import. *Dun & Bradstreet, supra,* at 760 (internal quotation marks omitted).

We noted a short time ago, in considering whether public employee speech addressed a matter of public concern, that "the boundaries of the public concern test are not well defined." *San Diego* v. *Roe,* 543 U. S. 77, 83 (2004) (*per curiam*). Although that remains true today, we have articulated some guiding principles, principles that accord broad protection to speech to ensure that courts themselves do not become inadvertent censors.

Speech deals with matters of public concern when it can "be fairly considered as relating to any matter of political, social, or other concern to the community," *Connick, supra,* at 146, or when it "is a subject of legitimate news interest; that is, a subject of general interest and of value and concern to the public," *San Diego, supra,* at 83–84. See *Cox Broadcasting Corp.* v. *Cohn,* 420 U. S. 469, 492–494 (1975); *Time, Inc.* v. *Hill,* 385 U. S. 374, 387–388 (1967). The arguably "inappropriate or controversial character of a statement is irrelevant to the question whether it deals with a matter of public concern." *Rankin* v. *McPherson,* 483 U. S. 378, 387 (1987).

Our opinion in *Dun & Bradstreet,* on the other hand, provides an example of speech of only private concern. In that case we held, as a general matter, that information about a particular individual's credit report "concerns no public issue." 472 U. S., at 762. The content of the report, we explained, "was speech solely in the individual interest of the speaker and its specific business audience." *Ibid.* That was confirmed by the fact that the particular report was sent to only five subscribers to the reporting service, who were bound not to disseminate it further. *Ibid.* To cite another example, we concluded in *San Diego* v. *Roe* that, in the context of a government employer regulating the speech of its employees, videos of an employee engaging in sexually explicit acts did not address a public concern; the videos "did nothing to inform the public about any aspect of the [employing agency's] functioning or operation." 543 U. S., at 84.

Deciding whether speech is of public or private concern requires us to examine the "'content, form, and context'" of that speech, "'as revealed by the whole record.'" *Dun & Bradstreet, supra,* at 761 (quoting *Connick, supra,* at 147–148). As in other First Amendment cases, the court is obligated "to 'make an independent examination of the whole record' in order to make sure that 'the judgment does not constitute a forbidden intrusion on the field of free expression.'" *Bose Corp.* v. *Consumers Union of United States, Inc.,* 466 U. S. 485, 499 (1984) (quoting *New York Times, supra,* at 284–286). In considering content, form, and context, no factor is dispositive, and it is necessary to evaluate all the circumstances of the speech, including what was said, where it was said, and how it was said.

The "content" of Westboro's signs plainly relates to broad issues of interest to society at large, rather than matters of "purely private concern." *Dun & Bradstreet, supra,* at 759. The placards read "God Hates the USA/Thank God for 9/11," "America is Doomed," "Don't Pray for the USA," "Thank God for IEDs," "Fag Troops," "Semper Fi Fags," "God Hates Fags," "Maryland Taliban," "Fags Doom Nations," "Not Blessed Just Cursed," "Thank God for Dead Soldiers," "Pope in Hell," "Priests Rape Boys," "You're Going to Hell," and "God Hates You." App. 3781–3787. While these messages may fall short of refined social or political commentary, the issues they highlight—the political and moral conduct of the United States and its citizens, the fate of our Nation, homosexuality in the military, and scandals involving the Catholic clergy—are matters of public import. The signs certainly convey Westboro's position on those issues, in a manner designed, unlike the private speech in *Dun & Bradstreet*, to reach as broad a public audience as possible. And even if a few of the signs—such as "You're Going to Hell" and "God Hates You"—were viewed as containing messages related to Matthew Snyder or the Snyders specifically, that would not change the fact that the overall thrust and dominant theme of Westboro's demonstration spoke to broader public issues.

Apart from the content of Westboro's signs, Snyder contends that the "context" of the speech—its connection with his son's funeral—makes the speech a matter of private rather than public concern. The fact that Westboro spoke in connection with a funeral, however, cannot by itself transform the nature of Westboro's speech. Westboro's signs, displayed on public land next to a public street, reflect the fact that the church finds much to condemn in modern society. Its speech is "fairly characterized as constituting speech on a matter of public concern," *Connick*, 461 U. S., at 146, and the funeral setting does not alter that conclusion.

Snyder argues that the church members in fact mounted a personal attack on Snyder and his family, and then attempted to "immunize their conduct by claiming that they were actually protesting the United States' tolerance of homosexuality or the supposed evils of the Catholic Church." Reply Brief for Petitioner 10. We are not concerned in this case that Westboro's speech on public matters was in any way contrived to insulate speech on a private matter from liability. Westboro had been actively engaged in speaking on the subjects addressed in its picketing long before it became aware of Matthew Snyder, and there can be no serious claim that Westboro's picketing did not represent its "honestly believed" views on public issues. *Garrison*, 379 U. S., at 73. There was no preexisting relationship or conflict between Westboro and Snyder that might suggest Westboro's speech on public matters was intended to mask an attack on Snyder over a private matter. Contrast *Connick, supra,* at 153 (finding public employee speech a matter of private concern when it was "no coincidence that [the speech] followed upon the heels of [a] transfer notice" affecting the employee).

Snyder goes on to argue that Westboro's speech should be afforded less than full First Amendment protection "not only because of the words" but also because the church members exploited the funeral "as a platform to bring their message to a broader audience." Brief for Petitioner 44, 40. There is no doubt that Westboro chose to stage its picketing at the Naval Academy, the Maryland State House, and Matthew Snyder's funeral to increase publicity for its views and because of the relation between those sites and its views—in the case of the military funeral, because Westboro believes that God is killing American soldiers as punishment for the Nation's sinful policies.

Westboro's choice to convey its views in conjunction with Matthew Snyder's funeral made the expression of those views particularly hurtful to many, especially to Matthew's father. The record makes clear that the applicable legal term—"emotional distress"—fails to capture fully the anguish Westboro's choice added to Mr. Snyder's already incalculable grief. But Westboro conducted its picketing peacefully on matters of public concern at a public place adjacent to a public street. Such space occupies a "special position in terms of First Amendment protection." *United States* v. *Grace*, 461 U. S. 171, 180 (1983). "[W]e have repeatedly referred to public streets as the archetype of a traditional public forum," noting that "'[t]ime out of mind' public streets and sidewalks have been used for public assembly and debate." *Frisby* v. *Schultz*, 487 U. S. 474, 480 (1988).[4]

That said, "[e]ven protected speech is not equally permissible in all places and at all times." *Id.,* at 479 (quoting *Cornelius* v. *NAACP Legal Defense & Ed. Fund, Inc.*, 473 U. S. 788, 799 (1985)). Westboro's choice of where and when to conduct its picketing is not beyond the Government's regulatory reach—it is "subject to reasonable time, place, or manner restrictions" that are consistent with the standards announced in this Court's precedents. *Clark* v. *Community for Creative Non-Violence*, 468 U. S. 288, 293 (1984). Maryland now has a law imposing restrictions on funeral picketing, Md. Crim. Law Code Ann. §10–205

---

[4] The dissent is wrong to suggest that the Court considers a public street "a free-fire zone in which otherwise actionable verbal attacks are shielded from liability." *Post,* at 10–11. The fact that Westboro conducted its picketing adjacent to a public street does not insulate the speech from liability, but instead heightens concerns that what is at issue is an effort to communicate to the public the church's views on matters of public concern. That is why our precedents so clearly recognize the special significance of this traditional public forum.

(Lexis Supp. 2010), as do 43 other States and the Federal Government. See Brief for American Legion as *Amicus Curiae* 18–19, n. 2 (listing statutes). To the extent these laws are content neutral, they raise very different questions from the tort verdict at issue in this case. Maryland's law, however, was not in effect at the time of the events at issue here, so we have no occasion to consider how it might apply to facts such as those before us, or whether it or other similar regulations are constitutional.[5]

We have identified a few limited situations where the location of targeted picketing can be regulated under provisions that the Court has determined to be content neutral. In *Frisby*, for example, we upheld a ban on such picketing "before or about" a particular residence, 487 U. S., at 477. In *Madsen* v. *Women's Health Center, Inc.*, we approved an injunction requiring a buffer zone between protesters and an abortion clinic entrance. 512 U. S. 753, 768 (1994). The facts here are obviously quite different, both with respect to the activity being regulated and the means of restricting those activities.

Simply put, the church members had the right to be where they were. Westboro alerted local authorities to its funeral protest and fully complied with police guidance on where the picketing could be staged. The picketing was conducted under police supervision some 1,000 feet from the church, out of the sight of those at the church. The protest was not unruly; there was no shouting, profanity, or violence.

The record confirms that any distress occasioned by Westboro's picketing turned on the content and viewpoint of the message conveyed, rather than any interference with the funeral itself. A group of parishioners standing at the very spot where Westboro stood, holding signs that

---

[5] The Maryland law prohibits picketing within 100 feet of a funeral service or funeral procession; Westboro's picketing would have complied with that restriction.

said "God Bless America" and "God Loves You," would not have been subjected to liability. It was what Westboro said that exposed it to tort damages.

Given that Westboro's speech was at a public place on a matter of public concern, that speech is entitled to "special protection" under the First Amendment. Such speech cannot be restricted simply because it is upsetting or arouses contempt. "If there is a bedrock principle underlying the First Amendment, it is that the government may not prohibit the expression of an idea simply because society finds the idea itself offensive or disagreeable." *Texas* v. *Johnson*, 491 U. S. 397, 414 (1989). Indeed, "the point of all speech protection . . . is to shield just those choices of content that in someone's eyes are misguided, or even hurtful." *Hurley* v. *Irish-American Gay, Lesbian and Bisexual Group of Boston, Inc.*, 515 U. S. 557, 574 (1995).

The jury here was instructed that it could hold Westboro liable for intentional infliction of emotional distress based on a finding that Westboro's picketing was "outrageous." "Outrageousness," however, is a highly malleable standard with "an inherent subjectiveness about it which would allow a jury to impose liability on the basis of the jurors' tastes or views, or perhaps on the basis of their dislike of a particular expression." *Hustler*, 485 U. S., at 55 (internal quotation marks omitted). In a case such as this, a jury is "unlikely to be neutral with respect to the content of [the] speech," posing "a real danger of becoming an instrument for the suppression of . . . 'vehement, caustic, and sometimes unpleasan[t]'" expression. *Bose Corp.*, 466 U. S., at 510 (quoting *New York Times*, 376 U. S., at 270). Such a risk is unacceptable; "in public debate [we] must tolerate insulting, and even outrageous, speech in order to provide adequate 'breathing space' to the freedoms protected by the First Amendment." *Boos* v. *Barry*, 485 U. S. 312, 322 (1988) (some internal quotation marks omitted). What Westboro said, in the whole context of how and where it chose to say it, is entitled to "special protection" under the First Amendment, and that protection cannot be overcome by a jury finding that the picketing was outrageous.

For all these reasons, the jury verdict imposing tort liability on Westboro for intentional infliction of emotional distress must be set aside.

III

The jury also found Westboro liable for the state law torts of intrusion upon seclusion and civil conspiracy. The Court of Appeals did not examine these torts independently of the intentional infliction of emotional distress tort. Instead, the Court of Appeals reversed the District Court wholesale, holding that the judgment wrongly "attache[d] tort liability to constitutionally protected speech." 580 F. 3d, at 226.

Snyder argues that even assuming Westboro's speech is entitled to First Amendment protection generally, the church is not immunized from liability for intrusion upon seclusion because Snyder was a member of a captive audience at his son's funeral. Brief for Petitioner 45–46. We do not agree. In most circumstances, "the Constitution does not permit the government to decide which types of otherwise protected speech are sufficiently offensive to require protection for the unwilling listener or viewer. Rather, . . . the burden normally falls upon the viewer to avoid further bombardment of [his] sensibilities simply by averting [his] eyes." *Erznoznik* v. *Jacksonville*, 422 U. S. 205, 210–211 (1975) (internal quotation marks omitted). As a result, "[t]he ability of government, consonant with the Constitution, to shut off discourse solely to protect others from hearing it is . . . dependent upon a showing that substantial privacy interests are being invaded in an essentially intolerable manner." *Cohen* v. *California*, 403 U. S. 15, 21 (1971).

As a general matter, we have applied the captive audience doctrine only sparingly to protect unwilling listeners from protected speech. For example, we have upheld a statute allowing a homeowner to restrict the delivery of offensive mail to his home, see *Rowan* v. *Post Office Dept.*, 397 U. S. 728, 736–738 (1970), and an ordinance prohibiting picketing "before or about" any individual's residence, *Frisby*, 487 U. S., at 484–485.

Here, Westboro stayed well away from the memorial service. Snyder could see no more than the tops of the signs when driving to the funeral. And there is no indication that the picketing in any way interfered with the funeral service itself. We decline to expand the captive audience doctrine to the circumstances presented here.

Because we find that the First Amendment bars Snyder from recovery for intentional infliction of emotional distress or intrusion upon seclusion—the alleged unlawful activity Westboro conspired to accomplish—we must likewise hold that Snyder cannot recover for civil conspiracy based on those torts.

IV

Our holding today is narrow. We are required in First Amendment cases to carefully review the record, and the reach of our opinion here is limited by the particular facts before us. As we have noted, "the sensitivity and significance of the interests presented in clashes between First Amendment and [state law] rights counsel relying on limited principles that sweep no more broadly than the appropriate context of the instant case." *Florida Star* v. *B. J. F.*, 491 U. S. 524, 533 (1989).

Westboro believes that America is morally flawed; many Americans might feel the same about Westboro. Westboro's funeral picketing is certainly hurtful and its contribution to public discourse may be negligible. But Westboro addressed matters of public import on public property, in a peaceful manner, in full compliance with the guidance of local officials. The speech was indeed planned to coincide with Matthew Snyder's funeral, but did not itself disrupt that funeral, and Westboro's choice to conduct its picketing at that time and place did not alter the nature of its speech.

Speech is powerful. It can stir people to action, move them to tears of both joy and sorrow, and—as it did here—inflict great pain. On the facts before us, we cannot react to that pain by punishing the speaker. As a Nation we have chosen a different course—to protect even hurtful speech on public issues to ensure that we do not stifle public debate. That choice requires that we shield Westboro from tort liability for its picketing in this case.

The judgment of the United States Court of Appeals for the Fourth Circuit is affirmed.

It is so ordered.

SUPREME COURT OF THE UNITED STATES

No. 09–751

ALBERT SNYDER, PETITIONER v. FRED W. PHELPS, SR., ET AL.

ON WRIT OF CERTIORARI TO THE UNITED STATES COURT OF APPEALS FOR THE FOURTH CIRCUIT

[March 2, 2011]

JUSTICE BREYER, concurring.

I agree with the Court and join its opinion. That opinion restricts its analysis here to the matter raised in the petition for certiorari, namely, Westboro's picketing activity. The opinion does not examine in depth the effect of television broadcasting. Nor does it say anything about Internet postings. The Court holds that the First Amendment protects the picketing that occurred here, primarily because the picketing addressed matters of "public concern."

While I agree with the Court's conclusion that the picketing addressed matters of public concern, I do not believe that our First Amendment analysis can stop at that point. A State can sometimes regulate picketing, even picketing on matters of public concern. See *Frisby* v. *Schultz*, 487 U. S. 474 (1988). Moreover, suppose that A were physically to assault B, knowing that the assault (being newsworthy) would provide A with an opportunity to transmit to the public his views on a matter of public concern. The constitutionally protected nature of the end would not shield A's use of unlawful, unprotected means. And in some circumstances the use of certain words as means would be similarly unprotected. See *Chaplinsky* v. *New Hampshire*, 315 U. S. 568 (1942) ("fighting words").

The dissent recognizes that the means used here consist

of speech. But it points out that the speech, like an assault, seriously harmed a private individual. Indeed, the state tort of "intentional infliction of emotional distress" forbids only conduct that produces distress "so severe that no reasonable man could be expected to endure it," and which itself is "so outrageous in character, and so extreme in degree, as to go beyond all possible bounds of decency, and to be regarded as atrocious, and utterly intolerable in a civilized community." *Post*, at 2–3 (opinion of ALITO, J.) (quoting *Harris* v. *Jones*, 281 Md. 560, 567, 571, 380 A. 2d 611, 614, 616 (1977); internal quotation marks omitted). The dissent requires us to ask whether our holding unreasonably limits liability for intentional infliction of emotional distress—to the point where A (in order to draw attention to his views on a public matter) might launch a verbal assault upon B, a private person, publicly revealing the most intimate details of B's private life, while knowing that the revelation will cause B severe emotional harm. Does our decision leave the State powerless to protect the individual against invasions of, *e.g.*, personal privacy, even in the most horrendous of such circumstances?

As I understand the Court's opinion, it does not hold or imply that the State is always powerless to provide private individuals with necessary protection. Rather, the Court has reviewed the underlying facts in detail, as will sometimes prove necessary where First Amendment values and state-protected (say, privacy-related) interests seriously conflict. Cf. *Florida Star* v. *B. J. F.*, 491 U. S. 524, 533 (1989); *Bose Corp.* v. *Consumers Union of United States, Inc.*, 466 U. S. 485, 499 (1984). That review makes clear that Westboro's means of communicating its views consisted of picketing in a place where picketing was lawful and in compliance with all police directions. The picketing could not be seen or heard from the funeral ceremony itself. And Snyder testified that he saw no more than the tops of the picketers' signs as he drove to the funeral. To uphold the application of state law in these circumstances would punish Westboro for seeking to communicate its views on matters of public concern without proportionately advancing the State's interest in protecting its citizens against severe emotional harm. Consequently, the First Amendment protects Westboro. As I read the Court's opinion, it holds no more.

Cite as: 562 U. S. ____ (2011) 1

ALITO, J., dissenting

SUPREME COURT OF THE UNITED STATES

No. 09–751

ALBERT SNYDER, PETITIONER v. FRED W. PHELPS, SR., ET AL.

ON WRIT OF CERTIORARI TO THE UNITED STATES COURT OF APPEALS FOR THE FOURTH CIRCUIT

[March 2, 2011]

JUSTICE ALITO, dissenting.

Our profound national commitment to free and open debate is not a license for the vicious verbal assault that occurred in this case.

Petitioner Albert Snyder is not a public figure. He is simply a parent whose son, Marine Lance Corporal Matthew Snyder, was killed in Iraq. Mr. Snyder wanted what is surely the right of any parent who experiences such an incalculable loss: to bury his son in peace. But respondents, members of the Westboro Baptist Church, deprived him of that elementary right. They first issued a press release and thus turned Matthew's funeral into a tumultuous media event. They then appeared at the church, approached as closely as they could without trespassing, and launched a malevolent verbal attack on Matthew and his family at a time of acute emotional vulnerability. As a result, Albert Snyder suffered severe and lasting emotional injury.[1] The Court now holds that the First Amendment protected respondents' right to brutalize Mr. Snyder. I cannot agree.

I

Respondents and other members of their church have

---

[1] See 580 F. 3d 206, 213–214, 216 (CA4 2009).

strong opinions on certain moral, religious, and political issues, and the First Amendment ensures that they have almost limitless opportunities to express their views. They may write and distribute books, articles, and other texts; they may create and disseminate video and audio recordings; they may circulate petitions; they may speak to individuals and groups in public forums and in any private venue that wishes to accommodate them; they may picket peacefully in countless locations; they may appear on television and speak on the radio; they may post messages on the Internet and send out e-mails. And they may express their views in terms that are "uninhibited," "vehement," and "caustic." *New York Times Co.* v. *Sullivan*, 376 U. S. 254, 270 (1964).

It does not follow, however, that they may intentionally inflict severe emotional injury on private persons at a time of intense emotional sensitivity by launching vicious verbal attacks that make no contribution to public debate. To protect against such injury, "most if not all jurisdictions" permit recovery in tort for the intentional infliction of emotional distress (or IIED). *Hustler Magazine, Inc.* v. *Falwell*, 485 U. S. 46, 53 (1988).

This is a very narrow tort with requirements that "are rigorous, and difficult to satisfy." W. Keeton, D. Dobbs, R. Keeton, & D. Owen, Prosser and Keeton on Law of Torts §12, p. 61 (5th ed. 1984). To recover, a plaintiff must show that the conduct at issue caused harm that was truly severe. See *Figueiredo-Torres* v. *Nickel*, 321 Md. 642, 653, 584 A. 2d 69, 75 (1991) ("[R]ecovery will be meted out sparingly, its balm reserved for those wounds that are truly severe and incapable of healing themselves" (internal quotation marks omitted)); *Harris* v. *Jones*, 281 Md. 560, 571, 380 A. 2d 611, 616 (1977) (the distress must be "'so severe that no reasonable man could be expected to endure it'" (quoting Restatement (Second) of Torts §46, Comment *j* (1963–1964))).

ALITO, J., dissenting

A plaintiff must also establish that the defendant's conduct was "'so outrageous in character, and so extreme in degree, as to go beyond all possible bounds of decency, and to be regarded as atrocious, and utterly intolerable in a civilized community.'" *Id.*, at 567, 380 A. 2d, at 614 (quoting Restatement (Second) of Torts §46, Comment *d*).

Although the elements of the IIED tort are difficult to meet, respondents long ago abandoned any effort to show that those tough standards were not satisfied here. On appeal, they chose not to contest the sufficiency of the evidence. See 580 F. 3d 206, 216 (CA4 2009). They did not dispute that Mr. Snyder suffered "'wounds that are truly severe and incapable of healing themselves.'" *Figueiredo-Torres*, *supra*, at 653, 584 A. 2d, at 75. Nor did they dispute that their speech was "'so outrageous in character, and so extreme in degree, as to go beyond all possible bounds of decency, and to be regarded as atrocious, and utterly intolerable in a civilized community.'" *Harris*, *supra*, at 567, 380 A. 2d, at 614. Instead, they maintained that the First Amendment gave them a license to engage in such conduct. They are wrong.

II

It is well established that a claim for the intentional infliction of emotional distress can be satisfied by speech. Indeed, what has been described as "[t]he leading case" recognizing this tort involved speech. Prosser and Keeton, *supra,* §12, at 60 (citing *Wilkinson* v. *Downton,* [1897] 2 Q. B. 57); see also Restatement (Second) of Torts §46, illustration 1. And although this Court has not decided the question, I think it is clear that the First Amendment does not entirely preclude liability for the intentional infliction of emotional distress by means of speech.

This Court has recognized that words may "by their very utterance inflict injury" and that the First Amendment does not shield utterances that form "no essential part of

ALITO, J., dissenting

any exposition of ideas, and are of such slight social value as a step to truth that any benefit that may be derived from them is clearly outweighed by the social interest in order and morality." *Chaplinsky* v. *New Hampshire*, 315 U. S. 568, 572 (1942); see also *Cantwell* v. *Connecticut*, 310 U. S. 296, 310 (1940) ("[P]ersonal abuse is not in any proper sense communication of information or opinion safeguarded by the Constitution"). When grave injury is intentionally inflicted by means of an attack like the one at issue here, the First Amendment should not interfere with recovery.

III

In this case, respondents brutally attacked Matthew Snyder, and this attack, which was almost certain to inflict injury, was central to respondents' well-practiced strategy for attracting public attention.

On the morning of Matthew Snyder's funeral, respondents could have chosen to stage their protest at countless locations. They could have picketed the United States Capitol, the White House, the Supreme Court, the Pentagon, or any of the more than 5,600 military recruiting stations in this country. They could have returned to the Maryland State House or the United States Naval Academy, where they had been the day before. They could have selected any public road where pedestrians are allowed. (There are more than 4,000,000 miles of public roads in the United States.[2]) They could have staged their protest in a public park. (There are more than 20,000 public parks in this country.[3]) They could have chosen any

---

[2] See Dept. of Transp., Federal Highway Administration, Highway Statistics 2008, Table HM–12M, http://www.fhwa.dot.gov/policyinformation/statistics/2008/hm12m.cfm (all Internet materials as visited Feb. 25, 2011, and available in Clerk of Court's case file).

[3] See Trust for Public Land, 2010 City Park Facts, http://www.tpl.org/content_documents/CityParkFacts_2010.pdf.

Catholic church where no funeral was taking place. (There are nearly 19,000 Catholic churches in the United States.[4]) But of course, a small group picketing at any of these locations would have probably gone unnoticed.

The Westboro Baptist Church, however, has devised a strategy that remedies this problem. As the Court notes, church members have protested at nearly 600 military funerals. *Ante,* at 1. They have also picketed the funerals of police officers,[5] firefighters,[6] and the victims of natural disasters,[7] accidents,[8] and shocking crimes.[9] And in advance of these protests, they issue press releases to ensure that their protests will attract public attention.[10]

This strategy works because it is expected that respondents' verbal assaults will wound the family and friends of the deceased and because the media is irresistibly drawn to the sight of persons who are visibly in grief. The more outrageous the funeral protest, the more publicity the Westboro Baptist Church is able to obtain. Thus, when the church recently announced its intention to picket the funeral of a 9-year-old girl killed in the shooting spree in Tucson—proclaiming that she was "better off dead"[11]—their announcement was national news,[12] and the church

---

[4] See United States Conference of Catholic Bishops, Catholic Information Project, http://www.usccb.org/comm/cip.shtml#toc4.

[5] See http://www.godhatesfags.com/fliers/20110124_St-Petersburg-FL-Dead-Police.pdf.

[6] See http://www.godhatesfags.com/fliers/20110120_Dead-Volunteer-Firefighter-Connecting_the_Dots-Baltimore-MD.pdf.

[7] See http://www.godhatesfags.com/fliers/20110104_Newburg-and-Rolla-MO-Tornado-Connecting-the-Dots.pdf.

[8] See http://www.godhatesfags.com/fliers/20101218_Wichita-KS-Two-Dead-Wichita-Bikers.pdf.

[9] See http://www.godhatesfags.com/fliers/20110129_Tampa-FL-God-Sent-Military-Mom-Shooter-to-Kill-Kids.pdf.

[10] See nn. 5–9, *supra.*

[11] See http://www.godhatesfags.com/fliers/20110109_AZ-Shooter-Connecting-the-Dots-Day-2.pdf.

[12] See, *e.g.,* Stanglin, Anti-Gay Church Group Plans to Picket Tucson

was able to obtain free air time on the radio in exchange for canceling its protest.[13] Similarly, in 2006, the church got air time on a talk radio show in exchange for canceling its threatened protest at the funeral of five Amish girls killed by a crazed gunman.[14]

In this case, respondents implemented the Westboro Baptist Church's publicity-seeking strategy. Their press release stated that they were going "to picket the funeral of Lance Cpl. Matthew A. Snyder" because "God Almighty killed Lance Cpl. Snyder. He died in shame, not honor—for a fag nation cursed by God .... Now in Hell—sine die." Supp. App. in No. 08–1026 (CA4), p. 158a. This announcement guaranteed that Matthew's funeral would be transformed into a raucous media event and began the wounding process. It is well known that anticipation may heighten the effect of a painful event.

On the day of the funeral, respondents, true to their word, displayed placards that conveyed the message promised in their press release. Signs stating "God Hates You"

Funerals, USA Today, Jan. 10, 2011, http://content.usatoday.com/communities/ondeadline/post/2011/01/anti-gay-church-group-plans-to-picket-tucston-funerals/1; Mohanani, Group to Picket 9-Year-Old Tucson Victim's Funeral, Palm Beach Post, Jan. 11, 2011, http://www.palmbeachpost.com/news/nation/group-to-picket-9-year-old-tucson-victims-1177921.html; Mehta & Santa Cruz, Tucson Rallies to Protect Girl's Family from Protesters, Los Angeles Times, Jan. 11, 2011, http://articles.latimes.com/2011/jan/11/nation/la-na-funeral-protest-20110112; Medrano, Funeral Protest: Arizona Rallies to Foil Westboro Baptist Church, Christian Science Monitor, Jan. 11, 2011, http://www.csmonitor.com/USA/2011/0111/Funeral-protest-Arizona-rallies-to-foil-Westboro-Baptist-Church.

[13] See Santa Cruz & Mehta, Westboro Church Agrees Not to Take Protest to Shooting Victims' Funerals, Los Angeles Times, Jan. 13, 2011, http://articles.latimes.com/2011/jan/13/nation/la-na-funeral-protest-20110113; http://www.godhatesfags.com/fliers/20110112_AZ-Shooter-Mike-Gallagher-Radio-Exchange.pdf.

[14] See Steinberg, Air Time Instead of Funeral Protest, N. Y. Times, Oct. 6, 2006, p. A14.

ALITO, J., dissenting

and "Thank God for Dead Soldiers" reiterated the message that God had caused Matthew's death in retribution for his sins. App. to Brief for Appellants in No. 08–1026 (CA4), pp. 3787, 3788 (hereinafter App.). Others, stating "You're Going to Hell" and "Not Blessed Just Cursed," conveyed the message that Matthew was "in Hell—sine die." *Id.,* at 3783.

Even if those who attended the funeral were not alerted in advance about respondents' intentions, the meaning of these signs would not have been missed. Since respondents chose to stage their protest at Matthew Snyder's funeral and not at any of the other countless available venues, a reasonable person would have assumed that there was a connection between the messages on the placards and the deceased. Moreover, since a church funeral is an event that naturally brings to mind thoughts about the afterlife, some of respondents' signs—*e.g.*, "God Hates You," "Not Blessed Just Cursed," and "You're Going to Hell"—would have likely been interpreted as referring to God's judgment of the deceased.

Other signs would most naturally have been understood as suggesting—falsely—that Matthew was gay. Homosexuality was the theme of many of the signs. There were signs reading "God Hates Fags," "Semper Fi Fags," "Fags Doom Nations," and "Fag Troops." *Id.,* at 3781–3787. Another placard depicted two men engaging in anal intercourse. A reasonable bystander seeing those signs would have likely concluded that they were meant to suggest that the deceased was a homosexual.

After the funeral, the Westboro picketers reaffirmed the meaning of their protest. They posted an online account entitled "The Burden of Marine Lance Cpl. Matthew A. Snyder. The Visit of Westboro Baptist Church to Help the Inhabitants of Maryland Connect the Dots!" *Id.,* at 3788.[15]

---

[15] The Court refuses to consider the epic because it was not discussed

ALITO, J., dissenting

Belying any suggestion that they had simply made general comments about homosexuality, the Catholic Church, and the United States military, the "epic" addressed the Snyder family directly:

> "God blessed you, Mr. and Mrs. Snyder, with a resource and his name was Matthew. He was an arrow in your quiver! In thanks to God for the comfort the child could bring you, you had a DUTY to prepare that child to serve the LORD his GOD—PERIOD! You did JUST THE OPPOSITE—you raised him for the devil.
>
> . . . . .
>
> "Albert and Julie RIPPED that body apart and taught Matthew to defy his Creator, to divorce, and to commit adultery. They taught him how to support the largest pedophile machine in the history of the entire world, the Roman Catholic monstrosity. Every dime they gave the Roman Catholic monster they condemned their own souls. They also, in supporting satanic Catholicism, taught Matthew to be an idolater.
>
> . . . . .
>
> "Then after all that they sent him to fight for the United States of Sodom, a filthy country that is in lock step with his evil, wicked, and sinful manner of life, putting him in the cross hairs of a God that is so mad

---

in Snyder's petition for certiorari. *Ante*, at 3, n. 1. The epic, however, is not a distinct claim but a piece of evidence that the jury considered in imposing liability for the claims now before this Court. The protest and the epic are parts of a single course of conduct that the jury found to constitute intentional infliction of emotional distress. See 580 F. 3d, at 225 ("[T]he Epic cannot be divorced from the general context of the funeral protest"). The Court's strange insistence that the epic "is not properly before us," *ante*, at 3, n. 1, means that the Court has not actually made "an independent examination of the whole record," *ante*, at 7 (internal quotation marks omitted). And the Court's refusal to consider the epic contrasts sharply with its willingness to take notice of Westboro's protest activities at other times and locations. See *ante*, at 9.

ALITO, J., dissenting

He has smoke coming from his nostrils and fire from his mouth! How dumb was that?" *Id.*, at 3791.

In light of this evidence, it is abundantly clear that respondents, going far beyond commentary on matters of public concern, specifically attacked Matthew Snyder because (1) he was a Catholic and (2) he was a member of the United States military. Both Matthew and petitioner were private figures,[16] and this attack was not speech on a matter of public concern. While commentary on the Catholic Church or the United States military constitutes speech on matters of public concern, speech regarding Matthew Snyder's purely private conduct does not.

JUSTICE BREYER provides an apt analogy to a case in which the First Amendment would permit recovery in tort for a verbal attack:

> "[S]uppose that A were physically to assault B, knowing that the assault (being newsworthy) would provide A with an opportunity to transmit to the public his views on a matter of public concern. The constitutionally protected nature of the end would not shield A's use of unlawful, unprotected means. And in some circumstances the use of certain words as means would be similarly unprotected." *Ante*, at 1 (concurring opinion).

This captures what respondents did in this case. Indeed, this is the strategy that they have routinely employed—and that they will now continue to employ—inflicting severe and lasting emotional injury on an ever growing list of innocent victims.

IV

The Court concludes that respondents' speech was protected by the First Amendment for essentially three

---

[16] See 533 F. Supp. 2d 567, 577 (Md. 2008).

reasons, but none is sound.

First—and most important—the Court finds that "the overall thrust and dominant theme of [their] demonstration spoke to" broad public issues. *Ante,* at 8. As I have attempted to show, this portrayal is quite inaccurate; respondents' attack on Matthew was of central importance. But in any event, I fail to see why actionable speech should be immunized simply because it is interspersed with speech that is protected. The First Amendment allows recovery for defamatory statements that are interspersed with nondefamatory statements on matters of public concern, and there is no good reason why respondents' attack on Matthew Snyder and his family should be treated differently.

Second, the Court suggests that respondents' personal attack on Matthew Snyder is entitled to First Amendment protection because it was not motivated by a private grudge, see *ante*, at 9, but I see no basis for the strange distinction that the Court appears to draw. Respondents' motivation—"to increase publicity for its views," *ibid.*—did not transform their statements attacking the character of a private figure into statements that made a contribution to debate on matters of public concern. Nor did their publicity-seeking motivation soften the sting of their attack. And as far as culpability is concerned, one might well think that wounding statements uttered in the heat of a private feud are less, not more, blameworthy than similar statements made as part of a cold and calculated strategy to slash a stranger as a means of attracting public attention.

Third, the Court finds it significant that respondents' protest occurred on a public street, but this fact alone should not be enough to preclude IIED liability. To be sure, statements made on a public street may be less likely to satisfy the elements of the IIED tort than statements made on private property, but there is no reason why a public street in close proximity to the scene of a funeral should be regarded as a free-fire zone in which otherwise actionable verbal attacks are shielded from liability. If the First Amendment permits the States to protect their residents from the harm inflicted by such attacks—and the Court does not hold otherwise—then the location of the tort should not be dispositive. A physical assault may occur without trespassing; it is no defense that the perpetrator had "the right to be where [he was]." See *ante*, at 11. And the same should be true with respect to unprotected speech. Neither classic "fighting words" nor defamatory statements are immunized when they occur in a public place, and there is no good reason to treat a verbal assault based on the conduct or character of a private figure like Matthew Snyder any differently.

One final comment about the opinion of the Court is in order. The Court suggests that the wounds inflicted by vicious verbal assaults at funerals will be prevented or at least mitigated in the future by new laws that restrict picketing within a specified distance of a funeral. See *ante*, at 10–11. It is apparent, however, that the enactment of these laws is no substitute for the protection provided by the established IIED tort; according to the Court, the verbal attacks that severely wounded petitioner in this case complied with the new Maryland law regulating funeral picketing. See *ante*, at 11, n. 5. And there is absolutely nothing to suggest that Congress and the state legislatures, in enacting these laws, intended them to displace the protection provided by the well-established IIED tort.

The real significance of these new laws is not that they obviate the need for IIED protection. Rather, their enactment dramatically illustrates the fundamental point that funerals are unique events at which special protection against emotional assaults is in order. At funerals, the emotional well-being of bereaved relatives is particularly vulnerable. See *National Archives and Records Admin.* v. *Favish*, 541 U. S. 157, 168 (2004). Exploitation of a funeral for the purpose of attracting public attention "intrud[es] upon their . . . grief," *ibid.*, and may permanently stain their memories of the final moments before a loved one is laid to rest. Allowing family members to have a few hours of peace without harassment does not undermine public debate. I would therefore hold that, in this setting, the First Amendment permits a private figure to recover for the intentional infliction of emotional distress caused by speech on a matter of private concern.

V

In reversing the District Court judgment in favor of petitioner, the Court of Appeals relied on several grounds not discussed in the opinion of this Court or in the separate opinion supporting affirmance. I now turn briefly to those issues.

First, the Court of Appeals held that the District Court erred by allowing the jury to decide whether respondents' speech was "'directed specifically at the Snyder family.'" 580 F. 3d, at 221. It is not clear whether the Court of Appeals thought that this was a question for the trial judge alone or a question on which the judge had to make a preliminary ruling before sending it to the jury. In either event, however, the submission of this question to the jury was not reversible error because, as explained above, it is clear that respondents' statements targeted the Snyders.

Second, the Court of Appeals held that the trial judge went astray in allowing the jury to decide whether respondents' speech was so "'offensive and shocking as to not be entitled to First Amendment protection.'" *Ibid.* This instruction also did respondents no harm. Because their speech did not relate to a matter of public concern, it was not protected from liability by the First Amendment, and the only question for the jury was whether the elements of the IIED tort were met.

Third, the Court of Appeals appears to have concluded that the First Amendment does not permit an IIED plaintiff to recover for speech that cannot reasonably be interpreted as stating actual facts about an individual. See *id.,* at 222. In reaching this conclusion, the Court of Appeals relied on two of our cases—*Milkovich* v. *Lorain Journal Co.,* 497 U. S. 1 (1990), and *Hustler,* 485 U. S. 46—but neither supports the broad proposition that the Court of Appeals adopted.

Milkovich was a defamation case, and falsity is an element of defamation. Nothing in *Milkovich* even hints that the First Amendment requires that this defamation element be engrafted onto the IIED tort.

Hustler did involve an IIED claim, but the plaintiff there was a public figure, and the Court did not suggest that its holding would also apply in a case involving a private figure. Nor did the Court suggest that its holding applied across the board to all types of IIED claims. Instead, the holding was limited to "publications such as the one here at issue," namely, a caricature in a magazine. 485 U. S., at 56. Unless a caricature of a public figure can reasonably be interpreted as stating facts that may be proved to be wrong, the caricature does not have the same potential to wound as a personal verbal assault on a vulnerable private figure.

Because I cannot agree either with the holding of this Court or the other grounds on which the Court of Appeals relied, I would reverse the decision below and remand for further proceedings.[17]

---

[17] The Court affirms the decision of the Fourth Circuit with respect to petitioner's claim of intrusion upon seclusion on a ground not addressed by the Fourth Circuit. I would not reach out to decide that issue but would instead leave it for the Fourth Circuit to decide on remand. I would likewise allow the Fourth Circuit on remand to decide whether

VI

Respondents' outrageous conduct caused petitioner great injury, and the Court now compounds that injury by depriving petitioner of a judgment that acknowledges the wrong he suffered.

In order to have a society in which public issues can be openly and vigorously debated, it is not necessary to allow the brutalization of innocent victims like petitioner. I therefore respectfully dissent.

---

the judgment on the claim of civil conspiracy can survive in light of the ultimate disposition of the IIED and intrusion upon seclusion claims.

NOTICE: This opinion is subject to motions for rehearing under Rule 22 as well as formal revision before publication in the New Hampshire Reports. Readers are requested to notify the Reporter, Supreme Court of New Hampshire, One Charles Doe Drive, Concord, New Hampshire 03301, of any editorial errors in order that corrections may be made before the opinion goes to press. Errors may be reported by E-mail at the following address: reporter@courts.state.nh.us. Opinions are available on the Internet by 9:00 a.m. on the morning of their release. The direct address of the court's home page is: http://www.courts.state.nh.us/supreme.

THE SUPREME COURT OF NEW HAMPSHIRE

_____

Hillsborough-northern judicial district
No. 2006-549

THE STATE OF NEW HAMPSHIRE

v.

MARSHALL ZIDEL

Argued: June 20, 2007
Opinion Issued: January 18, 2008

Kelly A. Ayotte, attorney general (Nicholas Cort, assistant attorney general, on the brief and orally), for the State.

Theodore Lothstein, assistant appellate defender, of Concord, on the brief and orally, for the defendant.

DUGGAN, J. The defendant, Marshall Zidel, appeals his conviction on nine counts of possession of child pornography, see RSA 649-A:3 (2007), arguing that the Superior Court (Lewis, J.) erred in denying his motions to dismiss. We reverse.

The following facts were found by the trial court for purposes of ruling upon the defendant's pretrial motion to dismiss or were stipulated to by the parties. At the time he was arrested, the defendant worked as a photographer at a camp in Amherst for children fifteen years old and younger. In that capacity, the defendant took pictures that were to be used to make an end-of-summer video yearbook or scrapbook for the children attending the camp.

On July 4, 2005, the defendant gave three CD-ROM discs to the camp director. On one of the discs, the director discovered images depicting heads and necks of minor females superimposed upon naked adult female bodies, with the naked bodies engaging in various sexual acts. One image shows an act of sexual intercourse; two images depict a person engaging in or about to engage in cunnilingus; two images depict a person digitally penetrating or touching a female's genitalia; and four images show comparably explicit sexual activity. The defendant and at least one of his family members appear in some of the images. The parties stipulated that, "[o]ther than necks and heads, there is no specific evidence that the images in question contain the body parts of actual children." In addition to these images, the CD-ROMs contained the original non-pornographic camp photographs of the minor females.

The camp director identified two of the faces in the images as those of campers from the summer of 2004, who would have been fifteen years old at the time the photographs were taken. He gave the discs to the Amherst Police Department. The parents of all the females involved were able to identify the individuals as girls under sixteen at the time the images were created. When questioned, the defendant told the police that the sexually explicit "photographs were only his 'personal fantasy' and that they were not real." The defendant was indicted for possession of child pornography.

Before trial, the defendant moved to dismiss, arguing that the prosecution pursuant to RSA 649-A:3, I(e) violated his rights under Part I, Article 22 of the New Hampshire Constitution and the First Amendment to the United States Constitution. Following the denial of his motion, the defendant was convicted based upon stipulated facts.

On appeal, the defendant argues that the trial court erred in denying his constitutional challenges to RSA 649-A:3. That statute provides, in relevant part, that "[a] person is guilty of a felony if such person . . . (e) Knowingly buys, procures, possesses, or controls any visual representation of a child engaging in sexual activity." RSA 649-A:3, I (2007). The defendant contends that, under both the Federal and State Constitutions, RSA 649-A:3 is facially overbroad, and as applied to his conduct, violates his right to free speech.

For purposes of this appeal, although we acknowledge that the images at issue may more properly be characterized as "composite images," see United States v. Rearden, 349 F.3d 608, 613 (9th Cir. 2003) (noting distinction between "composite" and "morphed" images), we adopt the terminology used by the United States Supreme Court in Ashcroft v. Free Speech Coalition, 535 U.S. 234, 242 (2002), and refer to the images in question as "morphed images." Ashcroft, 535 U.S. at 242. As the Supreme Court explained, in contrast to wholly computer-generated images, there is a "more common and lower tech means of creating virtual images, known as computer morphing. Rather than creating original images, pornographers can alter innocent pictures of real children so that the children appear to be engaged in sexual activity." Ashcroft, 535 U.S. at 242.

We first address the defendant's as-applied challenge. We review questions of constitutional law de novo. State v. Decato, 156 N.H. ___, ___ (decided December 18, 2007). As noted above, the defendant raises his claims under both the State and Federal Constitutions. Our settled rule is to first address the defendant's claims under the State Constitution, State v. Ball, 124 N.H. 226, 231 (1983), and cite federal opinions for guidance only. State v. MacElman, 154 N.H. 304, 307 (2006). Here, however, because United States Supreme Court precedents compel us to hold that criminalizing the defendant's mere possession of the images in question violates his First Amendment rights, and because we are required to follow federal constitutional law, an analysis under the State Constitution is unnecessary. We therefore decide this case under the First and Fourteenth Amendments to the Federal Constitution.

"The First Amendment commands, 'Congress shall make no law . . . abridging the freedom of speech.'" Ashcroft, 535 U.S. at 244. "As a general principle, the First Amendment bars the government from dictating what we see or read or speak or hear." Id. at 245. "[A] law imposing criminal penalties on protected speech is a stark example of speech suppression." Id. at 244. If a statute regulates speech based upon its content, application of the statute is subject to strict scrutiny. United States v. Playboy Entertainment Group, Inc., 529 U.S. 803, 813 (2000); see Sable Communications of Cal., Inc. v. FCC, 492 U.S. 115, 126 (1989). This places the burden upon the State to prove that the statute is "narrowly tailored to promote a compelling [state] interest. If a less restrictive alternative would serve the [state]'s purpose, the legislature must use that alternative." Playboy Entertainment Group, 529 U.S. at 813 (citation omitted).

The United States Supreme Court has determined that content-based restrictions on certain categories of speech satisfy strict scrutiny, and, thus, are not entitled to absolute constitutional protection. Ashcroft, 535 U.S. at 245-46; see People v. Alexander, 791 N.E.2d 506, 509 (Ill. 2003). This unprotected speech "includ[es] defamation, incitement, obscenity, and pornography produced with real children." Ashcroft, 535 U.S. at 246. Obscenity and child pornography are the two categories relevant here.

"The regulation of child pornography was initially rooted in the Supreme Court's obscenity doctrine." United States v. Williams, 444 F.3d 1286, 1290 (11th Cir. 2006). In Miller v. California, 413 U.S. 15 (1973), the Supreme Court reaffirmed that distribution of "obscene material is not protected by the First Amendment," id. at 36, and set forth a standard for determining what materials may be regulated as obscenity, id. at 24. Under this standard, "the Government must prove that the work, taken as a whole, appeals to the prurient interest, is patently offensive in light of community standards, and lacks serious literary, artistic, political, or scientific value." Ashcroft, 535 U.S. at 246 (citing Miller, 413 U.S. at 24).

While the government has "broad power to regulate obscenity," the Supreme Court held in Stanley v. Georgia, 394 U.S. 557 (1969), that this "power . . . does not extend to mere possession by the individual in the privacy of his own home." Stanley, 394 U.S. at 568. In so holding, the Court rejected all of Georgia's justifications for banning the mere possession of obscene materials. Id. at 565-68. First, the Court explained that the asserted "right to protect the individual's mind from the effects of obscenity" is "wholly inconsistent with the philosophy of the First Amendment." Id. at 565-66. Second, it rejected Georgia's assertion that "exposure to obscene materials may lead to deviant sexual behavior or crimes of sexual violence," because there was "little empirical basis for that assertion" and "the deterrents ordinarily to be applied to prevent crime are education and punishment for violations of the law." Id. at 566-67 (quotation omitted). Third, the Court found that, in a possession case, there is no "danger that obscene material might fall into the hands of children, or that it might intrude upon the sensibilities or privacy of the general public." Id. at 567 (citations omitted). Finally, the Court flatly rejected the argument that "prohibition of possession of obscene materials is a necessary incident to statutory schemes prohibiting distribution" as a result of "difficulties of proving an intent to distribute or in producing evidence of actual distribution." Id. It found that such difficulties, if they existed, did not "justify infringement of the individual's right to read or observe what he pleases." Id. at 568. Accordingly, the Supreme Court held that "the First and Fourteenth Amendments prohibit making mere private possession of obscene material a crime." Id.

With respect to child pornography, New York v. Ferber, 458 U.S. 747, 764-66 (1982), and Osborne v. Ohio, 495 U.S. 103, 111 (1990), together hold that a state may proscribe the distribution and mere possession of child pornography. Both cases recognized that states have a compelling interest "in safeguarding the physical and psychological well-being of a minor." Ferber, 458 U.S. at 756-57 (quotation omitted); see Osborne, 495 U.S. at 109.

In Ferber, the Court relied upon three justifications for a proscription on the distribution of child pornography. First, the Court reasoned, "The distribution of photographs and films depicting sexual activity by juveniles is intrinsically related to the sexual abuse of children in at least two ways": (1) "the materials produced are a permanent record of the children's participation and the harm to the child is exacerbated by their circulation"; and (2) "the distribution network for child pornography must be closed if the production of material which requires the sexual exploitation of children is to be effectively controlled." Ferber, 458 U.S. at 759. Second, the Court determined that "[t]he advertising and selling of child pornography provide an economic motive for and are thus an integral part of the production of such materials, an activity illegal throughout the Nation." Id. at 761. Finally, the Court found that "[t]he value of permitting live performances and photographic reproductions of children engaged in lewd sexual conduct is exceedingly modest, if not de minimus." Id. at 762. It noted that if "visual depictions of children performing sexual acts . . . were necessary for literary or artistic value, a person over the statutory age who perhaps looked younger could be utilized. Simulation outside of the prohibition of the statute could provide another alternative." Id. at 762-63.

Accordingly, because "[r]ecognizing and classifying child pornography as a category of material outside the protection of the First Amendment [wa]s not incompatible with [its] earlier decisions," id. at 763, the Court concluded that, generally, "[c]ontent-based restrictions on child pornography satisfy strict scrutiny," Alexander, 791 N.E.2d at 510 (citing Ferber, 458 U.S. at 756-59). The Court noted, however, that there are "limits on the category of child pornography which, like obscenity, is unprotected by the First Amendment." Ferber, 458 U.S. at 763. Thus, "distribution of descriptions or other depictions of sexual conduct, not otherwise obscene, which do not involve live performance or photographic or other visual reproduction of live performances, retains First Amendment protection." Id. at 764-65.

In Osborne, the Court extended Ferber's holding to allow states to proscribe the mere possession of child pornography. Osborne, 495 U.S. at 111. The Court noted that, in contrast to Stanley, where Georgia "was concerned that obscenity would poison the minds of its viewers," id. at 109 (citation omitted), Ohio did "not rely on a paternalistic interest in regulating Osborne's mind," id. Rather, Ohio proscribed possession of child pornography "to protect the victims of child pornography" by "destroy[ing] a market for the exploitative use of children." Id. Thus, the Court found that "the interests underlying child pornography prohibitions far exceed[ed] the interests justifying the Georgia law at issue in Stanley." Id. at 108.

Osborne additionally found that several interests justified Ohio's ban upon the possession of child pornography. First, "the use of children as subjects of pornographic materials is harmful to the physiological, emotional, and mental health of the child." Id. at 109. Second, it explained that "penaliz[ing] those who possess and view" child pornography will decrease its production, "thereby decreasing demand." Id. at 109-10. Third, relying upon Ferber, the Court reasoned: "[M]aterials produced by child pornographers permanently record the victim's abuse. The pornography's continued existence causes the child victims continuing harm by haunting the children in years to come. The State's ban on possession and viewing encourages the possessors of these materials to destroy them." Id. at 111 (citation omitted). Finally, the Court found that "encouraging the destruction of these materials is . . . desirable because evidence suggests that pedophiles use child pornography to seduce other children into sexual activity." Id. Accordingly, "[g]iven the gravity of the State's interests in this context," the Court held that Ohio could "constitutionally proscribe the possession and viewing of child pornography." Id.

In Ashcroft, the Supreme Court declared unconstitutional as overbroad section 2256(8)(B) of the Child Pornography Prevention Act of 1996 (CPPA), see 18 U.S.C. §§ 2251 et seq., which prohibited "any visual depiction, including any photograph, film, video, picture, or computer or computer-generated image or picture, that is, or appears to be, of a minor engaging in sexually explicit conduct." Ashcroft, 535 U.S. at 241 (quotations omitted; emphasis added). This "section capture[d] a range of depictions, sometimes called 'virtual child pornography,' which include computer-generated images, as well as images produced by more traditional means." Id. It also encompassed pornography "created by using adults who look like minors." Id. at 239-40.

In finding section 2256(8)(B) overbroad, the Supreme Court, although not explicitly, applied the strict scrutiny standard described above. See Alexander, 791 N.E.2d at 511 (concluding that, in Ashcroft, "section[] 2256(8)(B) . . . did not pass strict scrutiny because . . . [it was] not narrowly tailored to advance the government's compelling interest in protecting actual children from sexual abuse"); Note, Ashcroft v. Free Speech Coalition: How can Virtual Child Pornography be Banned Under the First Amendment, 31 Pepp. L. Rev. 825, 855 (2004) ("the Justices implicitly applied strict scrutiny"). The Court noted, "[T]he [Government's] speech ban is not narrowly drawn. The objective is to prohibit illegal conduct, but this restriction goes well beyond that interest by restricting the speech available to law-abiding adults." Ashcroft, 535 U.S. at 252-53.

The Government first argued that virtual child pornography fell within the category of child pornography unprotected by Ferber because it is "virtually indistinguishable from child pornography." Id. at 249. The Court rejected this contention for two reasons. First, in Ferber, "[t]he production of the work, not its content, was the target of the statute." Id. Thus, "[w]here the images are themselves the product of child sexual abuse, Ferber recognized that the State had an interest in stamping it out without regard to any judgment about its content." Id. (citation omitted). The Court clarified that Osborne "anchored its holding [that possession of child pornography is unprotected] in the concern for the participants, those whom it called the 'victims of child pornography.' It did not suggest that, absent this concern, other governmental interests would suffice." Id. at 250 (citation omitted).

Second, the Court rejected the Government's assertion that virtual child pornography "can lead to actual instances of child abuse." Id. It explained that, for virtual child pornography, "the causal link is contingent and indirect" because "[t]he harm does not necessarily follow from the speech, but depends upon some unquantified potential for subsequent criminal acts." Id. The Court found such indirect harms insufficient because, although "child pornography rarely can be valuable speech," id., "Ferber's judgment about child pornography was based upon how it was made, not on what it communicated," and "Ferber did not hold that child pornography is by definition without value," id. at 250-51. The Court concluded, "In contrast to the speech in Ferber, speech that itself is the record of sexual abuse, the CPPA prohibits speech that records no crime and creates no victims by its production. Virtual child pornography is not 'intrinsically related' to the sexual abuse of children, as were the materials in Ferber." Id. at 250. Accordingly, the Court rejected the government's assertion that virtual child pornography is unprotected speech under Ferber. Id. at 251.

Given its holding that virtual child pornography is protected speech, the Court went on to apply strict scrutiny to determine whether the Government could constitutionally proscribe this speech. Applying this demanding test, the Court flatly rejected the Government's justifications for banning virtual child pornography. First, the Government asserted that "the CPPA [wa]s necessary because pedophiles may use virtual child pornography to seduce children." Id. The Court disagreed and found that the CPPA was not "narrowly drawn" to achieve this objective. Id. at 252. It explained, "The Government cannot ban speech fit for adults simply because it may fall into the hands of children. The evil in question depends upon the actor's unlawful conduct, conduct defined as criminal quite apart from any link to the speech in question." Id. Thus, the restriction upon virtual child pornography went "well beyond" the interest in "prohibit[ing] illegal conduct" by "restricting the speech available to law-abiding adults." Id. at 252-53.

Second, the Government submitted that "virtual child pornography whets the appetites of pedophiles and encourages them to engage in illegal conduct." Id. at 253. This rationale could not sustain the ban on virtual child pornography because "[t]he mere tendency of speech to encourage unlawful acts is not a sufficient reason for banning it." Id. Quoting Stanley, 394 U.S. at 566, the Court explained that "[t]he government 'cannot constitutionally premise legislation on the desirability of controlling a person's private thoughts.'" Id. It also "may not prohibit speech because it increases the chance an unlawful act will be committed at some indefinite future time." Id. (quotation omitted). Accordingly, because "[t]he Government ha[d] shown no more than a remote connection between speech that might encourage thoughts or impulses and any resulting child abuse," id., the Court concluded that "the

Government [could] not prohibit speech on the ground that it may encourage pedophiles to engage in illegal conduct," id. at 253-54.

Third, the Government "argue[d] that its objective of eliminating the market for pornography produced using real children necessitates a prohibition on virtual images as well." Id. at 254. The Government submitted that since they are often indistinguishable and exchanged in the same market, the "virtual images promote the trafficking in works produced through the exploitation of real children." Id. Rejecting this market deterrence theory, the Court noted that "[i]n the case of the material covered by Ferber, the creation of the speech is itself the crime of child abuse; the prohibition deters the crime by removing the profit motive." Id. Because "there is no underlying crime at all" with virtual child pornography, the Government's market deterrence theory did not justify the statute. Id.

Finally, the Government maintained that virtual child pornography needed to be banned because advanced technology makes it difficult to determine whether "pictures were made by using real children or by using computer imaging," thus making it difficult "to prosecute those who produce pornography by using real children." Id. at 254-55. The Supreme Court found that this argument "turn[ed] the First Amendment upside down." Id. at 255. It explained: "Protected speech does not become unprotected merely because it resembles the latter. The Constitution requires the reverse." Id. Thus, the Government could not ban "unprotected speech if a substantial amount of protected speech [wa]s prohibited or chilled in the process." Id. Accordingly, because section 2256(8)(B) left "unprotected a substantial amount of speech not tied to the Government's interest in distinguishing images produced using real children from virtual ones," and "cover[ed] materials beyond the categories recognized in Ferber and Miller," the Court held that the provision was "overbroad and unconstitutional." Id. at 256.

Relying upon the foregoing cases, the defendant argues that applying RSA 649-A:3 to his private possession of morphed images, namely "images created by combining the head and shoulders of a real, existing child, with images of adult bodies, real or virtual, engaging in sexually explicit conduct," violates his right to free speech under both the Federal and State Constitutions. The defendant "does not claim that the state or federal constitutions preclude the government from criminalizing the distribution of such material." Rather, he contends that "Ashcroft, Ferber and Osborne, read together, mandate the conclusion that morphed images, that depict actual children but depict no children actually engaging in sexually [sic] activity, do not constitute child pornography." According to the defendant:

> [T]he overall set of rationales and principles relied
> upon by Ferber, and reinforced by Ashcroft's

> discussion of Ferber, support the narrow view that materials cannot be classified as child pornography unless children are involved in the production process – not the "post-production" process where images can be cut, pasted, and morphed – but the production process, the actual, sordid, filming or photography of child sexual abuse.

The State counters that because the defendant's images "incorporate identifiable pictures of real children," they "create harm to those children, even if the original pictures did not involve sexual activity, [since] those children are depicted as participating in such activity through manipulation of their likeness." The State argues that "harm is caused even when only one person views such an image," and, thus, "the State has a legitimate interest in preventing that harm, and no right of free speech is violated by prohibiting the possession of such images."

RSA 649-A:1 (2007) declares the legislature's purpose in criminalizing child pornography. It provides, in pertinent part:

> The legislature finds that there has been a proliferation of exploitation of children through their use as subjects in sexual performances. The care of children is a sacred trust and should not be abused by those who seek to profit through a commercial network based upon the exploitation of children. The public policy of the statute demands the protection of children from exploitation through sexual performances. . . . In accordance with the United States Supreme Court's decision in New York v. Ferber, this chapter makes the dissemination of visual representations of children under the age of 16 engaged in sexual activity illegal irrespective of whether the visual representations are legally obscene.

(Emphasis added.) Interpreting the identical legislative declaration in New York's statute, Ferber found that a state has a compelling interest "in safeguarding the physical and psychological health of a minor." Ferber, 458 U.S. at 756-57 (quotation omitted). As with our legislature's declaration, the focus in New York's statute was to combat the harm resulting to children from the distribution of depictions of sexual conduct involving live performance or visual reproduction of live performances by children. Id. at 764-65. Thus, the purpose of RSA 649-A:3 is to prevent harm to children resulting from their "use as subjects in sexual performances." RSA 649-A:1.

While this interest is undoubtedly compelling, Ferber, 458 U.S. at 756-57, criminalizing the possession of materials depicting heads and necks of identifiable minor females superimposed upon naked female bodies, where the naked bodies do not depict body parts of actual children engaging in sexual activity, does not promote this interest. Contrary to the State's assertion, when no part of the image is "the product of sexual abuse," Ashcroft, 535 U.S. at 249, and a person merely possesses the image, no demonstrable harm results to the child whose face is depicted in the image.

In Ashcroft, the Court emphasized that "Ferber's judgment about child pornography was based upon how it was made, not on what it communicated." Ashcroft, 535 U.S. at 250-51. Unlike the images in Ferber and Osborne, the images in this case do not "permanently record the [child]'s abuse." Osborne, 495 U.S. at 111. Although they may constitute a "permanent record" that if distributed may be harmful to the depicted child, such harm does not necessarily follow from the mere possession of these morphed images. Instead, the harm is contingent upon the occurrence of another arguably unlawful act; to wit, distribution. See Ashcroft, 535 U.S. at 250. The State "may not prohibit speech because it increases the chance an unlawful act will be committed at some indefinite future time." Id. at 253 (quotation omitted).

Further, while Osborne proscribes the mere possession of pornography produced with real children, see Ashcroft, 535 U.S. at 245-46; Osborne, 495 U.S. at 111, its holding is anchored in "the concern for the participants, those whom it called the 'victims of child pornography,'" Ashcroft, 535 U.S. at 250 (quoting Osborne, 495 U.S. at 110). These participants are the children who have been sexually abused or exploited in the production of the materials. Ferber, 458 U.S. at 759. The mere possession of morphed images depicting no victims of child pornography cannot "haunt[] the children in years to come," Osborne, 495 U.S. at 111, since the children do not know of their existence and did not participate in their production. Therefore, the foundation for Osborne's proscription on possession of child pornography is not present here.

Moreover, while a ban upon the possession of these morphed images may encourage possessors to destroy them, besides the indirect harm that may result from the potential distribution of these materials, the State has not advanced any additional narrow justification supporting this interest. As explained above, the possible circulation of these materials is insufficient justification for banning protected speech. Ashcroft, 535 U.S. at 250, 253. To the extent the State asserts that these morphed images require destruction because pedophiles use them to "seduce other children into sexual activity," Osborne, 495 U.S. at 111, the Supreme Court explicitly rejected this rationale in Ashcroft. Ashcroft, 535 U.S. at 253-54. Additionally, because they are not the product of the crime of child abuse, criminalizing the possession of these morphed images created from "innocent pictures" of actual children would not eliminate the market for pornography produced through the abuse of real children. Ashcroft, 535 U.S. at 254. Therefore, their possession is "not 'intrinsically related' to the sexual abuse of children, as were the materials in Ferber." Ashcroft, 535 U.S. at 250.

Finally, however distasteful, reprehensible, and valueless this conduct might seem, cf. Ferber, 458 U.S. at 762, the First Amendment protects "the individual's right to . . . observe what he pleases," Stanley, 394 U.S. at 567-68. This protection is central to our long and sacred tradition of prohibiting the government from intruding into the privacy of our thoughts and the contents of our homes. We cannot displace this guarantee simply because the materials at issue may express ideas that are unconventional and not shared by a majority. See id. at 566.

Although Ashcroft stated, in dicta, that morphed images "implicate the interests of real children and are in that sense closer to the images in Ferber," Ashcroft, 535 U.S. at 242, Ferber involved the distribution of child pornography, not its possession, Ferber, 458 U.S. at 751-52. Unlike a distribution case, in the private possession realm, neither the real child nor the general public observes the images; only the possessor views them. See Stanley, 394 U.S. at 567. Thus, while distribution of these morphed images might implicate the interests of real children, mere possession does not cause harm to the child. Accordingly, applying the standard articulated in Ashcroft, Ferber, and Stanley to the defendant, the statute is not narrowly tailored to achieve the State's asserted objectives.

The State cites United States v. Bach, 400 F.3d 622 (8th Cir. 2005), cert. denied, 546 U.S. 901 (2005), in support of its position that these morphed images may be criminalized. In Bach, "a photograph of the head of a well known juvenile, AC, was skillfully inserted onto the body of [a young] nude boy so that the resulting depiction appear[ed] to be a picture of AC engaging in sexually explicit conduct with a knowing grin." Bach, 400 F.3d at 632 (emphasis added). The Eighth Circuit Court of Appeals found:

> Although there is no contention that the nude body actually is that of AC or that he was involved in the production of the image, a lasting record has been created of AC, an identifiable minor child, seemingly engaged in sexually explicit activity. He is thus victimized every time the picture is displayed. Unlike . . . virtual child pornography or . . . pornography using youthful looking adults . . . , this image created an identifiable child victim of sexual exploitation.

Id. The Court noted, however, that "[t]his is not the typical morphing case in which an innocent picture of a child has been altered to appear that the child is engaging in sexually explicit conduct," and that "there may well be instances in which the [statute] violates the First Amendment." Id. at 632 (emphasis added).

Bach is distinguishable for two reasons. First, in Bach, the defendant challenged his conviction "for receipt of child pornography under [18 U.S.C.] § 2252A(a)(2)," id. at 629 (emphasis added), not possession of child pornography, see 18 U.S.C. § 2252A(a)(5). A conviction under 18 U.S.C. § 2252A(a)(2) requires that a person "knowingly receive[] or distribute[] . . . child pornography [or material that contains child pornography] that has been mailed, or shipped or transported in interstate or foreign commerce by any means, including by computer." 18 U.S.C. § 2252A(a)(2) (emphases added); see Bach, 400 F.3d at 630. Since these pictures do not remain within the privacy of a person's home, but instead disseminate into commerce, the interests of real children arguably may be implicated in such cases. Here, the defendant was not charged with receiving or distributing the images. See RSA 649-A:3(c)-(f). Therefore, we do not address whether we might reach the same result as Bach if presented with a case involving the receipt or distribution of morphed images.

Second, unlike these morphed images, the Bach picture depicted a young nude boy engaged in sexually explicit activity. Bach, 400 F.3d at 632. Thus, in Bach, the creation of the photograph involved the use and sexual exploitation of a real child. In contrast, the record here contains no evidence indicating that any of these morphed images depict similar conduct by a real child. Accordingly, while we might reach a different result if presented with the facts in Bach, this case constitutes one of those instances where application of a statute proscribing the possession of child pornography violates the First Amendment. Id.

Our finding that application of RSA 649-A:3(e) to the defendant's conduct violates his First Amendment right to free speech is limited to the facts of this particular case, where the defendant is charged with mere possession of morphed images that depict heads and necks of identifiable minor females superimposed upon naked female bodies, and the naked bodies do not depict body parts of actual children engaging in sexual activity. Given this finding, we do not reach the defendant's overbreadth challenge. Accordingly, the defendant's convictions are reversed.

Reversed.

BRODERICK, C.J., concurred; HICKS, J., dissented.

HICKS, J., dissenting. Because I believe that United States Supreme Court precedents do not compel the result the majority reaches and I believe that the State may constitutionally criminalize the defendant's mere possession of the images in question, I respectfully dissent. I would hold that the images possessed and controlled by the defendant are "visual representation[s] of a child engaging in sexual activity" as proscribed by RSA 649-A:3 (2007); that the statute is not fatally overbroad; and that its applicability to the defendant's conduct violates no free speech rights.

First, I cannot conclude that Ashcroft v. Free Speech Coalition, 535 U.S. 234 (2002), compels a finding that the defendant's morphed images are protected speech under the First Amendment to the United States Constitution in part because the Court explicitly left that question open. The respondents in Ashcroft did not challenge the provision of the Child Pornography Prevention Act of 1996 (CPPA), 18 U.S.C. §§ 2251 et seq., that prohibits morphed images. Id. at 242.

Writing for the majority in Ashcroft, Justice Kennedy explained:

> Section 2256(8)(C) [of the CPPA] prohibits a more common and lower tech means of creating virtual images, known as computer morphing. Rather than creating original images, pornographers can alter innocent pictures of real children so that the children appear to be engaged in sexual activity. Although morphed images may fall within the definition of virtual child pornography, they implicate the interests of real children and are in that sense closer to the images in [New York v. Ferber, 458 U.S. 747 (1982)]. Respondents do not challenge this provision, and we do not consider it.

Id. I believe that this is precisely the case left undecided by Ashcroft. Moreover, in my view, much of Ashcroft and Ferber is dicta, and, as such, does not compel any particular result in this case.

Although I believe that the majority correctly analyzes the Ferber factors, I would simply draw the opposite conclusion. For instance, the Ferber Court recognized that States have a compelling interest "in safeguarding the physical and psychological well-being of a minor." Ferber, 458 U.S at 756-57 (quotation omitted). I believe that this interest is implicated when pictures of identifiable real children are altered to make it appear as though the children are engaging in sexual activity. The Ferber Court noted the legislative and professional opinion that "the use of children as subjects of pornographic materials is harmful to the physiological, emotional, and mental health of the child." Id. at 758 (emphasis added). I believe that a child need not actually engage in the sexual activity depicted in morphed child pornography to be a victim of sexual exploitation. See United States v. Bach, 400 F.3d 622, 632 (8th Cir.), cert. denied, 546 U.S. 901 (2005) (concluding that image depicting the head of "AC, an identifiable minor child" on the nude body of an unidentified boy in a sexually explicit pose, "created an identifiable child victim [i.e., AC] of sexual exploitation"). I also believe that the State has a compelling interest in protecting children from such exploitation.

The Ferber Court noted that "[t]he distribution of photographs and films depicting sexual activity by juveniles is intrinsically related to the sexual abuse of children in at least two ways:" (1) "the materials produced are a permanent record of the children's participation and the harm to the child is exacerbated by their circulation;" and (2) "the distribution network for child pornography must be closed if the production of material which requires the sexual exploitation of children is to be effectively controlled." Ferber, 458 U.S. at 759. I acknowledge that the morphed images here do not implicate these concerns as directly as the images at issue in Ferber – images that the Ashcroft Court described as "speech that itself is the record of sexual abuse," Ashcroft, 535 U.S. at 250. Because they can be produced from "innocent pictures of real children," id. at 242, morphed images do not require the sexual abuse of a child for their production. Nevertheless, such images do produce a permanent record of the children's apparent participation in sexual activity. Cf. Ferber, 458 U.S. at 759. As discussed above, I believe that such images sexually exploit the real child whose image is used and I find the conclusion inescapable that "the harm to the child is exacerbated by their circulation." Id. Additionally, if one accepts the premise that morphed pornographic images of real children exploit those children, it logically follows that the production of such morphed images "requires the sexual exploitation of [those] children," id. Thus, I believe that morphed pornographic images of actual children sufficiently implicate the second Ferber rationale.

Another factor in the Ferber Court's reasoning was that "[t]he value of permitting live performances and photographic reproductions of children engaged in lewd sexual conduct is exceedingly modest, if not de minimis." Id. at 762. I believe that the value of permitting the exploitation of children by using their images to create virtual depictions of them engaged in sexual activity is de minimis at best.

Admittedly, not all of the Ferber factors obtain here; in my view, however, the absence of one or more of the Ferber factors is not fatal to this prosecution. The presence of those listed above is sufficient to warrant classifying the images possessed by the defendant as child pornography within the meaning of Ferber. Having reached that conclusion, I would hold that the images in question fall squarely within Osborne v. Ohio, 495 U.S. 103 (1990), in which the Supreme Court held that States may constitutionally criminalize the mere possession and viewing of child pornography, id. at 111. In addition, using the above-cited federal opinions for guidance only, see State v. Ball, 124 N.H. 226, 233 (1983), in the absence of controlling state precedent, I would hold that criminalizing the defendant's mere possession of the images at issue does not violate the State Constitution. Accordingly, I would reject the defendant's as-applied challenge and reach his facial challenge.

The defendant argues that this court's construction of RSA 649-A:3 in State v. Cobb, 143 N.H. 638 (1999), renders that statute substantially overbroad under the reasoning of Ashcroft. Although Ashcroft declared two provisions of the CPPA unconstitutional, only the first of those provisions, section 2256(8)(B), is relevant to this case. That section prohibited "any visual depiction, including any photograph, film, video, picture, or computer or computer-generated image or picture, that is, or appears to be, of a minor engaging in sexually explicit conduct." Ashcroft, 535 U.S. at 241 (quotations omitted). In concluding that section 2256(8)(B) was unconstitutionally overbroad, the Court declared that "[b]y prohibiting child pornography that does not depict an actual child, the statute goes beyond New York v. Ferber." Id. at 240.

The defendant contends that in Cobb, this court "construed [RSA 649-A:3] to extend to visual representations that did not involve any actual child engaging in sexual activity." The defendant cites the following language:

> There is no statutory requirement that the visual representation involve the use of an actual child. Furthermore, we see little meaningful distinction between sexually explicit material produced through the use of an actual child and such material that gives the appearance of having been produced through the use of an actual child.

Cobb, 143 N.H. at 644 (citations omitted).

As the trial court similarly concluded, however, the defendant takes the statement out of context. The defendant in Cobb argued that the statute did not apply to his "photographs because no children were used in sexual performances in order to create them." Id. This court's response, therefore, was focused upon the "use" of a child in a sexual performance. Thus, in saying that the statute did not require "the use of an actual child," id., the court held that the statute did not require that a child actually engage in the sexual activity depicted. In my view, that statement was not intended to decide whether or not the child depicted must be an actual child, as that question was not before the court.

Because I agree with the State that RSA 649-A:3 can be construed to apply only to images of real children, I would hold that the statute is not unconstitutionally overbroad. RSA 649-A:3, I, provides, in relevant part, that "[a] person is guilty of a felony if such person . . . (e) Knowingly buys, procures, possesses, or controls any visual representation of a child engaging in sexual activity." "Child" is defined to mean "any <u>person</u> under the age of 16 years." RSA 649-A:2, I (2007) (emphasis added). I conclude that construing the word "person" in RSA 649-A:2, I, to mean a real person, and the word "child" in RSA 649-A:3 to mean a real child, is a permissible interpretation of the statute. Cf. <u>Commonwealth v. Simone</u>, No. 03-0986, 2003 WL 22994238, at *15, *14 (Va. Cir. Ct. Nov. 12, 2003) (concluding that plain language of statute "confines its application to images utilizing actual children" where "[t]he statute specifically requires that the material at issue utilize or have as its subject a 'person'").

When RSA 649-A:2, I, is construed to refer to an actual child, RSA 649-A:3 does not reach the "virtual" pornography at issue in <u>Ashcroft</u>: images that look like real children but that are in fact wholly computer-generated. See <u>Ashcroft</u>, 535 U.S. at 241. In addition, because "[c]hild" is specifically defined to mean a "person under the age of 16 years," RSA 649-A:2, I, RSA 649-A:3 covers only images of actual persons who are, in fact, under sixteen years of age and does not reach images that appear to be of children but that are, in reality, of young-looking adults. Cf. <u>State v. Fingal</u>, 666 N.W.2d 420, 424 (Minn. Ct. App. 2003) ("'Minor' is defined [in the statute] as 'any person under the age of 18.' If the sexual performance depicted does not, in fact, involve a person under the age of 18, possession of the depiction is not prohibited."). Accordingly, under this construction, RSA 649-A:3 would not suffer the infirmities that rendered section 2256(8)(B) of the CPPA substantially, and therefore unconstitutionally, overbroad. Other courts have reached similar conclusions. See <u>id</u>. at 425 (concluding that where a statute prohibiting child pornography requires that "[t]he visual depiction must be of an identifiable minor, not a virtual child," the statute complies with <u>Ashcroft</u>); <u>State v. Tooley</u>, 872 N.E.2d 894, 907 (Ohio 2007) ("[M]orphed child pornography that uses images of real children . . . is not covered by the <u>Ashcroft</u> definition of protected virtual child pornography."), <u>cert. denied</u>, __ S. Ct. __, 2008 WL 59614 (U.S. Oct. 23, 2007) (No. 07-7366). I would also hold, using the above-cited federal opinions for guidance only, see <u>Ball</u>, 124 N.H. 233 (1983), in the absence of controlling state precedent, that RSA 649-A:3 is not fatally overbroad under the State Constitution.

The defendant's final challenge to his conviction alleges insufficiency of the evidence. That challenge is expressly conditioned, however, upon this court having "resolve[d] the constitutional issues by construing RSA 649-A:3 narrowly so that it does not reach [the defendant's] conduct." As I would not so construe the statute, I would not reach the defendant's final argument. Accordingly, I would uphold the trial court's denial of the defendant's motions and affirm the result below.

NOTICE: This opinion is subject to motions for rehearing under Rule 22 as well as formal revision before publication in the New Hampshire Reports. Readers are requested to notify the Reporter, Supreme Court of New Hampshire, One Charles Doe Drive, Concord, New Hampshire 03301, of any editorial errors in order that corrections may be made before the opinion goes to press. Errors may be reported by E-mail at the following address: reporter@courts.state.nh.us. Opinions are available on the Internet by 9:00 a.m. on the morning of their release. The direct address of the court's home page is: http://www.courts.state.nh.us/supreme.

THE SUPREME COURT OF NEW HAMPSHIRE

_____

4th Circuit Court-Laconia District Division
No. 2017-0116

THE STATE OF NEW HAMPSHIRE

v.

HEIDI C. LILLEY

THE STATE OF NEW HAMPSHIRE

v.

KIA SINCLAIR

THE STATE OF NEW HAMPSHIRE

v.

GINGER M. PIERRO

Argued: February 1, 2018
Opinion Issued: February 8, 2019

Gordon J. MacDonald, attorney general (Susan P. McGinnis, senior assistant attorney general, on the brief and orally), for the State.

Liberty Legal Services, of Manchester (Dan Hynes on the brief and orally), for the defendants.

American Civil Liberties Union of New Hampshire, of Concord (Gilles R. Bissonnette on the brief), as amicus curiae.

HANTZ MARCONI, J. The defendants, Heidi Lilley, Kia Sinclair, and Ginger Pierro, appeal a ruling of the Circuit Court (Carroll, J.) that they violated a City of Laconia ordinance prohibiting them from appearing in a state of nudity in a public place. See Laconia, N.H., Code of Ordinances ch. 180, art. I, § 180-2 (1998). We affirm.

I. Background

The following facts are drawn from the trial court's order on the defendants' motion to dismiss or are otherwise supported by the record. On May 28, 2016, Pierro went to Endicott Park Beach in Laconia. At the hearing on the defendants' motion to dismiss, Pierro testified that she "was topless" and was there "to enjoy the beach." She agreed with defense counsel that she was "performing yoga on the beach." She stated that she "was violently harassed" by "[s]everal citizens," but that "out of everybody on the beach, there were only actually a handful that were upset."

Sergeant Black of the Laconia Police Department testified that, on that same day, he and Officer Callanan responded to the beach because the department had "received several calls about a female . . . doing nude yoga." Callanan testified that they approached a woman, later identified as Pierro, who was "not wearing any shirt and her breasts, as well as her nipples, were both exposed." Callanan stated that she "made attempts to speak to" Pierro, but that Pierro "continued to do her yoga poses." She explained that "after about a minute or so, [Pierro] looked up and acknowledged that we were, in fact, trying to speak to her." She testified that they "explained to [Pierro] that the reason [they] were making contact with her was in reference to a Laconia City Ordinance, since her nipples were exposed on the beach in a public place." Callanan stated that they asked Pierro "multiple times to cover up, to put her bathing suit top back on, or put her shirt back on," but that Pierro "refused."

Callanan testified that Pierro was arrested for violating Laconia City Ordinance § 180-2 (the ordinance), which states, in relevant part, that "it shall be unlawful for any person to knowingly or intentionally, in a public place: . . . [a]ppear in a state of nudity." "Nudity" is defined as "[t]he showing of the human male or female genitals, pubic area or buttocks with less than a fully opaque covering, or the showing of the female breast with less than a fully opaque covering of any part of the nipple." Laconia, N.H., Code of Ordinances ch. 180, art. I, § 180-4 (1998).

In 2015, Sinclair became involved in the "Free the Nipple" movement. Sinclair testified that she was one of the people who "started" the movement in

New Hampshire after having her son and realizing "that there was a very big stigma on breastfeeding." She explained that she believed that breasts, specifically nipples, are "hypersexualize[d]" and "consider[ed] pornographic and taboo," which she stated results "in that stigma" and "contributes to the low breastfeeding rates that the United States has compared to the rest of the world." Sinclair told Lilley about the movement, which Lilley then joined. Lilley testified that she is "a feminist" and joined the movement because she "believe[s] in the equality of the male and female."

On May 31, 2016, Sinclair and Lilley went topless to Weirs Beach in Laconia. While at the beach, they were arrested for violating the ordinance. Sinclair testified that she "purposely engaged in civil disobedience knowing that the City of Laconia has an ordinance against the exposure of the female nipple and areola." She stated that she was "protesting [Pierro's] case where she had been arrested a few days prior." Lilley testified that she was also protesting Pierro's arrest and that she "announced to the arresting police officer that [she] was acting in a protest and that [she] did not believe that [she] could be arrested for protesting." She further agreed with the prosecutor that, on that day, she "chose to take it upon [herself] to violate the ordinance to give attention to [her] cause."

The defendants jointly moved to dismiss the charges against them. They argued that the ordinance violates the guarantee of equal protection and their right to free speech under the State and Federal Constitutions. They further contended that the City of Laconia lacked the authority to enact the ordinance and that the ordinance was preempted by RSA 645:1 (2016). Finally, the defendants maintained that the ordinance violates RSA chapter 354-A. See RSA ch. 354-A (2009 & Supp. 2017) (amended 2018). The State objected. Following a hearing, the court denied the defendants' motion. The court subsequently found the defendants guilty of violating the ordinance. This appeal followed.

On appeal, the defendants argue that the trial court erred by denying their motion to dismiss because the ordinance: (1) violates their right to equal protection under the State and Federal Constitutions; (2) violates their rights to free speech and expression under the State and Federal Constitutions; (3) does not fall within the regulatory authority granted to the City of Laconia by the legislature; (4) is preempted by RSA 645:1; and (5) violates RSA chapter 354-A. We will address each of the defendants' arguments in turn.

II. Equal Protection

The defendants first argue that the ordinance violates their right to equal protection under Part I, Article 2 of the New Hampshire Constitution and the Fourteenth Amendment to the United States Constitution. See N.H. CONST. pt. I, art. 2; U.S. CONST. amend. XIV. We review the constitutionality of local ordinances de novo. McKenzie v. Town of Eaton Zoning Bd. of Adjustment, 154 N.H. 773, 777 (2007). We first address the defendants' arguments under the State Constitution and cite federal opinions for guidance only. State v. Ball, 124 N.H. 226, 231-33 (1983).

We begin by addressing the scope of the defendants' challenge to the ordinance. An appellant may challenge the constitutionality of a statute or an ordinance[1] by asserting a facial challenge, an as-applied challenge, or both. See State v. Hollenbeck, 164 N.H. 154, 158 (2012). A facial challenge is a head-on attack of a legislative judgment, an assertion that the challenged statute violates the Constitution in all, or virtually all, of its applications. Id. To prevail on a facial challenge, the challenger must establish that no set of circumstances exists under which the challenged statute or ordinance would be valid. Id. On the other hand, an as-applied challenge concedes that the statute may be constitutional in many of its applications, but contends that it is not so under the particular circumstances of the case. Id.

Here, the defendants do not concede that the relevant portion of the ordinance is constitutional in any circumstance. They argue that "the ordinance makes a gender-based classification on its face." We construe their claim to be a facial challenge to the portion of the ordinance that prohibits "the showing of the female breast with less than a fully opaque covering of any part of the nipple" in a public place. See Laconia, N.H., Code of Ordinances ch. 180, art. I, §§ 180-2, 180-4. Thus, the defendants must demonstrate that there is no set of circumstances under which this ordinance might be valid. See Hollenbeck, 164 N.H. at 158.

Next, we must determine the appropriate standard of review to apply to the ordinance. In re Sandra H., 150 N.H. 634, 637 (2004). We do this by examining the purpose and scope of the State-created classification and the individual rights affected. Id. Classifications based upon suspect classes are subject to strict scrutiny: the government must show that the legislation is necessary to achieve a compelling government interest and is narrowly tailored. Cmty. Res. for Justice v. City of Manchester, 154 N.H. 748, 759 (2007). Classifications which affect a fundamental right may be subject to strict scrutiny depending on the nature of the right and the manner in which it is affected. See Estate of Cargill v. City of Rochester, 119 N.H. 661, 667 (1979); see also Bleiler v. Chief, Dover Police Dep't, 155 N.H. 693, 697-98 (2007); Lamarche v. McCarthy, 158 N.H. 197, 204 (2008). Below strict scrutiny is intermediate scrutiny, which is triggered when the challenged classification involves important substantive rights, Sandra H., 150 N.H. at 637-38, and which requires the government to show that the challenged legislation is substantially related to an important government interest. Cmty. Res., 154

---

[1] No party asserts that, for the purposes of considering their constitutional arguments, it makes any difference that we are dealing with an ordinance rather than a statute.

N.H. at 762. Finally, absent a classification based upon suspect classes, affecting fundamental rights, or involving important substantive rights, the constitutional standard of review is that of rationality. Sandra H., 150 N.H. at 638; cf. Gonya v. Comm'r, N.H. Ins. Dept., 153 N.H. 521, 532-33 (2006). Our rational basis test requires that legislation be rationally related to a legitimate government interest. Boulders at Strafford v. Town of Strafford, 153 N.H. 633, 639 (2006). Under this test, the party challenging the statute or ordinance must show that whatever classification is promulgated is arbitrary or without some reasonable justification. Id. at 640.

The defendants argue that the ordinance discriminates on the basis of gender and/or sex; thus, strict scrutiny is the appropriate standard of review. The State counters that the ordinance only distinguishes between men and women on the basis of their different physical characteristics; thus, the rational basis test applies.

Under federal equal protection law, pursuant to the Fourteenth Amendment, a classification based on gender triggers intermediate scrutiny. United States v. Virginia, 518 U.S. 515, 532-33 (1996). Part I, Article 2 of the New Hampshire Constitution states, however, "Equality of rights under the law shall not be denied or abridged by this state on account of race, creed, color, sex or national origin." N.H. CONST. pt. I, art. 2. Thus, under the New Hampshire Constitution, gender is a suspect class and classifications based thereon trigger strict scrutiny. See Cheshire Medical Center v. Holbrook, 140 N.H. 187, 189 (1995); see also LeClair v. LeClair, 137 N.H. 213, 222 (1993) ("We apply the strict scrutiny test . . . when the classification involves a suspect class based on race, creed, color, gender, national origin, or legitimacy . . . ." (quotation omitted)) (superseded by statute on other grounds). In Holbrook, we applied strict scrutiny to the common law doctrine of necessaries, which made husbands legally liable for essential goods or services provided to their wives by third parties. Holbrook, 140 N.H. at 189-90. We concluded that there was no compelling justification for the gender bias embodied in the traditional necessaries doctrine. Id. at 189. However, Holbrook did not address the type of legislation that is at issue here: a proscription that imposes requirements on both men and women, but applies to women somewhat differently. Thus, Holbrook, the only case in which we have applied strict scrutiny to a gender-based classification, does not necessarily establish that the Laconia ordinance triggers strict scrutiny.

Courts in other jurisdictions have generally upheld laws that prohibit women but not men from exposing their breasts against equal protection challenges. See generally Kimberly J. Winbush, Annotation, Regulation of Exposure of Female, but not Male, Breasts, 67 A.L.R.5th 431 (1999) (collecting cases). But see Free the Nipple Fort Collins v. City of Fort Collins, Colorado, 237 F. Supp. 3d 1126, 1133 (D. Colo. 2017) (concluding that equal protection challenge to ordinance prohibiting women but not men from exposing their breasts was likely to succeed on the merits). In so doing, however, they have often left unclear the applicable standard of review. See Tolbert v. City of Memphis, Tenn., 568 F. Supp. 1285, 1290 (W.D. Tenn. 1983); City of Jackson v. Lakeland Lounge, 688 So. 2d 742, 751-52 (Miss. 1996); State v. Turner, 382 N.W.2d 252, 255-56 (Minn. Ct. App. 1986); Free the Nipple – Springfield Residents Promoting Equality v. City of Springfield, Missouri, No. 15-3467-CV-S-BP, 2017 WL 6815041, at *2-3 (W.D. Mo. Oct. 4, 2017). Some courts have assumed without deciding that such laws are gender-based and thus trigger intermediate scrutiny under the Federal Constitution, and then upheld them on the grounds that the heightened requirements of intermediate scrutiny were satisfied. See Ways v. City of Lincoln, 331 F.3d 596, 600 (8th Cir. 2003); United States v. Biocic, 928 F.2d 112, 115 (4th Cir. 1991); J & B Soc. Club No. 1, Inc. v. City of Mobile, 966 F. Supp. 1131, 1139 (S.D. Ala. 1996). Others have explicitly held that laws which prohibit women but not men from exposing their breasts are gender-based and trigger intermediate scrutiny either under federal equal protection law or an analogous state constitutional provision. See Tagami v. City of Chicago, 875 F.3d 375, 380 (7th Cir. 2017), cert. denied, 138 S. Ct. 1577 (2018) (Federal Constitution); Buzzetti v. City of New York, 140 F.3d 134, 141-42 (2d Cir. 1998) (Federal Constitution); Craft v. Hodel, 683 F. Supp. 289, 299 (D. Mass. 1988) (Federal Constitution); City of Tucson v. Wolfe, 917 P.2d 706, 707 (Ariz. Ct. App. 1995) (state constitution); Dydyn v. Department of Liquor Control, 531 A.2d 170, 175 (Conn. App. Ct. 1987) (state constitution). Still others appear to have concluded that such laws do not trigger any form of heightened constitutional review. See Schleuter v. City of Fort Worth, 947 S.W.2d 920, 925-26 (Tex. App. 1997) (state constitution); City of Seattle v. Buchanan, 584 P.2d 918, 920-22 (Wash. 1978) (en banc) (state constitution); Eckl v. Davis, 124 Cal. Rptr. 685, 695-96 (Ct. App. 1975); see also Hang On, Inc. v. City of Arlington, 65 F.3d 1248, 1256-57 (5th Cir. 1995).

Among states, like New Hampshire, that define gender as a suspect class under their respective state constitutions, we are aware of none that apply strict scrutiny to ordinances similar to Laconia's.[2] See Buchanan, 584 P.2d at 921; City of Albuquerque v. Sachs, 92 P.3d 24, 27, 29 (N.M. Ct. App. 2004). Compare Williams v. City of Fort Worth, 782 S.W.2d 290, 296 (Tex. App. 1989) (recognizing that sex is a suspect class under Texas Constitution), with Schleuter, 947 S.W.2d at 925-26 (applying no heightened scrutiny to ordinance that restricted locations of businesses featuring female topless dancers).

In Buchanan, for example, the Washington Supreme Court held that an ordinance which prohibited both men and women from being nude in public, but defined nudity for women to include exposure of the breast, "d[id] not . . . impose unequal responsibilities on women" because the ordinance "applie[d] alike to men and women, requiring both to cover those parts of their bodies

---

[2] Relatedly, we are aware of no court with precedent-setting authority that has held such an ordinance unconstitutional. But cf. Free the Nipple Fort Collins, 237 F. Supp. 3d at 1133.

which are intimately associated with the procreation function." Buchanan, 584 P.2d at 921. The court noted, "It is true that [the ordinance] requires the draping of more parts of the female body than of the male, but only because there are more parts of the female body intimately associated with the procreative function. The fact that the ordinance takes account of this fact does not render it discriminatory." Id. at 922. Thus the ordinance did not "classify . . . on the basis of sex." Id. at 921.

The Eckl court reasoned similarly:

Nature, not the legislative body, created the distinction between that portion of a woman's body and that of a man's torso. Unlike the situation with respect to men, nudity in the case of women is commonly understood to include the uncovering of the breasts. Consequently, in proscribing nudity on the part of women it was necessary to include express reference to that area of the body. The classification is reasonable, not arbitrary, and rests upon a ground of difference having a fair and substantial relation to the object of the legislation, so that all persons similarly circumstanced are treated alike.

Eckl, 124 Cal. Rptr. at 696.

While Washington and California appear to address these considerations in the threshold analysis of the applicable standard of review, other courts that apply intermediate scrutiny to these types of laws have upheld them based on similar reasoning. See, e.g., Craft, 683 F. Supp. at 300 (quoting Eckl); see also Michael M. v. Sonoma County Superior Court, 450 U.S. 464, 468-69 (1981) (plurality opinion) ("[T]his court has consistently upheld statutes where the gender classification . . . realistically reflects the fact that the sexes are not similarly situated in certain circumstances.").

We conclude that the Laconia ordinance does not classify on the basis of gender. The ordinance prohibits both men and women from being nude in a public place. See Laconia, N.H., Code of Ordinances ch.180, art. 1, §§ 180-2, 180-4. "[T]he ordinance here does not prevent exposure by one sex only." Buchanan, 584 P.2d at 922. That the ordinance defines nudity to include exposure of the female but not male breast does not mean that it classifies based upon a suspect class. See id.; Gonya, 153 N.H. at 532. "Unlike the situation with respect to men, nudity in the case of women is commonly understood to include the uncovering of the breasts." Eckl, 124 Cal. Rptr. at 696. The ordinance merely reflects the fact that men and women are not fungible with respect to the traditional understanding of what constitutes nudity. See id.; Sachs, 92 P.3d at 29; see also Biocic, 928 F.2d at 115-16 (noting that female breasts have traditionally been regarded by society as an erogenous zone); Buzzetti, 140 F.3d at 143 (noting that, unlike the male breast, "public exposure of the female breast is rare under the conventions of our society, and almost invariably conveys sexual overtones"); cf. Virginia, 518 U.S. at 533 ("The two sexes are not fungible; a community made up exclusively of one sex is different from a community composed of both." (quotation and brackets omitted)).

Nor do we find that the ordinance affects a fundamental right. See Eckl, 124 Cal. Rptr. at 695. Although freedom of speech is a fundamental right, see McGraw v. Exeter Region Coop. Sch. Dist., 145 N.H. 709, 713 (2001), "[b]eing in a state of nudity is not an inherently expressive condition," Erie v. Pap's A.M., 529 U.S. 277, 289 (2000). Even assuming without deciding that the defendants' nudity in this case was expressive, not every restriction of a right classified as fundamental incurs strict scrutiny. Bleiler, 155 N.H. at 697-98. For limitations upon a fundamental right to be subject to strict scrutiny, there must be an actual deprivation of the right. Lamarche, 158 N.H. at 204; see also Estate of Cargill, 119 N.H. at 667. For the reasons discussed in Part III, infra, there was no such deprivation here. Similarly, intermediate scrutiny does not apply because the ordinance does not involve an important substantive right. Cf. LeClair, 137 N.H. at 222-23. Hence, rational basis is the appropriate standard of review for this ordinance.

Applying the standard, we have little trouble concluding that the defendants have not carried the heavy burden of mounting a successful facial attack to an ordinance analyzed only for rationality. The stated purpose of the ordinance is to uphold and support "public health, public safety, morals and public order." Laconia, N.H., Code of Ordinances ch. 180, art. I, § 180-1 (1998). Under the terms of the ordinance, "[t]he conduct prohibited . . . is deemed to be contrary to the societal interest in order and morality." Id. Federal courts have found these to be important or substantial interests under intermediate scrutiny, let alone legitimate ones under rational basis review. See Tagami, 875 F.3d at 379-80 (finding the purposes of "promoting traditional moral norms and public order" to be "important enough to survive [intermediate] scrutiny"); Biocic, 928 F.2d at 115-16 (finding "important" the "government interest . . . [in] protecting the moral sensibilities of that substantial segment of society that still does not want to be exposed" to parts of the body "that traditionally in this society have been regarded as erogenous zones"); Craft, 683 F. Supp. at 299-300 (finding a sufficient state interest in "protect[ing] the public from invasions of its sensibilities"); see also Barnes v. Glen Theatre, Inc., 501 U.S. 560, 569 (1991). We likewise conclude that they are legitimate government interests. "The traditional police power of the States is defined as the authority to provide for the public health, safety, and morals." Barnes, 501 U.S. at 569. Furthermore, the ordinance is rationally related to advancing those interests. See id. at 571-72; Craft, 683 F. Supp. at 300-01.

For these reasons, we hold that the ordinance does not violate Part I, Article 2 of the New Hampshire Constitution.[3]

The dissent faults us for seeking guidance from other courts in ascertaining whether Laconia's ordinance classifies based on gender. However, as demonstrated by the lack of any meaningful discussion of our precedent in the dissent, we have little in the way of help from our own cases in answering this question. Although we applied strict scrutiny to a gender-based classification in Holbrook, see Holbrook, 140 N.H. at 189-90, as already discussed, the law at issue in Holbrook did not impose requirements on both men and women. The dissent identifies no other instance, nor are we aware of any, in which we have concluded that a law challenged on equal protection grounds contained a gender-based classification and therefore was subject to strict scrutiny. But cf. In re Certain Scholarship Funds, 133 N.H. 227, 231 (1990) (concluding that the "State's participation in the administration of" certain scholarships established by trust but expressly limited to one gender "cannot even withstand the lowest level of judicial scrutiny," and thus declining to "determine what level of review should be employed in cases of gender . . . discrimination" under Part I, Article 2). Thus, our prior cases are not helpful in analyzing whether Laconia's ordinance is gender-based. In other words, to the extent the dissent contends that our precedent requires us to determine the standard of review in equal protection challenges by examining the purpose and scope of the State-created classification, we agree. The primary issue on which this case turns, however, is what that examination reveals when applied to the unique facts of this case.

We agree with the dissent, of course, that this court has a duty "to make an independent determination of the protections afforded in the New Hampshire Constitution." Ball, 124 N.H. at 231. However, where our previous cases have not had occasion to answer the question presented here, we fail to see how we depart from that duty by checking our work against other courts, many of them in states with equal protection provisions similar to our own. See TEX. CONST. art. 1, § 3a ("Equality under the law shall not be denied or abridged because of sex, race, color, creed, or national origin."); Schleuter, 947 S.W.2d at 925-26; WA. CONST. art. 31, § 1 ("Equality of rights and responsibility under the law shall not be denied or abridged on account of sex."); Buchanan, 584 P.2d at 920-22; N.M. CONST. art. 2, § 18 ("Equality of rights under law shall not be denied on account of the sex of any person."); Sachs, 92 P.3d at 29. Indeed, the dissent itself relies on out-of-jurisdiction cases to support its contention that the Laconia ordinance contains a gender-

---

[3] We reach the same result under the Federal Constitution as we do under the State Constitution. Federal courts applying federal equal protection analysis have near-uniformly upheld ordinances similar to Laconia's even when subjecting them to intermediate scrutiny. See Tagami, 875 F.3d at 379-80; Ways, 331 F.3d at 599-600; Buzzetti, 140 F.3d at 144; Biocic, 928 F.2d at 115-16; J & B Soc. Club No. 1, 966 F. Supp. at 1139-40; Craft, 683 F. Supp. at 299-301. But see Free the Nipple Fort Collins, 237 F. Supp. 3d at 1133.

based classification. To the extent the dissent simply finds those cases more persuasive, that is all the more reason for us, in fulfilling our obligation to independently interpret Part I, Article 2, to consider the full range of how courts have tackled this difficult question, lest we simply pick and choose from amongst courts whose holdings align with our own personal ideologies.

The dissent also contends that there is "no principled reason why" our approach to analyzing Laconia's ordinance "would not apply with equal force to other laws" that afford differing treatment to people of different races, religions, colors, or national origins. We disagree. The facts of this case, including the particular way in which men and women differ with respect to the traditional understanding of nudity, are unique. Indeed, the dissent does not even attempt to deny that nudity is simply different for men than for women. At the same time, it is undeniably true that classifications based on immutable characteristics have "long [been] recognized as in most circumstances irrelevant," Adarand Constructors, Inc. v. Pena, 515 U.S. 200, 227 (1995) (quotation omitted), and therefore are generally improper bases for differing treatment under the law. However, based on the unique way in which men and women differ with respect to nudity, we conclude that the ordinance does not afford different treatment for men and women based on gender. As for the dissent's assertion that, given our approach to analyzing Laconia's ordinance, we would not apply strict scrutiny in a case that concerned laws imposing more onerous retirement benefit requirements for women than for men, it suffices to say that any such case would be controlled by our analysis in Holbrook. See Holbrook, 140 N.H. at 189-90.

At various points throughout its opinion, the dissent lumps the ordinance, and our analysis of it, together with "pervasive and perverse discrimination," "romantic paternalism," "unexamined stereotypes," and "archaic prejudice." The resort to such hyperbole reveals the flawed nature of its reasoning. It assumes that, because the ordinance does not allow men and women to engage in precisely the same mode of dress, it must contain a gender-based classification. Respectfully, we find this approach deceptively simplistic. For strict scrutiny to apply, it is not enough that men and women be treated differently: they must be treated differently based upon a gender-based classification. See Buchanan, 584 P.2d at 921-22. For the reasons already discussed, we find no gender-based classification in the ordinance. It is telling that the dissent has identified no case, nor are we aware of any, in which a court sitting in a jurisdiction with an Equal Rights Amendment analogous to our own has applied strict scrutiny to an ordinance like Laconia's. Neither can we ignore that no court with precedent-setting authority has held such an ordinance unconstitutional.

Nor should the siren call of "equal rights" lead us to forget our constitutional role. In the absence of a suspect classification or a fundamental right, courts will not second guess legislative bodies as to the wisdom of a specific law. Winnisquam Reg. Sch. Dist. v. Levine, 152 N.H. 537, 539 (2005). That the ordinance may or may not "reflect sociological insight, or shifting social standards" is not determinative for our purposes. Buchanan, 584 P.2d at 921 (quotation omitted). "Our obligation" is to interpret and apply the law, "not to mandate our own moral code." Planned Parenthood of Southeastern PA v. Casey, 505 U.S. 833, 850 (1992). "We are told that concepts of morality and propriety are changing"; if so, then "it can reasonably be expected that public demand will soon make it imperative that this portion of the ordinance be repealed." Buchanan, 584 P.2d at 920-21. The people of Laconia may make such a decision, but this court will not make it for them.

III.   Freedom of Speech

The defendants next argue that the ordinance violates their rights to freedom of speech and expression under Part I, Article 22 of the New Hampshire Constitution and the First Amendment to the United States Constitution. They contend that, "[b]y appearing topless in public, [the defendants] engaged in speech and expression . . . to demonstrate to others [their] political viewpoint and message that the female nipple is not a sexual object." They further maintain that, by doing so, they sought "to bring attention to gender equality and how the female nipple is treated different[ly] than the male nipple," "to continue the advancement of women's rights[,] and to have the conduct of being topless be accepted and normalized."

We first address the defendants' claims under the State Constitution, and rely on federal law only to aid in our analysis. Ball, 124 N.H. at 231-33. Once again, our review of this constitutional question is de novo. McKenzie, 154 N.H. at 777.

Part I, Article 22 of the New Hampshire Constitution provides: "Free speech and liberty of the press are essential to the security of freedom in a state: They ought, therefore, to be inviolably preserved." N.H. CONST. pt. I, art. 22. Similarly, the First Amendment prevents the passage of laws "abridging the freedom of speech." U.S. CONST. amend. I. It applies to the states through the Fourteenth Amendment to the United States Constitution. Lovell v. Griffin, 303 U.S. 444, 450 (1938).

When assessing whether government restrictions impermissibly infringe on free speech, we must first address whether the speech or conduct at issue is protected by the State Constitution. State v. Bailey, 166 N.H. 537, 540-41 (2014). The State and Federal Constitutions contain robust guarantees of free speech, but they do not offer absolute protection to all speech under all circumstances and in all places. State v. Biondolillo, 164 N.H. 370, 373 (2012). We do not accept "the view that an apparently limitless variety of conduct can be labeled 'speech' whenever the person engaging in the conduct intends thereby to express an idea"; however, "we acknowledge that conduct may be sufficiently imbued with elements of communication to fall within the scope of constitutional protections." Bailey, 166 N.H. at 541 (quotation, brackets, and ellipsis omitted); see State v. Comley, 130 N.H. 688, 691 (1988) (noting that although statute did not specifically regulate speech, its application "may have such an effect where a prosecution under the statute concerns conduct encompassing expressive activity").

The State contends that the defendants' conduct did not constitute protected speech. Although "[b]eing in a state of nudity is not an inherently expressive condition," Pap's A.M., 529 U.S. at 289, under the circumstances of this case we will assume, without deciding, that the defendants engaged in constitutionally protected expressive conduct. See Clark v. Community for Creative Non-Violence, 468 U.S. 288, 293 (1984) (assuming, but not deciding, that overnight sleeping in connection with demonstration was constitutionally protected expressive conduct); Craft, 683 F. Supp. at 292 (assuming dubitante that plaintiffs' shirt-free appearances at Cape Cod National Seashore constituted "expressive conduct protected to some extent by the First Amendment" (quotation omitted)); see also Bailey, 166 N.H. at 541. We must, therefore, determine whether the ordinance violates their right to free speech.

"It is well settled that the government need not permit all forms of speech on property that it owns and controls." Bailey, 166 N.H. at 541 (quotation, brackets, and ellipsis omitted). "The standards by which limitations on speech must be evaluated differ depending on the character of the property." Id. at 542 (quotation and brackets omitted). Government property generally falls into three categories — traditional public forums, designated public forums, and limited public forums. Id. "A traditional public forum is government property which by long tradition or by government fiat has been devoted to assembly and debate." Id. (quotation omitted). In such forums, the government may impose reasonable time, place, and manner restrictions. Doyle v. Comm'r, N.H. Dep't of Resources & Economic Dev., 163 N.H. 215, 221 (2012). If a restriction is content-based, it must be narrowly tailored to serve a compelling government interest. Id.; Reed v. Town of Gilbert, Ariz., 135 S. Ct. 2218, 2226 (2015) ("Content-based laws—those that target speech based on its communicative content—are presumptively unconstitutional and may be justified only if the government proves that they are narrowly tailored to serve compelling state interests."). If a restriction is content-neutral, it must satisfy a slightly less stringent test — it must be narrowly tailored to serve a significant government interest. Doyle, 163 N.H. at 221; see Biondolillo, 164 N.H. at 373 (noting that federal precedent employs the same standard to assess constitutionality of restrictions on the time, place, and manner of expressive activities taking place in a public forum); see also Clark, 468 U.S. at 293.

The defendants suggest, and the State does not dispute, that the beaches at which the defendants were arrested constitute traditional public forums. Thus, for purposes of this appeal, we also will assume, without deciding, that the respective beaches constitute traditional public forums. Nonetheless, the defendants argue that "[t]ime, place, and manner analysis is not appropriate" because the ordinance regulates speech based upon its content and viewpoint. They contend, therefore, that we must subject the ordinance to strict scrutiny review. We disagree.

"Government regulation of speech is content based if a law applies to particular speech because of the topic discussed or the idea or message expressed." Reed, 135 S. Ct. at 2227; see also Biondolillo, 164 N.H. at 374. On the other hand, a law is a content-neutral speech regulation if it is "justified without reference to the content of the regulated speech." City of Renton v. Playtime Theatres, Inc., 475 U.S. 41, 48 (1986) (quotation and emphasis omitted).

We agree with the trial court that the ordinance is not content-based. The ordinance is, on its face, a general prohibition on public nudity. See Pap's A.M., 529 U.S. at 290 (concluding that ordinance banning public nudity was not related to the suppression of expression). As the United States District Court for the District of Massachusetts ruled regarding a National Park Service regulation prohibiting public nudity at the seashore, the ordinance is "plainly not based upon either the content or subject matter of speech." Craft, 683 F. Supp. at 293 (quotations omitted). There is nothing in the text of the ordinance itself that suggests "that one group's viewpoint is to be preferred at the expense of others." Id. (quotation omitted). It does not target nudity meant to advance women's rights or desexualize the female nipple. Rather, it prohibits all nudity, regardless of whether the nudity is accompanied by expressive activity. See Pap's A.M., 529 U.S. at 290. In that sense, the ordinance merely regulates the manner in which activities may be carried out in that they cannot be carried out in the nude. We, therefore, conclude that the ordinance is content-neutral.

As we stated, if a restriction is content-neutral, it must be narrowly tailored to serve a significant government interest. Doyle, 163 N.H. at 221. Content-neutral restrictions must also leave open ample alternative channels for communication. Id. On appeal, the defendants do not challenge the trial court's rulings that the ordinance meets these requirements. Rather, their only argument is that the ordinance is content-based and viewpoint discriminatory and, thus, should be subject to strict scrutiny review. Because we necessarily reject that argument by concluding that the ordinance is content-neutral, and the defendants have not otherwise demonstrated that the trial court's rulings were erroneous, we need not conduct a further constitutional analysis.

Finally, the defendants pose various scenarios in their brief regarding circumstances under which, they argue, the ordinance would be unlikely to be applied. For example, they state that "presumably Laconia would not be enforcing the ordinance against pre-pubescent females" and that it is "questionable if the City would be enforcing the ordinance against a female who had a double mastectomy who essentially lacks any breast tissue even if their nipples were exposed." Beyond these bare assertions, however, they do not develop a legal argument. Because a mere laundry list of complaints regarding adverse rulings by the trial court, without developed legal argument, is insufficient to warrant judicial review, we decline to respond to these assertions.[4] See State v. Ayer, 154 N.H. 500, 513 (2006) (declining to address defendant's due process argument as he had not explained how his rights were violated and had only argued in "conclusory terms").

Accordingly, for these reasons, we cannot say that the trial court erred by determining that the ordinance does not violate the defendants' rights to free speech and expression under the State Constitution. As the Federal Constitution affords the defendants no greater protection than the State Constitution under the circumstances presented here, see Tagami, 875 F.3d at 379 (citing Barnes, 501 U.S. at 568-69), we also find no violation of the Federal Constitution.

IV. Authorization to Enact the Ordinance

The defendants next argue that the ordinance is invalid because the City of Laconia did not have the statutory authority to enact the ordinance. We find this argument unpersuasive.

"[W]hile general statutes must be enacted by the legislature, it is plain the power to make local regulations, having the force of law in limited localities, may be committed to other bodies representing the people in their local divisions, or to the people of those districts themselves." State v. Grant, 107 N.H. 1, 3 (1966) (quotation omitted). "Our whole system of local government in cities, villages, counties and towns, depends upon that distinction. The practice has existed from the foundation of the state, and has always been considered a prominent feature in the American system of government." Id. (quotation omitted). Indeed, as a subdivision of the state, the City of Laconia may exercise such powers as are expressly or impliedly granted to it by the legislature. See Dover News, Inc. v. City of Dover, 117 N.H. 1066, 1068 (1977).

Although there exists no express authority for a city to enact an ordinance prohibiting females from exposing their nipples, RSA 47:17, VII (2012) grants the city the power "[t]o regulate all streets and public ways, wharves, docks, and squares, and the use thereof." Further, RSA 47:17, XIII

---

[4] RSA 132:10-d (2015) provides: "Breast-feeding a child does not constitute an act of indecent exposure and to restrict or limit the right of a mother to breast-feed her child is discriminatory." Although noting that the ordinance does not make any exception for breast-feeding, the defendants specifically acknowledge that "they are not seeking to invalidate the ordinance for its failure to exempt breastfeeding." We therefore have no occasion to address this issue.

(2012) grants the city the power "to regulate the times and places of bathing and swimming in the canals, rivers and other waters of the city, and the clothing to be worn by bathers and swimmers." In addition, RSA 47:17, XV (2012) gives the city the power to "make any other bylaws and regulations which may seem for the well-being of the city" so long as "no bylaw or ordinance" is "repugnant to the constitution or laws of the state."

Moreover, the governmental authority known as the police power is an inherent attribute of state sovereignty. Piper v. Meredith, 110 N.H. 291, 294 (1970). The police power is broad and "includes such varied interests as public health, safety, morals, comfort, the protection of prosperity, and the general welfare." Id. (quotation omitted). The express and implied powers granted to towns by the legislature must be interpreted and construed in light of the police powers of the state which grants them. Id. at 295.

We have held that towns are empowered under the authority granted by RSA 31:39 (Supp. 2017) to make bylaws for a variety of purposes which generally fall into the category of health, welfare, and public safety. See id. Specifically, RSA 31:39, I(a) empowers towns to make bylaws for "[t]he care, protection, preservation and use of the public cemeteries, parks, commons, libraries and other public institutions of the town."

We believe that these statutory provisions authorize the city to enact the ordinance. See Dover News, Inc., 117 N.H. at 1068. As we explained, the stated purpose of the ordinance is to uphold and support "public health, public safety, morals and public order." Laconia, N.H., Code of Ordinances ch. 180, art. 1, § 180-1. We agree with the State that the ordinance's prohibition on public nudity is substantially related to this purpose. See Grant, 107 N.H. at 3. Furthermore, we have found that the ordinance does not violate the defendants' constitutional rights to equal protection or freedom of speech under the State and Federal Constitutions. As such, it does not unduly restrict the defendants' fundamental rights. Accordingly, we agree with the trial court that the City had the authority to enact the ordinance.

V. Preemption

The defendants next contend that the ordinance is preempted by RSA 645:1, I (2016). It is well settled that towns cannot regulate a field that has been preempted by the State. Town of Rye Bd. of Selectmen v. Town of Rye Zoning Bd. of Adjustment, 155 N.H. 622, 624 (2007). The preemption doctrine flows from the principle that municipal legislation is invalid if it is repugnant to, or inconsistent with, state law. Id. State law expressly preempts local law when there is an actual conflict between state and local regulation. Id. at 624-25. An actual conflict exists when a municipal ordinance or regulation permits that which a state statute prohibits, or vice versa. Id. at 625. Moreover, even when a local ordinance does not expressly conflict with a state statute, it will be preempted when it frustrates the statute's purpose. Forster v. Town of Henniker, 167 N.H. 745, 756 (2015). Because preemption "is essentially a matter of statutory interpretation and construction," whether a state statute preempts local regulation is a question of law, which we review de novo. Id. (quotation omitted).

RSA 645:1, I, provides that "[a] person is guilty of a misdemeanor if such person fornicates, exposes his or her genitals, or performs any other act of gross lewdness under circumstances which he or she should know will likely cause affront or alarm." The defendants do not — and could not — argue that this statute specifically authorizes the public display of breasts by females. On the contrary, although we need not decide the issue, this statute at least arguably can be read to prohibit such conduct as an act of gross lewdness. See, e.g., Com. v. Quinn, 789 N.E.2d 138, 146 (Mass. 2003). Nor can it be said that this statute represents the kind of comprehensive regulatory scheme that is indicative of legislative intent to occupy the field of regulation of public safety and morals. See Prolerized New England Co. v. City of Manchester, 166 N.H. 617, 623 (2014). Therefore, there is simply no basis for a claim that the ordinance either expressly conflicts with RSA 645:1, I, or that it frustrates the purpose of the statute.

The defendants point to an unsuccessful effort by legislators to enact legislation that would have specifically prohibited the public exposure of female breasts, see 2016 HB 1525-FN, arguing that the failure of that measure demonstrates legislative intent not to prohibit such conduct. As we have noted, however, "[w]e can discern no clear meaning from the legislature's failure to enact the proposed amendment." Dover News, Inc., 117 N.H. at 1069; see also Appeal of House Legislative Facilities Subcom., 141 N.H. 443, 449 (1996) (rejecting as misguided argument that failure of proposed amendment to Public Employee Labor Relations Act that would have expressly excluded legislative and judicial employees from its coverage demonstrated legislative intent that such employees be covered, and observing that "the amendment's failure could as easily have resulted from the belief that those employees were not covered by the Act in the first place").

For these reasons, we find that the ordinance is not preempted by RSA 645:1, I.

VI. RSA Chapter 354-A

Finally, the defendants argue that the trial court erred by denying their motion to dismiss because the ordinance violates RSA chapter 354-A. Relying upon RSA 354-A:16 and :17, the defendants contend that by "mak[ing] it illegal to be a topless female in public while allowing a male to be topless in public," the ordinance discriminates by "exclud[ing] someone from being on public property based solely on that person's sex/gender."

This argument requires us to engage in statutory interpretation. We are the final arbiters of the legislature's intent as expressed in the words of the statute considered as a whole. EEOC v. Fred Fuller Oil Co., 168 N.H. 606, 608 (2016). "We first examine the language of the statute, and, when possible, we ascribe the plain and ordinary meanings to the words used." Eldridge v. Rolling Green at Whip-Poor-Will Condo. Owners' Association, 168 N.H. 87, 90 (2015) (quotation omitted).

RSA chapter 354-A, known as the "Law Against Discrimination," prohibits, as relevant here, unlawful discrimination based upon sex in places of public accommodation as provided therein. See RSA 354-A:1 (title and purposes of chapter), :16-:17 (public accommodation). RSA 354-A:16 provides, in pertinent part, that "[t]he opportunity for every individual to have equal access to places of public accommodation without discrimination because of age, sex, race, creed, color, marital status, physical or mental disability or national origin is hereby recognized and declared to be a civil right." RSA 354-A:17 states:

> It shall be an unlawful discriminatory practice for any person, being the owner, lessee, proprietor, manager, superintendent, agent or employee of any place of public accommodation, because of the . . . sex . . . of any person, directly or indirectly, to refuse, withhold from or deny to such person any of the accommodations, advantages, facilities or privileges thereof; or, directly or indirectly, to publish, circulate, issue, display, post or mail any written or printed communication, notice or advertisement to the effect that any of the accommodations, advantages, facilities and privileges of any such place shall be refused, withheld from or denied to any person on account of . . . sex . . . ; or that the patronage or custom thereat of any person belonging to or purporting to be of any particular . . . sex . . . is unwelcome, objectionable or acceptable, desired or solicited.

In advancing their statutory argument, the defendants do little more than rehash their constitutional equal protection argument that, by prohibiting the exposure of the female, but not the male, breast, the ordinance discriminates on the basis of sex. For the reasons already discussed, we do not find that the ordinance constitutes unlawful discrimination in violation of RSA 354-A:16 or :17. Rather, we agree with the trial court that the ordinance merely prohibits those who access public places from doing so in the nude, and makes a permissible distinction between the areas of the body that must be covered by each gender.[5] See Sachs, 92 P.3d at 29 (holding that, in addition to

---

[5] The defendants cite cases from several jurisdictions that hold that various forms of preferences given to women, such as car wash discounts and discounted drink prices for women at a bar or racetrack, violated the respective jurisdiction's anti-discrimination laws or ordinances. See Koire

not violating the New Mexico Constitution, the ordinance at issue in that case did not contravene the New Mexico Human Rights Act).

Affirmed.

LYNN, C.J., and DONOVAN, J., concurred; BASSETT, J., with whom HICKS, J., joined, concurred in part and dissented in part.

BASSETT, J., with whom HICKS, J., joins, concurring in part and dissenting in part. We agree with our colleagues in most respects: Laconia's ordinance does not violate the defendants' rights to freedom of speech and expression; it falls within the regulatory authority of the City of Laconia; it is not preempted by statute; and it does not violate RSA chapter 354-A. However, we part company with the majority when it rejects the defendants' equal protection claim. We strongly disagree that rational basis is the lens through which the defendants' equal protection challenge should be analyzed. Laconia's ordinance facially classifies on the basis of gender: if a woman and a man wear the exact same clothing on the beach, on Laconia's main street, or in a backyard "visible to the public," the woman is engaging in unlawful behavior — but the man is not. Laconia, N.H., Code of Ordinances ch. 180, art. I, §§ 180-2, 180-4 (1998). This is a gender-based classification. Accordingly, the court must apply strict scrutiny. See In re Sandra H., 150 N.H. 634, 637 (2004) ("Classifications based upon suspect classes or affecting a fundamental right are subject to the most exacting scrutiny . . . ." (quotation omitted)); Cheshire Medical Center v. Holbrook, 140 N.H. 187, 189 (1995) ("Our constitution guarantees that 'equality of rights . . . shall not be denied or abridged by this state on account of . . . sex.' N.H. CONST. pt. I, art. 2. In order to withstand scrutiny under this provision, a common law rule that distributes benefits or burdens on the basis of gender must be necessary to serve a compelling State interest."); LeClair v. LeClair, 137 N.H. 213, 222 (1993) ("We apply the strict scrutiny test, in which the government must show a compelling State interest in order for its actions to be valid, when the classification involves a suspect class based on race, creed, color, gender, national origin, or legitimacy . . . ." (quotation omitted) (superseded by statute on other grounds). Were this court to subject Laconia's ordinance to this exacting standard, given that the government failed to present sufficient evidence in the trial court to satisfy its burden of proof, we would be compelled to find the ordinance unconstitutional.

---

v. Metro Car Wash, 707 P.2d 195, 204 (Cal. 1985); City of Clearwater v. Studebaker's D. Cl., 516 So. 2d 1106, 1108-09 (Fla. Dist. Ct. App. 1987); Ladd v. Iowa West Racing Ass'n, 438 N.W.2d 600, 602 (Iowa 1989); Peppin v. Woodside Delicatessen, 506 A.2d 263, 267 (Md. Ct. Spec. App. 1986); Com., Pa. Liquor Control Bd. v. Dobrinoff, 471 A.2d 941, 943 (Pa. Commw. Ct. 1984). These cases are readily distinguishable from the case at bar because, unlike in this case, they did not involve a distinction based upon the common understanding of what constitutes nudity.

Laconia's ordinance makes it "unlawful for any person to knowingly or intentionally, in a public place: . . . [a]ppear in a state of nudity." Laconia, N.H., Code of Ordinances ch. 180, art. I, § 180-2. Laconia defines "public place" to include "[a]ny public street, . . . beach, or other property or public institution of the City"; "[a]ny outdoor location, whether publically or privately owned, which is visible to the public at the time the prohibited conduct occurs"; and "[a]ny area within any . . . place of public accommodation or other private property which is generally frequented by the public." Laconia, N.H., Code of Ordinances ch. 180, art. I § 180-4. It defines nudity as "the showing of the human male or female genitals, pubic area or buttocks with less than a fully opaque covering, or the showing of the female breast with less than a fully opaque covering of any part of the nipple." Id. The defendants argue that the latter portion of the ordinance violates their constitutional rights to equal protection because, even though both men and women have nipples, the ordinance does not treat men and women equally.

"In considering an equal protection challenge under our State Constitution, we must first determine the correct standard of review by examining the purpose and scope of the State-created classification and the individual rights affected." Cmty. Res. for Justice v. City of Manchester, 154 N.H. 748, 758 (2007) (quotation and brackets omitted). The significance of the threshold determination as to the proper standard of review cannot be overstated. Classifications based upon suspect classes or that affect fundamental rights are subject to strict scrutiny: the government must prove that the legislation is "necessary to serve a compelling State interest," Holbrook, 140 N.H. at 189, and that it is "narrowly tailored to meet that end," Cmty. Res., 154 N.H. at 759 (quotation omitted). Below strict scrutiny is intermediate scrutiny, which is triggered when the challenged classification involves important substantive rights, Sandra H., 150 N.H. at 637-38, and which requires the government to show that the challenged legislation is substantially related to an important government interest. Cmty. Res., 154 N.H. at 762. Under either strict or intermediate scrutiny, the government bears the burden of proof, and "may not rely upon justifications that are hypothesized or invented post hoc in response to litigation, nor upon overbroad generalizations." Id. (quotations omitted); see also Fisher v. University of Texas at Austin, 570 U.S. 297, 310-12 (2013). On the other end of the spectrum, if legislation does not classify based on a suspect class, affect fundamental rights, or involve important substantive rights, the constitutional standard of review is rational basis. Sandra H., 150 N.H. at 638. "The rational basis test under the State Constitution requires that legislation be only rationally related to a legitimate government interest." Boulders at Strafford v. Town of Strafford, 153 N.H. 633, 641 (2006). The rational basis test puts the burden of proof on the party challenging the legislation and "contains no inquiry into whether legislation unduly restricts individual rights." Id. at 641-42.

The majority acknowledges — as it must — that under the New Hampshire Constitution, gender-based classifications trigger strict scrutiny. Yet the majority declines to apply strict scrutiny in this case, reasoning that, because "men and women are not fungible with respect to the traditional understanding of what constitutes nudity," the Laconia ordinance does not classify on the basis of gender. The conclusion that the ordinance does not classify on the basis of gender, and therefore can be analyzed by applying the rational basis test, does not find support in the plain language of the ordinance, the New Hampshire Constitution, or our precedent.

That the ordinance classifies on the basis of gender is self-evident. The ordinance defines "nudity" differently for females and males. By the plain text of the ordinance, a person who appears in a public place showing "the female breast with less than a fully opaque covering of any part of the nipple" violates the ordinance; a male who appears in the same public place without such a covering does not. Laconia, N.H., Code of Ordinances ch. 180, art. I, §§ 180-2, 180-4 (emphasis added). The challenged portion of the ordinance creates a public dress code which only one gender can violate. This is a gender-based classification.

Indeed, the Seventh Circuit Court of Appeals recently held that a public nudity ordinance that defines nudity differently for men and women classifies on the basis of gender. Tagami v. City of Chicago, 875 F.3d 375, 379-80 (7th Cir. 2017), cert. denied, 138 S. Ct. 1577 (2018). In Tagami, a woman who had been found guilty of violating a public-nudity ordinance that criminalized public display of "the breast at or below the upper edge of the areola thereof of any female person" if "not covered by an opaque covering," sued the City alleging that the ordinance discriminates on the basis of sex in violation of the Federal Constitution. Id. at 377 (quotation omitted). The City asserted that the ordinance did not classify on the basis of sex because it "treats men and women alike by equally prohibiting the public exposure of the male and female body parts that are conventionally considered to be intimate, erogenous, and private." Id. at 379-80. The City contended that "the list of intimate body parts is longer for women than men, but that's wholly attributable to the basic physiological differences between the sexes." Id. at 380. The Seventh Circuit summarily dismissed the City's contention, stating that the City's argument was "a justification for this classification rather than an argument that no sex-based classification is at work here at all." Id. The court concluded that, "[o]n its face, the ordinance plainly does impose different rules for women and men," and then proceeded to analyze the ordinance under the heightened scrutiny required by the Federal Constitution for gender-based classifications. Id.

The Seventh Circuit is not an outlier. Many courts have held that ordinances such as Laconia's do, in fact, classify on the basis of gender. See, e.g., Craft v. Hodel, 683 F. Supp. 289, 299 (D. Mass. 1988) (concluding that, under the Federal Constitution, a regulation prohibiting display of female but not male breasts "does, of course, distinguish between males and females" and thus was "subject to scrutiny under the Equal Protection Clause" (quotation omitted)); City of Tucson v. Wolfe, 917 P.2d 706, 707 (Ariz. Ct. App. 1995) (applying heightened scrutiny "[b]ecause this ordinance creates a different standard of conduct for each gender"); Dydyn v. Department of Liquor Control, 531 A.2d 170, 175 (Conn. App. Ct. 1987) ("We are not persuaded, however, by the argument that the regulation does not classify on the basis of sex. When a statute or regulation distinguishes between male and female anatomy, we hold that [the level of scrutiny required for gender-based classifications] must be applied."). But see Eckl v. Davis, 124 Cal. Rptr. 685, 695-96 (Ct. App. 1975) (holding that the ordinance did not classify based on sex because "nudity in the case of women is commonly understood to include the uncovering of the breast"); City of Seattle v. Buchanan, 584 P.2d 918, 920-22 (Wash. 1978) (en banc) (same).

We agree with the reasoning of the Seventh Circuit. Public nudity ordinances such as the ordinances in Chicago and Laconia — i.e., those that use explicit, gendered language to make it unlawful for a female to engage in certain behavior, while the same behavior is lawful for a male — clearly classify by gender. The majority asserts that such reasoning is "flawed" and "deceptively simple." We fail to see the flaw or deception in our simple reasoning: when a law uses the word "female" to classify between those who can violate the ordinance — females — and those who cannot — males — it contains a gender-based classification. We freely acknowledge that the question of whether basic physiological differences between the sexes justify disparate treatment of men and women is a more nuanced and complicated question. But classification and justification present different questions. Respectfully, we find the reasoning of the majority — which obscures the simple threshold question — needlessly convoluted and artificially complex.

Indeed, a court upends the safeguards of equal protection if it reasons that, because a law is premised upon physiological or anatomical differences between the sexes, the law does not classify by gender and therefore it need not be analyzed under strict scrutiny. For example, because women have a longer life expectancy than men, by the majority's reasoning, a hypothetical law that mandates that women work four years longer than men in order to qualify for a pension, or prevents women from retiring until age 70 as opposed to age 66 for men, or reduces a woman's social security benefits if she retires at the same age as a man, does not classify on the basis of gender. Such a law would be constitutional so long as it was "rationally related to a legitimate government interest." Boulders, 153 N.H. at 641. Analyzing whether a law comports with equal protection does not require that the court be blind to basic physiological or anatomical differences. In some cases, applying the constitutionally required level of scrutiny, this court might conclude that such differences justify disparate treatment under the law. However, a court subverts the basic guarantee of equal protection if it concludes that, because men and women have physiological or anatomical differences, a law that classifies on the basis of those differences does not trigger strict scrutiny.

The New Hampshire Constitution states: "Equality of rights under the law shall not be denied or abridged by this state on account of race, creed, color, sex or national origin." N.H. CONST. pt. I, art. 2. This guarantee became part of our State Constitution in 1974 after the people of New Hampshire passed the Equal Rights Amendment by an overwhelming margin. There is no counterpart to New Hampshire's Equal Rights Amendment in the United States Constitution. Accordingly, we, like courts in other states whose citizens have adopted an Equal Rights Amendment, do not "equate our [Equal Rights Amendment] with the equal protection clause of the federal constitution" as doing so "would negate its meaning given that our state adopted an [Equal Rights Amendment] while the federal government failed to do so." Doe v. Maher, 515 A.2d 134, 160-61 (Conn. Super. Ct. 1986). We "find inescapable the conclusion that [our Equal Rights Amendment] was intended to supplement and expand the guaranties of the equal protection provision . . . and requires us to hold that a classification based on sex is a 'suspect classification' which, to be held valid, must withstand 'strict judicial scrutiny.'" People v. Ellis, 311 N.E.2d 98, 101 (Ill. 1974). "Any other view would mean the people intended to accomplish no change in the existing constitutional law governing sex discrimination" when they enacted the amendment. Darrin v. Gould, 540 P.2d 882, 889 (Wash. 1975) (en banc). Our amended Constitution, and subsequent precedent, now require the State to bear a heavy burden when it seeks to treat people differently under the law "on account of race, creed, color, sex or national origin." N.H. CONST. pt. I, art. 2; see, e.g., Sandra H., 150 N.H. at 637; Holbrook, 140 N.H. at 189; LeClair, 137 N.H. at 222. As we have previously observed:

> Part I, article 2 of the New Hampshire Constitution forbids the State to discriminate on the basis of . . . gender. The New Hampshire voters, in ratifying this amendment, have firmly established public policy that demands equal protection for all, regardless of . . . gender.

In re Certain Scholarship Funds, 133 N.H. 227, 232 (1990).

The majority's conclusion that a lesser standard applies turns the clock back to the era before the adoption of the Equal Rights Amendment — a bygone era when women were the victims of pervasive discrimination and this court rejected challenges to laws that treated men and women differently. Indeed, the New Hampshire Supreme Court held more than sixty years ago — but within the lifetimes of judges now sitting on this court — that a regulation which banned women from playing golf on a municipal course during certain hours did not violate the New Hampshire Constitution's equal protection guarantee. See Allen v. Manchester, 99 N.H. 388, 390-92 (1955). We reasoned that because it was not "plainly mistaken or arbitrary" that "women golfers, on the average, progress about the course more slowly than men," and separating slow groups from fast groups might improve "the safety of players, and of women and children golfers in particular," the law did not create an "invalid classification." Id. at 391-92. "Women were separately classified with children, not because of sex, but because of a manner of playing golf thought to be characteristic of them as a group." Id. at 392. The majority's position in this case — that strict scrutiny is not required here because women are thought to be different from men with regard to nudity — harkens back to that bygone era.

The majority misconstrues the equal protection guarantee when it reasons that our precedent "does not necessarily establish that the Laconia ordinance triggers strict scrutiny" because it "does not address the type of legislation that is at issue here: a proscription that imposes requirements on both men and women, but applies to women somewhat differently." The threshold inquiry as to the proper level of review is not whether the law classifies by gender in all respects: it is whether the law classifies by gender in any respect. As the United States Supreme Court has explained: "Whenever the government treats any person unequally because of [a suspect classification], that person has suffered an injury that falls squarely within the language and spirit of the Constitution's guarantee of equal protection." Adarand Constructors, Inc. v. Pena, 515 U.S. 200, 229-30 (1995). It is precisely because Laconia's ordinance "applies to women somewhat differently" that we must apply strict scrutiny.

The majority reasons that a lesser standard is applicable here in part because "[c]ourts in other jurisdictions have generally upheld laws that prohibit women but not men from exposing their breasts," but have "often left unclear the applicable standard of review." It observes that no court has held that an ordinance like Laconia's triggers strict scrutiny, and that no appellate court has held such an ordinance unconstitutional. However, "[t]he New Hampshire Constitution is the fundamental charter of our State." State v. Ball, 124 N.H. 226, 231 (1983). "Our constitution will often afford greater protection against the action of the State than does the Federal Constitution." State v. Settle, 122 N.H. 214, 217 (1982). Therefore, "this court has a responsibility to make an independent determination of the protections afforded under the New Hampshire Constitution." Ball, 124 N.H. at 231. "If we ignore this duty, we fail to live up to our oath to defend our constitution . . . ." Id.

We recognize that courts in other jurisdictions, applying less exacting levels of scrutiny, have upheld the constitutionality of ordinances similar to Laconia's. See, e.g., Tagami, 875 F.3d at 380. But see Free the Nipple Fort Collins v. City of Fort Collins, Colorado, 237 F. Supp. 3d 1126, 1130, 1133 (D. Colo. 2017) (concluding that equal protection challenge to ordinance prohibiting women but not men from exposing their breasts was likely to succeed on the merits when analyzed under intermediate scrutiny, as required by the Federal Constitution, because the ordinance "is based on an impermissible gender stereotype that results in a form of gender-based discrimination"). However the Federal Constitution, and the majority of other state constitutions, materially differ from New Hampshire's Constitution because they do not explicitly provide that equal rights under the law shall not be denied because of sex. See Leslie W. Gladstone, Cong. Research Serv., RS20217, Equal Rights Amendments: State Provisions (2004) (discussing and listing state Equal Rights Amendments). In those jurisdictions, gender-based classifications never trigger strict scrutiny review. See, e.g., Tagami, 875 F.3d at 380 (Federal Constitution); Wolfe, 917 P.2d at 707 (state constitution). By contrast, in New Hampshire, gender-based classifications always trigger strict scrutiny review. Therefore, to the extent that the majority relies upon the outcome of cases decided through application of less rigorous standards to determine the issue central to this case — whether Laconia's ordinance contains a gender-based classification — it shrinks from the court's duty to ensure that "Equality of rights under the law shall not be denied or abridged by this state on account of race, creed, color, sex or national origin." N.H. CONST. pt. I, art. 2.

For the reasons discussed above, we conclude that Laconia's ordinance classifies on the basis of gender. We recognize that a handful of courts, including two sitting in states that have adopted equal rights provisions similar to Part I, Article 2, have concluded that ordinances like Laconia's do not classify on the basis of gender. See Eckl, 124 Cal. Rptr. at 696; Buchanan, 584 P.2d at 920-22. However, the reasoning employed by these courts is unsound and cannot withstand scrutiny.

In Eckl, the California Court of Appeal reasoned that a public nudity ordinance that defined nudity differently for men and women did not contain a gender-based classification because "[n]ature, not the legislative body, created the distinction between that portion of the woman's body and that of a man's torso," Eckl, 124 Cal. Rptr. at 696; see also Buchanan, 584 P.2d at 920 ("[C]ommon knowledge tells us . . . that there is a real difference between the sexes with respect to breasts . . . ."). However, the fact that "nature" has created distinctions between men and women does not lessen the level of scrutiny demanded by our constitution. Our precedent is clear: in order to "determine the correct standard of review," the court must "examin[e] the purpose and scope of the State-created classification and the individual rights affected." Cmty. Res., 154 N.H. at 758 (quotations and brackets omitted). The critical threshold determination as to the proper standard of review should not — and does not — include a judicial inquiry into whether "nature" or "the legislative body" created distinctions among those classified.

Indeed, "natural" distinctions between people — including differences in skin color, gender, and country of origin — have historically served as justifications for pervasive and perverse discrimination. That is precisely why the constitution requires us to subject legislation that distinguishes between people on the basis of such differences to heightened scrutiny. The "basic concept of our system [is] that legal burdens should bear some relationship to individual responsibility." Frontiero v. Richardson, 411 U.S. 677, 686 (1973) (plurality opinion) (quotation omitted). Gender, skin color, and country of origin are "immutable facts that bear no relation to ability, disadvantage, moral culpability, or any other characteristics of constitutionally permissible interest to government." Fullilove v. Klutznick, 448 U.S. 448, 525 (1980) (Stewart, J., dissenting); see also Frontiero, 411 U.S. at 686. Accordingly, when a legislative body enacts a law that distributes benefits or burdens on the basis of any of these immutable characteristics, that legislation triggers strict scrutiny review. See Holbrook, 140 N.H. at 189. The Equal Rights Amendment was intended as a shield to protect people from disparate treatment under the law on the basis of "natural" or immutable characteristics. But here the majority concludes that because "nature, not the legislative body," has distinguished between men and women, Laconia's ordinance does not classify on the basis of gender. In so doing, the majority turns a constitutional shield into a sword: it wields "immutable characteristics" as a weapon to attack the very protections that the Equal Rights Amendment was intended to guarantee.

Perhaps recognizing this truth, the majority, quoting Buchanan and Eckl, attempts to further justify its conclusion by asserting that the ordinance "merely reflects the fact that men and women are not fungible with respect to the traditional understanding of what constitutes nudity." Buchanan, 584 P.2d at 920-22 ("It is true that [the ordinance] requires the draping of more parts of the female body than of the male, but only because there are more parts of the female body intimately associated with the procreative function. The fact that the ordinance takes account of this fact does not render it discriminatory."); Eckl, 124 Cal. Rptr. at 696 ("Unlike the situation with respect to men, nudity in the case of women is commonly understood to include the uncovering of the breasts. Consequently, in proscribing nudity on the part of women it was necessary to include express reference to that area of the body."). However, "traditional" or "common" moral understandings do not determine constitutional guarantees.

"[O]ur Nation has had a long and unfortunate history of sex discrimination." Frontiero, 411 U.S. at 684. "Traditionally, such discrimination was rationalized by an attitude of 'romantic paternalism' which, in practical effect, put women, not on a pedestal, but in a cage." Id. The law no longer accepts stereotypical notions about women's abilities, interests, and proper place in the public sphere as justifications to treat men and women differently under the law with regard to their ability to serve on juries, see J.E.B. v. Alabama ex rel. T.B., 511 U.S. 127, 130-31 (1994), administer estates, see Reed v. Reed, 404 U.S. 71, 76 (1971), or learn as military cadets, see United States v. Virginia, 518 U.S. 515, 557-58 (1996). A court would no longer say, as a Supreme Court Justice did over 100 years ago, that a woman did not have a right to practice law because "the civil law, as well as nature herself, has always recognized a wide difference in the respective spheres and destinies of man and woman. . . . This is the law of the Creator. . . . [T]he rules of civil society must be adapted to the general constitution of things . . . ." Bradwell v. The State, 83 U.S. 130, 141-42 (1872) (Bradley, J., concurring). We revisit that bygone era, and thwart the very protections the Equal Rights Amendment was enacted to provide, if we allow stereotypical notions about women's bodies to alter our analysis of the straightforward question of whether Laconia's ordinance classifies on the basis of gender. This is precisely why the New Hampshire Constitution requires that legislation which discriminates on the basis of a suspect classification be subject to strict scrutiny.

The law has often been used to perpetuate discrimination based on "public sensibilities" or "common understandings" about individuals on the basis of immutable characteristics — however misinformed or ill-motivated those understandings might be. "One of the most important purposes to be served by the Equal Protection Clause is to ensure that 'public sensibilities' grounded in prejudice and unexamined stereotypes do not become enshrined as part of the official policy of government." People v. Santorelli, 600 N.E.2d 232, 236 (N.Y. 1992) (Titone, J., concurring). "Thus, where 'public sensibilities' constitute the justification for a gender-based classification, the fundamental question is whether the particular 'sensibility' to be protected is, in fact, a reflection of archaic prejudice or a manifestation of a legitimate government objective." Id. When the majority takes judicial notice of a common moral understanding about an immutable physical characteristic, and allows it to alter and lessen a constitutional guarantee, it erodes the protections the Equal Rights Amendment was enacted to provide. We see no principled reason why the majority's approach would not apply with equal force to other laws that treat people differently "on account of race, creed, color, sex or national origin." N.H. CONST. pt. I, art. 2. This is a significant change to New Hampshire's equal protection guarantee that gives us great pause. As the United States Supreme Court has observed:

> The point of carefully examining the interest asserted by the government in support of a [suspect] classification, and the evidence offered to show that the classification is needed, is precisely to distinguish legitimate from illegitimate uses of [immutable characteristics] in governmental decisionmaking. . . . [The fact that] some cases may be difficult to classify [is] all the more reason, in our view, to examine [suspect] classifications carefully. . . . By requiring strict scrutiny of [suspect] classifications, we require courts to make sure that a governmental

classification based on [a suspect class] . . . is legitimate, before permitting unequal treatment . . . to proceed.

Adarand, 515 U.S. at 228 (quotation omitted).

We now analyze Laconia's ordinance under the applicable standard of review, strict scrutiny, to determine whether the State adduced sufficient evidence to meet its exacting burden. We have no choice but to conclude that it did not. During the hearing on the petitioners' motion to dismiss, the State argued that equal protection is not strictly applicable to this case, and that "the burden is on the petitioner to show that [the ordinance] is unconstitutional. . . . It's not on the State." In light of the State's position that the ordinance does not trigger strict scrutiny, it is not surprising that the State failed to introduce sufficient evidence to support a finding that the ordinance is "necessary to serve a compelling State interest," Holbrook, 140 N.H. at 189, or that it is "narrowly tailored to meet that end." Cmty. Res., 154 N.H. at 759 (quotation omitted).

The ordinance's stated purpose is to uphold and support "public health, public safety, morals and public order." Laconia, N.H., Code of Ordinances ch. 180, art. I, § 180-1 (1998). In the trial court, the City asserted that because the defendants were topless, they caused a "disturbance" which "has the potential for violence." The City also asserted that, because people think of "female breasts in a sexualized manner," topless women may present other beachgoers with "a mental health issue." Turning to the ordinance's other stated purposes, "morals and public order," the City argued to the trial court that women who do not cover their nipples act contrary to "the City's character" and "morals as determined by the city council."

However we, like the United States Supreme Court, "have never held that moral disapproval, without any other asserted state interest, is a sufficient rationale under the Equal Protection Clause to justify a law that discriminates among groups of persons." Lawrence v. Texas, 539 U.S. 558, 582 (2003) (O'Connor, J., concurring in the judgment). Indeed, the State has not cited — nor are we aware of — any case that holds that a government's interest in morality rises to the level of a compelling government interest. "[T]he fact that the governing majority in a State has traditionally viewed a particular practice as immoral is not a sufficient reason for upholding a law prohibiting the practice." Id. at 577 (quotation omitted) (majority opinion). Accordingly, we do not conclude that the State has met its burden of proving that the government's interests in morals and public order are, in fact, compelling. "Our obligation is to define the liberty of all, not to mandate our own moral code." Planned Parenthood of Southern PA v. Casey, 505 U.S. 833, 850 (1992).

Even if we assume that the government's asserted interests are compelling, a review of the evidence presented to the trial court establishes that the State has not met its burden to prove that the ordinance is necessary and narrowly tailored. See Holbrook, 140 N.H. at 189; Cmty. Res., 154 N.H. at 759. "Although narrow tailoring does not require exhaustion of every conceivable [gender]-neutral alternative, . . . [t]he reviewing court must ultimately be satisfied that no workable [gender]-neutral alternatives" would suffice. Fisher, 570 U.S. at 312 (quotation, citation, and brackets omitted). Here, there is no evidence that the City of Laconia considered gender-neutral alternatives and the State has made no argument and presented no evidence as to why gender-neutral alternatives would not suffice. At oral argument the State asserted that the ordinance was "fairly narrowly tailored" because a woman need only "wear pasties" including "pasties that look like nipples." However, it failed to explain why the ordinance was necessary in the first place or why a less restrictive ordinance, perhaps one more narrow in time or place, would be insufficient. By the ordinance's plain language, it is perfectly lawful for a post-pubescent female to wear pasties with tassels walking down Laconia's Main Street, even though a four-year-old girl playing on the beach wearing only shorts, or an adult woman sunbathing without a top in her own back yard, engages in unlawful behavior if her nipples are "visible to the public." Laconia, N.H., Code of Ordinances ch. 180, art. I, § 180-4. Without evidence that gender-neutral or less restrictive alternatives would be unworkable, we cannot conclude that the State has met its burden to prove that Laconia's ordinance is necessary and narrowly tailored to accomplish the government's asserted interests.

In sum, applying the strict scrutiny standard required by Part I, Article 2, we conclude that the State has not carried its burden to prove that its asserted interests are compelling and that Laconia's ordinance is necessary and narrowly tailored. We reach this conclusion after objectively applying strict scrutiny as required by our precedent and Part I, Article 2. In so concluding, we do not mean to imply that all legislation that classifies on the basis of gender would not survive the strict scrutiny test, nor that Laconia's ordinance might not have passed constitutional muster had the State accepted that it bore the burden of proof; rather, we find that the State's proof in this case falls far short of satisfying strict scrutiny.

Although laws that classify on the basis of gender are subject to strict scrutiny under the New Hampshire Constitution, it does not follow that all such laws will be invalidated by application of that exacting standard. "The fact that strict scrutiny applies says nothing about the ultimate validity of any particular law; that determination is the job of the court applying strict scrutiny." Johnson v. California, 543 U.S. 499, 515 (2005) (quotation omitted). Therefore, if the State meets its burden to demonstrate that a law that classifies on the basis of gender is necessary and narrowly tailored to further a compelling government interest, this court would find — as have others — that such a law is constitutional. See People v. Carranza, No. B240799, 2013 WL 3866506, at *7-8 (Cal. Ct. App. July 24, 2013) (concluding that a sexual battery statute which criminalized non-consensual touching of the breast of a female, but not of a male, did not violate the state's constitutional equal protection guarantee when analyzed under strict scrutiny because "there is a compelling government interest in protecting females from non-consensual touching of their breasts"); Michael M. v. Superior Court of Sonoma Cty., 601 P.2d 572, 573-74 (Cal. 1979) (en banc), aff'd, 450 U.S. 464 (1981) (applying strict scrutiny and holding that a statute which criminalized sexual intercourse with a minor female, but not a male, classified by sex but did not violate equal protection because the law was "supported not by mere social convention but by the immutable physiological fact that it is the female exclusively who can become pregnant," and the State had a "compelling . . . interest in minimizing both the number of [teen] pregnancies and their disastrous consequences").

Finally, the majority concludes its equal protection analysis by stating that we as a court should not allow any feelings we may have as judges about the ordinance to "lead us to forget our constitutional role" because "'[o]ur obligation' is to interpret and apply the law, 'not to mandate our own moral code.'" (Quoting Casey, 505 U.S. at 850.) The suggestion is that we, as judges, should interpret and apply the constitution as it exists, not as we think it ought to exist. On this point, we agree. However, the constitution — as it has existed for the past 45 years — includes an Equal Rights Amendment: "Equality of rights under the law shall not be denied or abridged by this state on account of race, creed, color, sex or national origin." N.H. CONST. pt. I, art. 2. Surely the citizens thought they were accomplishing something important when they changed the constitution. Our "constitutional role" is, therefore, to interpret and apply Part I, Article 2.

In service of that role, over four decades, we have fashioned an analytical framework which subjects laws that distinguish on the basis of gender to the highest level of constitutional scrutiny: strict scrutiny. See Holbrook, 140 N.H. at 189; Sandra H., 150 N.H. at 637; LeClair, 137 N.H. at 222. However, perhaps mindful of the State's obvious failure to present evidence sufficient to meet the exacting burden of strict scrutiny in this case, the majority strains to conclude that an ordinance that prohibits women — but not men — from engaging in certain behavior does not discriminate on the basis of sex, but is, in fact, gender-neutral. Such an approach is not in service of our constitutional role: it is an abdication of it. Based upon the record before us, we conclude that Laconia's ordinance violates Part I, Article 2 of the New Hampshire Constitution. We respectfully dissent.

LINDSAY HECOX, et al., Plaintiffs,
v.
BRADLEY LITTLE, et al.; Defendants.
Case No. 1:20-cv-00184-DCN
UNITED STATES DISTRICT COURT FOR THE DISTRICT OF IDAHO
August 17, 2020

MEMORANDUM DECISION AND ORDER

This matter is before the Court on Plaintiffs' Motion for Preliminary Injunction, proposed intervenors' Motion to Intervene, and Defendants' Motion to Dismiss. The Court held oral argument on July 22, 2020 and took the matters under advisement.

Upon review, and for the reasons stated below, the Court GRANTS the Motion for Preliminary Injunction (Dkt. 22); GRANTS the Motion to Intervene (Dkt. 30); and GRANTS in PART and DENIES in PART the Motion to Dismiss (Dkt. 40).

I. OVERVIEW

Plaintiffs in this case challenge the constitutionality of a new Idaho law which excludes transgender women from participating on women's sports teams. Defendants assert Plaintiffs lack standing, that their claims are not ripe for review, that certain of their claims fail as a matter of law, and that they are not entitled to injunctive relief. The proposed intervenors seek to intervene to advocate for their interests as female athletes and to defend the law Plaintiffs challenge. The United States has also filed a Statement of Interest in support of Idaho's law. Dkt. 53.

The primary question before the Court—whether the Court should enjoin the State of Idaho from enforcing a newly enacted law which precludes transgender female athletes from participating on women's sports—involves complex issues relating to the rights of student athletes, physiological differences between the sexes, an individual's ability to challenge the gender of other student athletes, female athlete's rights to medical privacy and to be free from potentially invasive sex identification procedures, and the rights of all students to have complete access to educational opportunities, programs, and activities available at school. The debate regarding transgender females' access to competing on women's sports teams has received nationwide attention and is currently being litigated in both traditional courts and the court of public opinion.

Despite the national focus on the issue, Idaho is the first and only state to categorically bar the participation of transgender women in women's student athletics. This categorical bar to girls and women who are transgender stands in stark contrast to the policies of elite athletic bodies that regulate sports both nationally and globally—including the National Collegiate Athletic Association ("NCAA") and the International Olympic Committee ("IOC")—which allow transgender women to participate on female sports teams once certain specific criteria are met.

In addition to precluding women and girls who are transgender and many who are intersex from participating in women's sports, Idaho's law establishes a "dispute" process that allows a currently undefined class of individuals to challenge a student's sex. Idaho Code § 33-6203(3). If the sex of any female student athlete—whether transgender or not—is disputed, the student must undergo a potentially invasive sex verification process. This provision burdens all female athletes with the risk and embarrassment of having to "verify" their "biological sex" in order to play women's sports. *Id.* Similarly situated men and boys—whether transgender or not—are not subject to the dispute process because Idaho's law does not restrict individuals who wish to participate on men's teams.

Finally, as an enforcement mechanism, Idaho's law creates a private cause of action against a "school or institution of higher education" for any student "who is deprived of an athletic opportunity" or suffers any harm, whether direct or indirect, due to the participation of a woman who is transgender on a women's team. *Id.* § 33-6205(1). Idaho schools are also precluded from taking any "retaliation or other adverse action" against those who report an alleged violation of the law, regardless of whether the report was made in good faith or simply to harass a competitor. *Id.* at § 33-6205(2).

Plaintiffs seek a preliminary injunction which would enjoin enforcement of Idaho's law pending trial on the merits. The Court will ultimately be required to decide whether Idaho's law violates Title IX and/or is unconstitutional, but that is not the question before the Court today. The question currently before the Court is whether Plaintiffs have met the criteria for enjoining enforcement of Idaho's law *for the present time* until a trial on the merits can be held. To issue an injunction preserving the status quo by enjoining the law's enforcement, the Court must primarily decide whether Plaintiffs have constitutional and prudential standing to challenge the law, whether they state facial or only as-applied constitutional challenges, and whether they are likely to succeed on their claim, based upon the current record, that the law violates the Equal Protection Clause of the Fourteenth Amendment.

II. BACKGROUND

On March 30, 2020, Idaho Governor Bradley Little ("Governor Little") signed the Fairness in Women's Sports Act (the "Act") into law. Idaho Code Ann. § 33-6201-6206.[1] Plaintiffs' Complaint challenges the constitutionality of the Act. Among other things, Plaintiffs contend that the Act violates their constitutional rights to equal protection, due process, and the right to be free from unconstitutional searches and seizures. Plaintiffs seek preliminary relief solely on their equal protection claim, arguing the Act discriminates on the basis of transgender status by categorically barring transgender women from participating in women's sports, and also discriminates on the basis of sex by subjecting all women student-athletes to the risk of having to undergo invasive, unnecessary tests to "verify" their sex, while permitting all men student-athletes to participate in men's sports without such risk. Plaintiffs seek a preliminary injunction to enjoin enforcement of the Act pending trial on the merits.

A. Definitions

As the Third Circuit recently explained, in the context of issues such as those raised in the instant case, "such seemingly familiar terms as 'sex' and 'gender' can be misleading." *Doe ex rel. Doe v. Boyertown Area Sch. Dist.*, 897 F.3d 518, 522 (3d Cir. 2018). The Court accordingly begins by defining relevant terms utilized in this decision.

"Sex" is defined as the "anatomical and physiological processes that lead to or denote male or female. Typically, sex is determined at birth based on the appearance of external genitalia." *Id.*

A person's "gender identity" is his or her "deep-core sense of self as being a particular gender." *Id.* "Although the detailed mechanisms are unknown, there is a medical consensus that there is a significant biologic component underlying gender identity." Dkt. 22-9, ¶ 18.[2]

The term "cisgender" refers to a person who identifies with the sex that person was determined to have at birth. *Boyertown*, 897 F.3d at 522.

"Transgender" refers to "a person whose gender identity does not align with the sex that person was determined to have at birth." *Id.* A transgender woman "is therefore a person who has a lasting, persistent female gender identity, though the person's sex was determined to be male at birth." *Id.*

Transgender individuals may experience "gender dysphoria," which is "characterized by significant and substantial distress as result of their birth-determined sex being different from their gender identity." *Id.* "In order to be diagnosed with gender dysphoria, the incongruence must have persisted for at least six months and be accompanied by clinically significant distress or impairment in social, occupational, or other important areas of functioning." Dkt. 22-2, ¶ 19. If left untreated, symptoms of gender dysphoria can include severe anxiety and depression, suicidality, and other serious mental health issues. *Id.* at ¶ 20. Attempted suicide rates in the transgender community are over 40%. Dkt. 1, at ¶ 103.

The term "intersex" is an umbrella term for a person "born with unique variations in certain physiological characteristics associated with sex, "such as chromosomes, genitals, internal organs like testes or ovaries, secondary sex characteristics, or hormone production or response." Dkt. 22-1, at 2 (citing Dkt. 22-2, ¶ 41). Some intersex traits are identified at birth, while others may not be discovered until puberty or later in life, if ever. *See generally* Dkt. 22-2, at 11-16.

B. The Parties

1. Plaintiffs

Plaintiffs in this action include Lindsay Hecox, and Jean and John Doe on behalf of their minor daughter, Jane Doe (collectively "Plaintiffs").[3] Lindsay is a transgender woman athlete who lives in Idaho and attends Boise State University ("BSU"). As part of her treatment for gender dysphoria, Lindsay has undergone hormone therapy by being treated with testosterone suppression and estrogen, which lower her circulating testosterone levels and affect her bodily systems and secondary sex characteristics. Dkt. 1, ¶ 29. Lindsay is a life-long runner who intends to try out for the BSU women's cross-country team in fall 2020, and for the women's track team in spring 2021. *Id.* at ¶ 33. Under current NCAA rules, Lindsay could compete at NCAA events in September—when she has completed one year of hormone treatment.[4] *Id.* at ¶ 32.

Jane is a 17-year old girl and athlete who is cisgender. Dkt. 1, ¶¶ 39, 42. Jane has played sports since she was four and competes on the soccer and track teams at Boise High School, where she is a rising senior. *Id.* at ¶¶ 40, 45. After tryouts in August, Jane intends to play on Boise High's soccer team again in fall 2020.[5] *Id.* Because most of her closest friends are boys, she has an athletic build, rarely wears skirts or dresses, and has at times been thought of as "masculine," Jane worries that one of her competitors may dispute her sex pursuant to section 33-6203(3) of the Act. *Id.* at ¶ 47.

2. Defendants

The defendants named in this action (collectively "Defendants") include Governor Little; Idaho Superintendent of Public Instruction Sherri Ybarra; the individual members of the Idaho State Board of Education (Debbie Critchfield, David Hill, Emma Atchley, Linda Clark, Shawn Keough, Kurt Liebich, and Andrew Scoggin); Idaho state educational institutions BSU and Independent School District of Boise City #1 ("Boise School District"); BSU's President, Dr. Marlene Tromp; Superintendent of the Boise School District, Coby Dennis; the individual members of the Boise

School District's Board of Trustees (Nancy Gregory, Maria Greeley, Dennis Doan, Alicia Estey, Dave Wagers, Troy Rohn, and Beth Oppenheimer); and the individual members of the Idaho Code Commission (Daniel Bowen, Andrew Doman, and Jill Holinka).

3. Proposed Intervenors

Proposed intervenors Madison ("Madi") Kenyon and Mary ("MK") Marshall (collectively "Madi and MK" or the "Proposed Intervenors") are Idaho cisgender female athletes. Like Lindsay and Jane, Madi and MK are "female athletes for whom sports is a passion and life-defining pursuit." Dkt. 30-1, at 2. Madi and MK both run track and cross-country on scholarship at Idaho State University ("ISU") in Pocatello, Idaho. *Id*. Both competed against a transgender woman athlete last year at the University of Montana and had "deflating experiences" of running against and losing to that athlete. *Id*., at 3; Dkt. 30-2, ¶¶ 12, 14-15; Dkt. 30-3, ¶ 11. The Proposed Intervenors support the Act and wish to have their personal concerns fully set forth and represented in this case.

C. The Act

1. Overview

Idaho passed House Bill 500 ("H.B. 500"), the genesis for the Act, on March 16, 2020. Dkt. 1, ¶ 90. In the United States, high school interscholastic athletics are generally governed by state interscholastic athletic associations, such as the Idaho High School Activities Association ("IHSAA"). *Id*. at ¶ 66. The NCAA sets policies for member colleges and universities, including BSU. *Id*. at ¶ 67. Prior to the passage of H.B. 500, the IHSAA policy allowed transgender girls in K-12 athletics in Idaho to compete on girls' teams after completing one year of hormone therapy suppressing testosterone under the care of a physician for purposes of gender transition.

Id. at ¶ 71. Similarly, the NCAA policy allows transgender women attending member colleges and universities in Idaho to compete on women's teams after one year of hormone therapy suppressing testosterone. *Id.* at ¶ 75.

2. Legislative History

On February 13, 2020, H.B. 500 was introduced in the Idaho House by Representative Barbara Ehardt ("Rep. Ehardt"). On February 19, 2020, the House State Affairs Committee heard testimony on H.B. 500. *Id.* at ¶ 80. Ty Jones, Executive Director of the IHSAA, answered questions at that hearing and noted that no Idaho student had ever complained of participation by transgender athletes, and no transgender athlete had ever competed under the IHSAA policy regulating inclusion of transgender athletes. *Id.* at ¶ 81. In addition, millions of student-athletes have competed in the NCAA since it adopted its policy in 2011 of allowing transgender women to compete on women's teams after one year of hormone therapy suppressing testosterone, with no reported examples of any disturbance to women's sports as a result of transgender inclusion. *Id.* at ¶ 76. Rep. Ehardt admitted during the hearing that she had no evidence any person in Idaho had ever challenged an athlete's eligibility based on gender. *Id.* at ¶ 80.

On February 21, 2020, H.B. 500 was passed out of the House committee. *Id.* at ¶ 82. On February 25, 2020, Idaho Attorney General Lawrence Wasden ("Attorney General Wasden") warned in a written opinion letter that H.B. 500 raised serious constitutional and other legal concerns due to the disparate treatment and impact it would have on both transgender and intersex athletes, as well as its potential privacy intrusion on all female student athletes. *Id.* at ¶ 83. On February 26, 2020, the House debated the bill. Rep. Ehardt referred to two high school athletes in Connecticut and one woman in college who are transgender and who participated on teams for women and girls. *Id*. at ¶ 84. Rep. Ehardt argued that the mere fact of these athletes' participation exemplified the "threat" the bill sought to address. *Id*. The bill passed the House floor after the debate. *Id*.

After passage in the House, H.B. 500 was heard in the Senate State Affairs Committee and was passed out of Committee on March 9, 2020. *Id*. at ¶ 85. The next day, the bill was sent to the Committee of the Whole Senate for amendment, and minor amendments were made. *Id*. at ¶ 86. One day later, on March 11, 2020, the World Health Organization declared COVID-19 a pandemic and many states adjourned state legislative sessions indefinitely. *Id*. at ¶ 89. By contrast, the Idaho Senate remained in session and passed H.B. 500 as amended on March 16, 2020. *Id*. at ¶ 90. After the House concurred in the Senate amendments, the bill was delivered to Governor Little on March 19, 2020. *Id*.

Professor Dorianne Lambelet Coleman, whose work was cited in the H.B. 500 legislative findings, urged Governor Little to veto the bill, explaining her research was misused and that "there is no legitimate reason to seek to bar all trans girls and women from girls' and women's sport, or to require students whose sex is challenged to prove their eligibility in such intrusive detail." *Id*. at ¶ 91. Professor Coleman endorsed the existing NCAA rule, which mirrors the IHSAA policy, and stated: "No other state has enacted such a flat prohibition against transgender athletes, and Idaho shouldn't either." *Id*.

Five former Idaho Attorneys General likewise urged Governor Little to veto the bill "to keep a legally infirm statute off the books." *Id*. at ¶ 92. They urged Governor Little to "heed the sound advice" of Attorney General

Wasden, who had "raised serious concerns about the legal viability and timing of this legislation." *Id.* Nevertheless, based on legislative findings that, *inter alia*, "inherent, physiological differences between males and females result in different athletic capabilities," Governor Little signed H.B. 500 into law on March 30, 2020.[6] Idaho Code § 33-6202(8); Dkt. 1, ¶ 93.

For purpose of the instant motions, the Act contains three key provisions. First, the Act provides that "interscholastic, intercollegiate, intramural, or club athletic teams or sports that are sponsored by a public primary or secondary school, a public institution of higher education, or any school or institution whose students or teams compete against a public school or institution of higher education" shall be "expressly designated as one (1) of the following based on biological sex: (a) Males, men, or boys; (b) Females, women, or girls; or (c) Coed or mixed." Idaho Code § 33-6203(1). The Act mandates, "[a]thletic teams or sports designated for females, women, or girls shall not be open to students of the male sex." *Id.* at § 33-6203(2). The Act does not contain comparable limitation for any individuals—whether transgender or cisgender—who wish to participate on a team designated for males.

Second, the Act creates a dispute process for an undefined class of individuals who may wish to "dispute" any transgender or cisgender female athlete's sex. This provision provides:

> A dispute regarding a student's sex shall be resolved by the school or institution by requesting that the student provide a health examination and consent form or other statement signed by the student's personal health care provider that shall verify the student's biological sex. The health care

provider may verify the student's biological sex as part of a routine sports physical examination relying only on one (1) or more of the following: the student's reproductive anatomy, genetic makeup, or normal endogenously produced testosterone levels. The state board of education shall promulgate rules for schools and institutions to follow regarding the receipt and timely resolution of such disputes consistent with this subsection.

Id. at § 33-6203(3).

Third, the Act creates an enforcement mechanism to ensure compliance with its provisions. Specifically, the Act creates a private cause of action for any student negatively impacted by violation of the Act, stating:

(1) Any student who is deprived of an athletic opportunity or suffers any direct or indirect harm as a result of a violation of this chapter shall have a private cause of action for injunctive relief, damages, and any other relief available under law against the school or institution of higher education.

(2) Any student who is subject to retaliation or other adverse action by a school, institution of higher education, or athletic association or organization as a result of reporting a violation of this chapter to an employee or representative of the school, institution, or athletic association or organization, or to any state or federal agency with oversight of schools or institutions of higher education in the state, shall have a private cause of action for injunctive relief, damages, and any other relief available under law against the school,

institution, or athletic association or organization.

(3) Any school or institution of higher education that suffers any direct or indirect harm as a result of a violation of this chapter shall have a private cause of action for injunctive relief, damages, and any other relief available under law against the government entity, licensing or accrediting organization, or athletic association or organization.

(4) All civil actions must be initiated within two (2) years after the harm occurred. Persons or organizations who prevail on a claim brought pursuant to this section shall be entitled to monetary damages, including for any psychological, emotional, and physical harm suffered, reasonable attorney's fees and costs, and any other appropriate relief.

Id. at § 33-6205.

D. Procedural Background

Plaintiffs filed the instant suit on April 15, 2020. The lawsuit primarily seeks: (1) a judgment declaring that the Act violates the United States Constitution and Title IX, and also violates such rights as applied to Plaintiffs; (2) preliminary and permanent injunctive relief enjoining the Act's enforcement; and (3) an award of costs, expenses, and reasonable attorneys' fees. *Id.* at 53-54. On April 30, 2020, Plaintiffs filed the instant Motion for Preliminary Injunction, seeking preliminary relief on their Equal Protection Claim. Dkt. 22. The Proposed Intervenors filed a Motion to Intervene on May 26, 2020 (Dkt. 30), and Defendants filed a Motion to Dismiss on June 1, 2020. Dkt. 40. After each was fully briefed, the

Court held oral argument on all three motions on July 22, 2020.

III. ANALYSIS

Since there are three pending motions with different applicable legal standards, the Court will set forth the appropriate legal standard when addressing each motion. Because the Court's decision on the Motion to Intervene will determine the parties in this action, and its decision on the Motion to Dismiss will determine whether Plaintiffs may bring their Motion for a Preliminary Injunction, the Court begins with the Motion to Intervene, follows with Defendants' Motion to Dismiss, and, since the Court finds the Motion to Dismiss is appropriately denied in part and granted in part, concludes with consideration of the Motion for Preliminary Injunction.

A. Motion to Intervene (Dkt. 30)

The Proposed Intervenors seek to intervene to advocate for their interests and to defend the Act, arguing they "face losses to male athletes" and "stand opposed to any legally sanctioned interference with the opportunities that they have enjoyed as female competitors, and that would deprive them and other young women of viable avenues of competitive enjoyment and success within a context that acknowledges and honors them as females." Dkt. 30-1, at 4. The Proposed Intervenors request intervention as a matter of right, or, alternatively, permissive intervention, under Federal Rule of Civil Procedure 24. Plaintiffs oppose the Motion to Intervene. Dkt. 45; Dkt. 51-1. Defendants are in favor of intervention and suggest the Proposed Intervenors' perspectives "can help inform the Court when it balances hardships and determines the public consequences of the relief Plaintiffs seek." Dkt. 44, at 2.

1. Legal Standard

Where, as here, an unconditional right to intervene in not conferred by federal statute,[7] Federal Rule of Civil Procedure 24 authorizes intervention as of right or permissive intervention.

Rule 24(a) contains the standards for intervention as of right, and provides that a court must permit anyone to intervene who, on timely motion: "claims an interest relating to the property or transaction that is the subject of the action, and is so situated that disposing of the action may as a practical matter impair or impede the movant's ability to protect its interest, unless existing parties adequately represent that interest." Fed. R. Civ. P. 24(a)(2).

The Ninth Circuit has distilled the aforementioned provision into a four-part test for intervention as of right: (1) the application for intervention must be timely; (2) the applicant must have a "significantly protectable" interest relating to the property or transaction that is the subject of the action; (3) the applicant must be so situated that the disposition of the action may, as a practical matter, impair or impede the applicant's ability to protect that interest; and (4) the applicant's interest must be inadequately represented by existing parties in the lawsuit. *Sw. Ctr. for Biological Diversity v. Berg*, 268 F.3d 810, 817 (9th Cir. 2001) ("*Berg*") (citation omitted).

The Court must construe Rule 24(a)(2) liberally in favor of intervention. *Id.* at 818. In assessing interventions, courts are "guided primarily by practical and equitable considerations." *Arakaki v. Cayetano*, 324 F.3d 1078, 1083 (9th Cir. 2003) (citing *Donnelly v. Glickman*, 159 F.3d 405, 409 (9th Cir. 1998)). However, it is the movant's burden to show that it satisfies each of the four criteria for intervention as of right. *Prete v. Bradbury*, 438 F.3d 949, 954 (9th Cir. 2006).

In general, Rule 24(b) also gives the court discretion to allow permissive intervention to anyone who has a claim or defense that shares with the main action a common question of law or fact. Fed. R. Civ. P. 24(b)(1)(B). In addition, in exercising its discretion under Rule 24(b), the Court must consider whether intervention will unduly delay or prejudice the adjudication of the original parties' rights. Fed. R. Civ. P. 24(b)(3).

2. *Analysis*

a. Intervention as of Right

Plaintiffs argue intervention as of right should be denied because the Proposed Intervenors claim interests that are neither cognizable under the law nor potentially impaired by the disposition of the present lawsuit. Plaintiffs also argue intervention as of right is unavailable because Defendants adequately represent the Proposed Intervenors' interests.

i. Timeliness of Application

In support of their arguments against permissive intervention, Plaintiffs suggest the Proposed Intervenors' participation will likely delay and prejudice the adjudication of Plaintiffs' claims. Dkt. 45, at 17. Plaintiffs do not, however, contest the timeliness of the application to intervene with respect to intervention as of right. To the extent necessary, the Court will accordingly address the timeliness of the application when assessing permissive intervention.

ii. Protectable Interest

To warrant intervention as of right, a movant must show both "an interest that is protected under some law" and "a 'relationship' between its legally protected interest and the plaintiff's claims." *California ex rel. Lockyer v. United States*, 450 F.3d 436, 441 (9th Cir. 2006) ("*Lockyer*") (quoting *Donnelly*, 159 F.3d at 409). "Whether an applicant for intervention demonstrates sufficient interest in an action is a practical, threshold inquiry. No specific legal or equitable interest need be established." *Berg*, 268 F.3d at 818 (citing *Greene v. United States*, 996 F.2d 973, 976 (9th Cir. 1993)).

The Proposed Intervenors claim a significant and protected interest in having and maintaining "female-only competitions and a competitive environment shielded from physiologically advantaged male participants to whom they stand to lose." Dkt. 30-1, at 7; *see also* Dkt. 52, at 4 n. 1. Plaintiffs characterize this interest as a mere desire to exclude transgender students from single-sex sports, which is not significantly protectable. Dkt. 45, at 10-11. As Plaintiffs note, the Ninth Circuit has held cisgender students do not have a legally protectable interest in excluding transgender students from single-sex spaces. *Parents for Privacy v. Barr*, 949 F.3d 1210, 1228 (9th Cir. 2020) (rejecting Title IX and constitutional claims of cisgender students based on having to share single sex restrooms and locker facilities with transgender students).

However, the Ninth Circuit has also held that redressing past discrimination against women in athletics and promoting equality of athletic opportunity between the sexes is unquestionably a legitimate and important interest, which is served by precluding males from playing on teams devoted to female athletes. *Clark, ex rel. Clark v. Arizona Interscholastic Ass'n*, 695 F.2d 1126, 1131 (9th Cir. 1982) ("*Clark*"). Regardless of how the Proposed Intervenors' interest is characterized—either as a right to a level playing field or as a more invidious desire to exclude transgender athletes—they do claim a protectable interest in ensuring equality of athletic opportunity. The importance of this interest is the basic premise of almost fifty years of Title IX law as it applies to athletics, and, as recognized by the Ninth

Circuit, is unquestionably a legitimate and important interest. *Clark*, 695 F.2d at 1131. The Proposed Intervenors argue the only way to protect equality in sports is through sex segregation without regard to gender identity. Whether this argument is accurate or constitutional is not dispositive of the issue of whether the Proposed Intervenors have an interest in this suit.

Just as Plaintiffs have an interest in seeking equal opportunity for transgender female student athletes, the Proposed Intervenors have an interest in seeking equal opportunity for cisgender female student athletes. As such, to find the Proposed Intervenors are without a protactable interest in the subject matter of this litigation would be to hold that no party has an interest in this litigation. *See, e.g., Johnson v. San Francisco Unified Sch. Dist.*, 500 F.2d 349, 353 (9th Cir. 1974) (explaining all students and parents have an interest in a sound educational system, and that interest is surely no less significant where it is entangled with the constitutional claims of a racially defined class).

Further, Defendants acknowledged at oral argument what seems beyond dispute—Idaho passed the Act to protect cisgender female student athletes like Madi and MK. Because the Proposed Intervenors are the "intended beneficiaries" of the Act, their interest is neither "undifferentiated" nor "generalized." *Lockyer*, 450 F.3d at 441 (citation omitted); *see also Cty. of Fresno v. Andrus*, 622 F.2d 436, 438 (9th Cir. 1980) (finding small farmers had a protectable interest in action seeking to enjoin a federal statute passed regarding lands receiving federally subsidized water where the small farmers were "precisely those Congress intended to protect" with the statute). If the Act is declared unconstitutional or substantially narrowed as result of this litigation, Madi and MK may be more likely to have to choose between competing against transgender athletes or not competing at all. Such an interest is sufficiently "direct, non-contingent, [and] substantial" to constitute a significant protectible interest in this action. *Lockyer*, 450 F.3d at 441 (alteration in original) (quoting *Dilks v. Aloha Airlines*, 642 F.2d 1155, 1157 (9th Cir. 1981)).[8]

iii. Impairment of Interest

The "significantly protectable interest" requirement is closely linked with the requirement that the outcome of the litigation may impair the proposed intervenors' interests. *Lockyer*, 450 F.3d at 442 ("Having found that [intervenors] have a significant protectable interest, we have little difficulty concluding that disposition of this case, may, as a practical matter, affect [them]."). If a proposed intervenor "'would be substantially affected in a practical sense by the determination made in an action, he should, as a general rule, be entitled to intervene.'" *Berg*, 268 F.3d at 822 (quoting Fed. R. Civ. P. 24 advisory committee note to 1966 amendment).

The relief requested by Plaintiffs may affect the Proposed Intervenors' interests. Should Plaintiffs prevail in this lawsuit, the Proposed Intervenors will not have the protection of the law they claim is vital to ensure their right to equality in athletics. Further, they "will have no legal means to challenge [any] injunction" that may be granted by this Court. *Forest Conservation Council v. U.S. Forest Serv.*, 66 F.3d 1489, 1498 (9th Cir. 1995) (abrogated by further broadening of intervention as of right for claims brought under the National Environmental Policy Act in *Wilderness Soc'y v. U.S. Forest Serv.*, 630 F.3d 1173 (9th Cir. 2011)); *see also Lockyer*, 450 F.3d at 443 (finding impairment where proposed intervenors would have no alternative forum to contest the interpretation of a law that was "struck down" or had its "sweep substantially narrowed"). Under such circumstances, the Proposed Intervenors satisfy the impairment requirement for intervention as of right.

iv. Adequacy of Representation

The "most important factor" to determine whether a proposed intervenor is adequately represented by an existing party to the action is "how the [proposed intervenor's] interest compares with the interests of existing parties." *Arakaki*, 324 F.3d at 1086 (citations omitted). When an existing party and a proposed intervenor share the same ultimate objective, a presumption of adequacy of representation applies. *Id.* There is also an assumption of adequacy where, as here, the government is acting on behalf of a constituency that it represents. *United States v. City of Los Angeles*, 288 F.3d 391, 401 (9th Cir. 2002). In the absence of a "very compelling showing to the contrary, it will be presumed that a state adequately represents its citizens when the applicant shares the same interest." *Arakaki*, 324 F.3d at 1086 (internal quotation marks and citation omitted).

Despite their individual interests in the instant litigation, even "interpret[ing] the requirements broadly in favor of intervention," it is clear that the ultimate objective of both the Proposed Intervenors and Defendants is to defend the constitutionality of the Act. *Perry v. Proposition 8 Official Proponents*, 587 F.3d 947, 955 (9th Cir. 2009) (alteration in original) (quoting *Donnelly*, 159 F.3d at 409); *see also Prete*, 438 F.3d at 958-959 (holding that a public interest organization seeking intervention to defend a state constitutional ballot initiative failed to defeat the presumption of adequate representation when the ultimate objective of both the organization and the defendant government was to uphold the measure's validity).[2] Given this shared objective, the presumption of adequacy of representation applies, and the Proposed Intervenors must make "a very compelling showing" to defeat this presumption. *Arakaki*, 324 F.3d at 1086.

The Ninth Circuit has identified three factors for evaluating the adequacy of representation: (1) whether the interest of an existing party is such that it will undoubtedly make all of a proposed intervenor's arguments; (2) whether the existing party is capable and willing to make such arguments; and (3) whether a proposed intervenor would offer any necessary elements to the proceeding that existing parties would neglect. *Id.* "The prospective intervenor bears the burden of demonstrating that existing parties do not adequately represent its interests." *Nw. Forest Res. Council v. Glickman*, 82 F.3d 825, 838 (9th Cir. 1996). However, this burden is satisfied if a proposed intervenor shows that representation "may be" inadequate. *Trbovich v. United Mine Workers*, 404 U.S. 528, 538 n. 10 (1972)).

The Proposed Intervenors argue that their participation in this lawsuit is necessary because Defendants include "multiple agencies and voices of the Idaho government that represent multiple constituencies including constituencies with views and interests more aligned with Plaintiffs than proposed intervenors." Dkt. 30-1, at 10. The Proposed Intervenors also suggest they bring a unique perspective the government cannot adequately represent because the "personal distress and other negative effects suffered by female athletes from the inequity of authorized male competition against females is not felt by institutional administrators." *Id.* Neither of these arguments is convincing.

First, regardless of the "multiple constituencies" represented, or beliefs of individual constituents voiced before H.B. 500 was passed,[10] there is no reason to believe that Defendants cannot be "counted on to argue vehemently in favor of the constitutionality of [the Act]."

League of United Latin Am. Citizens v. Wilson, 131 F.3d 1297, 1306 (9th Cir. 1997). Defendants' retention of an expert witness, "proactive filing of a motion to dismiss and the arguments they have advanced in support of that motion," and fervent opposition to Plaintiffs' Motion for a Preliminary Injunction, "suggest precisely the opposite conclusion." *Animal Legal Defense Fund v. Otter*, 300 F.R.D. 461, 465 (D. Idaho 2014). As even the Proposed Intervenors observe in their proposed opposition to Plaintiffs' Motion for Preliminary Injunction, the "legal authorities, standards, and arguments" in opposing Plaintiffs' motion for a preliminary injunction are "well covered" by Defendants. Dkt. 46, at 5.

Likewise, the Proposed Intervenors' "particular expertise in the subject of the dispute" as cisgender female athletes who have competed against a transgender woman athlete does not amount to a compelling showing of inadequate representation by Defendants. *Prete*, 438 F.3d at 958-959. To the extent they lack personal experience, Defendants can "acquire additional specialized knowledge through discovery (*e.g.*, by calling upon intervenor-defendants to supply evidence) or through the use of experts." *Id.* at 958. Defendants have also already referred to the experiences of both Madi and MK in opposing Plaintiffs' Motion for a Preliminary Injunction. Dkt. 41, at 19-20. Thus, the Proposed Intervenors' personal experience is insufficient to provide the showing necessary to overcome the presumption of adequate representation. *Prete*, 438 F.3d at 959.

However, the Court cannot find Defendants "will undoubtedly make" all of the Proposed' Intervenors' arguments. *Arakaki*, 324 F.3d at 1086. Specifically, there are two limiting constructions that Defendants could, and in fact have, advocated to support dismissal of Plaintiffs' suit and/or assuage constitutional doubts clouding the

Act: (1) the Act is not self-executing and requires another individual to invoke the "dispute process" before any transgender athlete will be precluded from playing on a women's team; and (2) to verify her sex, a transgender female athlete need only submit a form from her health care provider verifying that she is female. Defendants invoked such limiting constructions in their briefing on the Motion to Dismiss and reaffirmed them during oral argument. *See, e.g.*, Dkt. 40-1, at 3, 6-7; Dkt. 59, at 5-6; Dkt. 62, at 44:13-25, 66:21-25. Thus, that the "the government will offer . . . a limiting construction of [the Act] is not just a theoretical possibility; it has already done so." *Lockyer*, 450 F.3d at 444.

In contrast to Defendants' attempt to narrow the Act, the Proposed Intervenors suggest the Act must be read broadly to categorically preclude transgender women from ever playing on female sports teams, regardless of whether they become the target of a dispute or whether they can obtain a sex verification letter from a health care provider. These are far more than differences in litigation strategy between Defendants and the Proposed Intervenors. *City of Los Angeles*, 288 F.3d at 402-403 ("[M]ere differences in strategy . . . are not enough to justify intervention as of right."). This conflicting construction goes to the heart of interpretation and enforcement of the Act.

The Court therefore concludes that the Proposed Intervenors have "more narrow, parochial interests" than the Defendants. *Lockyer*, 450 F.3d at 445 (finding proposed intervenors overcame the presumption of adequacy of representation where the government suggested a limiting construction of a law in its motion for summary judgment); *Citizens for Balanced Use v. Montana Wilderness Ass'n*, 647 F.3d 893, 899 (9th Cir. 2011) (holding proposed intervenors overcame presumption of adequate representation where they sought to secure the broadest possible interpretation of the Forest Service's Interim Order, while the Forest Service argued that a much narrower interpretation would suffice to comply with the Interim Order). Through the presentation of direct evidence that Defendants "will take a position that actually compromises (and potentially eviscerates) the protections of [the Act]," the Proposed Intervenors have overcome the presumption that Defendants will act in their interests. *Lockyer*, 450 F.3d at 445.

Liberally construing Rule 24(a), the Court finds that the Proposed Intervenors have met the test for intervention as a matter of right. Alternatively, however, the Court finds permissive intervention is also appropriate.

b. Permissive Intervention

The Court's discretion to grant or deny permissive intervention is broad. *Spangler v. Pasadena City Bd. of Educ.*, 552 F.2d 1326, 1329 (9th Cir. 1977) (citation omitted). The Ninth Circuit has "often stated that permissive intervention requires: (1) an independent ground for jurisdiction; (2) a timely motion; and (3) a common question of law and fact between the movant's claim or defense and the main action." *Freedom from Religion Found., Inc. v. Geithner*, 644 F.3d 836, 843 (9th Cir. 2011) (citations omitted). "In exercising its discretion," the Court must also "consider whether the intervention will unduly delay or prejudice the adjudication of the original parties' rights." Fed. R. Civ. P. 24(b)(3). When a proposed intervenor has otherwise met the requirements, "[t]he court may also consider other factors in the exercise of its discretion, including the nature and extent of the intervenors' interest and whether the intervenors' interests are adequately represented by other parties." *Perry*, 587 F.3d at 955 (quoting *Spangler*, 552 F.2d at 1329).

Plaintiffs do not dispute that the Proposed Intervenors have an independent ground for jurisdiction and share a common question of law and fact with the defense of the main action. Plaintiffs instead argue that permissive intervention should be denied because existing parties adequately represent the Proposed Intervenors' interests, and because intervention would unduly delay or prejudice the adjudication of the rights of the original parties. Dkt. 45, at 16-19. As explained above, the Proposed Intervenors have shown Defendants may not adequately represent their interests because Defendants have advanced a limiting construction of the Act and thus *undoubtedly will not* make all of the arguments Madi and MK will make. *Arakaki*, 324 F.3d at 1086. The Court accordingly rejects Plaintiffs' contention that permissive intervention should be denied because Defendants adequately represent the Proposed Intervenors' interests.

Plaintiffs also argue the Proposed Intervenors' participation will likely delay and prejudice the adjudication of Plaintiffs' claims because Madi and MK waited six weeks after Plaintiffs filed their Complaint to seek intervention. This argument fails because the Ninth Circuit has held an application to intervene is timely where, as here, it is filed less than three months after the complaint. *See, e.g., Idaho Farm Bureau Fed'n v. Babbitt*, 58 F.3d 1392, 1397 (9th Cir. 1995) (finding motion to intervene filed four months after initiation of a lawsuit to be timely); *Citizens for Balanced Use v. Montana Wilderness Ass'n*, 647 F.3d 893, 897 (9th Cir. 2011) (deeming motion to intervene timely when it was filed "less than three months after the complaint was filed and less than two weeks after [Defendant] filed its answer to the complaint.").

Plaintiffs next contend they will be prejudiced if they are unable to obtain a ruling from this Court before the fall sports season begins, and that the any disruption of the briefing schedule to accommodate the Motion to Intervene could delay resolution of Plaintiffs' request for emergency relief. This concern is moot because the Motion to Intervene was fully briefed prior to oral argument on July 22, 2020, and the Court is issuing the instant decision on all three pending motions before the fall sports season begins.

Finally, Plaintiffs argue intervention could prejudice the adjudication of their claims because counsel for the Proposed Intervenors have a history of utilizing misgendering tactics that will delay and impair efficient resolution of litigation. For instance, the Motion to Intervene is replete with references to Lindsay using masculine pronouns and refers to other transgender women by their former male names. The Court is concerned by this conduct, as other courts have denounced such misgendering as degrading, mean, and potentially mentally devastating to transgender individuals. *T.B., Jr. ex rel. T.B. v. Prince George's Cty. Bd. of Educ.*, 897 F.3d 566, 577 (4th Cir. 2018) (describing student's harassment of transgender female teacher by referring to her with male gender pronouns as "pure meanness."); *Hampton v. Baldwin*, 2018 WL 5830730, at *2 (S.D. Ill. Nov. 7, 2018) (referencing expert testimony that "misgendering transgender people can be degrading, humiliating, invalidating, and mentally devastating.").

Counsel for the Proposed Intervenors responds that they have used such terms not to be discourteous, but to differentiate between "immutable" categories of sex versus "experiential" categories of gender identity, and that the terms they use simply reflect "necessary accuracy." Dkt. 52, at 8 (quoting *Frontiero v. Richardson*, 411 U.S. 677, 686 (1973)). Such "accuracy," however, is not compromised by simply referring to Lindsay and other transgender females as "transgender women," or by adopting Lindsay's preferred gender pronouns.[11] *See, e.g., Edmo v. Corizon*, 935 F.3d 757 (9th Cir. 2019) (consistently referring to transgender female prisoner using her chosen name and female gender pronouns); *Canada v. Hall*, 2019 WL 1294660, at *1 n. 1 (N.D. Ill. March 21, 2019) ("Although immaterial to this ruling, the Court would be derelict if it failed to note the defendants' careless disrespect for the plaintiff's transgender identity, as reflected through . . . the consistent use of male pronouns to identify the plaintiff. The Court cautions counsel against maintaining a similar tone in future filings."); *Lynch v. Lewis*, 2014 WL 1813725, at *2 n. 2 (M.D. Ga. May 7, 2014) ("The Court and Defendants will use feminine pronouns to refer to the Plaintiff in filings with the Court. Such use is not to be taken as a factual or legal finding. The Court will grant Plaintiff's request as a matter of courtesy, and because it is the Court's practice to refer to litigants in the manner they prefer to be addressed when possible.").[12]

Ultimately, however, that the Proposed Intervenors' counsel used gratuitous language in their briefs is not a reason to deny Madi and MK the opportunity to intervene to support a law of which they are the intended beneficiaries. Moreover, during oral argument, counsel for the Proposed Intervenors was respectful in advocating for Madi and MK without needlessly attempting to shame Lindsay or other transgender women. That counsel did so illustrates there is no need to misgender Lindsay or others in order to "speak coherently about the goals, justifications, and validity of the Fairness in Women's Sports Act." Dkt. 52, at 8. Counsel should continue this practice in future filings and arguments before the Court.

In sum, the Court will allow Madi and MK to intervene as of right, and, alternatively, finds permissive intervention is also appropriate. The Court will accordingly collectively refer to Madi and MK hereinafter as the "Intervenors."

B. Motion to Dismiss (Dkt. 40)

Defendants filed a Motion to Dismiss Plaintiffs' action, contending Plaintiffs lack standing, that their claims are not ripe for review, and that their facial challenges fail as a matter of law.

1. Legal Standard

A motion to dismiss based on a lack of Article III standing arises under Federal Rule of Civil Procedure 12(b)(1). *Maya v. Centex Corp.*, 658 F.3d 1060, 1067 (9th Cir. 2011); *Valentin v. Hosp. Bella Vista*, 254 F.3d 358, 362-63 (1st Cir. 2001) (applying Rule 12(b)(1) to a motion to dismiss on grounds of ripeness or mootness). A motion to dismiss for lack of subject matter jurisdiction under Rule 12(b)(1) may challenge jurisdiction either on the face of the pleadings or by presenting extrinsic evidence for the court's consideration. *Safer Air for Everyone v. Meyer*, 373 F.3d 1035, 1039 (9th Cir. 2004) (holding a jurisdictional attack may be facial or factual). "In a facial attack, the challenger asserts that the allegations contained in the complaint are insufficient on their face to invoke federal jurisdiction. By contrast, in a factual attack, the challenger disputes the truth of the allegations that, by themselves, would otherwise invoke federal jurisdiction." *Id.* Where, as here, an attack is facial, the court confines its inquiry to allegations in the complaint. *White v. Lee*, 227 F.3d 1214, 1242 (9th Cir. 2000).

When ruling on a facial jurisdictional attack, courts must "accept as true all material allegations of the complaint and must construe the complaint in favor of the complaining party." *De La Cruz v. Tormey*, 582 F.2d 45, 62 (9th Cir. 1978) (citing *Warth v. Seldin*, 422 U.S. 490, 501 (1975)). However, the plaintiff bears the burden of alleging facts that are legally sufficient to invoke the court's jurisdiction. *Leite v. Crane Co.*, 749 F.3d 1117, 1121 (9th Cir. 2014).

Rule 12(b)(6) permits a court to dismiss a case if the plaintiff has "fail[ed] to state a claim upon which relief can be granted." Fed. R. Civ. P. 12(b)(6). A Rule 12(b)(6) dismissal may be based on either a 'lack of a cognizable legal theory' or 'the absence of sufficient facts alleged under a cognizable legal theory.'" *Johnson v. Riverside Healthcare Sys., LP*, 534 F.3d 1116, 1121 (9th Cir. 2008) (citation omitted). In deciding whether to grant a motion to dismiss, the court must accept as true all well-pled factual allegations made in the pleading under attack. *Ashcroft v. Iqbal*, 556 U.S. 662, 678 (2009). A court is not, however, "required to accept as true allegations that are merely conclusory, unwarranted deductions of fact, or unreasonable inferences." *Sprewell v. Golden State Warriors*, 266 F.3d 979, 988 (9th Cir. 2001). However, a "complaint should not be dismissed unless it appears beyond doubt that the plaintiff can prove no set of facts in support of the claim that would entitle the plaintiff to relief." *Id.* (citing *Morley v. Walker*, 175 F.3d 756, 759 (9th Cir. 1999)).

Dismissal without leave to amend is inappropriate unless it is beyond doubt that the complaint could not be saved by amendment. *See Harris v. Amgen, Inc.*, 573 F.3d 728, 737 (9th Cir. 2009) (citations omitted). The

Ninth Circuit has held that "in dismissals for failure to state a claim, a district court should grant leave to amend even if no request to amend the pleading was made, unless it determines that the pleading could not possibly be cured by the allegation of other facts." *Cook, Perkiss and Liehe, Inc. v. N. California Collection Serv., Inc.*, 911 F.2d 242, 247 (9th Cir. 1990) (citations omitted).

2. *Analysis*

a. Standing

The "irreducible constitutional minimum" of Article III standing consists of three elements: (1) the plaintiff must have suffered an injury in fact; (2) that is fairly traceable to the challenged conduct of the defendant and not the result of the independent action of some third party not before the court; and (3) that is likely to be redressed by a favorable judicial decision. *Lujan v. Defenders of Wildlife*, 504 U.S. 555, 560 (1992). To survive a Rule 12(b)(1) motion at the pleading stage (a facial challenge to subject-matter jurisdiction), the complaint must clearly allege facts demonstrating each element of standing. *Spokeo, Inc. v. Robins*, 136 S. Ct. 1540, 1547 (2016).

Defendants suggest Plaintiffs lack standing because they have failed to allege that they have suffered an injury in fact.[13] Dkt. 40-1, at 6. "To establish injury in fact, a plaintiff must show that he or she has suffered 'an invasion of a legally protected interest' that is 'concrete and particularized' and 'actual or imminent, not conjectural or hypothetical.'" *Spokeo*, 136 S. Ct. at 1548 (quoting *Lujan*, 504 U.S. at 560). "A plaintiff threatened with future injury has standing to sue if the threatened injury is 'certainly impending,' or there is a 'substantial risk that the harm will occur.'" *In re Zappos.com, Inc.*, 888 F.3d 1020, 1024 (9th Cir. 2018) (quoting *Susan B. Anthony List v. Driehaus*, 573 U.S. 149, 158 (2014)). A plaintiff cannot establish standing by alleging a threat of future harm based on a chain of speculative contingencies. *Nelsen v. King Cty.*, 895 F.2d 1248, 1252 (9th Cir. 1990).

Defendants argue Plaintiffs have not alleged an injury in fact because all alleged harms are conjectural, hypothetical, or based on a chain of speculative contingencies. Specifically, Defendants suggest that Lindsay's alleged harm of being subject to exclusion from participation on a women's sport teams, and Jane's alleged harm of being required to verify her sex, cannot occur unless each Plaintiff first makes a women's athletic team, and a third party then disputes either Plaintiffs' sex according to regulations that the State Board of Education has not yet promulgated.[14] Dkt. 40-1, at 6. This argument fails with respect to both Plaintiffs.

i. Lindsay

The Act categorically bars Lindsay from participating on BSU's women's cross-country and track teams. Idaho Code § 33-6203(2) ("Athletic teams or sports designated for females, women, or girls *shall* not be open to students of the male sex.") (emphasis added). Although Defendants contend Lindsay will not be harmed unless she first makes the BSU team and someone then seeks to exclude her through a sex verification challenge, the Act prevents BSU from allowing Lindsay to try out for the women's team at all.

The Act also subjects BSU to a risk of civil suit by any student "who is deprived of an athletic opportunity or suffers any direct or indirect harm," if BSU allows a transgender woman to participate on its athletic teams. Idaho Code § 33-6205(1). A student who prevails on a claim brought pursuant to this section "shall be entitled to monetary damages, including for any psychological, emotional, and physical harm suffered, reasonable attorney's fees and costs, and any other appropriate relief." *Id.* at 6205(4). Defendants' claim that the Act's categorical bar against Lindsay's participation on BSU's women's teams is not "self-executing" because it "has no independent enforcement mechanism," is meritless in light of the risk of significant civil liability the Act imposes on any school that allows a transgender woman to participate in women's sports. Dkt. 59, at 5.

The harm Lindsay alleges—the inability to participate on women's teams—arose when the Act went into effect on July 1, 2020. That Lindsay has not yet tried out for BSU athletics or been subject to a dispute process is irrelevant because the Act bars her from trying out in the first place. The Supreme Court has long held that the "injury in fact" required for standing in equal protection cases is denial of equal treatment resulting from the imposition of a barrier, not the ultimate inability to obtain the benefit. *Ne. Florida Chapter of Associated Gen. Contractors of Am. v. City of Jacksonville*, 508 U.S. 656, 664 (1993) ("When the government erects a barrier that makes it more difficult for members of one group to obtain a benefit than it is for members of another group, a member of the former group seeking to challenge the barrier need not allege that he would have obtained the benefit but for the barrier in order to establish standing"); *Clements v. Fashing*, 457 U.S. 957, 962 (1982) (finding political officers had standing to challenge provision of Texas Constitution requiring automatic resignation for some officeholders upon their announcement of candidacy for another office because injury was the "obstacle to [their] candidacy" for a new office, not the fact that they would have been elected to a new office but for the law's prohibition); *Regents of Univ. of California v. Bakke*, 438 U.S. 265, 281 n. 14 (1978) (holding twice-rejected white male applicant had standing to challenge medical school's admissions program which reserved 16 of 100 places in the entering class for minority applicants, because the requisite "injury" was plaintiff's inability to *compete* for all 100 places in the class, simply because of his race, not that he would have been *admitted* in the absence of the special program). Lindsay has adequately alleged an injury because she cannot compete for a position on BSU's women's cross-country and track teams in the first place, regardless of whether or not she would ultimately make such teams.[15]

In addition, even if BSU risked civil liability and allowed Lindsay to try out for, or join, a women's team, it is not speculative to suggest Lindsay's sex would be disputed. Lindsay is a nineteen-year-old transgender woman who has bravely become the public face of this litigation, and, in doing so, has captured the attention of local and national news. *See, e.g.*, James Dawson, *Idaho Transgender Athlete Law To Be Challenged in Federal Court*, https://www.boisestatepublicradio.org/post/idaho-transgender-athlete-law-be-challenged-federal-court#stream/0 (Apr. 15, 2020); Julie Kliegman, SPORTS ILLUSTRATED, *Idaho Banned Trans Athletes from Women's Sports. She's Fighting Back*, https://www.si.com/sports-illustrated/2020/06/30/idaho-transgender-ban-fighting-back (June 30, 2020); Roman Stubbs, THE WASHINGTON POST, *As transgender rights debate spills into sports, one runner finds herself at the center of a pivotal case* https://www.washingtonpost.com/sports/2020/07/27/idaho-transgender-sports-lawsuit-hecox-v-little-hb-500/ (July 27, 2020).[16]

In addition to such headlines, prominent athletes, including Billie Jean King and Megan Rapinoe, have, due to the Act, called for the NCAA to move men's basketball tournament games scheduled to be played in

Idaho next March to another state. *Id.* On the other side of the coin, advocates in favor of the Act, including 300 high-profile female athletes, signed a letter asking the NCAA not to boycott Idaho over passing the Act. Ellie Reynolds, THE FEDERALIST, *More Than 300 Female Athletes, Olympians Urge NCAA to Protect Women's Sports*, https://thefederalist.com/2020/07/30/more-than-300-female-athletes-olympians-urge-ncaa-to-protect-womens-sports/ (July 30, 2020). In light of the extensive attention this case has already received, and widespread knowledge that Lindsay is transgender, it is untenable to suggest she would *not* be subject to a sex dispute if BSU allowed her the opportunity to try out for, or join, a women's team.[17]

Defendants also argue Lindsay lacks standing because she has not alleged facts to show she could compete under the current NCAA rules, such as dates showing she has undergone hormone treatment for one calendar year prior to participation on women's sports teams. However, Lindsay alleged in the Complaint that she is being treated with both testosterone suppression and estrogen, and that she is eligible to compete in women's sports in fall 2020 under existing NCAA rules for inclusion of transgender athletes. Dkt. 1, at ¶¶ 29, 32. Because the Court must accept such allegations as true and construe them in Lindsay's favor, Lindsay has adequately alleged she is eligible to participate on women's teams under the NCAA's regulations despite the Complaint's omission of the exact dates of her treatment. *De la Cruz*, 582 F.2d at 62.

Nonetheless, Defendants claim Lindsay has not adequately alleged she is otherwise eligible to play on women's teams because the U.S. Department of Education Office of Civil Rights ("OCR") recently issued a Letter of Impending Enforcement Action ("OCR

Letter") opining that allowing transgender high school athletes in Connecticut to participate in women's sports violated the rights of female athletes under Title IX.[18] Dkt. 40-1, at 7 n. 1, 10 n. 2. However, the OCR Letter itself states that "it is not a formal statement of OCR policy and should not be relied upon, cited, or construed as such." Dkt. 41, at 68. Because it is expressly not the OCR's formal policy and may not be cited or construed as such, the OCR Letter does not render Lindsay ineligible from participating on women's teams. In addition, the OCR Letter is also of questionable validity given the Supreme Court's recent holding in *Bostock v. Clayton Cty., Georgia*, 140 S. Ct. 1731, 1741 (2020) (clarifying that the prohibition on discrimination because of sex in Title VII includes discrimination based on an individual's transgender status); *see also Emeldi v. Univ. of Oregon*, 698 F.3d 715, 724 (9th Cir. 2012) (interpreting Title IX provisions in accordance with Title VII). The Court accordingly rejects Defendants' claim that Lindsay may not otherwise be eligible to play women's sports due to the OCR Letter.

Defendants also imply Lindsay cannot establish an injury in fact because the State Board of Education has not yet promulgated regulations governing third-party sex verification disputes. Dkt. 40-1, at 3, 6. Regardless of how they are written, any future regulations cannot alter the Act's categorical bar against transgender women participating on women's teams. Under the Act, women's teams "shall not be open to students of the male sex." *Id.* at § 33-6203(2). Future regulations could not alter this mandate without eliminating a key component of the Act by overriding specific language of the statute.

In essence, Defendants' argument regarding Lindsay's standing is essentially a claim that Lindsay has not suffered any injury because there is no guarantee the

Act will be enforced. Defendants have not identified any "principal of standing," or "any case that stands for the proposition that [the Court] should deny standing on the assumption that the regulated entity under the statute will simply violate the law and not do what the law says." Dkt. 62, at 52:5-9. In fact, the Supreme Court rejected a similar argument by the State of Georgia in *Turner v. Fouche*, 396 U.S. 346, 361 (1970). In *Turner*, the Supreme Court held a non-property owner had standing to raise an, equal protection claim against a state law requiring members of the board of education to be property owners. The Court addressed Georgia's contention that the non-property owner lacked standing to challenge the law in the absence of evidence that the law had been enforced, noting: "Georgia also argues the question is not properly before us because the record is devoid of evidence that [the property ownership requirement] has operated to exclude any [non-property owners] from the Taliaferro County board of education." *Id.* at 361 n. 23. The *Turner* Court neatly rejected this contention, stating, "Georgia can hardly urge that her county officials may be depended on to ignore a provision of state law." *Id.* Moreover, given the civil liability and significant damages any regulated entity in Idaho now faces if they allow a transgender woman to participate on woman's sport teams, the Act's enforcement is essentially guaranteed. Idaho Code § 33-6205.

In addition to the injury of being barred from playing women's sports, Lindsay also claims an injury of being forced to turn over private medical information to the government if her sex was challenged. Dkt. 1, at ¶¶ 157, 168. Defendants argue this injury is "not based in [the Act's] text, which requires a 'health examination and consent form or other statement signed by the student's personal health provider' when there is a dispute, and does not require that the health care provider expound further or disclose any underlying health information." Dkt. 40-1, at 8. However, if BSU violates the Act by allowing Lindsay to participate in women's sports and another student challenges Lindsay's sex, the Act also provides a health care provider can verify Lindsay's sex relying *only* on one or more of the following: her reproductive anatomy, genetic makeup, or normal endogenously produced testosterone levels. Idaho Code § 33-6203(3). Evaluating any of these criteria would require invasive examination and/or testing and would also necessarily reveal extremely personal health information such as Lindsay's precise genetic makeup. Moreover, it would be impossible for Lindsay to demonstrate a "biological sex" permitting participation on a women's team based on any of these three criteria. Dkt. 55, at 7-8.

Defendants counter that Plaintiffs' concerns are overblown and that the verification process is not an invasive as Plaintiffs make it out to be. They suggest a health care provider may verify a student's "biological sex" based on something other than the three expressly listed criteria due to the "health examination and consent form or other statement provision" language outlined in the Act. Dkt. 40-1, at 3 (claiming that the Act does not require the health care provider "to use the three specified factors in providing an 'other statement' verifying 'the students biological sex.'") During oral argument, defense counsel confirmed that Lindsay can play on female sport's teams if her health care provider simply signs an "other statement" stating that Lindsay is female. Dkt. 62, at 66:21-25; 67:4-9.

It is "a cardinal principle of statutory construction" that "a statute ought, upon the whole, to be so construed that, if it can be prevented, no clause, sentence, or word shall be superfluous, void, or insignificant." *Duncan v. Walker*, 533 U.S. 167, 174 (2001) (internal quotation marks and citations omitted); *United States v. Menasche*, 348 U.S. 528, 538-539 (1955) ("It is our duty to give effect, if possible, to every clause and word of a statute." (internal quotation marks omitted); *Beck v. Prupis*, 529 U.S. 494, 506 (2000) (it is a "longstanding canon of statutory construction that terms in a statute should not be construed so as to render any provision of that statute meaningless or superfluous.")

If the Court were to adopt Defendants' aforementioned construction of the statute, the entire legislative findings and purpose section of the Act would be rendered meaningless. Idaho Code § 33-6202 (explaining inherent physiological differences put males at an advantage in sports, requiring sex-specific women's teams to promote sex equality). So too would the Act's mandate that athletic teams or sports designated for females, women, or girls "shall not be open to students of the male sex." *Id.* at § 33-6203(2). Defendants' contention that Lindsay would not be subject to the invasive and potentially cost-prohibitive medical examination codified in Idaho Code section 33-6203(3) because her health care provider could simply verify that she is female is impossible to reconcile with the rest of the Act's provisions.[19] As such, Lindsay has also alleged a non-speculative risk of suffering an invasion of privacy if BSU violated the law and allowed her to try out for the women's cross-country or track team.

ii. Jane

Jane has also alleged an injury in fact because, by virtue of the Act's passage, she is now subject to disparate, and less favorable, treatment based on sex. As a female student athlete, Jane risks being subject to the "dispute process," a potentially invasive and expensive medical exam, loss of privacy, and the embarrassment of having her sex challenged, while male student athletes who play on male teams do not face such risks. The Supreme Court has long recognized that unequal treatment because of gender like that codified by the Act "is an injury in fact" sufficient to convey standing. *Heckler v. Mathews*, 465 U.S. 728, 738 (1984) (finding plaintiff claimed a judicially cognizable injury where a statute subjected him to unequal treatment solely because of his gender); *Davis v. Guam*, 785 F.3d 1311, 1315 (9th Cir. 2015) ("[Plaintiff's] allegation—that Guam law provides a benefit to a class of persons that it denies him—is 'a type of personal injury [the Supreme Court] has long recognized as judicially cognizable.'") (quoting *Heckler*, 465 U.S. at 738).

The male appellee in *Heckler* challenged a provision of the Social Security Act that required certain male workers (but not female workers) to make a showing of dependency as a condition for receiving full spousal benefits. *Heckler*, 465 U.S. at 731-35. However, the statute also "prevent[ed] a court from redressing this inequality by increasing the benefits payable to" male workers. *Id.* at 739. Thus, the lawsuit couldn't have resulted in any tangible benefit to plaintiff. The Supreme Court nevertheless held that appellee's claimed injury of being subject to unequal treatment solely because of his gender was "a type of personal injury we have long recognized as judicially cognizable." *Id.* at 738. The *Heckler* Court explained plaintiff had standing to challenge the provision because he sought to vindicate the "right to equal treatment," which isn't necessarily "coextensive with any substantive rights to the benefits denied the party discriminated against." *Id.* at 739. In *Davis*, the Ninth Circuit read *Heckler* "as holding that equal treatment under law is a judicially cognizable inquiry that satisfies the case or controversy requirement of Article III, even if it brings no tangible benefit to the party asserting it." *Davis*, 785 F.3d at 1315.

As a cisgender girl who plays on the Boise High soccer team and who will run track on the girl's team in the spring, Jane is subject to worse and differential treatment than are similarly situated male students who play for boy's teams in Idaho.[20] Jane has suffered an injury because she is subject to disparate rules for participation on girls' teams, while boys can play on boys' teams without such rules. *Id.* (holding Guam's alleged denial of equal treatment on the basis of race through voter registration law was a judicially cognizable injury); *see also Melendres v. Arpaio*, 695 F.3d 990, 998 (9th Cir. 2012) (holding that Latino plaintiffs had standing to challenge policy targeting Latinos in connection with traffic stops based on their "[e]xposure to this policy while going about [their] daily li[ves]," even though "the likelihood of a future stop of a particular individual plaintiff may not be 'high'") (citation omitted).[21] That Jane has not had her sex challenged does not change the fact that she is subject to different, and less favorable, rules for participation on girls' teams that similarly situated boys are not.

In addition to being subject to disparate treatment on the basis of her sex, Jane reasonably fears that her sex will be disputed and that she will suffer the further injury of having to undergo the sex verification process. Dkt. 1, ¶¶ 46-50. In *Krottner v. Starbucks Corp.*, 628 F.3d 1139 (9th Cir. 2010), the Ninth Circuit addressed the Article III standing of victims of data theft where a thief stole a laptop containing "the unencrypted names, addresses, and social security numbers of approximately 97,000 Starbucks employees." *Id.* at 1140. Some employees sued, and the only harm that most alleged was an "increased risk of future identity theft." *Id.* at 1142. There was no evidence that the thief had actually used plaintiffs' specific identities. The Ninth Circuit determined this was sufficient for Article III standing, holding that the plaintiffs had "alleged a credible threat of real and immediate harm" because the laptop and their personal information had been stolen. *Id.* at 1143.

Jane also alleges a credible threat of being forced to undergo a sex verification process. Jane has identified why she is more likely than other female athletes to be subjected to the dispute process. Specifically, Jane "worries that one of her competitors may decide to 'dispute' her sex" because she "does not commonly wear skirts or dresses," "most of her closest friends are boys," she has "an athletic build," and because "people sometimes think of her as masculine." Dkt. 1, at ¶¶ 46-47. Further, even in the absence of Jane's specific characteristics, her general fear of being subjected to the dispute is credible because the Act currently provides that essentially anyone can challenge another female athlete's sex and protects any challenger from adverse action regardless of whether the dispute is brought in good faith or simply to bully or harass. Although, as Defendants note, the State Board of Education may promulgate regulations that narrow the Act's dispute process, Jane risks being subject to the currently unlimited process as soon as she tries out for Boise High's soccer team on or around August 17, 2020.

Under the Act's dispute process, Jane may have to verify that she is female in order to play girls' sports, and, given the clear meaning of the statute, such verification must be based on her reproductive anatomy, genetic makeup, or normal endogenously produced testosterone levels. Idaho Code § 33-6203(3). As discussed above,

Defendants' claim that Jane can simply provide a health examination and consent form from her sports physical, or "other statement" from her personal health care provider, appears impossible to reconcile with the clear language of the Act. Dkt. 40-1, at 7. Jane's risk of being forced to undergo an invasion of privacy simply to play sports represents an "injury in fact" sufficient to confer standing. *Babbitt v. United Farm Workers Nat'l Union*, 442 U.S. 289, 298 (1979) ("A plaintiff who challenges a statute must demonstrate a realistic danger of sustaining a direct injury as a result of the statute's operation or enforcement. But one does not have to await the consummation of threatened injury to obtain preventive relief.") (internal quotation marks, alterations, and citations omitted).

Because it finds both Lindsay and Jane have alleged an injury in fact, the Court turns to Defendants' ripeness argument.

b. Ripeness[22]

Defendants also seek dismissal because this case is purportedly unripe. Ripeness is a question of timing. *Thomas v. Anchorage Equal Rights Comm'n*, 220 F.3d 1134, 1138 (9th Cir. 2000). It is a doctrine "designed to prevent the courts, through avoidance of premature adjudication, from entangling themselves in abstract disagreements." *Id.* (internal quotation marks and citation omitted).

The "ripeness inquiry contains both a constitutional and prudential component." *Portman v. Cty. of Santa Clara*, 995 F.2d 898, 902 (9th Cir. 1993). As Defendants acknowledge, the constitutional component of the ripeness injury is generally coextensive with the injury element of standing analysis. Dkt. 40-1, at 9; *California Pro-Life Council, Inc. v. Getman*, 328 F.3d 1088, 1094 n. 2 (9th Cir. 2003) (noting, "the constitutional component of ripeness is synonymous with the injury-in-fact prong of the standing inquiry"); *see also Duke Power Co. v. Carolina Envtl. Study Grp., Inc.*, 438 U.S. 59, 81 (1978) (finding that an "injury in fact" satisfies the constitutional ripeness inquiry). Defendants' constitutional ripeness arguments fail for the same reasons that their standing arguments fail.

The prudential component of ripeness "focuses on whether there is an adequate record upon which to base effective review." *Portman*, 995 F.2d at 903. In evaluating prudential ripeness, the Court must consider "the fitness of the issues for judicial decision and the hardship to the parties of withholding court consideration." *Thomas*, 220 F.3d at 1141. Ultimately, prudential considerations of ripeness are discretionary. *Id.* at 1142.

i. Fitness for Judicial Review

The Supreme Court and Ninth Circuit have recognized the difficulty of deciding constitutional questions without the necessary factual context. *See, e.g., W.E.B. DuBois Clubs of Am. v. Clark*, 389 U.S. 309, 313 (1967); *Thomas*, 220 F.3d at 1141. In *Thomas*, several landlords challenged an Alaska statute that banned discrimination on the basis of marital status, arguing the statute violated their First Amendment rights. 220 F.3d at 1137. For instance, the landlords claimed, *inter alia*, that the City's prohibition on any advertising referencing a marital status preference violated their right to free speech. The Ninth Circuit found the free speech claim was not ripe because no "concrete factual scenario" demonstrated how the law, as applied, infringed the landlords' constitutional rights. *Id.* at 1141. Specifically, the landlords had never advertised or published a reference to marital status preference in the past in connection with their rental real estate activities, nor had expressed any intent of doing so in the future. *Id.* at 1140 n. 5. On this record, the Ninth Circuit held the alleged free speech violation did not rise to the level of a justiciable controversy. *Id.*

Here, unlike in *Thomas*, Plaintiffs' claims are concrete and Plaintiffs clearly delineate how the Act harms them in their specific circumstances. Specifically, Jane is a life-long student athlete who will try out for Boise High School's girls' soccer team in August 2020. Because of various identified traits that have led others to classify her as masculine, Jane reasonably fears she may be subject to a sex dispute challenge. That a specific individual has not threatened such challenge is immaterial because the Act has never been in effect during a school sport's season and the sex dispute challenge has thus never before been available, and, by virtue of being a female student athlete, Jane risks being subject to a sex dispute challenge as soon as she tries out for Boise High's girls' soccer team. Lindsay is also a life-long athlete who has alleged a desire and intent to try out for BSU's women's cross-country team this fall. If BSU permitted her to try out, Lindsay would meet the rules under the NCAA, and the rules in Idaho prior to the Act's passage, to participate by the time BSU will have its first NCAA meet. However, Lindsay is now categorically barred from trying out for the cross-country team under the Act.

Defendants have not addressed such as-applied challenges and have not identified any factual questions that preclude consideration of such challenges at this juncture.[23]

Further, legal questions that require little factual development are more likely to be ripe. *Thomas v. Union Carbide Agric. Products Co.*, 473 U.S. 568, 581 (1985). The issues Lindsay and Jane raise are primarily legal:

whether the Act violates the Constitution and Title IX in light of its categorical exclusion of transgender women and girls from school sports and its sex-verification scheme for all female student athletes. As such, the Act's legality involves a "pure question of law" and Plaintiffs claims are fit for judicial review now. *Freedom to Travel Campaign v. Newcomb*, 82 F.3d 1431, 1435 (9th Cir. 1996) (finding claims were ripe and issue was purely legal where organization which arranged trips to Cuba challenged regulation restraining right to travel to Cuba, even though organization had not applied for, and had not been denied, the specific license required under regulation).

ii. Hardship to the Parties should the Court Withhold Consideration

When a plaintiff challenges a statute or regulation, hardship is more likely if the statute has a direct effect on the plaintiff's daily life. *Texas v. United States*, 523 U.S.296, 301 (1998). Hardship is less likely if the statute's effect is abstract. *Id.* at 302 (rejecting argument that ongoing "threat to federalism" could constitute hardship).

Here, the Court is satisfied that the Plaintiffs stand to suffer a hardship should the Court withhold its decision. If the Court declines jurisdiction over this dispute, Lindsay will be categorically barred from participating on BSU's women's teams this fall and will also lose at least a season of NCAA eligibility, which she can never get back. Dkt. 1, at ¶ 34. Similarly, as soon as she tries out for fall soccer, Jane is subject to disparate rules and risks facing a sex verification challenge. If the Court withholds its decision, both Plaintiffs risk being forced to endure a humiliating dispute process and/or invasive medical examination simply to play sports.[24] Given the reasonable threat that the Act will be enforced within days of this decision, as well as the hardship such enforcement will impose on Lindsay and Jane, the Court exercises its discretion to accept jurisdiction over this dispute.

c. Facial Challenge[25]

Finally, Defendants argue Plaintiffs' facial challenges fail as a matter of law because the Act's provisions can be constitutionally applied. Facial challenges are "disfavored" because they: (1) "raise the risk of premature interpretation of statutes on factually barebone records;" (2) run contrary "to the fundamental principle of judicial restraint"; and (3) "threaten to short circuit the democratic process by preventing laws embodying the will of the people from being implemented in a manner consistent with the Constitution." *Washington State Grange v. Washington State Republican Party*, 552 U.S. 442, 451 (2008) (internal quotation marks and citations omitted). As such, the Supreme Court has held, a "facial challenge to a legislative Act is, of course, the most difficult challenge to mount successfully, since the challenger must establish that *no set of circumstances* exists under which the Act would be valid." *United States v. Salerno*, 481 U.S. 739, 745 (1987) (emphasis added). As previously discussed, the Ninth Circuit has held that an Arizona policy of excluding boys from playing on girls' sports teams was constitutionally permissible. *Clark*, 659 F.2d at 1131. Thus, Defendants argue the Act can clearly be constitutionally applied to cisgender boys, and Plaintiffs' facial challenges fail.

Plaintiffs counter that the *Salerno* language does not represent the Supreme Court's standard for adjudicating facial challenges. Dkt. 55, at 17 (citing *City of Chicago v. Morales*, 527 U.S. 41, 51-52, 55 n. 22 (1999) (plurality) (finding an ordinance was facially invalid even though it also had constitutional applications and observing that, "[t]o the extent we have consistently articulated a clear standard for facial challenges, it is not the *Salerno* formulation, which has never been the decisive factor in any decision of this Court, including *Salerno* itself."). As Plaintiffs point out, *Salerno's* "no set of circumstances" test was called into question by the Supreme Court in *Morales* and has been the subject of considerable debate. *Morales*, 527 U.S. at 55 n. 22; *see also Janklow v. Planned Parenthood, Sioux Falls Clinic*, 517 U.S. 1174, 1175 (1996) (stating that the "dicta in *Salerno* does not accurately characterize the standard for deciding facial challenges[.]"); *Washington State Grange*, 552 U.S. at 449 (noting that some Members of the Supreme Court have criticized the *Salerno* formulation); *Almerico v. Denney*, 378 F. Supp. 3d 920, 924-926 (D. Idaho 2019) (outlining debate regarding viability of *Salerno's* "no set of circumstances" test); *Does 1-134 v. Wasden*, 2018 WL 2275220, at *4 (D. Idaho May 17, 2018) (noting the ongoing debate regarding *Salerno* and "what types of constitutional claims would warrant a facial challenge, when a facial challenge becomes ripe, and the level of scrutiny that should be applied to the challenged statute").

Notwithstanding such controversy, the Ninth Circuit has consistently held that *Salerno* is the appropriate test for most facial challenges.[26] *S.D. Myers, Inc. v. City & Cty. of San Francisco*, 253 F.3d 461, 467 (9th Cir. 2001) (explaining that the Ninth Circuit will not reject *Salerno* in contexts other than the First Amendment or abortion "until the majority of the Supreme Court clearly directs us to do so."); *Almerico*, 378 F. Supp. 3d at 925 ("Time and again, plaintiffs have attempted to escape the effect of the *Salerno* standard, only to see their path foreclosed by the Ninth Circuit."). The Supreme Court also continues to apply *Salerno* to most facial challenges, albeit with some limited exceptions. *See, e.g., Washington State Grange*, 552 U.S. at 449 (holding a plaintiff can succeed on a facial challenge only by establishing that no set of circumstances exists under which the law could be valid).

However, Plaintiffs suggest an exception to the *Salerno* test, recently applied by the Supreme Court in *City of Los Angeles v. Patel*, 576 U.S. 409, 418 (2015), is applicable. In *Patel*, the Supreme Court cited *Salerno* with approval, but also explained that when assessing whether a statute meets the "no set of circumstances" standard, the Supreme Court "has considered only applications of the statute in which it actually authorizes or prohibits conduct." *Id*. In addressing a facial challenge to a statute authorizing warrantless searches, the *Patel* Court held the "proper focus of the constitutional inquiry is the group for whom the law is a restriction, not the group for whom the law is irrelevant." *Id*. (quoting *Casey*, 505 U.S. at 894). Plaintiffs argue a facial challenge is appropriate here because transgender and cisgender girls and women, are those for "whom the law is a restriction," while the Act is "irrelevant" to cisgender boys. Dkt. 55, at 18 (quoting *Patel*, 576 U.S. at 418).

While the Court recognizes *Patel* implied that the "method for defining the relevant population" test may apply to all facial challenges, *Patel* unfortunately did not explain when such test is applicable, whether it is appropriate in contexts other than abortion or the Fourth Amendment, or how to distinguish those cases where the test is appropriately used for facial adjudication from others where it is not. Nothing in the *Patel* opinion "even explains why *Casey's* method of defining the relevant population to which a statute applies should be transplanted to adjudicate Fourth Amendment unreasonableness claims, especially when *Casey* was confined to the abortion context before *Patel*." *Facial Versus As Applied Challenges*, 129 HARV. L. REV. at 250. Plaintiffs do not cite, and the Court has not located, any subsequent Ninth Circuit or Supreme Court case where *Patel*'s method for defining the relevant population has been used outside the abortion or Fourth Amendment context. Absent such guidance, the Court declines to extend *Patel* to create a new exception to *Salerno's* "no set of circumstances test" here.

Plaintiffs also suggest that a motion to dismiss is not the proper vehicle for Defendants' opposition to their facial challenge, as the distinction between facial and as-applied challenges "goes to the breadth of the remedy employed by the Court, not what must be pleaded in a complaint." *Citizens United v. Fed. Election Comm'n*, 558 U.S. 310, 331 (2010). However, *Citizens United* involved a facial challenge to a federal statute which purportedly violated plaintiffs' First Amendment rights. As noted *supra*, note 26, *Salerno* does not apply to facial challenges under the First Amendment. *Lawall*, 180 F.3d at 1026. As such, *Citizens United* appears inapplicable to cases where, as here, Plaintiffs facial challenges do not involve the First Amendment.

Further, the District of Idaho has frequently dismissed facial challenges at the Motion to Dismiss stage under *Salerno*, including facial challenges brought under the Fourteenth Amendment. *See, e.g., Almerico*, 378 F. Supp. 3d at 926 (dismissing facial due process and equal protection challenge to Idaho statute requiring any healthcare directive executed by women in Idaho to contain provision rendering directive without force during pregnancy); *Williams v. McKay*, 2020 WL 1105087, at *5 (D. Idaho March 6, 2020) (dismissing prisoner's facial First Amendment challenge to prison's grievance policy); *Wasden*, 2018 WL 2275220 at *18 (dismissing all facial constitutional challenges to Idaho's Sexual Offender Registration and Community Right-to-Know Act).

In sum, the Court is not convinced an exception to *Salerno* applies to Plaintiffs' facial Fourteenth Amendment challenges and will dismiss such claims. The Court will not dismiss Plaintiffs' as-applied Fourteenth Amendment challenges to the Act.[27]

C. Motion for Preliminary Injunction (Dkt. 22)

1. Legal Standard

Injunctive relief "is an extraordinary remedy that may only be awarded upon a clear showing that the plaintiff is entitled to such relief." *Winter v. Nat. Res. Def. Council, Inc.*, 555 U.S. 7, 22 (2008) (citing *Mazurack v. Armstrong*, 520 U.S. 968, 972 (1997)). A party seeking a preliminary injunction must establish: (1) a likelihood of success on the merits; (2) likely irreparable harm in the absence of a preliminary injunction; (3) that the balance of equities weighs in favor of an injunction; and (4) that an injunction is in the public interest. *Id.* at 20. Where, as here, "the government is a party, these last two factors merge." *Drakes Bay Oyster Co. v. Jewell*, 747 F.3d 1073, 1092 (9th Cir. 2014) (citing *Nkhen v. Holder*, 556 U.S. 418, 436 (2009)).

A preliminary injunction can take two forms. A prohibitory injunction prohibits a party from taking action and "preserve[s] the status quo pending a determination of the action on the merits." *Chalk v. U.S. Dist. Court*, 840 F.2d 701, 704 (9th Cir. 1988). A mandatory injunction "orders a responsible party to take action." *Meghrig v. KFC W., Inc.*, 516 U.S. 479, 484 (1996). A mandatory injunction "'goes well beyond simply maintaining the status quo,'" requires a heightened burden of proof, and is "'particularly disfavored.'" *Marlyn*

Nutraceuticals, Inc. v. MucosPharma GmbH & Co., 571 F.3d 873, 879 (9th Cir. 2009) (quoting *Anderson v. U.S.*, 612 F.2d 1112, 1114 (9th Cir. 1980)). In general, mandatory injunctions "'are not granted unless extreme or very serious damage will result and are not issued in doubtful cases or where the injury complained of is capable of compensation in damages.'" *Id.* (quoting *Anderson*, 612 F.2d at 111).

While the parties do not address the issue, the relevant "status quo" for purposes of an injunction "refers to the legally relevant relationship between the parties before the controversy arose." *Arizona Dream Act Coal. v. Brewer*, 757 F.3d 1053, 1061 (9th Cir. 2014) (emphasis in original); *see also Regents of Univ. of California v. Am. Broad. Companies, Inc.*, 747 F.2d 511, 514 (9th Cir. 1984) (for purposes of injunctive relief, the status quo means "the last uncontested status which preceded the pending controversy") (internal quotation marks and citation omitted). Here, Plaintiffs' motion for preliminary injunction was filed to contest the enforceability of H.B. 500—Idaho's new Act. The status quo, therefore, is the policy in Idaho prior to H.B.500's enactment. Injunctions that prohibit enforcement of a new law or policy are prohibitory, not mandatory. *Arizona Dream Act*, 757 F.3d at 1061; *Bay Area Addiction Research & Treatment, Inc. v. City of Antioch*, 179 F.3d 725, 732 n. 13 (9th Cir. 1999) (requested preliminary injunction against enforcement of new zoning ordinance was not subject to heightened burden of proof since relief sought was prohibitory injunction that preserved the status quo pending a decision on the merits). Thus, if the Court grants Plaintiffs' preliminary injunction, it will be issuing a prohibitory injunction to preserve the status quo pending trial on the merits, rather than forcing Defendants to take action.

2. Analysis

a. Equal Protection Clause

The Equal Protection Clause of the Fourteenth Amendment requires that all similarly situated people be treated alike. *City of Cleburne Living Ctr., Inc.*, 473 U.S. 432, 439 (1985). Equal protection requirements restrict state legislative action that is inconsistent with core constitutional guarantees, such as equality in treatment. *Obergefell v. Hodges*, 135 S. Ct. 2584, 2603 (2015). However, the Fourteenth Amendment's "promise that no person shall be denied the equal protection of the laws must coexist with the practical necessity that most legislation classifies for one purpose or another, with resulting disadvantage to various groups or persons." *Romer v. Evans*, 517 U.S. 620, 631 (1996). The Supreme Court has attempted to reconcile this reality with the equal protection principle by developing tiers of judicial scrutiny. *Latta v. Otter*, 19 F. Supp. 3d 1054, 1073 (D. Idaho) ("*Latta I*"), aff'd, *Latta v. Otter*, 771 F.3d 456 (9th Cir. 2014) ("*Latta II*"). "The level of scrutiny depends on the characteristics of the disadvantaged group or the rights implicated by the classification." *Latta I*, 19 F. Supp. 3d at 1073.

When a state restricts an individual's access to a fundamental right, the policy must withstand strict scrutiny, which requires that the government action serves a compelling purpose and that it is the least restrictive means of doing so. *San Antonio Indep. Sch. Dist. v. Rodriguez*, 411 U.S. 1, 16-17 (1973). The Supreme Court has recognized that the Constitution protects a number of fundamental rights, including the right to privacy concerning consensual sexual activity, *Lawrence v. Texas*, 539 U.S. 558, 578 (2003), the right to marriage, *Obergefell*, 135 S. Ct. at 2599, and the right to reproductive autonomy, *Eisenstadt v. Baird*, 405 U.S.

438, 455 (1972). Access to interscholastic sports is not, however, a constitutionally recognized fundamental right. *See, e.g, Walsh v. La. High Sch. Athletic Ass'n*, 616 F.2d 152, 159-60 (5th Cir. 1980) (explaining that a student's interest in playing sports "amounts to a mere expectation rather than a constitutionally protected claim of entitlement[.]").

When a fundamental right is not at stake, a court must analyze whether the government policy discriminates against a suspect class. *Cleburne*, 473 U.S. at 440 (identifying race, alienage, and national origin as suspect classifications vulnerable to pernicious discrimination). Because government policies that discriminate on the basis of race or national origin typically reflect prejudice, such policies will survive only if the law survives strict scrutiny. *Id.* Strict scrutiny review is so exacting that most laws subjected to this standard fail, leading one former Supreme Court Justice to quip that strict scrutiny review is "strict in theory, but fatal in fact." *Fullilove v. Klutznick*, 448 U.S. 448, 519 (1980).

Statutes that discriminate on the basis of sex, a "quasi-suspect" classification, need to withstand the slightly less stringent standard of "heightened" scrutiny.[28] *Craig v. Boren*, 429 U.S. 190, 197 (1976); *United States v. Virginia*, 518 U.S. 515, 533 (1996) ("*VMI*"). To withstand heightened scrutiny, classification by sex "must serve important governmental objectives and must be substantially related to achievement of those objectives." *Craig*, 429 U.S. at 197. "The purpose of this heightened level of scrutiny is to ensure quasi-suspect classifications do not perpetuate unfounded stereotypes or second-class treatment." *Latta I*, 19 F. Supp. 3d at 1073 (citing *VMI*, 518 U.S. at 533).

The District of Idaho determined transgender individuals qualify as a quasi-suspect class in *F.V. v. Barron*, 286 F. Supp. 3d 1131, 1143-1145 (2018) ("*Barron*").[29] While not specifically stating that transgender individuals constitute a quasi-suspect class, the Ninth Circuit has also held that heightened scrutiny applies if a law or policy treats transgender persons in a less favorable way than all others. *Karnoski v. Trump*, 926 F.3d 1180, 1201 (2019). Further, although in the context of Title VII, the Supreme Court has, as mentioned, recently stated, "it is impossible to discriminate against a person for being . . . transgender without discriminating against that individual based on sex." *Bostock v. Clayton Cty., Ga.*, 140 S. Ct. 1731, 1741 (2020).

Finally, the least stringent level of scrutiny is rational basis review. Rational basis review is applied to laws that impose a difference in treatment between groups but do not infringe upon a fundamental right or target a suspect or quasi-suspect class. *Heller v. Doe*, 509 U.S. 312, 319-321 (1993). "[A] classification neither involving fundamental rights nor proceeding along suspect lines is accorded a strong presumption of validity." *Id.* at 319 (citations omitted). Rational-basis review in equal protection analysis "is not a license for courts to judge the wisdom, fairness, or logic of legislative choices." *Id.* (quoting *FCC v. Beach Communications, Inc.*, 508 U.S. 307, 313 (1993)). Under rationale basis review, a classification "must be upheld against equal protection challenge if there is any reasonably conceivable state of facts that could provide a rational basis for the classification." *Id.* at 320 (quoting *Beach*, 508 U.S. at 313).[30]

b. <u>Appropriate level of scrutiny</u>

Plaintiffs argue heightened scrutiny is appropriate in this case because the Act discriminates on the basis of both transgender status and sex. Dkt. 22-1, at 12 (citing *VMI*, 518 U.S. at 55). Defendants acknowledge that the Act may be subject to heightened scrutiny but suggest the Act does not discriminate on the basis of transgender status or sex because it simply "treats all biological males the same and prohibits them from participating in female sports to protect athletic opportunities for biological females." Dkt. 41, at 13 n. 8. While contending, "[n]either the Supreme Court nor the Ninth Circuit has recognized 'gender identity' as a suspect class,"[31] the Intervenors argue the Act nonetheless passes heightened scrutiny. Dkt. 46, at 13-18. Finally, the United States contends that even assuming, *arguendo*, that the Act triggers heightened scrutiny, it "readily withstand[s] this form of review." Dkt. 53, at 5.

Because all parties focus their arguments on the Act's ability to withstand heightened scrutiny, and because the Court finds heightened scrutiny is appropriate pursuant to *Craig*, 429 U.S. at 197, *VMI*, 518 U.S. at 533, *Barron*, 286 F. Supp. 3d at 1144, and *Karnoski*, 926 F.3d at 1201, the Court applies this level of review.[32]

c. Likelihood of Success on the Merits-Lindsay

i. Discrimination based on transgender status

Defendants and the United States suggest the Act does not discriminate against transgender individuals because it does not expressly use the term "transgender" and because the Act does not ban athletes on the basis of transgender status, but rather on the basis of the innate physiological advantages males generally have over females. Dkt. 41, at 13 n. 8; Dkt. 53, at 13. The Ninth Circuit rejected a similar argument in *Latta II*, 771 F.3d at 468. In *Latta II*, the Ninth Circuit considered defendants' claim that Idaho and Nevada's same-sex marriage bans did not discriminate on the basis of sexual orientation, but rather on the basis of procreative capacity. The Ninth Circuit rebuffed this contention, explaining:

> Effectively if not explicitly, [defendants] assert that while these laws may disadvantage some same-sex couples and their children, heightened scrutiny is not appropriate because differential treatment by sexual orientation is an incidental effect of, but not the reason for, those laws. However, the laws at issue distinguish on their face between opposite-sex couples, who are permitted to marry and whose out-of-state marriages are recognized, and same-sex couples, who are not permitted to marry and whose marriages are not recognized. Whether facial discrimination exists 'does not depend on why' a policy discriminates, 'but rather on the explicit terms of the discrimination.' Hence, while the procreative capacity distinction that defendants seek to draw could represent a *justification* for the discrimination worked by the laws, it cannot overcome the inescapable conclusion that Idaho and Nevada do discriminate on the basis of sexual orientation.

Id. at 467-68 (emphasis in original) (quoting *Int'l Union, United Auto., Aerospace & Agr. Implement Workers of Am., UAW v. Johnson Controls, Inc.*, 499 U.S. 187, 199 (1991)).

Similarly, the Act on its face discriminates between cisgender athletes, who may compete on athletic teams consistent with their gender identity, and transgender women athletes, who may not compete on athletic teams consistent with their gender identity. Hence, while the physiological differences the Defendants suggest support the categorical bar on transgender women's participation in women's sports may justify the Act, they do not overcome the inescapable conclusion that the Act discriminates on the basis of transgender status. *Id.* at 468.

As mentioned, the Ninth Circuit has held that classifications based on transgender status are subject to heightened scrutiny. *Karnoski*, 926 F.3d at 1201. The Court accordingly applies heightened scrutiny to the Act. Under this level of scrutiny, four principles guide the Court's equal protection analysis. The Court: (1) looks to the Defendants to justify the Act; (2) must consider the Act's actual purposes; (3) need not accept hypothetical, *post hoc* justifications for the Act; and (4) must decide whether Defendants' proffered justifications overcome the injury and indignity inflicted on Plaintiffs and others like them. *Latta I*, 19 F. Supp. 3d at 1077. When applying heightened scrutiny, the Court does not adopt the strong presumption in favor of constitutionality or heavy deference to legislative judgments characteristic of rational basis review. *SmithKline Beecham Corp. v. Abbott Laboratories*, 740 F.3d 471, 483 (9th Cir. 2014). Further, under heightened scrutiny review, the Court must examine the Act's "actual purposes and carefully consider the resulting inequality to ensure that our most fundamental institutions neither send nor reinforce messages of stigma or second-class status." *Latta II*, 771 F.3d at 468 (quoting *SmithKline*, 740 F.3d at 483).

ii. The Ninth Circuit's holding in *Clark*

At the outset, the Court recognizes that sex-discriminatory policies withstand heightened scrutiny when sex classification is "not invidious, but rather realistically reflects the fact that the sexes are not similarly situated in certain circumstances." *Michael M. v. Superior Ct. of Sonoma Cty.*, 450 U.S. 462, 469 (1981) (upholding law that held only males criminally liable for statutory rape because the consequences of teenage pregnancy essentially fall only on girls, so applying statutory rape law solely to men was justified since men suffer fewer consequences of their conduct). The Equal Protection Clause does not require courts to disregard the physiological differences between men and women. *Michael M.*, 450 U.S. at 481; *Clark*, 695 F.2d at 1131.

As repeatedly highlighted by Defendants, the Intervenors, and the United States (collectively hereinafter the Act's "Proponents"), the Ninth Circuit in *Clark* held that there "is no question" that "redressing past discrimination against women in athletics and promoting equality of athletic opportunity between the sexes" is "a legitimate and important governmental interest" justifying rules excluding males from participating on female teams. *Clark*, 695 F.2d at 1131. In *Clark*, the Ninth Circuit determined a policy in Arizona of excluding boys from girls' teams simply recognized "the physiological fact that males would have an undue advantage competing against women," and would diminish opportunity for females. *Id.* at 1131. The *Clark* Court also explained that "even wiser alternatives to the one chosen" did not invalidate Arizona's policy since it was "substantially related to the goal" of providing fair and equal opportunities for females to participate in athletics. *Id.* at 1132.

While the Court recognizes and accepts the principals outlined in *Clark*, *Clark*'s holding regarding general sex separation in sport, as well as the justifications for such separation, do not appear to be implicated by allowing transgender women to participate on women's teams. In *Clark*, the Ninth Circuit held that it was lawful to exclude cisgender boys from playing on a girls' volleyball team because: (1) women had historically been deprived of athletic opportunities in favor of men; (2) as a general matter, men had equal athletic opportunities to women; and (3) according to stipulated facts, average physiological differences meant that "males would displace females to a substantial extent" if permitted to play on women's volleyball teams. *Clark*, 695 F.2d at 1131. These principals do not appear to hold true for women and girls who are transgender.

First, like women generally, women who are transgender have historically been discriminated against, not favored. *See, e.g., Barron*, 286 F. Supp. 3d at 1143-1145. In a large national study, 86% of those perceived as transgender in a K-12 school experienced some form of harassment, and for 12%, the harassment was severe enough for them to leave school. National Center for Transgender Equality, 2015 U.S. Transgender Survey: Idaho State Report 1-2, https://www.transequality.org/sites/default/files/docs/usts/USTSIDStateReport%281017%29.pdf (October 2017). According to the same study, 48% of transgender people in Idaho have experienced homelessness in their lifetime, and 25% were living in poverty. *Id.* Rather than a general separation between a historically advantaged group (cisgender males) and a historically disadvantaged group (cisgender women), the Act excludes a historically disadvantaged group (transgender women) from participation in sports, and further discriminates against a historically disadvantaged group (cisgender women) by subjecting them to the sex dispute process. The first justification for the Arizona policy at issue in *Clark* is not present here.

Second, under the Act, women and girls who are transgender will not be able to participate in any school sports, unlike the boys in *Clark*, who generally had equal athletic opportunities. *Clark*, 695 F.2d at 1131; Dkt. 58-3, at ¶¶ 24-28 (explaining that forcing a transgender woman to participate on a men's team would be forcing her to be cisgender, which is "associated with adverse mental health outcomes."); *see also* Dkt. 22-6, ¶¶ 35-37. Participating in sports on teams that contradict one's gender identity "is equivalent to gender identity conversion efforts, which every major medical association has found to be dangerous and unethical." Dkt. 58, at 11 (citing Dkt. 58-3, ¶¶ 24-28).[33] As such, the Act's categorical exclusion of transgender women and girls entirely eliminates their opportunity to participate in school sports—and also subjects all cisgender women to unequal treatment simply to play sports—while the men in *Clark* had generally equal athletic opportunities.

Third, it appears transgender women have not and could not "displace" cisgender women in athletics "to a substantial extent." *Clark*, 695 F.2d at 1131. Although the ratio of males to females is roughly one to one, less than one percent of the population is transgender. Dkt. 22-1, at 22. Presumably, this means approximately one half of one percent of the population is made up of transgender females. It is inapposite to compare the potential displacement allowing approximately half of the population (cisgender men) to compete with cisgender women, with any potential displacement one half of one percent of the population (transgender women) could cause cisgender women. It appears untenable that allowing transgender women to compete on women's teams would substantially displace female athletes.[34]

And fourth, it is not clear that transgender women who suppress their testosterone have significant physiological advantages over cisgender women. The

Court discusses the distinction between physical differences between men and women in general, and physical differences between transgender women who have suppressed their testosterone for one year and women below. However, the interests at issue in *Clark*—Defendants' central authority—pertained to sex separation in sport generally and are not necessarily determinative here.[35]

iii. The Act's justifications

The legislative findings and purpose portion of the Act suggests it fulfills the interests of promoting sex equality, providing opportunities for female athletes to demonstrate their skill, strength, and athletic abilities, and by providing female athletes with opportunities to obtain college scholarship and other accolades. Idaho Code § 33-6202(12). Plaintiffs do not dispute that these are important governmental objectives. They instead argue that the Act is not substantially related to such important governmental interests. At this stage of the litigation, and without further development of the record, the Court is inclined to agree.

(1) Promoting Sex Equality and Providing Opportunities for Female Athletes

As discussed, *supra*, section II.C, the legislative record reveals no history of transgender athletes ever competing in sports in Idaho, no evidence that Idaho female athletes have been displaced by Idaho transgender female athletes, and no evidence to suggest a categorical bar against transgender female athlete's participation in sports is required in order to promote "sex equality" or to "protect athletic opportunities for females" in Idaho. Idaho Code § 33-6202(12); *see* Dkt. 1, at ¶¶ 80-83. Rather than presenting empirical evidence that transgender inclusion will hinder sex equality in sports or athletic opportunities for women, both the Act itself and

Proponents' rely exclusively on three transgender athletes who have competed successfully in women's sports.

Specifically, during the entire legislative debate over the Act, the only transgender women athletes referenced were two high school runners who compete in Connecticut, and who were, notably, also defeated by cisgender girls in recent races.[36] Dkt. 22-3, Ex. B, at 8; *see also* Associated Press, *Cisgender female who sued beats transgender athlete in high school race*, https://www.fox61.com/article/news/local/transgender-athlete-loses-track-race-lawsuit-ciac-high-school-sports/520-df66c6f5-5ca9-496b-a6ba-61c828655bc6 (Feb. 15, 2020). Notably, unlike the IHSAA and NCAA rules in place in Idaho before the Act, Connecticut does not require a transgender woman athlete to suppress her testosterone for any time prior to competing on women's teams. Dkt. 41, at 33; Dkt. 45, at 7.

The Intervenors identify a third transgender athlete, June Eastwood, and argue that their athletic opportunities were limited by Eastwood's participation in women's sports. Dkt. 46, at 8. The State also highlights this example. Dkt. 41, at 18. However, Eastwood was not an Idaho athlete and the competition at issue took place at the University of Montana. Dkt. 45, at 10 n. 7. So, the Idaho statute would have no impact on Eastwood. More importantly, although the Intervenors lost to Eastwood, Eastwood was also ultimately defeated by her cisgender teammate. *Id*. And, losing to Eastwood at one race did not deprive the Intervenors from the opportunity to compete in Division I sports, as both continue to compete on the women's cross-country and track teams with ISU. Dkt. 30-1, at 2.

The evidence cited during the House Debate on H.B. 500 and in the briefing by the Proponents regarding three transgender women athletes who have each lost to cisgender women athletes does not provide an "exceedingly persuasive" justification for the Act. *VMI*, 518 U.S. at 533 ("To summarize the Court's current directions for cases of official classification based on gender: Focusing on the differential treatment for denial of opportunity for which relief is sought, the reviewing court must determine whether the proffered justification is 'exceedingly persuasive.'"). Heightened scrutiny requires that a law solves an actual problem and that the "justification must be genuine, not hypothesized." *VMI*, 518 U.S. at 533. In the absence of any empirical evidence that sex inequality or access to athletic opportunities are threatened by transgender women athletes in Idaho, the Act's categorical bar against transgender women athletes' participation appears unrelated to the interests the Act purportedly advances.

Plaintiffs have also presented compelling evidence that equality in sports is *not* jeopardized by allowing transgender women who have suppressed their testosterone for one year to compete on women's teams. Plaintiffs' medical expert, Dr. Joshua Safer, suggests that physiological advantages are not present when a transgender woman undergoes hormone therapy and testosterone suppression. Before puberty, boys and girls have the same levels of circulating testosterone. Dkt. 22-9, at ¶ 23. After puberty, the typical range of circulating testosterone for cisgender women is similar to before puberty, and the circulating testosterone for cisgender men is substantially higher. *Id*.

Dr. Safer contends there "is a medical consensus that the difference in testosterone is generally the primary known driver of differences in athletic performance between elite male athletes and elite female athletes." Dkt. 22-9, at ¶ 25. Dr. Safer highlights the only study examining the effects of gender-affirming hormone therapy on the athletic performance of transgender athletes. *Id.* at ¶ 51. The small study showed that after undergoing gender affirming intervention, which included lowering their testosterone levels, the athletes' performance was reduced so that relative to cisgender women, their performance was proportionally the same as it had been relative to cisgender men prior to any medical treatment. *Id.* In other words, a transgender woman who performed 80% as well as the best performer among men of that age before transition would also perform at about 80% as well as the best performer among women of that age after transition. *Id.*

Defendants' medical expert, Dr. Gregory Brown, also confirms that male's performance advantages "result, in large part (but not exclusively), from higher testosterone concentrations in men, and adolescent boys, after the onset of male puberty." Dkt. 41-1, at ¶ 17. While Dr. Brown maintains that hormone and testosterone suppression cannot fully eliminate physiological advantages once an individual has passed through male puberty, the Court notes some of the studies Dr. Brown relies upon actually held the opposite. *Compare* Dkt. 41-1, at ¶ 81 *with* Dkt. 58-2, at ¶ 7 (highlighting that the Handelsman study upon which Dr. Brown relies states that "evidence makes it highly likely that the sex difference in circulating testosterone of adults explains most, if not all, of the sex differences in sporting performance."). Further, the majority of the evidence Dr. Brown cites, and most of his declaration, involve the differences between male and female athletes in general, and contain no reference to, or information about, the difference between cisgender women athletes and transgender women athletes who have suppressed their testosterone. Dkt. 41-1, at ¶¶ 12-112, 114-125.

Yet, the legislative findings for the Act contend that even after receiving hormone and testosterone suppression therapy, transgender women and girls have "an absolute advantage" over non-transgender girls. Idaho Code § 33-6202(11). In addition to the evidence cited above, several factors undermine this conclusion. For instance, there is a population of transgender girls who, as a result of puberty blockers at the start of puberty and gender affirming hormone therapy afterward, never go through a typical male puberty at all. Dkt. 22-9, ¶ 47. These transgender girls never experience the high levels of testosterone and accompanying physical changes associated with male puberty, and instead go through puberty with the same levels of hormones as other girls. *Id.* As such, they develop typically female physiological characteristics, including muscle and bone structure, and do not have an ascertainable advantage over cisgender female athletes. *Id.* Defendants do not address how transgender girls who never undergo male puberty can have "an absolute advantage" over cisgender girls. Nor do Defendants address why transgender athletes who have never undergone puberty should be categorically excluded from playing women's sports in order to protect sexual equality and access to opportunities in women's sports.

The Act's legislative findings do claim the "benefits that natural testosterone provides to male athletes is not diminished through the use of puberty blockers and cross-sex hormones." Idaho Code § 33-6202(11). However, the study cited in support of this proposition was later altered after peer review, and the conclusions the legislature relied upon were removed. Dkt. 58, at 17; Dkt. 58-2, at ¶ 19; Dkt. 62 at 80:10-25; 81:1-10; 95:24-25, 96. Defendants provide no explanation as to why the Legislators relied on the pre-peer review version of the article or why Defendants did not correct this fact in their briefing after the peer reviewed version was published. In fact, the study did not involve transgender athletes at all, but instead considered the differences between transgender men who increased strength and muscle mass with testosterone treatment, and transgender women who lost some strength and muscle mass with testosterone suppression. Dkt. 58, at 17. The study also explicitly stated it "is important to recognize that we only assessed proxies for athletic performance . . . it is still uncertain how the findings would translate to transgender athletes." Anna Wiik et. al, *Muscle Strength, Size, and Composition Following 12 months of Gender-affirming Treatment in Transgender Individual*, J. CLIN. METAB., 105(3):e805-e813 (2020).[37]

In addition, several of the Act's legislative findings which purportedly demonstrate the "absolute advantage" of transgender women are based on a study by Doriane Lambelet Coleman. Idaho Code § 33-6202(5), (10). Professor Coleman herself urged Governor Little to veto H.B. 500 because her work was misused, and she also endorsed the NCAA's rule of allowing transgender women to participate after one year of hormone and testosterone suppression. Betsy Russell, *Professor whose work is cited in HB500a, the transgender athletes bill, says bill misuses her research and urges veto*, IDAHO PRESS https://www.idahopress.com/eyeonboise/professor-whose-work-is-cited-in-hb-a-the-transgenderarticle_0e800202-cacl-5721-a7690328665316a8.html (Mar. 19, 2020).

The policies of elite athletic regulatory bodies across the world, and athletic policies of most every other state in the country, also undermine Defendants' claim that transgender women have an "absolute advantage" over other female athletes. Specifically, the International Olympic Committee and the NCAA require transgender women to suppress their testosterone levels in order to compete in women's athletics. *Id.* at ¶ 45. The NCAA policy was implemented in 2011 after consultation with medical, legal, and sports experts, and has been in effect since that time. Dkt. 1, ¶ 76. Millions of student-athletes have competed in the NCAA since 2011, with no reported examples of any disturbance to women's sports as a result of transgender inclusion.[38] *Id.* Similarly, every other state in the nation permits women and girls who are transgender to participate under varying rules, including some which require hormone suppression prior to participation. The Proponents' failure to identify any evidence of transgender women causing purported sexual inequality other than four athletes (at least three of whom who have notably lost to cisgender women) is striking in light of the international and national policy of transgender inclusion.

Finally, while general sex separation on athletic teams for men and women may promote sex equality and provide athletic opportunities for females, that separation preexisted the Act and has long been the status quo in Idaho. Existing rules already prevented boys from playing on girls' teams before the Act. IHSAA Non-Discrimination Policy, http://idhsaa.org/asset/RULE%2011.pdf ("If a sport is offered for both boys and girls, girls must play on the girls team and boys must play on the boys team. . . If a school sponsors only a single team in a sport. . . Girls are eligible to participate on boys' teams. . . . Boys are not eligible to participate on girls' teams."). However, the IHSAA policy also allows transgender girls to participate on girls' teams after one year of hormone suppression. Similarly, the existing NCAA rules also preclude men from playing on women's teams but allow transgender women to compete after one year of testosterone suppression. Because Proponents fail to show that participation by transgender women athletes threatened sexual equality in sports or opportunities for women under these preexisting policies, the Act's proffered justifications do not appear to overcome the inequality it inflicts on transgender women athletes.

The Ninth Circuit in *Clark* ruled that sex classification can be upheld only if sex represents "a legitimate accurate proxy." *Clark*, 695 F.2d at 1129. The *Clark* Court further explained the Supreme Court has soundly disapproved of classifications that reflect "archaic and overbroad generalizations," and has struck down gender-based policies when the policy's proposed compensatory objective was without factual justification. *Id.* Given the evidence highlighted above, it appears the "absolute advantage" between transgender and cisgender women athletes is based on overbroad generalizations without factual justification.

Ultimately, the Court must hear testimony from the experts at trial and weigh both their credibility and the extent of the scientific evidence. However, the incredibly small percentage of transgender women athletes in general, coupled with the significant dispute regarding whether such athletes actually have physiological advantages over cisgender women when they have undergone hormone suppression in particular, suggest the Act's categorical exclusion of transgender women athletes has no relationship to ensuring equality and opportunities for female athletes in Idaho.

(2) Ensuring Access to Athletic Scholarships

The Act also identifies an interest in advancing access to athletic scholarships for women. Idaho Code § 33-6202(12). Yet, there is no evidence in the record to suggest that the Act will increase scholarship opportunities for girls. Just as the head of the IHSAA testified during the legislative debate on H.B. 500 that he was not aware of any transgender girl ever playing high school girls' sports in Idaho, there is also no evidence of a transgender person ever receiving any athletic scholarship in Idaho. Idaho Education News, *Lawmakers hear emotional testimony but take no action on transgender bill*, Idaho News 6, https://www.kivitv.com/news/education/making-the-grade/lawmakers-hear-emotional-testimony-but-take-no-action-on-transgender (Feb. 20, 2020). Nor have the scholarships of the Intervenors—the only identified Idaho athletes who have purportedly been harmed by competing against a transgender woman athlete—been jeopardized. Both Intervenors continue to run track and cross-country on scholarship with ISU, despite their loss to a transgender woman athlete at the University of Montana. Dkt. 30-1, at 2.

The Act's incredibly broad sweep also belies any genuine concern with an impact on athletic scholarships. The Act broadly applies to interscholastic, intercollegiate, intramural, or club athletic teams or sports that are sponsored by a public primary or secondary school, or a public institution of higher education, or any school or institution whose students or teams compete against a public school or institution of higher education. Idaho Code § 33-6203(1). Thus, any female athlete, from kindergarten through college, is generally subject to the Act's provisions. Clearly, the need for athletic scholarships is not implicated in primary school and intramural sports in the same way that it may be for high school and college athletes. As such, "the breadth of the [law] is so far removed from [the] particular justifications" put forth in support of it, that it is "impossible to credit them." *Romer*, 517 U.S. at 635.

Based on the dearth of evidence in the record to show excluding transgender women from women's sports supports sex equality, provides opportunities for women, or increases access to college scholarships, Lindsay is likely to succeed in establishing the Act violates her right to equal protection. This likelihood is further enhanced by Defendants' implausible argument that the Act does not actually ban transgender women, but instead only requires a health care provider's verification stating that a transgender woman athlete is female. *See, e.g*, Dkt. 40-1, at 3; Dkt. 41, at 4; Dkt. 62, at 66:21-25; 67:1-25; 68:1-17.

Defense counsel confirmed during oral argument that if Lindsay's health care provider signs a health form stating that she is female, Lindsay can play women's sports. Dkt. 62, at 66:21-25. In turn, Plaintiffs' counsel affirmed that Lindsay's health care provider will sign a form verifying Lindsay is female. *Id*. at 70:5-21. If this is indeed the case, then each of the Proponents' arguments claiming that the Act ensures equality for female athletes by disallowing males on female teams falls away. Under this interpretation, the Act does not ensure sex-specific teams at all and is instead simply a means for the Idaho legislature to express its disapproval of transgender individuals. If "equal protection of the laws means anything, it must at the very least mean that a bare congressional desire to harm a politically unpopular group cannot constitute a legitimate governmental interest." *Moreno*, 413 U.S. at 534.

(3) The Act's Actual Purpose

The Act's legislative findings reinforce the idea that the law is directed at excluding women and girls who are transgender, rather than on promoting sex equality and opportunities for women. For instance, the Act's criteria for determining "biological sex" appear designed to exclude transgender women and girls and to reverse the prior IHSAA and NCAA rules that implemented sex-separation in sports while permitting transgender women to compete. Idaho Code § 33-6203(3).

Specifically, an athlete subject to the Act's dispute process may "verify" their sex using three criteria: (1) reproductive anatomy, (2) genetic makeup, or (3) endogenous testosterone, i.e., the level of testosterone the body produces without medical intervention. *Id.* This excludes some girls with intersex traits because they cannot establish a "biological sex" of female based on these verification metrics. Dkt. 22-9, ¶ 41. It also completely excludes transgender girls.

Girls under eighteen generally cannot obtain gender-affirming genital surgery to treat gender dysphoria, and therefore will not have female reproductive anatomy. Dkt. 22-2, ¶ 13. Many transgender women over the age of eighteen also have not had genital surgery, either because it is not consistent with their individualized treatment plan for gender dysphoria or because they cannot afford it. *Id.* With respect to genetic makeup, the overwhelming majority of women who are transgender have XY chromosomes, so they cannot meet the second criteria. And, by focusing on "endogenous" testosterone levels, rather than actual testosterone levels after hormone suppression, the Act excludes transgender women whose circulating testosterone levels are within the range typical for cisgender women.

Thus, the Act's definition of "biological sex" intentionally excludes the one factor that a consensus of the medical community appears to agree drives the physiological differences between male and female athletic performance. Dkt. 22-9, at ¶ 25. Significantly, the preexisting Idaho and current NCAA rules instead focus on that factor. That the Act essentially bars consideration of circulating testosterone illustrates the Legislature appeared less concerned with ensuring equality in athletics than it was with ensuring exclusion of transgender women athletes.

In addition, it is difficult to ignore the circumstances under which the Act was passed. As COVID-19 was declared a pandemic and many states adjourned state legislative session indefinitely, the Idaho Legislature stayed in session to pass H.B. 500 and become the first and only state to bar all women and girls who are transgender from participating in school sports. *Id.* at ¶ 89. At the same time, the Legislature also passed another bill, H.B. 509, which essentially bans transgender individuals from changing their gender marker on their birth certificates to match their gender identity. Governor Little signed H.B. 500 and H.B. 509 into law on the same day. That the Idaho government stayed in session amidst an unprecedented national shut down to pass two laws which dramatically limit the rights of transgender individuals suggests the Act was motivated by a desire for transgender exclusion, rather than equality for women athletes, particularly when the national shutdown preempted school athletic events, making the rush to the pass the law unnecessary.

Finally, the Proponents turn the Act on its head by arguing that transgender people seek "special" treatment by challenging the Act. Dkt. 53, at 9-10; Dkt. 62, at 92:16-22. This argument ignores that the Act excludes *only* transgender women and girls from participating in sports, and that Lindsay simply seeks the status quo prior to the Act's passage, rather than special treatment. Further, the Proponents' argument that Lindsay and other transgender women are not excluded from school sports because they can simply play on the men's team is analogous to claiming homosexual individuals are not prevented from marrying under statutes preventing same-sex marriage because lesbians and gays could marry someone of a different sex. The Ninth Circuit rejected such arguments in *Latta*, 771 F.3d at 467, as did the Supreme Court in *Bostock*, 140 S. Ct. at 1741-42.

In short, the State has not identified a legitimate interest served by the Act that the preexisting rules in Idaho did not already address, other than an invalid interest of excluding transgender women and girls from women's sports entirely, regardless of their physiological characteristics. As such, Lindsay is likely to succeed on the merits of her equal protection claim. Again, at this stage, the Court only discusses the "likelihood" of success based on the information currently in the record. Actual success—or failure—on the merits will be determined at a later stage.

d. Likelihood of Success-Jane

The Act additionally triggers heightened scrutiny by singling out members of girls' and women's teams for sex verification. *VMI*, 518 U.S. at 555 (["A]ll gender-based classifications today warrant heightened scrutiny") (internal quotation marks and citation omitted). Defendants argue that the Act does not treat females differently because "it requires any athlete subject to dispute, whether male or female, to verify his or her sex." Dkt. 41, at 13 n. 8. Defendants suggest males are equally subject to the sex verification process because they may try to participate on a woman's team. *Id*. This claim ignores that all cisgender women are subject to the verification process in order to play on the team matching their gender identity, while only a limited few (if any) cisgender men will be subject to the verification process if they try to play on a team contrary to their gender identity.

Defendants' argument also contradicts the express language of the Act, which mandates, "[a]thletic teams or sports designated for females, women, or girls *shall* not be open to students of the male sex." *Id.* at § 33-6203(2) (emphasis added). Males are not subject to the dispute process because female teams are not open to them under the Act.[39] By arguing that people of any sex who seek to play women's sports would be subject to sex verification, Defendants ignore that the Act creates a different, more onerous set of rules for women's sports when compared to men's sports. Where spaces and activities for women are "different in kind . . . and unequal in tangible and intangible ways from those for men, they are tested under heightened scrutiny." *VMI*, 518 U.S. at 540.

It is also clear that a sex verification examination is unequal to the physical sports exam a male must have in order to play sports. Being subject to a sex dispute is itself humiliating. The Act's dispute process also creates a means that could be used to bully girls perceived as less feminine or unpopular and prevent them from participating in sports. And if, as the Act states, sex must be verified through a physical examination relying "only on one (1) or more of the following: the student's reproductive anatomy, genetic makeup, or normal endogenously produced testosterone levels," girls like Jane may also have to endure invasive medical tests that could constitute an invasion of privacy in order to "verify" their sex. Idaho Code § 33-6302(3).

As Plaintiffs' expert, Dr. Sara Swoboda, a pediatrician in Boise with approximately 1,500 patients across Idaho, explains, none of the aforementioned physiological characteristics are tested for in any routine sports' physical examination. Dkt. 22-10, ¶ 21. If a health care provider was to verify a patient's sex related to their reproductive anatomy, genes or hormones, none of that testing is straightforward or ethical without medical indication. *Id.* at ¶ 22. Nor would it actually "verify biological sex," "either alone or in any combination," as this "would not be consistent with medical science." *Id.* at ¶ 21.

For example, "'reproductive anatomy' is not a medical term. That could include internal reproductive organs, external genitalia, or other body systems." *Id.* at ¶ 28. Further, "medically unnecessary pelvic examination would be incredibly intrusive and traumatic for a patient" and would not be conducted. *Id.* at ¶ 29. Pelvic examinations in "pediatric patients are limited to patients with specific concerns such as acute trauma or infection," and are not conducted as a general practice. *Id.* at ¶ 27. "In young patients, such an exam would often be done with sedation and appropriate comfort measures to limit psychological trauma." *Id.* "Pediatric consensus recognizes that genitalia exams are always invasive and carry the risk of traumatizing patients if not done with careful consideration of medical utility, discussion about the purpose and subsequent findings of any exam with the patient and their family, and explicit consent of the patient." *Id.* In addition, determining whether an individual has ovaries or a uterus may also require more intrusive testing including "transvaginal ultrasounds and may require referral to pediatric gynecologists, endocrinologists, and geneticists. None of this testing would be a necessary part of a sports physical or any standard medical examination absent medical concerns and indications of underlying health conditions necessitating treatment." *Id.* at ¶ 30.

Similarly, determining a patient's "genetic makeup" would require genetic testing. Such testing is complicated and personal and reveals a significant amount of information. *Id.* at ¶ 23. It is done by a specialist and would require a pediatric endocrinologist if performed on a minor like Jane. *Id.* at ¶ 24. Where a patient presents with a constellation of medical concerns that indicate a need for genetic testing, they are referred to a pediatric endocrinologist for a chromosomal microarray:

> This type of testing reveals a significant amount of very sensitive and private medical information. A chromosomal microarray looks at all 23 pairs of chromosomes that an individual has and would reveal things beyond just whether a person has 46-XX, 46-XY, or some combination of sex chromosomes. In ordering genetic testing of this kind, a range of genetic conditions could be revealed to a patient and a patient's family. [Dr. Swoboda does] not do genetic testing as a routine part of any medical evaluation and [is] not aware of any pediatric practice that would (absent specific medical indications). Even in cases where a patient presents with possible medical or genetic conditions based off of medical or family history that would warrant genetic testing, such testing is complex and often requires insurance preauthorization.

Id. at ¶ 25.

Nor would hormone testing be conducted as a part of a normal physical examination, or without clear medical indication. *Id.* at ¶¶ 21-22. Hormone testing would also require a referral to a pediatric endocrinologist and could reveal sensitive information. *Id.* at ¶¶ 24, 31. "Specific testing of genetics, internal or external reproductive anatomy, and hormones could reveal information that an individual was not looking to find out about themselves and then could result in having to disclose information to a school and community that could be deeply upsetting to pediatric patients." *Id.*

Given the significant burden the Act's dispute process places on all women athletes, the Court must decide whether Defendants' proffered justifications overcome the injury and indignity inflicted on Jane and all other female athletes through the dispute process. *SmithKline*, 740 F.3d at 481-83. Instead of ensuring "long-term benefits that flow from success in athletic endeavors for women and girls," it appears that the Act hinders those benefits by subjecting women and girls to unequal treatment, excluding some from participating in sports at all, incentivizing harassment and exclusionary behavior, and authorizing invasive bodily examinations. Idaho Code § 33-6202(12). Because, as discussed above, Defendants have not offered evidence that the Act is substantially related to its purported goals of promoting sex equality, providing opportunities for female athletes, or increasing female athlete's access to scholarship, Jane is also likely to succeed on her equal protection claim. Idaho Code § 33-6202(12).

e. Irreparable Harm

Lindsay and Jane both face irreparable harm due to violations of their rights under the Equal Protection Clause. "It is well established that the deprivation of constitutional rights unquestionably constitutes irreparable injury." *Hernandez v. Sessions*, 872 F.3d 976, 994 (9th Cir. 2017) (internal citations omitted); *Monterey Mech. Co. v. Wilson*, 125 F.3d 702, 715 (9th Cir. 1997) (holding that an equal protection violation constitutes irreparable harm).

Beyond this dispositive presumption, Lindsay and Jane will both suffer specific "harm for which there is no adequate legal remedy" in the absence of an injunction. *Ariz. Dream Act Coal. v. Brewer*, 757 F.3d 1053, 1068

(9th Cir. 2014). If Lindsay is denied the opportunity to try out for and compete on BSU's women's teams, she will permanently lose a year of NCAA eligibility that she can never get back. Lindsay is also subject to an Act that communicates the State's "moral disproval" of her identity, which the Constitution prohibits. *Lawrence v. Texas*, 539 U.S. 558, 582-83 (2003). When Jane tries out for Boise High's women's soccer team, she will be subject to the possibility of embarrassment, harassment, and invasion of privacy through having to verify her sex. Such violations are irreparable. *Obergefell*, 135 S. Ct. at 2606 ("Dignitary wounds cannot always be healed with the stroke of a pen."). Lindsay and Jane both also face the injuries detailed *supra*, section III.B.2, if the Act is not enjoined.[40]

The Court accordingly finds Plaintiffs will likely suffer irreparable harm if the Act is not enjoined. *Alliance for the Wild Rockies*, 632 F.3d at 1131 (noting plaintiffs must establish irreparable harm is likely, not certain, in order to obtain an injunction).

f. Balance of the Equities and Public Interest

Where, as here, the government is a party, the "balance of the equities" and "public interest" prongs of the preliminary injunction test merge. *Drakes Bay Oyster Co.*, 747 F.3d at 1092. In evaluating the balance of the equities, courts "must balance the competing claims of injury and must consider the effect on each party of the granting or withholding of the requested relief." *Winter*, 555 U.S. at 24. As explained above, Plaintiffs' harms weigh significantly in favor of injunctive relief.

In stark contrast to the deeply personal and irreparable harms Plaintiffs face, a preliminary injunction would not harm Defendants because it would merely maintain the status quo while Plaintiffs pursue their claims. If an injunction is issued, Defendants can continue to rely on the NCAA policy for college athletes and IHSAA policy for high school athletes, as they did for nearly a decade prior to the Act. In the absence of any evidence that transgender women threatened equality in sports, girls' athletic opportunities, or girls' access to scholarships in Idaho during the ten years such policies were in place, neither Defendants nor the Intervenors would be harmed by returning to this status quo.

Further, the Intervenors are themselves subject to disparate treatment under the Act. While the Intervenors have never competed against a transgender woman athlete from Idaho, or in Idaho, they risk being subject to the Act's sex dispute process simply by playing sports. As Plaintiffs' counsel noted during oral argument, the Act "isn't a law that pits some group of women against another group of women. This is a law that harms all women in the state, all women who are subject to . . . the sex verification process, and, of course, particularly women and girls who are transgender and are now singled out for categorical exclusion." Dkt. 62, at 89:23-25; 90:1-4.

Moreover, it is "always in the public interest to prevent the violation of a party's constitutional rights." *Melendres*, 695 F.3d at 1002. By establishing a likelihood that the Act violates the Constitution, Plaintiffs "have also established that both the public interest and the balance of the equities favor a preliminary injunction." *Ariz. Dream Act*, 757 F.3d at 1069 ("[T]he public interest and the balance of the equities favor preven[ting] the violation of a party's constitutional rights.") (internal quotation marks and citation omitted).

g. Bond Requirement

Finally, Plaintiffs request that the Court waive the bond requirement under Federal Rule of Civil Procedure

65(c). The Ninth Circuit has held that requiring a bond "to issue before enjoining potentially unconstitutional conduct by a governmental entity simply seems inappropriate because . . . protection of those rights should not be contingent upon an ability to pay." *Johnson v. Couturier*, 572 F.3d 1067, 1086 (9th Cir. 2009). In any event, Defendants do not contest Plaintiffs' request that the Court waive the bond. The Court will accordingly grant Plaintiff's request.

IV. CONCLUSION

The Court recognizes that this decision is likely to be controversial. While the citizens of Idaho are likely to either vehemently oppose, or fervently support, the Act, the Constitution must always prevail. It is the Court's role—as part of the third branch of government—to interpret the law. At this juncture, that means looking at the Act, as enacted by the Idaho Legislature, and determining if it may violate the Constitution. In making this determination, it is not just the constitutional rights of transgender girls and women athletes at issue but, as explained above, the constitutional rights of every girl and woman athlete in Idaho. Because the Court finds Plaintiffs are likely to succeed in establishing the Act is unconstitutional as currently written, it must issue a preliminary injunction at this time pending trial on the merits.

V. ORDER

Now, therefore IT IS HEREBY ORDERED:

1. The Motion to Intervene (Dkt. 30) is GRANTED;

2. The Motion to Dismiss (Dkt. 40) is GRANTED IN PART and DENIED IN PART. It is GRANTED with respect to Plaintiffs' facial Fourteenth Amendment

constitutional challenges, it is DENIED with respect to Plaintiffs' as-applied constitutional claims and in all other respects;

3. The Motion for Preliminary Injunction (Dkt. 22) is GRANTED.

DATED: August 17, 2020

/s/_____

David C. Nye
Chief U.S. District Court Judge

Footnotes:

[1] The Act went into effect on July 1, 2020. Idaho Code § 33-6201.

[2] The Court relies on various declarations filed in support of the Motion for Preliminary Injunction and Motion to Intervene for medical definitions of the terms used herein, and to identify the proposed intervenors and their arguments. The Court also considers extra-pleading materials when assessing Plaintiffs' Motion for Preliminary Injunction. The Court does not, however, rely on extra-pleading materials (other than those of which it takes judicial notice) in its assessment of Defendants' Motion to Dismiss, and accordingly does not treat the Motion to Dismiss as a Motion for Summary Judgment. *Olsen v. Idaho State Bd. of Med.*, 363 F.3d 916, 921-22 (9th Cir. 2004) (finding a represented party's submission of extra-pleading materials justified treating the motion to dismiss as a motion for summary judgment). Pursuant to Federal Rule of Evidence 201(c), the Court has discretionary authority to take judicial notice, regardless of whether it is requested to do so by a party, and does in fact do so in this case as it relates to certain materials identified below. Fed. R. Evid. 201.

3. Plaintiffs Jean, John, and Jane Doe have been granted permission to proceed under pseudonyms. Dkt. 48.

4. Due to the COVID-19 pandemic, the Mountain West conference in which BSU participates recently postponed sports competitions for fall sports. However, as of the date of this decision, BSU has not announced whether it will alter the training programs or tryouts for the cross-country team, and the Court has been advised by Plaintiffs' counsel that Lindsay is continuing her individual training program in preparation for tryouts.

5. Although try-outs for the Boise High soccer team have recently been postponed, the Court has been advised that small group training for the girls' soccer team may begin as early as August 17, 2020.

6. On the same day, Governor Little also signed another bill into law, H.B. 509, which essentially bans transgender individuals from changing their gender marker on their birth certificates to match their gender identity. *Id.* at ¶ 93-94. Enforcement of H.B. 509 is currently being litigated in *F.V. and Dani Martin v. Jeppesen et al.*, 1:17-cv-00170-CWD, because another judge of this Court previously permanently enjoined Idaho from enforcing a prior law that restricted transgender individuals from altering the sex designation on their birth certificates. *F.V. v. Barron*, 286 F. Supp. 3d 1131, 1146 (D. Idaho 2018).

7. While a federal statute does not authorize intervention by the Proposed Intervenors, the United States is statutorily authorized to intervene in cases of general public importance involving alleged denials of equal protection on the basis of sex. 28 U.S.C. § 517; *see also United States v. Virginia*, 518 U.S. 515, 523 (1996). The United States filed its Statement of Interest in support of the Act pursuant to 28 U.S.C. § 517. Dkt. 53.

8. Plaintiffs also argue the outcome of this lawsuit will not advance the Proposed Intervenors' claimed interests because Madi and MK, as collegiate athletes, will still be required to compete against non-Idaho teams and athletes who are subject to the rules of the NCAA, which allow participation of women who are transgender after one year of testosterone suppression. Yet, the fact that a challenged law may only partially protect an intervenor from harm does not mean that the intervenor does not have an interest in preserving that partial protection, and Plaintiffs do not cite any authority to the contrary.

9. In *Prete*, the Court explained that while "it is unclear whether this 'assumption' rises to the level of a second presumption, or rather is a circumstance that strengthens the first presumption, it is clear that 'in the absence of a very compelling showing to the contrary,' it will be presumed that the Oregon government adequately represents the interests of the intervenor-defendants." *Id.* at 957 (quoting *Arakaki*, 324 F.3d at 1086).

10. As Plaintiffs note, although Attorney General Wasden issued an opinion letter explaining that H.B. 500 was likely unconstitutional at the request of a legislator, Attorney General Wasden is statutorily required to represent the State in all courts, Idaho Code section 67-1401(1), and his Deputy Attorney General vigorously defended the Act in both briefing on the pending motions and during oral argument. As such, there is no evidence to suggest that Attorney General Wasden will not fulfill his statutory duties. In addition, the Proposed Intervenors contend BSU will not adequately represent their interests because BSU has a Gender Equality Center that advances the interests of transgender students. Dkt. 30-1, at 11-13. However, as Plaintiffs highlighted during oral argument, BSU could have realigned itself as a party if it felt it

could not support the Act, but instead gave over representation to the State and has accordingly adopted the positions of the State. Dkt. 62, at 28: 10-15. The Proposed Intervenors' arguments regarding Attorney General Wasden and BSU are not a compelling showing of inadequate representation.

[11.] The Court does not take issue with identifying Lindsay (or any other transgender women) as a transgender woman or transgender female, a male-to-female transgender athlete or individual, or as a person whose sex assigned at birth (male) differs from her gender identity (female). *Edmo*, 935 F.3d at 772. Each of these descriptions makes counsel's point without doing so in an inflammatory and potentially harmful manner.

[12.] Personal preferences or beliefs and organizational perceptions or positions notwithstanding, the Court expects courtesy between all parties in this litigation. In an ever contentious social and political world, the Courts will remain a haven for fairness, civility, and respect—even in disagreement.

[13.] Defendants do not challenge the causation and redressability elements of standing.

[14.] Defendants also maintain that "because HB 500 has not yet come into effect, all alleged harm is future harm—and Plaintiffs have not shown that the alleged injuries are certainly impending, or that there is substantial risk of harm occurring." Dkt. 40-1, at 6. Since the Act went into effect July 1, 2020, this argument is moot.

[15.] Citing *Braunstein v. Arizona Dep't of Transp.*, 683 F.3d 1177, 1185 (9th Cir. 2012), Defendants argue that even where the government discriminates on the basis of a protected category, only those who are "personally denied equal treatment have a cognizable injury under Article III." Dkt. 59, at 3. In *Braunstein*, the

Ninth Circuit considered a white male engineer's lawsuit alleging the Arizona Department of Transportation violated his right to equal protection by giving general contractors a financial incentive to hire minority-owned subcontractors. *Braunstein*, 683 F.3d at 1184. Braunstein alleged that these preferences prevented him, as a non-minority business owner, from competing for subcontracting work on an equal basis. *Id.* at 1185. However, Braunstein did not submit a quote or attempt to secure subcontract work from any of the prime contractors who bid on the government contract. *Id.* at 1185. The Ninth Circuit held that because Braunstein's surviving claim was for damages, rather than for declaratory and injunctive relief, Braunstein had to show more than that he was "able and ready" to seek subcontracting work. *Id.* at 1186. The Court determined Braunstein had not established an injury for purposes of his claim for damages because Braunstein had "done essentially nothing to demonstrate that he [was] in a position to compete equally with the other contractors." *Id.* By contrast, Lindsay seeks declaratory and injunctive relief, and has demonstrated she is "able and ready" to join the BSU cross-country and track teams. *Id.* at 1186 (citing *Gratz v. Bollinger*, 539 U.S. 244, 261-62 (2003) (holding plaintiff had standing to challenge university's race-conscious transfer admissions policy, even though he never applied as a transfer student, because he demonstrated that he was "able and ready to do so.") Lindsay has adequately alleged that she is ready and able to join BSU's women's cross-country and women's track teams and also that she is in a position to compete with other students who try out for BSU's women's track and cross-country teams. Specifically, Lindsay alleges she has been training hard to qualify for such teams, that she is a life-long runner who competed on track and cross-country teams in high school, and that she will try out for the cross-country team in fall 2020 and track team in spring 2020 if BSU allows her to do so. Dkt. 1, at ¶¶ 6, 25, 33. Such allegations are sufficient to establish standing for Lindsay's claims. *Braunstein*, 683 F.3d at 1185-86.

[16.] The Court takes judicial notice of such articles because they are matters in the public realm. "When a court takes judicial notice of publications like websites and newspaper article, the court merely notices what was in the public realm at the time, not whether the contents of those articles were in fact true." *Prime Healthcare Services, Inc. v. Humana Ins. Co.*, 230 F. Supp. 3d 1194, 1201 (citing *Heliotrope Gen. Inc. v. Ford Motor Co.*, 189 F.3d 971, 981 n. 118 (9th Cir. 1999)). The Court references such articles solely to illustrate that this case has received local and national attention, and not for the truth of the contents of the articles. *Id.*

[17.] As mentioned, BSU cannot allow Lindsay this opportunity under section 33-6203(2) of the Act. Given BSU's awareness that Lindsay is a transgender woman, the Act directs that BSU "shall not" permit her to join the women's team, regardless of whether a third-party challenges Lindsay's sex. Idaho Code § 33-6203(2).

[18.] The OCR Letter was filed by the OCR in Connecticut court cases involving claims by three high school student-athletes and their parents due to the Connecticut Interscholastic Athletic Conference's policy of permitting transgender women to compete on women's teams. Dkt. 41, at 25. Although the parties do not raise the issue, the Court takes judicial notice of the OCR Letter, filed by Defendants in support of their Opposition to the Motion for Preliminary Injunction, and cited by Defendants in their Motion to Dismiss, because the Court may take judicial notice of "proceedings in other courts, both within and without the federal judicial system, if those proceedings have a direct relation to the matters at issue." *United States ex rel. Robinson Rancheria Citizens Council v. Borneo, Inc.*, 971 F.2d 244, 248 (9th Cir. 1992).

[19.] During oral argument, Plaintiffs' counsel stated that they would be happy to consider entering into a consent decree if Defendants were willing to agree that this interpretation of the statute was authoritative and binding in Idaho. Dkt. 62, at 70:16-21. Defendants did not respond to this suggestion, and the parties have not notified the Court of any subsequent talks regarding a potential consent decree.

[20.] The Court uses the specific terms "girl" and "girl's teams" for Jane, and "transgender woman" and "woman's teams" for Lindsay, due to their respective ages and year in school. The terms are generally interchangeable, however, since the Act applies to nearly all girls and women student athletes in Idaho. Idaho Code § 33-6203(1).

[21.] Defendants suggest *Melendres* is inapposite because each of the plaintiffs in *Melendres* had been subjected to targeted traffic stops, and because plaintiffs presented evidence that the defendants had an ongoing policy of targeting Latinos. Dkt. 59, at 2-3 n. 1. Defendants argue this case is distinguishable because no one has challenged either Plaintiff's sex, and because Defendants have no policy or practice to mount such challenges in the future. *Id.* This argument ignores that regulated entities, such as BSU and Boise High, are statutorily required to ensure that transgender women or girls do not play on female sports' teams, are also responsible for resolving sex disputes, and risk significant civil liability if they fail to comply with the statute. Idaho Code §§ 33-6203(3), 6205. The requirements the statute itself places on regulated entities is evidence that the policy will be enforced.

[22.] Standing and ripeness are closely related. *Colwell v. Dep't of Health and Human Services*, 558 F.3d 1112, 1123 (9th Cir. 2009). "But whereas standing is primarily concerned with *who* is a proper party to litigate a particular matter, ripeness addresses *when* that litigation may occur." (emphasis in original) (internal quotation marks and citations omitted).

[23.] Although Defendants again highlight that the Department of Education has not yet established the rules and regulations applicable to the sex verification process, Defendants do not articulate how the forthcoming rules and regulations could possibly change the Act's core prohibitions and requirements; could allow transgender women athletes to participate on women's teams; could exempt a girl or woman whose sex is disputed from the verification process; or could add to the narrow list of criteria that can be used to verify a girl's or woman's biological sex. Defendants are simply mistaken that impending regulations could possibly alleviate Plaintiffs' concerns, or that such rules must be established before Lindsay can be excluded from women's sports and before Jane can be subjected to a sex verification challenge.

[24.] Lindsay will not have even this choice unless BSU violates the Act, exposing itself to civil suit, and allows her to join the women's team.

[25.] "Facial and as-applied challenges do not enjoy a neat demarcation, but conventional wisdom defines facial challenges as 'ones seeking to have a statute declared unconstitutional in all possible applications,' while as-applied challenges are 'treated as the residual, although ostensibly preferred and larger, category.'" *Standing--Facial Versus As Applied Challenges--City of Los Angeles v. Patel*, 129 HARV. L. REV. 241, 246

(2015)("*Facial Versus As Applied Challenges*") (quoting Richard H. Fallon, Jr., *Fact and Fiction About Facial Challenges*, 99 CAL. L. REV. 915, 923 (2011)). However, as many scholars note, the distinction, if any, between a facial and an as-applied challenge is difficult to explain because there is a disconnect between what the Supreme Court has outlined and what happens in actual practice. *Facial Versus As Applied Challenges*, 129 HARV. L. REV. at 247; *see also* Gillian E. Metzger, *Facial Challenges and Federalism*, 105 COLUM. L. REV. 873, 882 (2005).

[26.] Exceptions to *Salerno's* "no set of circumstances" test have been developed but are not applicable here. For instance, *Salerno* does not apply to certain facial challenges to statutes under the First Amendment. *Planned Parenthood of S. Arizona v. Lawall*, 180 F.3d 1022, 1026 (9th Cir. 1999). The Supreme Court also held *Salerno's* "no set of circumstances" test does not apply to "undue burden" challenges to statutes regulating abortion in *Planned Parenthood of Se. Pennsylvania v. Casey*, 505 U.S. 833, 895 (1992).

[27.] Plaintiffs also bring facial challenges under the Fourth Amendment. Given the confusion created by *Patel* and uncertainty as to whether *Patel* applies here, the Court will deny dismissal of Plaintiffs' facial Fourth Amendment challenges without prejudice. However, even if the Court later determines that all of Plaintiffs' facial challenges fail, the Court rejects Defendants' suggestion that if the Court dismisses all facial challenges, all of Plaintiffs' other requests for relief, including all requests for injunctive relief, should be dismissed. Dkt. 59, at 8. Plaintiffs seek preliminary and permanent injunctive relief enjoining enforcement of the Act both facially and as applied. Dkt. 1, at 53 (Prayer for Relief, paragraph D, requesting injunctive relief "as discussed above" which includes reference to Plaintiffs' as-applied challenges in paragraphs A and B). Dismissal of Plaintiffs' facial challenges does not require dismissal of their requests for injunctive relief.

<u>28.</u> Heightened scrutiny is also referred to as "intermediate scrutiny." *See, e.g., Clark v. Jeter*, 486 U.S. 456, 461 (1988). The Court uses the term "heightened" scrutiny for consistency.

<u>29.</u> As the *Barron* Court explained, the Supreme Court employs a four-factor test to determine whether a class qualifies as suspect or quasi-suspect: (1) when the class has been "historically subjected to discrimination;" (2) has a defining characteristic bearing no "relation to ability to perform or contribute to society;" (3) has "obvious, immutable, or distinguishing characteristics;"" and (4) is "a minority or is politically powerless." *Id.* at 1144 (quoting *United States v. Windsor*, 570 U.S. 744 (2003)). The *Barron* Court determined transgender individuals meet each of these criteria. *Id*. This test has also been employed by district courts in other states to find transgender people are a quasi-suspect class. For instance, in *Adkins v. City of New York*, 143 F. Supp. 3d 134, 139 (S.D.N.Y.), the court determined: (1) transgender individuals have a history of persecution and discrimination and, moreover, "this history of persecution and discrimination is not yet history"; (2) transgender status bears no relation to ability to contribute to society; (3) transgender status is a sufficiently discernible characteristic to define a discrete minority class; and (4) transgender individuals are a politically powerless minority. *Id*. at 139.

<u>30.</u> Yet, even under rational basis review, if a court finds that a classification is "born of animosity toward the class of persons affected," a law that implicates neither a suspect classification nor a fundamental right

may be ruled constitutionally invalid. *Romer*, 517 U.S. at 634; *United States Department of Agriculture v. Moreno*, 413 U.S. 528 (1973) (striking down provision of Food Stamp Act that denied food stamps to households of unrelated individuals where the legislative history suggested Congress passed the provision in an effort to prevent "hippie communes" from receiving food stamps). Thus, even under rational basis review, a policy that is primarily motivated by animus will not pass constitutional muster. *Id.* at 534.

31. However, as noted *supra*, the Ninth Circuit has explicitly held heightened scrutiny applies if a law or policy treats transgender persons in a less favorable way than all others. *Karnoski*, 926 F.3d at 1201.

32. While maintaining heightened scrutiny is appropriate, Plaintiffs also argue the Act fails even rational basis review. Dkt. 22-1, at 12, 25-26. Because the Court finds provisions of the Act fail to withstand heightened scrutiny, it does not further address this argument.

33. The Intervenors rely on an expert opinion from Dr. Stephen Levine claiming gender-affirming policies (such as allowing transgender individuals to play on sports teams consistent with their gender identity) are instead harmful to transgender individuals. *See generally*, Dkt. 46-2. However, another judge of this Court previously determined that Dr. Levine is an outlier in the field of gender dysphoria and placed "virtually no weight" on his opinion in a case involving a transgender prisoner's medical care. *Edmo v. Idaho Dep't of Corr.*, 258 F. Supp. 3d 1103, 1125 (D. Idaho 2018) (*vacated in part on other grounds in Edmo v. Corizon*, 935 F.3d 757 (9th Cir. 2019)); *see also Norsworthy v. Beard*, 87 F. Supp. 3d 1164, 1188-89 (N.D. Cal. 2015) (noting Dr. Levine's expert opinion overwhelmingly relied on

generalizations about gender dysphoria, contained illogical inferences, and admittedly included references to a fabricated anecdote). At this stage of the proceedings, the Court accepts Plaintiffs' evidence regarding the harm forcing transgender individuals to deny their gender identity can cause.

[34.] The United States suggests the Ninth Circuit held participation by just one cisgender boy on the girls' volleyball team would "set back" the "goal of equal participation by females in interscholastic sports." Dkt. 52, at 10 (citing *Clark by and through Clark v. Arizona Interscholastic Ass'n*, 886 F.2d 1191, 1193 (1989) ("*Clark II*"). The part of *Clark II* the United States references responded to plaintiff's "mystifying" argument that the Arizona school association had been "wholly deficient in its efforts to overcome the effects of past discrimination against women in interscholastic athletics, and that this failure vitiate[d] its justification for a girls-only volleyball team." *Id*. The Ninth Circuit noted that it was true that participation in Arizona interscholastic sports was still far from equal. *Id*. In light of this inequity, the *Clark II* Court could not see how plaintiff's "remedy" of allowing him to play on the girl's team would help. *Id*. Thus, the *Clark II* Court's statement regarding participation by one male athlete was in the context of plaintiff's argument that he should be permitted to play on the girl's team because there was no justification for women's teams. *Id*. The *Clark II* Court remained focused on the risk that a ruling in plaintiff's favor would extend to all boys and would engender substantial displacement of girls in school sports. *Id*. (observing that the issue of "males . . . outnumber[ing] females in sports two to one" in school sports would "not be solved by opening the girls' team to Clark *and other boys*.") (emphasis added); *see also id*. ("Clark does not dispute our conclusion in *Clark I* that 'due to physiological differences, *males would displace females to a substantial extent if they were* allowed to compete for positions on the volleyball team.") (quoting *Clark*, 695 F.2d at 1131) (emphasis added).

35. As Attorney General Wasden advised the legislature before it passed the Act: "The issue of a transgender female wishing to participate on a team with other women requires considerations beyond those considered in *Clark* and presents issues that courts have not yet resolved." Letter from Attorney General Wasden to Rep. Rubel (Feb. 25, 2020), https://www.idahostatesman.com/latest-newsarticle240619742.ece/BINARY/HB%20500%20Idaho%20AG%20response.pdf.

36. Rep. Ehardt also vaguely referenced a college transgender athlete, but it is not clear from the record who this athlete is or where she competed. Dkt. 22-3, Ex. B, at 8.

37. The legislative findings and the citations in the Proponents' briefs cite this study as Tommy Lundberg et al., *Muscle strength, size and composition following 12 months of gender-affirming treatment in transgender individuals: retained advantage for transwomen*, Karolinska Institute (Sept. 26, 2019). The correct reference for the published study is Anna Wiik et al., *Muscle Strength, Size, and Composition following 12 Months of Gender-affirming Treatment in Transgender Individuals*, J. CLIN. METAB., 105(3):e805-e813 (2020).

38. In their Response to the Motion for Preliminary Injunction, Defendant's highlight the circumstances of one transgender woman athlete who competed in women's sports after suppressing her hormones, Cece Telfer, to suggest testosterone suppression does not

eliminate the physiological advantages of transgender women athletes. Dkt. 41, at 17-18. The Court finds, and Defendants concede, that such anecdotal evidence does not establish that hormone therapy is ineffective in reducing athletic performance advantages in transgender women athletes. *Id.* at 18.

39. Moreover, males were already excluded from female sports teams under the long-standing rules in Idaho prior to the Act's passage. Defendants do not explain why women must risk being subject to the onerous sex verification process in the name of equality in sports when women already had single sex teams without the risk of a sex dispute prior to the Act's passage.

40. The Intervenors outrageously contend that Lindsay has not shown she will suffer irreparable harm because she has not alleged that she will commit suicide if she is not permitted to participate on BSU's women's sports teams. Dkt. 46, at 2. Clearly, a risk of suicide is not required to establish irreparable harm. The Intervenors' attempt to twist the tragically high suicide rate of transgender individuals into a requirement that Lindsay must be suicidal to establish irreparable harm is distasteful.